Social Justice and the Modern Athlete

Social Justice and the Modern Athlete

Exploring the Role of Athlete Activism in Social Change

Edited by

Mia Long Anderson

LEXINGTON BOOKS
Lanham • Boulder • New York • London

Published by Lexington Books
An imprint of The Rowman & Littlefield Publishing Group, Inc.
4501 Forbes Boulevard, Suite 200, Lanham, Maryland 20706
www.rowman.com

86-90 Paul Street, London EC2A 4NE, United Kingdom

British Library Cataloguing in Publication Information Available

Library of Congress Cataloging-in-Publication Data

Names: Anderson, Mia Long, 1977– editor.
Title: Social justice and the modern athlete : exploring the role of athlete activism in
   social change / edited by Mia Long Anderson.
Description: Lanham, Maryland : Lexington Books, [2023] | Includes bibliographical
   references. | Summary: "Social Justice and the Modern Athlete: Exploring the Role
   of Athlete Activism in Social Change is an edited volume that illuminates the power
   athletes have to influence and rectify social injustices. It highlights athlete activism in
   the areas of politics, gender equity, nonviolent protest, mental health, and the online
   sphere"—Provided by publisher.
Identifiers: LCCN 2022040437 (print) | LCCN 2022040438 (ebook) | ISBN
   9781666904574 (cloth) | ISBN 9781666904581 (epub) | ISBN 978-1-66690-
   459-8 (paper)
Subjects: LCSH: Social justice and sports—United States. | Social change—United
   States. | Social movements—United States. | Athletes—Political activity—
   United States.
Classification: LCC GV706.5 .S6416 2023 (print) | LCC GV706.5 (ebook) | DDC
   306.4/83—dc23/eng/20221104
LC record available at https://lccn.loc.gov/2022040437
LC ebook record available at https://lccn.loc.gov/2022040438

Contents

Acknowledgments

The idea for this project developed in an interesting time—one year into a global pandemic and nearly a year following the murder of George Floyd. The outrage and action that converged following Mr. Floyd's murder illuminated the activism of athletes within the United States and beyond its borders. Sports became an outlet and a catalyst. Athletes reminded us of the strength of their influence—on and off their field of play. This book explores that perception.

I would first like to thank God for providing direction on this collection. I am grateful to the contributors for their thoughtful work in bringing this project to fruition. I am constantly indebted to my husband, Walter, and my daughter, Eden, for their encouragement and patience with every project.

I dedicate this book to my parents, Ray and Mary, for their boundless love and support.

Introduction

Mia Long Anderson

In 2016, former NFL player Colin Kaepernick was heavily criticized for taking a knee during the playing of the national anthem at a pre-season NFL game. Those who eventually joined him in drawing attention to systemic oppression, police brutality, and injustice drew ire from the media, the public, and even the President of the United States. The adverse sentiments echoed Fox Sports anchor Laura Ingraham's message to LeBron James months earlier that he should "shut up and dribble" instead of involving himself in politicized issues. In the midst of an environment already agitated by a fast-spreading pandemic, 2020 saw the silent protests turn into heightened athlete activism as outrage at racially motivated violence extended beyond the field of play. Meanwhile, college athletes around the nation marched in the streets of their college towns, protesting a need for change in race relations in American society. The 2020 election season also saw athletes actively participating in efforts to increase voter registration and turnout.

These efforts build upon the legacy of athlete activism addressing many societal factors. From Muhammad Ali's Cleveland Summit in 1967 to John Carlos and Tommie Smith's raised fists during the 1968 Olympics to WNBA star Maya Moore's more recent fight for Jonathan Irons' freedom, athletes have been at the forefront of social movements. In reflecting on his participation in the Cleveland Summit, former NFL player Walter Beach stated, "It was very important that you let people understand that you're more than a football player. Football is what I did, it wasn't who I was. Muhammad Ali was a boxer. That's what he did. That wasn't who he was" (Lartey, 2017, para. 11). Beach's sentiments have reverberated in word and deed over the past decade. Perhaps Carmelo Anthony, Chris Paul, Dwyane Wade, and LeBron James said it best in their intro to the 2016 ESPYS broadcast:

Generations ago, legends like Jesse Owens, Jackie Robinson, Muhammad Ali, John Carlos and Tommie Smith, Kareem Abdul-Jabbar, Jim Brown, Billie Jean King, Arthur Ashe and countless others, they set a model for what athletes should stand for. So we choose to follow in their footsteps.

The system is broken, the problems are not new, the violence is not new, and the racial divide definitely is not new, but the urgency for change is at an all-time high . . .

Tonight we're honoring Muhammad Ali, the GOAT. But to do his legacy any justice, let's use this moment as a call to action to all professional athletes to educate ourselves, explore these issues, speak up, use our influence and renounce all violence, and most importantly, go back to our communities, invest our time, our resources, help rebuild them, help strengthen them, help change them. We all have to do better. (ESPN.com, 2016)

The NBA players' 2016 call to action speaks to the impact athletes have on raising awareness and leading change in various areas of society. As athletes before them, today's "modern" athlete is carrying the baton to advance efforts that result in a more equitable social structure. Anthony, Paul, and Wade launched the Social Change Fund which seeks equality along racial lines in the areas of police brutality, criminal justice reform, voting access, education, health equity, economic investment, and the arts (Medina, 2021). LeBron James partnered with Akron Public Schools to launch the I Promise School, a school "dedicated to those students who are already falling behind and in danger of falling through the cracks" (I Promise, n.d.). WNBA star Renee Montgomery retired from the sport, becoming co-owner of the Atlanta Dream franchise for which she played, following a year of watching former Dream owner and former U.S. Senator Kelly Loeffler denounce the racial justice issues for which many WNBA players stood (Hinchliffe, 2021). Tennis standout Naomi Osaka donned seven different masks bearing the names of "victims of racial injustice" during the 2020 U.S. Open to increase awareness of violence against unarmed African Americans (Mansoor, 2020). In 2021, she shed light on mental health when she dropped out of the French Open, citing her own struggles with anxiety and depression (Chen, 2021).

The NCAA defines activism as "the practice of taking intentional action to bring about social, political, economic or environmental change" (NCAA, n.d.). It further states, "it can take many forms but often relies on a strategic, organized and action-oriented approach to address persistent systemic issues in society" (NCAA, n.d.). The strategic and action-oriented nature of athlete activism is visible in the t-shirts donned by WNBA and NBA players in silent protest to issues impacting minorities in America. The organization of athlete activism is seen in the University of Missouri football team's response to racist acts taking place on their campus (McKnight, 2020). There are more examples–many featured in this book–of athletes taking a stand for the sake of societal reforms. Fortunately, athlete activism benefits from the global celebrity of athletes. When LeBron speaks (or tweets), people listen.

That said, athlete activism did not begin with LeBron James nor did it start in the 1960s with Muhammad Ali and Jim Brown. According to sociologist Harry Edwards, there are four waves of athlete activism (Edwards, 2017). The First Wave, from 1900 to 1946, "related to broader issues of Black freedom, justice, and equality in America" (p. 158). During this time, athletes like Joe Louis and Jesse Owens struggled with the fact that they could represent the country globally yet be prohibited from interracial contests (and overall civil rights) in their home country. The Second Wave, from 1946 to 1965, "encompass[ed] an all-out struggle for *access*" (p. 158). It was during this time period that African American athletes began to break the color barrier on professional teams in the United States. The Third Wave, beginning in 1965, "focused on compelling respect, dignity, and equality of treatment and justice for Black athletes in particular and for Black people more generally" (p. 159). It was during this time that Tommie Smith and John Carlos raised their fists in protest. Following a period of seeming silence among African American athletes in the 1980s and 1990s, we have witnessed a revival of athlete activism in recent years (Edwards, 2017). This Fourth Wave "brought about unprecedented independence and influence as high-profile athletes began to speak out against the racial injustice taking place at an alarming rate in America" (Williams, 2022, p. 268).

Coinciding with the Black Lives Matter movement, the ongoing fight for the actualization of Title IX, and arguments for prison reform and trans rights, athletes are again front and center in the battle for human rights. That being the case, Williams, building upon Edwards' (2017) work, asserts that we are now in the Fifth Wave of athlete activism. Williams (2022) contends that this Fifth Wave "harnessed the power of dialogical practices (and, the power of the athlete) exhibited by the 2015 University of Missouri football team by instituting a work stoppage until their demands were met" (i.e., NBA player work stoppage; p. 270). As Williams states, the Fifth Wave "also combined the efforts of the ESPYS call-to-action with Kaepernick's demonstrations by garnering dialogical attention in the media and being willing to stand up for what they believe in, even if it meant that their athletic ventures could be negatively affected" (p. 271).

Mirroring the scope of issues that envelope us all, this edited collection illuminates the myriad ways in which athletes have conducted their social justice work. As our society encompasses a spectrum of marginalization based on gender, sexual orientation, race, religion, ability, and poverty, so too the current collection addresses the role athletes play in righting wrongs impacting diverse segments of society. To that end, the book contains five sections addressing (1) the foundations of athlete activism, (2) athletes' refusal to "stick to sports," (3) the voice of the student-athlete, (4) gender equity and issues, and (5) the role of social media in athlete activism.

Part I provides a foundation for athletes' decision to become activists. The decision to become an activist is not an easy one and often comes with repercussions. Athletes must consider their reputation and finances. For instance, though he worked out for the Las Vegas Raiders in 2022, at the time of this publication, Colin Kaepernick remained an unsigned NFL quarterback, despite (1) the NFL's assertion that Kaepernick's unemployment is unrelated to his silent protests and (2) the league's shift to supporting athlete protests in 2020 (Beaton, 2020). Chapter 1 seeks to address the question of what motivates athletes to or deters athletes from social justice work in the current racial and political climate. Such factors as (1) athlete marketability, (2) the ubiquity of social media, and (3) the intersection of racial and athlete identities seem to provide some insight. In addition, the first section highlights the differences between athlete activism of the Third Wave and athlete activism of the Fourth Wave, as Chapter 2 provides the basis for why Kaepernick's actions should not be so easily, and perhaps thoughtlessly, compared to the actions of Tommie Smith and John Carlos years prior.

Part II focuses on athletes' refusal to "stick to sports." Even in the midst of a pandemic, NBA players felt compelled to express themselves, using their platform–though they themselves were in isolation–to bring attention to societal issues. Chapter 3 investigates the interplay of players using their voice within the constraints placed on them in the NBA bubble. It also considers the rhetoric of space/place in light of those constraints. Finally, it looks at the relationship between corporate influence and athlete activism and the potential impact that relationship may have on athlete-activist legitimacy. Chapter 4 discusses Maya Moore's decision to forgo her WNBA career to center her attention on prison reform. In doing so, it highlights the role religion played in Moore's decision and how that religious foundation shaped media coverage of Moore's social justice work. Chapter 5 examines the ways in which Naomi Osaka has expressed her political convictions on the court. Specifically, the chapter explores the role of authenticity in Osaka's advocacy for racial justice and mental health awareness.

Part III appropriately draws attention to the heightened activism of student-athletes. Using tempered radicalism as its framework, Chapter 6 focuses on how athletic department staff use their roles to encourage, support, and engage in student-athlete activism. The chapter uses interviews with staff members to illuminate the varied approaches taken by athletic staff in choosing to act as tempered radicals in social movements. Chapter 7 speaks to the power of one person's actions in influencing widespread societal change. The chapter explores the impact of Mississippi State football player Kylin Hill's tweet calling for a change to the Mississippi state flag. Hill's 98 characters contributed to a movement that stimulated actions from the NCAA and the Mississippi state legislature. In continuing discussion of the power of voice, Chapter 8 delves into how University of Alabama football players used their voices to express their civic and political ideas during the height of the Black Lives Matter movement in 2020. Ultimately, members of the team used their influence to offer dissent to racial injustice, calling for everyone to take a stand in creating "a better world" and reminding everyone that "All lives can't matter until Black lives matter." Chapter 9 discusses the crisis that took place at Oklahoma State when a tweet showed head football coach Mike Gundy wearing a One America News (OAN) shirt. Oklahoma State football players (and others) took offense to what seemed to be Gundy's support of OAN, a network that had consistently been more critical of the protests taking place after George Floyd's murder. Using Hearit's model of apologetic ethics as a foundation, the chapter explores Gundy's response to the crisis.

Part IV addresses gender equity and issues in sport. Chapter 10 applies the Theory of Planned Behavior in exploring Nike's sponsorship of athlete-mothers. Specifically, the chapter describes (1) the role of workplace norms in Nike's discriminatory practices, (2) the ways in which perceived controls and norms are harmful to elite athlete-mothers, and (3) how Alysia Montaño and Allyson Felix used their platforms to shift public opinion, thereby forcing Nike to develop more inclusive practices. Chapter 11 offers a comparative analysis of the international conversation on pay equity. Using examples from the WNBA, U.S. Women's National Soccer Team, and U.S. Women's Hockey, the chapter illustrates how women athletes are using various forms of activism to challenge pay inequities in their respective sports. Chapter 12 provides insight on Twitter and intersectionality, particularly as it relates to Caster Semenya's fight against International Association of Athletics Federations' (IAAF) "differences on sex development" (DSD) policy. Relying on critical discourse analysis, the chapter examines how Twitter users entreat Semenya to regard the categories of race and sex, while also exploring how users exert their support or opposition to the IAAF regulations.

Part V highlights athlete activism in the online space. Chapter 13 focuses on NCAA athlete activism on TikTok. In particular, it examines three instances in which athletes used TikTok as a platform for social justice activism: (1) Oregon women's basketball player Sedona Prince's exposure of the stark contrast of women's and men's NCAA facilities; (2) UCONN women's basketball player Christyn Williams's viral "Black Lives Matter" post; and (3) LSU middle distance runner TJ Bleichner's LGBTQ+ advocacy. Chapter 14 discusses Formula 1 driver Lewis Hamilton's use of Instagram to raise awareness of global development challenges, particularly as they relate to the Sustainable Development Goals (SDGs) of the United Nations. Chapter 15 takes a broader look at how athletes and sports organizations use their influence to advance online conversations about social justice issues. Specifically, the chapter relies on social network analysis of Twitter data to examine how athletes, sports organizations, and media personalities are positioned in the social media conversation and how such positioning impacts the overall network. Finally, Chapter 16 delves into fan response to online athlete activism, providing practical implications for athletes' use of social media as a platform for social movements.

Together, this edited collection reflects on the powerful history of athlete activism while acknowledging the many ways activism has evolved through the years. In addition, the chapters each contribute to the fabric that is woven into the larger tapestry that is athlete activism which proves multifaceted in the areas of social justice it covers. In this way, the book extends the conversation surrounding activism, building upon the historical foundation set by athlete activism experts such as journalist Howard Bryant (2018) and sociologist Harry Edwards (2017).

REFERENCES

Beaton, A. (2020, September 11). The NFL protests with Colin Kaepernick, who's still unsigned. *Wall Street Journal.* Retrieved from https://www.wsj.com/articles/the-nfl-protests-with-colin-kaepernick-whos-still-unsigned-11599827958

Bryant, H. (2018). *The heritage: Black athletes, a divided America, and the politics of patriotism.* Boston: Beacon Press.

Chen, T. P. (2021, June 3). What happens when mental-health issues get in the way of work. *Wall Street Journal.* Retrieved from https://www.wsj.com/articles/what-happens-when-mental-health-issues-get-in-the-way-of-work-11622719860

Edwards, H. (2017). *The revolt of the Black athlete: 50th anniversary edition.* Urbana: University of Illinois Press.

ESPN.com. (2016). LeBron James on social activism: "We all have to do better." ESPN.com. Retrieved from https://www.espn.com/espys/2016/story/_/id/17060953/espys-carmelo-anthony-chris-paul-dwyane-wade-lebron-james-call-athletes-promote-change

Hinchliffe, E. (2021, May 17). How Renee Montgomery pivoted from WNBA player to owner. *Fortune.* Retrieved from https://fortune.com/2021/05/17/how-renee-montgomery-pivoted-from-wnba-player-to-owner/

I Promise. (n.d.). The I promise school. Retrieved from https://ipromise.school/#slide-1

Lartey, J. (2017, October 23). The "Ali summit": A turning point in sports' fight against injustice. *The Guardian.* Retrieved from https://www.theguardian.com/sport/2017/oct/23/colin-kaepernick-muhammad-ali-summit-sports-activism

Mansoor, S. (2020, September 13). Naomi Osaka says she wore 7 masks about Black lives during this year's U.S. Open to "make people start talking." *Time.* Retrieved from https://time.com/5888583/naomi-osaka-masks-black-lives-matter-us-open/

McKnight, M. (2020, November 5). How the Missouri football protest changed college sports forever. *Sports Illustrated.* Retrieved from https://www.si.com/college/2020/11/05/missouri-protests-daily-cover

Medina, M. (2021, January 18). Carmelo Anthony, Chris Paul, and Dwyane Wade have led on social justice causes. Their fund pushes for social change. *USA Today.* Retrieved from https://www.usatoday.com/story/sports/nba/2021/01/18/chris-paul-carmelo-anthony-dwyane-wade-social-change-fund/4199714001/

NCAA. (n.d.). Student-athlete activism. NCAA.com. Retrieved from https://www.ncaa.org/sports/2021/7/23/student-athlete-activism.aspx

Williams, A. L. (2022). The heritage strikes back: Athlete activism, Black Lives Matter, and the iconic fifth wave of activism in the (W)NBA bubble. *Cultural Studies Critical Methodologies, 22*(3), 266–275.

PART I

Historical Foundations

Chapter 1

A Model Framework for Analysis of Elite Athletes' Social Responsibility

A. Michelle Clemon

Athlete activism in the United States has historically tracked along the overall sociopolitical climate, reaching what was regarded as its zenith in the height of the civil rights movement in the 1960s. In that season and into the 1970s, athletes such as Jackie Robinson, Muhammad Ali, Bill Russell, and Arthur Ashe were viewed as standard-bearers as athletes and activists.

Except for Craig Hodges and Mahmoud Abdul-Rauf (Norris, 2020; Washington, 2016), athlete engagement in social justice took a downturn in the last decades of the twentieth century and that trend appeared to be continuing into the 21st century. That was until the highly publicized deaths of countless people of color at the hands of law enforcement over the last decade prompted a reawakening of consciousness and activism among athletes, a reawakening that includes a broader spectrum of athletes and social justice causes than previous seasons of activism in sports.

The increased engagement in activism begs several questions, including, "What drives or deters athletes from activism in this current climate?" To address this question, this chapter will provide an extensive review of relevant literature and a conceptual model that frames the issues associated with professional athletes and social responsibility. Three research questions will guide the review and integrate the effects of social responsibility activities on (1) career planning and marketability, (2) social media as a social activism tool, and (3) the intersection of racial and athlete identities for athlete-activists. For this chapter, the terms "athlete-activist" and "activist-athlete" may be used interchangeably and are defined as athletes who "use sport or their role as athletes to promote social and political change" (Kaufman, 2008, p. 220). The chapter will address athlete-activists at both the collegiate and professional levels, although less is known about collegiate athlete-activists and their perspectives on race, racism, activism, and their inclination to engage in activism (MacIntosh et al., 2020). The proposed conceptual model provides athlete development specialists and scholars of athlete development with a greater understanding of how to best advise and assist athletes and facilitate their navigation of this intersection of their high-profile roles.

REVIEW OF LITERATURE

Recent history has demonstrated that high profile athletes who speak out on social issues tend to encounter backlash and controversy (Schmidt, Shreffler, Hambrick & Gordon, 2018). After Colin Kaepernick completed the season in which he protested social injustice by taking a knee at every game, he opted out of his contract with the San Francisco 49ers in 2017 (Wagoner, 2017). Four years later, he has yet to be signed to a team despite countless teams needing a quarterback of his caliber. Given the increase in athlete activism since Kaepernick "took a knee," it is important to examine how such activism has affected their employability and marketing opportunities.

Schmidt et al. (2018) studied the effect of activism type and activism effort on a sponsor's brand image and purchase intention of a product the athlete endorses. The study distinguished between "safe" activism (e.g., an anti-obesity campaign) and "risky" activism (e.g., a racial injustice campaign; Schmidt et al., 2018). Schmidt et al. defined "high" effort of activism as creating an organization and "low" effort as posting on social media. The results indicated that there was no statistical interaction effect between activism effort and risk but that there was a statistical difference between risky and safe activism types (Schmidt et al.). Risky activism resulted in decreases in brand image and purchase intention compared to safe activism, which did not (Schmidt et al., 2018). Moreso, Schmidt et al. found that athlete fear of financial backlash from risky activism was possibly warranted based on these findings (Schmidt et al., 2018).

More recently, Niven (2020) conducted a study to determine whether there was any difference in treatment in the next contracts of NFL players who knelt during the anthem during the 2017 season and those who did not, with the pool involving players with comparable performances during that season. Specifically, Niven (2020) examined changes in guaranteed money and non-guaranteed money as well as whether players moved to a different team after the season. To assure that the performances of the players were comparable, Niven (2020) relied upon the approximate value measure, which is a metric used to assess an individual player's contribution to team success across all positions in football and emphasizes excellence over any given position. The study found that players who protested were more likely to take a pay cut (less guaranteed money), experienced slower salary growth and were more likely to be traded to another team (Niven, 2020).

The literature suggests that athletes who engage in social activism should factor in the type of activism and level of effort when assessing the impact that the activism will have on their earning ability in the near and long terms. Furthermore, athletes who are contemplating engaging in "risky" activism will likely want to confer with their financial advisor to devise a financial strategy with several contingencies should the activism have a deleterious effect on their income. Likewise, the athlete development specialist should assist the athlete in their assessment of the risk and refer them to the appropriate financial services providers. As such, the current research asks the first research question.

RQ 1: What impact does professional athletes' social activism have on their careers and marketability?

With the power of social media as a tool to illustrate social injustices being irrefutable (Sanderson et al., 2016), professional athletes have utilized it to express their personal opinions around various social justice issues. Following George Zimmerman's acquittal for killing Trayvon Martin, Dwyane Wade posted a picture of himself wearing a hoodie on Facebook and Twitter and LeBron James posted a picture of him and his Miami Heat teammates wearing hoodies (Sanderson et al., 2016). Additionally, athletes use social media, Twitter specifically, to convey different messages around social justice. Schmittel and Sanderson (2015) studied NFL's players' usage of Twitter after the Zimmerman acquittal in 2013. Their examination revealed that players discussed the case in at least one of seven ways: (1) anticipation, (2) disbelief, (3) critiques of the American justice system, (4) social commentary, (5) condolences and support, (6) responding to fans, and (7) freedom of speech arguments (Schmittel & Sanderson, 2015). The study also revealed that Twitter is a viable option for players of color to express themselves around social justice issues and to start critical conversations on such topics. Furthermore, it concluded that fans and teams for which the athletes play may be uncomfortable with players championing social justice causes (Schmittel & Sanderson, 2015).

LeBron James is likely viewed as the most vocal NBA player when it comes to social justice issues and politics. Coombs and Cassilo (2017) explored the role of James as an activist and found four themes that emerged in his Black Lives Matter related messaging: (1) Brand LeBron, (2) Established Voice,

Higher Expectations; (3) Attention, Not Aggression; and (4) Community Versus Protest. It was found that James is careful and deliberate in his messaging as an activist and tends to avoid revolutionary content, all the while keeping in mind his reputation and future goals (Coombs & Cassilo, 2017). Given James' stature in the sports world, his social media strategies and messaging in the context of activism could be instructive for athletes contemplating utilizing social media for similar purposes.

Social media will continue to be a primary instrument through which athlete-activists express themselves. The literature suggests that athlete development specialists are well served to have a sufficiently strong rapport with athletes and stay informed on how the athlete intends to utilize social media and to counsel him or her on content before it is posted, particularly as it relates to content around social justice issues. Furthermore, just as employers constantly monitor athletes' social media accounts, it would benefit the specialist to do so as well. To that end, the second research question is posed.

RQ 2: What role does social media play in professional athletes' social activism?

While there is a scarcity of research specifically on social activism and the intersection of the dual identities of race and athlete (Beachy et al., 2018), there is literature that addresses self-identity, the interplay between racial and athlete identity, and how those factors affect athletes, particularly athletes of color (Beachy et al., 2018; Bimper & Harrison, 2011). Athletes who are engaged in social responsibility activities appear to have a strong sense of self and a firm sense of their interests and values. Self-identity is a cornerstone of effective athlete development (Miller & Kerr, 2002). It can be harmful for athletes not to develop a sense of self independent of sport and to be unaware of what their interests are beyond sport. Student-athletes who over-identify with being an athlete and fail to experiment with other roles can be susceptible to a range of developmental disadvantages such as limited exploration of interests outside of sport, emotional distress upon withdrawal from sport roles, willingness to engage in risk behaviors, and immature career and lifestyle planning (Miller & Kerr, 2002). Holstein, Jones, and Koonce (2015) address this phenomenon in their discussion of elite collegiate players becoming "engulfed" in their identities as athletes. This engulfment trend appears to be one to which African-American athletes are particularly susceptible.

According to Beamon (2012), Black collegiate football and basketball players have the highest rates of identity foreclosure, as they have tended to over-emphasize their identities as athletes above all else. In an examination of African-American athletic and racial identity, Bimper and Harrison (2011) asserted that Black athletes have a dual consciousness as black and athlete, identities that the athlete may struggle to negotiate and balance.

Black athletes also face the reality that fans and other stakeholders, most of whom are not black, expect them to choose their athletic identity over their racial identity (Bimper & Harrison, 2011). The opposition to athletes as socially responsible activists is grounded in the notion that athletes, particularly those of color, should just "shut up and dribble" (Sullivan, 2018). These fans watch sports to escape what's occurring in the world and when athletes insert societal issues into the playing field, their enjoyment of the sport is diminished. Smith and Hattery (2011) assert that anyone who is surprised to hear that the SportsWorld reflects the real world is not interested in a discussion about the SportsWorld as a site of privilege, race, class and gender.

MacIntosh et al. (2020), using a series of MANOVAs and the social justice scale, examined collegiate student-athletes' perceptions of activism and found that student-athletes of color "held higher perceptions on most of the subscales related to activism" (p. 1) relative to white student-athletes. Specifically, student-athletes of color had stronger positive attitudes towards activism and stronger inclinations to engage in activism (MacIntosh et al., 2020). It was further found that student-athletes from less privileged backgrounds (people of color and women) were more likely to hold favorable views of activism because they themselves had likely encountered discrimination and felt moved to act as a result (MacIntosh et al., 2020).

The literature suggests that athlete development specialists will need to have increased awareness of the fact that African American athlete-activists may be more invested in their identities as black men and women than their identities as athletes. This should inform how they engage such athlete-activists. Athlete development specialists should also be prepared to direct resources towards the mental well-being of athlete-activists, as activism and the opposition to it can take an emotional toll on those in high profile roles (MacIntosh et al., 2020). While this has focused on collegiate student-athletes, their views are germane to those of professional athletes, as most professional athletes played collegiately. In 2021, 83% of active NFL rosters came from FBS schools (Putnik, 2021). In 2020, 84% of the NBA's roster consisted of college players (Pekale, 2020) and 94% of the WNBA's roster consisted of college players (2020). Accordingly, when speaking of professional athlete-activists, we are speaking of a group that overwhelmingly has experience as collegiate student-athletes. In turn, the final research question is asked.

RQ 3: What role do racial and athlete identity play in athletes' activism?

ANALYTICAL MODEL

This framework presented here is based upon one articulated by Cunningham (2010) in the context of understanding the under-representation of African-American coaches at the collegiate level. Cunningham (2010) asserts that concentrating on only one explanation for the lack of African American coaches is insufficient because sports organizations are multilevel, complex entities that are influenced by myriad factors and that frameworks should account for those complex realities. Similarly, the factors influencing elite athletes' decisions around social activism are multilevel in nature and are influenced just as much by the individual athletes as they are by the sports organizations for which they play. Accordingly, it is appropriate to apply a similar approach when examining such decisions.

The Original Framework (2018)

The proposed model framework has three levels: macro, meso, and micro. Respectively, the levels account for factors that exist at the societal, organizational and individual levels (Melton & Cunningham, 2014). These factors don't exist independently of one another (Cunningham, 2010). In fact, they interact with and influence one another (Cunningham, 2010).

Macro-Level Factors

Factors at the macro level are those that exist within larger society but can affect an individual athlete's attitude and behaviors (Melton & Cunningham, 2014). According to Melton and Cunningham (2014), the factors include "prevailing norms, customs and ideals" (p. 191). Macro level factors frequently observed in the context of analyzing athletes' social responsibility include institutionalized practices and the political climate.

Institutionalized Practices

Cunningham (2010) asserts that practices become institutionalized when over time and due to "habit, history and tradition," they become the standard way in which things are done. Racism and sexism are examples of institutionalized practices that have existed throughout the history of this country (Feagin,

2006; Howard, 1998). Both exist within the sports industry (Burton, 2014; Cunningham, 2010) and have historically driven athlete activism from figures that include Paul Robeson, Muhammad Ali, Arthur Ashe, Wilma Rudolph, Wyomia Tyus, and Billie Jean King.

In the 21st century, athlete-activists continue to bring awareness to racism and sexism (and other practices such as homo/transphobia, xenophobia, and ableism). Relative to previous generations of athlete-activists, this group has taken an approach that targets specific manifestations of racism and sexism in sports and frequently in real-time, due to the proliferation and convenience of social media (Schmittel & Sanderson, 2015).

In October 2015, the University of Missouri football team, in protest of a racially charged campus climate that included racial epithets and swastikas, refused to play another game until the university president was terminated or resigned (Peralta, 2015). The team, with the support of its coach, leveraged social media in its protest efforts (Peralta, 2015). The president resigned before the team's next game (Peralta, 2015). Six years later, Sedona Prince, a member of Oregon's women's basketball team, posted a video on Instagram and Twitter that highlighted the disparities between the NCAA's March Madness men's basketball tournament and the women's tournament (Bachman & Higgins, 2021). While the video focused on the stark difference in facilities and equipment, it brought to light other disparities in branding, COVID-19 testing, and amenities between the two tournaments, triggering a broader conversation about sexism and gender inequities in sports and other professions (Bachman & Higgins, 2021). The NCAA subsequently commissioned an independent investigation that concluded that it has historically failed to invest in the women's tournament on the same level as it has the men's tournament (Bachman & Higgins, 2021).

Institutionalized practices, perhaps more than any of the factors to be addressed in this chapter, are the most pervasive and immovable. Racism and sexism systemically drive discriminatory hiring practices, inequitable wage structures, and homogeneity in senior and executive leadership in sports and other professions (Cunningham, 2010). Given how rooted these two institutionalized practices are in the American experience, it can be anticipated that these and similar practices will continue to prompt activism amongst athletes.

Political Climate

The political climate at any given moment in the country can have a profound effect on sports organizations. Cunningham (2010) asserts, "The prevailing political climate and social dynamics of a particular time or administrations have the potential to influence a sport organization in a number of ways, including the emphasis placed on competitive and participant sport opportunities (Coakley, 2009), the provision of funding for sports facilities (Crompton, 1995), empowerment (or lack thereof) of unions (Abercrombie, Hill, & Turner, 2000), [and] education (West & Currie, 2008)" (p.398). The climate can also have a profound effect on athletes' engagement in social activism.

President Donald Trump created a political climate that engendered animus toward athletes who knelt in protest of racial injustice. During his presidency, he referred to protesting NFL players as "son(s) of bitch(es)" and called for their termination, attacked high profile, vocal athletes such as LeBron James, Megan Rapinoe, and Steph Curry on Twitter, and politicized White House ceremonies for championship teams (Seifert, 2017; Menon, 2020). The climate he cultivated spurred like-minded conservative politicians to express their dissatisfaction with such activities as well. Former U.S. senator and then co-owner of the Atlanta Dream Kelly Loeffler was one of those politicians. Her explicit objection to Black Lives Matter and protesting athletes led members of the Dream to actively campaign for her opponent in the upcoming 2020 election, Rev. Raphael Warnock (Gregory, 2021). Warnock's profile and fundraising substantially increased in part because of the Dream amplifying him, which ultimately led to him successfully defeating Loeffler in the runoff election in January 2021 (Gregory, 2021). Loeffler ultimately sold her stake in the Dream as well (Booker, 2021).

When examining athlete activism past and present, it can be argued that the more charged the political climate, the more engagement occurs. The historical analog to this current season of activism is the athlete activism of the 1960s, which occurred in the context of a highly unpopular war and shifting sociopolitical winds. What seems clear is that where the political climate of the country goes, athlete activism inevitably follows. Divisive climates increase activism and less charged ones decrease it.

Meso-Level Factors

Factors at this level are those that exist within the organization and are related to how structure, decisions and processes influence an athlete's assessment of the efficacy of protesting (Cunningham, 2010). Meso-level factors include the organizational culture and team location.

Organizational (League/Team) Culture

The league for which an athlete plays and the culture it promotes can have a role in whether he or she engages in activism. Schein (1990) defines culture as:

(a) a pattern of basic assumptions, (b) invented, discovered, or developed by a given group, (c) as it learns to cope with its problems of external adaptation and internal integration, (d) that has worked well enough to be considered valid, and therefore (e) is to be taught to new members as the (f) correct way to perceive, think and feel in relation to those problems. (p. 111)

People within the organization strongly shape the culture (Cunningham, 2010). For professional sports leagues and teams, team culture can be driven by the ideologies and philosophies of teams' owners and upper management (Schrotenboer, 2019; Belson, 2020). Their support of athlete activism, or lack thereof, can influence athletes' decisions around such matters.

Athlete-activists tend to flourish in organizations whose cultures accept activism as a form of social responsibility. Of the American professional leagues, the WNBA is illustrative of how league support foments player activism. Over the last five years, this league has evolved from fining players for wearing shirts that brought attention to police shootings (a penalty that was ultimately rescinded) to creating a social justice council and dedicating the 2020 season to Breonna Taylor (Berkman, 2021). Commissioner Cathy Engelbert believes that partners are happy to work with the league because the players stand up for their individual principles (Berkman, 2021). From Minnesota Lynx Semoine Augustus's campaign for LGBTQ marriage equality to players such as Maya Moore, Renee Montgomery, and Natasha Cloud taking sabbaticals to pursue various social justice reforms, WNBA players are at the forefront of activism (Abrams & Weiner, 2020). The WNBA, through its progression from penalizing athlete-activists for their on-the-job protests to embracing athlete activism and creating infrastructure to support it, has demonstrated how organizational culture can either suppress or cultivate such activism.

Team Location

An athlete's geographic proximity to social justice events is another factor that can influence decisions around activism. Colin Kaepernick's paradigm shifting 2016 social justice campaign was prompted by the December 2015 murder of Mario Woods, who was shot at least 21 times by San Francisco police officers (Carroll, 2019). Kaepernick had been playing for the San Francisco Forty-Niners for five seasons at the time of the Woods murder, having led the team to two conference championship games and a Super Bowl appearance (Wagoner, 2017). In the same month in which Woods was killed, five St. Louis Rams protested the lack of charges against the Ferguson officer who shot Mike Brown by entering the field for a game with their hands in the "don't shoot" posture ("No fines for Rams," 2014). Kenny Britt, one of the participants, offered an explanation that suggests that proximity was a driving factor in the group's action. He stated, "We wanted to show that we are organized for a great cause and something positive comes out of it. That's what we hope we can make happen. That's our community. We wanted to let the community know that we support the community" ("No fines for Rams," 2014).

Similarly, the WNBA's Minnesota Lynx donned "Black Lives Matter" shirts during warm-ups in a 2016 game against the Dallas Wings following the shooting deaths of Philando Castile and Alton Sterling by the police (Shoichet, 2017). Castile was shot by police in St. Anthony, a suburb in the greater Minneapolis-St. Paul metropolitan area. The Milwaukee Bucks' 2020 work stoppage was triggered by the shooting of Jacob Blake in Kenosha, a bedroom community between Milwaukee and Chicago (Baer & Berman, 2020). Increasingly, athletes appear to be more inclined to engage in activism when incidents "hit close to home." This trend only has the potential to continue, especially as more incidents occur in or near cities with professional teams. Given the unpredictable nature of when such incidents may occur, sports organizations are well served to be prepared for athletes to take visible roles in opposing social injustices in the cities in which they play.

Micro-Level Factors

Micro-level factors are those which are specific to the individual athlete and influence decisions around engagement in activism. The intersection of identity, personal experiences, and financial security are the factors that fall at this level.

Identity and Personal Experiences

Identity and personal experiences are micro-level factors that could easily warrant individual discussion. However, due to their intersection in influencing activism behavior, they will be addressed jointly. Identity is defined as "either (a) a special category, defined by membership rules and (alleged) characteristic attributes or expected behaviors, or (b) socially distinguishing features that a person takes a special pride in or views as unchangeable but socially consequential" (Fearon, 1999, p. 1). Elite athletes can find themselves extremely tied to their identities as athletes (Miller & Kerr, 2002). In addition to race or gender, identity can include religion, sexual orientation and disability status (Anderson, Smith, & Stokowski, 2019; Anderson, 2009).

Student-athletes of color and female student-athletes have stronger positive attitudes towards activism, perceived behavioral control and behavioral intentions to engage in activism relative to white student-athletes and male student-athletes of color, respectively (MacIntosh et al., 2020). Furthermore, those of privileged backgrounds were found to not view racism as a prevalent issue and were less likely to participate in activism (MacIntosh et al., 2020). Put simply, those student-athletes in groups that were likely to encounter systemic oppression and discrimination (people of color, women, members of the LGBTQ community) were more likely to have positive views of activism and engaging in it. Among the NCAA's Division 1 revenue generating sports—football and basketball—48% and 52% of the players are black, respectively (Burns, 2019). The most elite student-athletes ascend to the professional ranks, where their positive views of activism appear to convert into actual activism. Over the last decade, the leagues that have been the most vocal from a social justice standpoint are the NFL, NBA, and the WNBA, leagues whose players are primarily black men or women. According to Lapchick (2020), players of color make up 69.4%, 83.1%, and 79.6% of the NFL, NBA, and WNBA, respectively.

That the professional leagues consisting primarily of people of color and women are also the leagues that have the most engaged athlete-activists is likely because those demographics enter their respective leagues holding positive views of activism (Harnois, 2017; Ball, 2020). It also follows that leagues that are predominantly white and consist of athletes who are more likely to come from privileged backgrounds, are less likely to view activism as necessary (MacIntosh et al., 2020) and have lower rates of players engaging in activism. In other words, league affiliation can be a possible indicator of a player's likelihood of engaging in activism.

How athletes personally experience the world can be largely impacted by their identities, all of which can play a role in steering them toward or away from activism. Personal experiences can include any number of things—an individual's background, connection to history, or a connection or perceived connection to traumatic events. Following the shooting of Jacob Blake in August 2020, four-time Grand Slam winner Naomi Osaka announced that she would not play in the semi-finals of the Western & Southern Open, citing the fact that she was a black woman as the reason she was sitting out the match. She explained, "As a black woman I feel as though there are much more important matters at hand that need immediate attention rather than watching me play tennis. I don't expect anything drastic to happen with me not playing but if I can get a conversation started in a majority white sport, I consider that a step in the right direction" (Fieldstadt, 2020, para 5). NBA player Sterling Brown is someone whose activism is driven by a confluence of personal experiences. Brown is from Chicago and attended the same high school as revolutionary Black Panther Fred Hampton, who was assassinated in 1969 by the FBI and Chicago Police Department (Woodyard, 2020). That exposure to Hampton led him to research and learn more about him and better understand his cause, which has informed his own activism (Woodyard, 2020). Brown has also experienced brutality at the hands of the police, after being tackled to the ground and tasered over a parking violation by Milwaukee police officers in 2018, when he played for the Milwaukee Bucks. He subsequently sued the city and ultimately settled for terms that included financial compensation and most importantly, changes to the Milwaukee Fire and Police Commission's Standard Operating Procedures, including more thorough documentation of occasions when officers draw their weapons (Hart, 2021).

Identity and personal experiences can hold a powerful sway over athletes as they determine whether to engage in activism. Collegiate programs and professional leagues with players who primarily come from historically marginalized communities are well served to be aware of this fact and implement strategies that serve to create space to allow their voices to be heard.

Financial Security

The potential financial consequences for speaking up for social justice are an undeniable micro-level factor in athletes' decision making on activism. Muhammad Ali, Craig Hodges, and Colin Kaepernick serve as examples of how activism can lead to decreased economic opportunities (i.e., jobs and endorsements; Gonyea, 2016; Schmidt et al., 2018; Norris, 2020). Student-athletes potentially jeopardize their athletic scholarships when they engage in activism as well. Fear of financial repercussions is real, as evidenced by these comments from retired safety D'Angelo Hall:

> I'm not getting into a pissing match with nobody-the president and all these other owners, the owner I work for now and others that I might be working for one day. If your boss doesn't believe in one thing and you really do, do you want to get into a pissing match with him? I told someone the other day: "Man, I love my family and my kids and the financial stability I have more than anything in the world." And so, to jeopardize that for them, it's going to take a lot for me to do that. (Niven, 2020, p. 643)

There is no doubt that Hall is not alone in his view, particularly in a climate in which the immediate past president encouraged NFL owners to fire protesting players.

Accordingly, elite athletes must navigate this piece carefully and engage a cost-benefit analysis before becoming activists. The cost-benefit analysis should account for the kind of activism the athlete intends to engage in and whether it could jeopardize their current or future earnings. The counsel of a certified financial planner is advised to assure that the athlete is equipped to weather any negative financial consequences. The analysis should also account for the fact that as employees of private entities, professional athletes' speech is not protected under the First Amendment; there are, however, protections under the National Labor Relations Act (NLRA).

Updated Framework (2020)

Events in 2020 changed the game in athlete engagement in social justice. The murders of George Floyd, Ahmaud Arbery, and Breonna Taylor and the arrival of a worldwide pandemic aggravated an already volatile political climate. Sports came to a halt in March 2020 due to COVID-19 and did not return until July. When they did return, the landscape had materially shifted, and the multi-level framework along with it.

The racial reckoning triggered specifically by George Floyd's murder was seemingly a tipping point for athletes who had remained silent around issues of social justice. For the first time, football players from the Power 5 conferences were not only demanding racial justice in society generally but advocating for better treatment as players. From Mississippi State star running back and Mississippi native Kylin Hill declaring that he would not play another game for the school if the Confederacy-aligned stars and bars remained on the state flag (Lee, 2021) to players in the PAC-12 forming a unity group that demanded improved COVID safety protocols, revenue sharing among players and infrastructure to address social justice issues (PAC-12 football players' letter, 2020), college football players found and asserted their voices on individual and collective levels. Student-athletes on campuses throughout the country marched in protest of racial injustices, with coaches joining them in some instances.

The most cataclysmic event was the work stoppage initiated by the Milwaukee Bucks during the NBA playoffs after the shooting of Jacob Blake. Their actions triggered a domino effect in which the remaining teams in the bubble refused to take the court for their games that night and the next several days. Other major league teams soon followed suit, resulting in an unprecedented work stoppage across all major professional major sports leagues in the U.S.

What we saw in the Bucks's actions as a team reflected an overlapping of the three levels of factors, making them almost indistinguishable from each other. Where they were once distinct yet influencing one another, this incident saw the national reckoning around race (macro), close geographic proximity to Jacob Blake's shooting (meso), and personal experiences of teammates like Sterling Brown (micro) intersect in such a way that it was difficult to determine which level had the most influence over the course of action. Figure 1.1 captures the shift in the framework.

The observed shifting within the framework's dynamic suggests that the model should be periodically revisited so that it can be appropriately

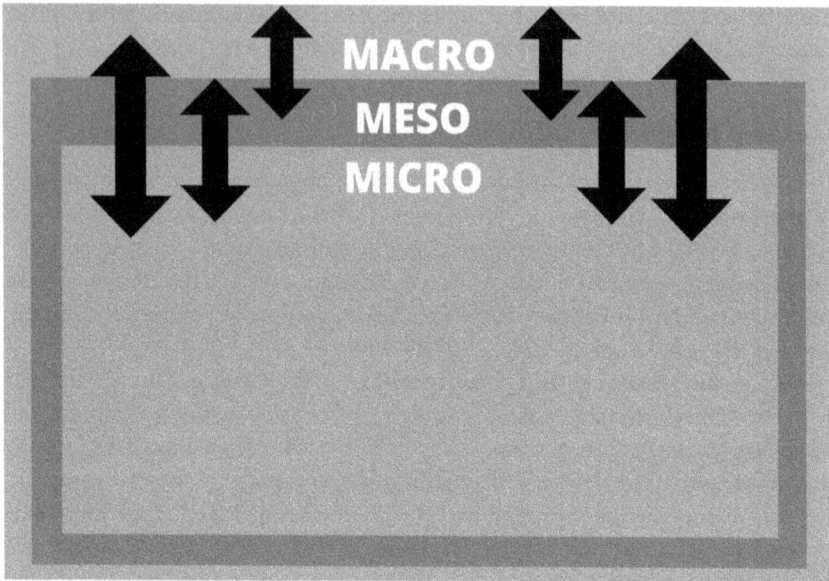

Figure 1.1: Shift of factors, 2020–2022. Source: A. Michelle Clemon

adjusted to reflect changes that may occur at the various levels, including adding/removing factors that may gain or lose influence over time. By way of example, the recent emphasis on mental health as highlighted by Naomi Osaka and Simone Biles may be an indication that mental health should be included among the micro level factors. For the model to be instructive, it should remain current to reflect real-time dynamics.

CONCLUSION

Over the last thirty years, there's been a profound shift in how athlete-activists express themselves as socially conscious citizens. Equipped with smart phones and social media platforms that can reach millions with a touch of a button, today's athlete-activist wields a level of influence and access unimaginable to the likes of Paul Robeson, Muhammad Ali, and Arthur Ashe. This paradigm shift underscores the importance of examining what prompts or discourages athletes' engagement in activism. The framework outlined here addresses the issue by acknowledging that there are factors at the systemic/national, local and individual levels that are vital in any assessment of an athlete's likelihood of becoming an athlete-activist. Each level is layered and interplays with the other levels. The last two years have shown that under certain circumstances, the levels that are usually distinct from one another can overlap and become almost indistinguishable. This framework has practical implications for invested stakeholders (athletes, sports managers, agents, athlete development specialists, and sports scholars) seeking greater comprehension of the factors that can drive or deter athlete activism.

REFERENCES

Abrams, J., Weiner, N. (2020, October 16). How the most socially progressive pro league got that way. *New York Times*. https://www.nytimes.com/2020/10/16/sports/basketball/wnba-loeffler-protest-kneeling.html?action=click&module=RelatedLinks&pgtype=Article

Agyemang, K., Singer, J. N., & DeLorme, J. (2010). An exploratory study of black male college athletes' perceptions on race and athlete activism. *International Review for the Sociology of Sport, 45*(4), 419–435.

Anderson, A. R., Smith, C. M., & Stokowski, S. E. (2019). The impact of religion and ally identity on individual sexual and gender prejudice at an NCAA Division II institution. *Journal of Issues in Intercollegiate Athletics, 12,* 154–177.

Anderson, D. (2009). Adolescent girls' involvement in disability sport: Implications for identity development. *Journal of Sport and Social Issues, 33*(4), 427–449.

Associated Press. (2021, June 2). The NFL will stop assuming racial differences when assessing brain injuries. *NPR*. https://www.npr.org/2021/06/02/1002627309/nfl-says-it-will-halt-race-norming-and-review-brain-injury-claims

Bachman, R., L, Higgins. (2021, August 3). NCAA undervalued women's basketball tournament by millions while prioritizing men's tourney, report finds. *Wall Street Journal*. https://www.wsj.com/articles/ncaa-undervalued-womens-basketball-tournament-11628018560?st=zauv8quvw4oaxqs&reflink=article_imessage_share

Baer, S., Berman, M. (2020, August 26). The Milwaukee Bucks set off a postponement of NBA playoff games in protest of the shooting of Jacob Blake. *Buzz Feed*. Retrieved on January 12, 2022, from https://www.buzzfeednews.com/article/skbaer/milkwaukee-bucks-boycott-jacob-blake

Ball, J. C. (2020). The identity of activism: How gender and racial identity relate to activism among African Americans. https://doi.org/10.17615/dw8a-sy68

Beachy, E. G., Brewer, B. W., Van Raalte, J. L., & Cornelius, A. E. (2018). Associations between activist and athletic identities in college students. *Journal of Sport Behavior, 41*(4), 369-389.

Beamon, K. (2012). "I'm a baller": Athletic identity foreclosure among African-American former student-athletes. *Journal of African American Studies, 16*(2), 195–208.

Berkman, S. (2021, July 5). The Liberty's role in making W.N.B.A. players "top dogs" of activism. *New York Times*.https://www.nytimes.com/2021/07/05/sports/basketball/wnba-social-activism-protests-new-york-liberty.html?referringSource=articleShare

Bieler, D. (2020, August 27). Bill Russell led an NBA boycott in 1961. Now he's saluting others for "getting in good trouble." *Washington Post*. https://www .washingtonpost.com/sports/2020/08/27/bill-russell-nba-boycott/

Bimper, A. Y., & Harrison, L. (2011). Meet me at the crossroads: African American athletic and racial identity. *Quest, 63*(3), 275–288.

Booker, B. (2021, February 26). WNBA team co-owned by Ex-Sen. Kelly Loeffler is sold after players' criticism. *NPR*. Retrieved on December 27, 2021, from https://www.npr.org/2021/02/26/971877660/wnba-team-co-owned-by-ex-sen -kelly-loeffler-is-sold-after-players-criticism

Boren, C. (2019, June 19). Trump invites USWNT to White House after Megan Rapinoe says she's 'not going.' *Washington Post*. https://www.washingtonpost.com /sports/2019/06/26/megan-rapinoe-says-shes-not-going-white-house/

Busbee, Jay. (2019, November 5). When did championship teams start visiting the White House? *Yahoo Sports*. Retrieved on June 23, 2021, from https://sports.yahoo.com/ when-did-championship-teams-start-visiting-the-white-house-190309190.html

Chiari, M. (2017, September 23). LeBron James responds to Donald Trump unin- viting Stephen Curry to White House. *Bleacher Report*. Retrieved on June 25, 2021, from https://bleacherreport.com/articles/2734713-lebron-james-responds-to -donald-trump-uninviting-stephen-curry-to-white-house

Cohen, M. (2020, November 2). Step into my oval office: An oral history of White House visits under Trump. *Sports Illustrated*. Retrieved on June 23, 2020, from https://www.si.com/more-sports/2020/11/02/donald-trump-white-house-visits -daily-cover

Conway, T. (2017, February 8). Stephen Curry responds to Under Armour CEO Kevin Plank's support of Donald Trump. *Bleacher Report*. Retrieved on June 29, 2021, from https://bleacherreport.com/articles/2692044-stephen-curry-responds-to -under-armour-ceo-kevin-planks-support-of-donald-trump

Cunningham, G. B., and Regan Jr., M. R. (2012). Political activism, racial iden- tity and the commercial endorsement of athletes. *International Review for the Sociology of Sport, 47*(6), 657–669.

Edwards, F., Lee, H., and Esposito, M. (2019). Risk of being killed by police use of force in the United States by age, race–ethnicity, and sex. *Proceedings of the National Academy of Sciences, 116*(34), 16793–16798.

ESPN.com news services. (2015, December 1). No fines for Rams players' salute. https://www.espn.com/nfl/story/_/id/11963218/the-five-st-louis-rams-players -saluted-slain-teenager-michael-brown-sunday-game-not-fined

Feagin, J. (2013). Systemic racism: A theory of oppression. London: Routledge.

Fearon, J. D. (1999). *What is identity (as we now use the word)* [Unpublished manu- script]. Stanford, CA: Stanford University.

Fieldstadt, E. (2020, August 27). Osaka won't play Western & Southern Open semifi- nal in stance for racial justice, tournament paused. *NBC News*. Retrieved on August 10, 2021, from https://www.nbcnews.com/news/sports/osaka-won-t-play-western -southern-open-semifinal-stance-racial-n1238402

Frank, M. (2017, September 7). Eagles owner on Kaepernick: Anthem pro- tests must be "respectful." *Delaware Online*. Retrieved on August 9,

2021, from https://www.delawareonline.com/story/sports/nfl/eagles/2017/09/07/eagles-owner-kaepernick-anthem-protests-respectful/644120001/

Gaines, C. (2019, June 29). Championship teams visiting the White House has turned into a mess. *Business Insider*. Retrieved on June 24, 2021, from https://www.businessinsider.com/championship-teams-trump-white-house-2019-4

Garcia, S. (2017, October 20). The woman who created #MeToo long before hashtags. *New York Times*. https://www.nytimes.com/2017/10/20/us/me-too-movement-tarana-burke.html

Gibbs, C., & Haynes, R. (2013). A phenomenological investigation into how Twitter has changed the nature of sport media relations. International Journal of Sport Communication, 6(4), 394–408.

Goldberg, R. (2017, October 8). Jerry Jones says any Cowboys player who "disrespects" the flag won't play. www.bleacherreport. Retrieved on August 9, 2021, from https://bleacherreport.com/articles/2737631-jerry-jones-says-a-cowboys-player-who-disrespects-the-flag-wont-play

Gonyea, D. (2016, June 10). In political activism, Ali pulled no punches—and paid a heavy price. www.npr.com. Retrieved on December 6, 2021, from https://www.npr.org/2016/06/10/481523465/in-political-activism-ali-pulled-no-punches-and-paid-a-heavy-price

Gregory, S. (2021, January 7). WNBA's strategy to support Raphael Warnock-and help Democrats win the Senate. www.time.com. Retrieved on July 15, 2021, from https://time.com/5927075/atlanta-dream-warnock-loeffler/

Harnois, C. E. (2017). Intersectional masculinities and gendered political consciousness: How do race, ethnicity and sexuality shape men's awareness of gender inequality and support for gender activism? *Sex Roles, 77*(3), 141–154.

Hart, M. (2021, April 27). City of Milwaukee approves settlement with former Bucks players Sterling Brown. www.wpr.org. Retrieved on August 12, 2021, from https://www.wpr.org/city-milwaukee-committee-approves-settlement-former-bucks-player-sterling-brown

Holstein, J., Jones, R., & Koonce, G. (2015). Is there life after football? Surviving the NFL. New York: NYU Press.

Howard, J. A. (1998, September). The more things change, the more they stay the same? Reflections on the state of sexism. In *Sociological Forum* (pp. 545–555). Eastern Sociological Society.

Jenkins, A. (2017, September 23). Read President Trump's NFL speech on national anthem protests. time.com. Retrieved on June 25, 2021, from https://time.com/4954684/donald-trump-nfl-speech-anthem-protests/

Joseph, A. (2020, September 15). Dallas Cowboys owner Jerry Jones spoke about Dontari Poe's decision to kneel during national anthem. www.usatoday.com. Retrieved on August 9, 2020, from https://www.usatoday.com/story/sports/ftw/2020/09/15/dallas-cowboys-jerry-jones-dontari-poe-national-anthem-protest/114033760/

Kaufman, P. (2008). Boos, bans, and other backlash: The consequences of being an activist athlete. *Humanity & Society, 32*(3), 215–237.

Littlefield, B. (2017, May 12). Craig Hodges: NBA activism, confronting MJ and a letter for President Bush. Retrieved on June 23, 2021, from https://www.wbur.org/onlyagame/2017/05/12/craig-hodges-nba-activism

Lockhart, P. (2018, January 11). What Serena Williams's scary childbirth story says about medical treatment of black women. www.vox.com. Retrieved on August 10, 2021, from https://www.vox.com/identities/2018/1/11/16879984/serena-williams-childbirth-scare-black-women

Machota, J. (2017, August 22). Jerry Jones feels "very strongly" players shouldn't protest anthem; "I like the way the Cowboys do it." www.dallasnews.com. Retrieved on July 2, 2021, from https://www.dallasnews.com/sports/cowboys/2017/08/22/jerry-jones-feels-very-strongly-players-shouldn-t-protest-anthem-i-like-the-way-the-cowboys-do-it/

Mac Intosh, A., Martin, E. M., & Kluch, Y. (2020). To act or not to act? Student-athlete perceptions of social justice activism. *Psychology of Sport and Exercise*, *51*, 101766

Martin, Jonathan. (2020, June 10). LeBron James and other stars form a voting rights group. nytimes.com. Retrieved on June 21, 2021, from https://www.nytimes.com/2020/06/10/us/politics/lebron-james-voting-rights.html

Martin, R. (2017, June 28). Former tennis player James Blake on athletes and activism. www.npr.com. Retrieved on August 12, 2021, from https://www.npr.org/2017/06/28/534671434/former-tennis-player-james-blake-on-athletes-and-activism

Menon, S. (2020, November 3). LeBron James, Steph Curry, Megan Rapinoe and others who raised their voices against Trump. www.republicworld.com. Retrieved on August 4, 2021, from https://www.republicworld.com/sports-news/other-sports/lebron-james-steph-curry-megan-rapinoe-and-others-who-raised-their-voices-against-trump.html

Miller, P. S., & Kerr, G. A. (2002). Conceptualizing excellence: Past, present, and future. *Journal of Applied Sport Psychology*, 14(3), 140–153.

Niven, D. (2020). Stifling workplace activism: The consequences of anthem protests for NFL players. *Social Science Quarterly*, *101*(2), 641–655.

Nadkarni, R., Nieves, A. (2015, November 9). Why Missouri's football team joined a protest against school administration. www.si.com. Retrieved on August 9, 2021, from https://www.si.com/college/2015/11/09/missouri-football-protest-racism-tim-wolfe

Norris, L. (2020, September 16). Like Colin Kaepernick in the NFL, Craig Hodges was essentially blackballed from the NBA for his social activism. www.sportscasting.com. Retrieved on December 6, 2021, from https://www.sportscasting.com/like-colin-kaepernick-in-the-nfl-craig-hodges-was-essentially-blackballed-from-the-nba-for-his-social-activism/

Orkand, B. (2017, June 27). "I Ain't got no quarrel with them Vietcong." nytimes.com. Retrieved on June 22, 2021, from https://www.nytimes.com/2017/06/27/opinion/muhammad-ali-vietnam-war.html

Peralta, E. (2015, November 8). Missouri football players strike to demand ouster of university president. www.npr.org. Retrieved on August 11,

2021, from https://www.npr.org/sections/thetwo-way/2015/11/08/455216375/missouri-football-players-strike-to-demand-ouster-of-university-president

Pekale, Z. (2020, July 27). Colleges, conferences with the most players on 2020 WNBA rosters. www.ncaa.com. Retrieved on January 15, 2022, from https://www.ncaa.com/news/basketball-women/article/2020-07-24/colleges-conferences-most-players-2020-wnba-rosters

Pekale, Z. (2020, December 21). Colleges with the most players on 2020–21 NBA opening day rosters. www.ncaa.com. Retrieved on January 15, 2022, from https://www.ncaa.com/news/basketball-men/article/2020-12-19/colleges-most-players-2020-21-nba-rosters

Putnik, G. (2021, September 121). NFL players by college on 2021 rosters. www.ncaa.com. Retrieved on January 15, 2022, from https://www.ncaa.com/news/football/article/2021-09-06/nfl-players-college-2021-rosters

Sanderson, J., Frederick, E., & Stocz, M. (2016). When athlete activism clashes with group values: Social identity threat management via social media. *Mass Communication and Society, 19*(3), 301–322.

Schmidt, S. H., Shreffler, M. B., Hambrick, M. E., & Gordon, B. S. (2018). An experimental examination of activist type and effort on brand image and purchase intentions. *Sport Marketing Quarterly, 27*(1), 31–43. DOI: 10.32731/SMQ.271.032018.03.

Schmittel, A., & Sanderson, J. (2015). Talking about Trayvon in 140 characters: Exploring NFL players' tweets about the George Zimmerman verdict. *Journal of Sport and Social Issues, 39*(4), 332–345.

Seifert, K. (2017, September 22). President Trump criticizes NFL player protests, says fans should exit stadiums. www.espn.com. Retrieved on June 30, 2021, from https://www.espn.com/nfl/story/_/id/20788354/president-donald-trump-speaks-nfl-player-protests

Shoichet, C., Martin, J. (2016, July 12). Off-duty cops walk out over WNBA players' Black Lives Matter shirts. www.cnn.com. Retrieved on July 6, 2021, from https://www.cnn.com/2016/07/12/us/wnba-minnesota-lynx-black-lives-matter-shirts/index.html

Skiver, K. (2017, December 5). Look: LeBron's tweet calling Trump a bum is the most retweeted athlete post in 2017. cbssports.com. Retrieved on April 28, 2017, from https://www.cbssports.com/nba/news/look-lebrons-tweet-calling-trump-a-bum-the-is-most-retweeted-athlete-post-in-2017

Smith, E. & Hattery, A. (2011). Race Relations Theories: Implications for Sport Management. Journal of Sport Management, 25, 107–117.

Sullivan, E. (2018, February 18). Laura Ingraham told LeBron James to shut up and dribble; He went to the hoop. www.npr.org. Retrieved on April 25, 2018, from https://www.npr.org/sections/thetwo-way/2018/02/19/587097707/laura-ingraham-told-lebron-james-to-shutup-and-dribble-he-went-to-the-hoop

Wagoner, N. (2017, March 1). Colin Kaepernick to opt out, become free agent. www.espn.com. Retrieved on November 3, 2021, from https://www.espn.com/nfl/story/_/id/18796373/colin-kaepernick-san-francisco-49ers-opts-contract

Washington, J. (2016, September 1). Still no anthem, still no regrets for Mahmoud Abdul-Rauf. www.andscape.com. Retrieved on April 11, 2022, from https://andscape.com/features/abdul-rauf-doesnt-regret-sitting-out-national-anthem/

Williams, S. (2018, February 20). Serena Williams: What my life-threatening experience taught me about giving birth. www.cnn.com. Retrieved on July 9, 2021, from https://www.cnn.com/2018/02/20/opinions/protect-mother-pregnancy-williams-opinion/index.html

Wilson, R. (2018, June 5). Report: No Eagles players took a knee or stayed in the locker room during anthem last season. www.cbssports.com. Retrieved on August 9, 2021, from https://www.cbssports.com/nfl/news/report-no-eagles-players-took-a-knee-or-stayed-in-the-locker-room-during-anthem-last-season/

Woodyard, E. (2020, February 28). Bucks' Sterling Brown carries on legacy of late activist Fred Hampton: "It's in his DNA." www.theundefeated.com. Retrieved on August 12, 2021, from https://theundefeated.com/features/bucks-sterling-brown-carries-on-legacy-of-late-activist-fred-hampton-its-in-his-dna/

Chapter 2

One Knee Does Not Equal Two Gloves

The Flaws in Equating Colin Kaepernick to Tommie Smith and John Carlos

Anthony J. Moretti

Former San Francisco 49ers quarterback Colin Kaepernick's protest against police brutality of African Americans became news in 2016 when he stopped standing for the national anthem prior to National Football League (NFL) games. "I am not going to stand to show pride in a flag for a country that oppresses black people and people of color," he said, in explaining his decision (Wyche, 2016, para. 3). Within months, Kaepernick, who is biracial and was adopted by a Caucasian couple when he was a child, went from being the team's starting quarterback to out of a job. Martin and McHendry Jr. (2016), shortly after Kaepernick's actions drew attention, stated that Kaepernick's expulsion from the NFL resulted from violating "the culture of compulsory patriotism that permeates much of contemporary U.S. culture—in particular at sporting events" (p. 88). Viewed another way, standing for the national anthem was seen as a mandatory act for any athlete who wishes to remain in his or her professional league.

Kaepernick has remained out of football since 2016. He and a former teammate reached an out-of-court settlement with the NFL in February 2019; both men had sued the NFL contending the league and its owners were colluding against them because of their decisions to kneel during the national anthem (Draper & Belson, 2019).

Kaepernick's criticism of the treatment of Blacks drew parallels to what happened at the 1968 Olympics in Mexico City, where American track stars

Tommie Smith and John Carlos each raised a fist covered in a black glove during the medal ceremony for the 200-meter race in which they finished first and third, respectively. They were looking to make a statement about the status of Blacks and other underrepresented groups in America and around the world. Smith described what Carlos and he did as a "socially generated act that happened to culminate on the world's biggest athletic stage" (Smith, 2007, p. 7). Smith's words might seem sarcastic, but his and Carlos's actions were anything but. The response to what they did also had no trace of sarcasm.

Within hours of their protest, the two Black men were expelled from the Games and later flown back to the U.S. well before the closing ceremonies. The United States Olympic Committee issued a statement in which it expressed "profound regrets to the International Olympic Committee, to the Mexican Organizing Committee and to the people of Mexico for the discourtesy displayed" by the two athletes (Sheehan, 1968, p. 45). Smith and Carlos returned to San Jose State College (it was renamed San Jose State University in the early 1970s and continues to operate with that designation today), where they were students, and according to Smith, "At best, we were considered outside the mainstream . . . at worst, we were simply infamous" (Smith, 2007, p. 18). Carlos was blunter, stating that as the years went by: "I was lonelier than a raindrop in the Sahara. No one wanted to talk to me" (Carlos, 2011, p. 1).

And both men suffered far worse than merely being booted from the Olympic Games: Smith already had been fired from his job before the Games because his employer was worried he might do something in Mexico City that would embarrass the company (Smith, 2007); Carlos' wife committed suicide a few years after the 1968 Games (Barra, 2008). Carlos (2011) traced the initial signs of his wife's suffering to what happened in the aftermath of the Mexico City Olympics. For both men, professional opportunities were limited. Smith and Carlos' relationship, which was never close, was fractured for many years (Amdur, 2011).

Beginning in 2016, a media narrative developed in the United States as Kaepernick drew more attention by continuing his protest during the national anthem. That narrative equated the actions of the multi-million dollar quarterback to two blue-collar runners. The *New York Times'* Jere Longman put forward Kaepernick as a "direct activist descendant" to Smith and Carlos (Longman, 2018, para. 4). *The Atlantic*'s Vann R. Newkirk II (2017) stated Kaepernick's decision to kneel "carried the same kind of defiance" (para. 6) as Smith and Carlos' raised fists. *The Washington Post*'s Kevin Blackistone (2016) reported Kaepernick had the conviction to do what Smith and Carlos also had done: "he dared to protest in the athletic arena, where we wrap sporting events in a prophylactic of patriotism used to demand political conformity and suppress discourse" (para. 6).

This chapter examines that narrative and suggests it is flawed. There are critical differences among the men, and between what Kaepernick did in 2016 and what Smith and Carlos did 48 years earlier; these differences mitigate the association between the men and their actions. Moreover, the media reaction to what took place in 2016 and 1968 was different. Delinking the activities of the three athletes, as this chapter will do, does not question the importance of what each man did and should not suggest one form of protest was more appropriate or necessary than the other. Rather, such separation is required because asserting a linkage and a chronology with Smith and Carlos on one end and Kaepernick on the other does not stand up to scrutiny.

1968: SMITH, CARLOS, AND THE OLYMPIC PROJECT FOR HUMAN RIGHTS

Smith and Carlos were not independent actors in 1968. Both men were members of the Olympic Project for Human Rights (OPHR), an organization founded in the United States, made up mostly of African-American male athletes, and which threatened a boycott of that summer's Mexico City Olympics. Smith (2007) emphasized the group supported human rights "even [for] those [people] who denied us ours" (p. 161). Its members had multiple demands, one being the removal of Avery Brundage as head of the International Olympic Committee (IOC; Zirin, n.d.); another was the expulsion of South Africa from the Olympic Games (Carlos, 2011). OPHR's leader was sociologist Harry Edwards, who considered Brundage "a devout anti-Semitic and an anti-Negro personality" (Bass, in Bloom & Willard, 2002, p. 185). Smith (2007) described Brundage as "just another racist white man" (p. 165). When several dozen Black athletes met with Edwards in 1967 to begin discussions of a potential Olympics boycott, Edwards knew "many of the athletes felt that despite their athletic accomplishments and the potential spoils their victories would bring to the U.S., they were still treated as less than equals by white Americans" (Peterson, 2009, p. 100). Carlos was more direct, stating, "We are nothing but show horses for white people" (p. 102).

Brundage was the former president of America's Olympic committee, and he had been president of the IOC since 1952. He passionately endorsed the "traditional concept of Olympism" (Quick, 1990, p. 21), which meant that politics and professionalism had no place in the Olympics. But, as Zukas (1992) notes, "Brundage's insistence on his romantic vision for the Games contradicted real world events" (p. 345), which included unrest in Eastern Europe, the continuing shame of apartheid in South Africa, the Vietnam War, and increased tensions about civil rights in the United States. Nevertheless, in 1968, Brundage saw two American athletes not as activists seeking to

highlight and improve the social and economic standing of countless numbers of people around the world but instead as polluters of idealism. Defining
their protest as "nasty demonstrations by Negroes" (Henderson, 2010, p. 78),
Brundage led the effort to get Carlos and Smith immediately returned to the
U.S. He succeeded.

2016: A QUARTERBACK TAKES A
STAND BY REFUSING TO STAND

Colin Kaepernick almost completed a remarkable rally in Super Bowl XLVII
in early February 2013. The 49ers trailed the Baltimore Ravens 28–6 early
in the third quarter before a furious comeback led by Kaepernick made the
score 28–23 before the quarter ended. However, Kaepernick and the 49ers
couldn't complete the rally, losing 34–31. In the immediate aftermath of the
loss, the team's fans were told with Kaepernick at quarterback they should
be "very excited about the future" (Bien, 2013, para. 1). In 2014, he signed
a six-year, $126 million contract (Gaines, 2017), a sure sign he would be the
team's quarterback for years to come. However, between 2013 and 2015,
the 49ers stalled, winning twelve games in 2013, eight in 2014, and five in
2015, and they did not return to the Super Bowl. As the 2016 season drew
near, Kaepernick's position as starting quarterback was in doubt (Wagoner,
2016). Though he started eleven games that season, his refusal to stand for the
national anthem, not his play on the field, dominated the headlines. The NFL
front office acknowledged before the season that "players are encouraged but
not required to stand during the playing of the National Anthem" (Fucillo,
2016, para. 2), an announcement that did not temper the negative emotions
directed at Kaepernick, who received death threats over his protest activities (Al Jazeera, 2016). His and his team's 2016 season ended with a 2–14
record. He opted out of his contract in March 2017 (49ers.com), which in the
end paid him only $39 million (Gaines, 2017). *TIME* suggested in 2017 that
Kaepernick was set to become "the first star athlete since the Vietnam era to
lose his career because of his beliefs" (Gregory, 2017, p. 102). That statement
was in reference to Muhammad Ali, who was stripped of his championship
boxing title for refusing to join the U.S. military and fight in Vietnam.

    Sports Illustrated noted when it named Kaepernick the 2017 recipient of
its "Sports Illustrated Muhammad Ali Legacy Award" that it took two weeks
for anyone in the media to ask Kaepernick why he had stopped standing. The
magazine's account noted, "It is a rare person who gives up what he loves
for what he believes" (Rosenberg, 2017, p. 62). Martin and McHendry Jr.
(2016) stated that as criticism of Kaepernick grew, one uncomfortable truth
became ever clearer: The people who opposed what he did were telling the

quarterback that he "can protest . . . but only in exactly a manner that offends no one," which meant they wanted him to do nothing at all (p. 97).

The brief overview above affirms Kaepernick's personal and professional situation bears little resemblance to that of Smith and Carlos from almost 50 years earlier. Nevertheless, the media in 2016 wanted their audiences to believe that the quarterback was akin to an heir to the track stars. The three men, their circumstances and the media's response to what they did undermine any realistic claim that Kaepernick, Smith, and Carlos deserve the linkage associated with them.

DISCONNECT 1: THE ACTORS

The biographies of Tommie Smith, John Carlos, and Colin Kaepernick are the first reason that a Smith/Carlos-Kaeprenick linkage ought to be more carefully considered.

Smith, born in 1944, was the seventh of 12 children who grew up "picking and chopping cotton in east Texas" (Smith, 2007, p. 4). Segregation was ripe; opportunities for his family were not. He wrote in his autobiography that he "never did know where the school that white kids went to was located" (Smith, 2007, p. 49), and no white children considered themselves to be Smith's friend. Smith indicated he learned as a boy that race relations were not good and that blacks were second to whites, and this was true in Texas and later in California, where his family had moved when he was 5.

Carlos also felt the sting of racism in Texas. Poor grades in high school necessitated he go to East Texas State Junior College. Arriving on a plane from New York, he noticed one airport bathroom marked "whites" and another "colored." He deliberately walked into the former, seeing how clean it was as he did. Then he walked into the latter, "and the toilets looked like they hadn't been cleaned since the Alamo" (Carlos, 2011, p. 63). He quickly learned that in New York, the racist white person would be called out and scorn heaped on him or her; but in Texas, the racist white person was surrounded by hundreds of people who thought the same thing ensuring the Black person was defenseless against the hate (Carlos, 2011).

Carlos, who was born in 1945 in New York, also had a difficult upbringing. In his autobiography, Carlos identifies the need for the "hustle," because "Black men, in particular, just couldn't make it off the salaries that they were earning at that particular time" (Carlos, 2011, p. 6). And in many Black families, "there were a lot of fathers that were MIA" (p. 19). Sometimes the hustle meant trying to escape the police, "which was at the heart of my extra-curricular activities," he wrote, and involved Carlos and friends stealing food from a freight train and handing it out to the needy in Harlem (p. 19). Carlos justified what he was doing by stating, "I couldn't turn my back when I saw evidence of discrimination in the community" (p. 27), which he said included the police and the fire department failing to protect Black families and their places of residence.

Carlos also was attracted to the message being disseminated by Malcolm X, who Carlos followed whenever the Nation of Islam leader was in Harlem. "Maybe it was because he made time for me on the streets," Carlos wrote. "Maybe it was because he made me raise my head up high" (Carlos, 2011, p. 31). From Malcolm X, Carlos found an example of how to stand up and demand change. "We could project our will, and if we had strength and unity, we could move mountains," he declared (p. 37). At age 18, and just one week after Malcolm X was murdered, Carlos "felt this urge to move forward, to grow up, to be my own man" (Carlos, 2011, p. 57). He married and about 10 months later, he became a father.

Carlos suffered from dyslexia, and one of his teachers "literally made [him] wear a dunce cap in the corner" (Carlos, 2011, p. 11). Needless to say, like Smith, Carlos was exposed to racism at a young age; the most bitter example came not when he had to wear a dunce cap but when his father said that he could not be a swimmer in the Olympics because "they don't allow the blacks to join the private clubs" (p. 15).

Tommie Smith and John Carlos experienced prejudice and racism from the day they were born. Their childhoods were not fun and games; Smith's family needed him to work in the fields, and Carlos' had to look the other way when he began stealing. It was not until both matured and began showing prowess in athletics that opportunities for a better life appeared. However, both men believed they would never reap the full benefits of any athletic accomplishments because of the color of their skin. Smith wrote it was when he was a student at San Jose State College that "I put it all together . . . I was clearly considered a second-class citizen" (Smith, 2007, p. 80).

Kaepernick's upbringing was much different; opportunities for a better life came to him almost immediately after he was born in 1987, and he has offered no hint in his conversations with the media that in his youth he was subjected to racial taunts that came anywhere close to what Smith and Carlos experienced. The biological child of a white mother and black father, Kaepernick was adopted by Rick and Teresa Kaepernick when he was five weeks old. The Caucasian couple, who lived in Wisconsin, had lost two children to congenital heart failure but did have two other biological children (Johnson, 2016). The Kaepernicks moved to Turlock, California, a few years after the adoption. The *New York Times* described the central California city as "pleasant and unremarkable" and "overwhelmingly white" (Branch, 2017, para. 16). Mr. Kaepernick eventually became the vice president of the company he worked for in the city (Branch, 2017).

Kaepernick excelled as an athlete and a student, graduating from high school with a 4.0 GPA (Klemko, 2012). Mrs. Kaepernick described her adopted son as the "perfect child" (Johnson, 2016, para. 9). In a story in which Kaepernick's parents responded to one columnist criticizing him for his multiple tattoos, *USA Today* noted "he was never arrested" as a young man (Klemko, 2012, para. 7). His preference for football led him to accept a scholarship to the University of Nevada; Kaepernick was the team's starting quarterback for four straight seasons. He graduated with a degree in business and had perfect grades in at least one semester (Branch, 2017). At Nevada, he also discovered a "deeper connection to his own roots and a broader understanding of the lives of others" (Branch, 2017, para. 3).

Kaepernick credited his parents for "let[ting] me be who I needed to be," especially because his skin color made it clear he was "different to my parents and my older brother and sister" (Lee, 2015, para. 3). He also noted whenever his family would travel on vacation that "somebody would walk up to me, a real nervous [motel] manager, and say: 'Excuse me. Is there something I can help you with?'" (Lee, 2015, para. 4). Kaepernick acknowledged that being himself meant identifying as an African American. "I do want to be representative of the African community," he said, and he wanted to be a positive role model for African-American kids (Lee, 2015, para. 7).

Unlike Smith and Carlos, Kaepernick did not grow up poor and often hungry. He most definitely did not need to steal. And the only fields he knew were those from baseball; as a teenager, Kaepernick's fastball reached 95 miles per hour, and at the time he was considered a better baseball player than football player (Corsello, n.d.). These differences among Smith, Carlos, and Kaepernick affirm that a media-created linkage among them deserves more scrutiny. Kaepernick's socioeconomic conditions guaranteed he never lacked for a good meal and a good school. Smith and Carlos did. Kaepernick appears to have never faced direct racist taunts or ridicule. Smith and Carlos did. Kaepernick's attempts at succeeding as an athlete and as a student were not limited because of a family's need for the additional income he could provide even from the most menial of jobs. Smith's and Carlos' were.

DISCONNECT 2: THE CIRCUMSTANCES

Tommie Smith (2009) and John Carlos (2011) have acknowledged not planning their exact form of protest at the Mexico City Olympics, but they were part of a group that intended to use the Games to advance a political agenda. The Olympic Project for Human Rights (OPHR) found success in the months leading up to the Mexico City Olympics. Its triumphs included forcing the cancellation of one college football game; the mass boycott of a prominent track-and-field competition; and building public support for Muhammad Ali, the heavyweight division boxing champion who, as mentioned, had refused to enlist for the Vietnam War (Jackson, 2018).

Hoffer (2009) noted the IOC also inadvertently aided OPHR because it chose to admit South Africa into the 1968 Games, only to change its mind a couple months later because of the country's apartheid policies. Brundage, as IOC president, stubbornly refused to acknowledge the organization had capitulated to international pressure, ensuring that OPHR's message seemed more aligned with the times (Hoffer, 2009). Compared to the seemingly elitist and out-of-touch IOC, OPHR appeared keenly aware of inequality around the world and determined to end it. OPHR was an organization asserting that the plight of more than just Blacks needed to be addressed. Smith (2007) acknowledged that as early as 1965—three years before the Mexico City Olympics—he was interested more in human rights rather than civil rights. He described it as a "system that needed changing" (p. 100).

Carlos (2011) has argued that any plans for an OPHR-led boycott of the 1968 Summer Olympics dissolved in the spring of that year. Nevertheless, Smith and Carlos were determined to do something to call attention to OPHR's work around the world. Smith said, "I have to preserve the honor of Tommie Smith. I'm an American until I die, and to me that means I have to do something" (Hoffer, 2009, p. 100).

What they chose to do in Mexico City has been well documented. As they approached the medal stand after the 200-meter race, each wore beads around their necks to call attention to the history of lynching; each wore one black glove to symbolize strength and unity; and each carried their running shoes to highlight poverty. As the national anthem played, Smith's right fist, covered in a black glove, was raised; Carlos did the same with a black glove on his left fist. Booed during and after the anthem, the track stars knew they would face Brundage's wrath: "This didn't surprise me at all," Carlos wrote (2011, p. 126). Smith said, "You'd think I committed murder," in assessing what happened after his and Carlos' protest (Hoffer, 2009, pp. 176–177). Smith and Carlos were soon on their way home because Brundage insisted they had committed the worst possible crime: infecting the Olympics with politics. The entire U.S. delegation got the message: Do something out of line and you, too, would be done (Hoffer, 2009).

Kaepernick was on his own when he began his protest almost 50 years later. He was part of no organized group that had held conversations about boycotts when he chose to take a knee during the national anthem. He began seeking answers to his questions about the oppression of Blacks as a student at Nevada. When Kaepernick walked into the Kappa Alpha Psi fraternity house on the Nevada campus, Olumide Ogundimu, a member of the predominately African-American fraternity, wondered why. Ogundimu told the *New*

York Times, "I thought: 'You're the star quarterback. What are you still miss-ing that you're looking for membership into our fraternity?'" (Branch, 2017, para. 2). Ogundimu added that it soon became clear Kaepernick "realized that things weren't always so easy for the rest of us" (Branch, 2017, para. 15).

Kaepernick entered the NFL in 2011 and kept hidden whatever agenda he had. That remained true for about four years, a period of time that included the aforementioned 49ers' Super Bowl appearance. However, teammates and others around the NFL began to notice a change in him around 2015. The affable, smiling (and now rich) quarterback appeared to detest the media's questions; he altered his messaging on social media; he audited a course at the University of California examining the representation of blacks in popular culture; and he began dating a woman who "has had a measure of influence on Kaepernick's views," a *New York Times'* reporter stated (Branch, 2017, para. 50). In 2016, Kaepernick equated the shooting of an African-American man by police in Louisiana to "what lynchings look like" (Kaepernick, 2016a), and he reacted similarly to the shooting of another African-American man by police in Minnesota, stating, "We are under attack!" (Kaepernick, 2016b). Within weeks, his protest during the playing of the national anthem commenced. "I have to stand up for people that are oppressed," he said. "If they take football away, my endorsements from me, I know that I stood up for what is right" (Wyche, 2016, para. 11). He also used his position of prominence—and his money—to support multiple charities (Branch, 2017). By 2018, he had given away $1 million (Barca, 2018).

When he began his protest in 2016, Kaepernick had not rallied dozens of athletes to his cause. He had no organization behind him. He had no fear of being assassinated inside a crowded stadium. There was no Avery Brundage-type figure immediately ousting him from a sporting event. His demands focused on calling attention to the difficulties faced by Blacks in the U.S. and to the history of oppression against Africans dating back to the slav-ery era. Moreover, unlike the IOC, dogged by criticism because it refused to powerfully endorse human rights in 1968, the NFL in 2016 was dealing with questions about deflated footballs, the return of the Rams to Los Angeles and whether another team soon would join them there. The league also continued to be nagged by questions of whether it was doing enough to protect play-ers from head injuries and concussions (Belson, 2016). Nevertheless, it was not considered at best blinded by idealism or at worst racist, as the IOC was in 1968. Thus, the circumstances faced by Smith and Carlos are in no way similar to what Kaepernick faced.

Jackson (2018) concluded that OPHR, at its core, was a boycott move-ment. Tommie Smith and John Carlos were part of it. Colin Kaepernick was not seeking a boycott of the NFL or of any other domestic or international sporting league when he knelt during the National Anthem. OPHR was about boycotting, but Kaepernick was about protesting. This important difference provides another reason why linking Smith and Carlos to Kaepernick is dubious. Smith and Carlos had no economic means to financially support organizations that sought to improve human rights around the world; Kaepernick had received $39 million over four years, ensuring that he could generously give money to agencies assisting in making life better for African Americans. This difference among the three men also must be highlighted.

DISCONNECT 3: THE FALLOUT

Hoffer (2009) has suggested that Smith and Carlos's protest would never have become a major media story if Brundage and other IOC leaders had done nothing to the two runners. However, when they demanded U.S. Olympic officials send the two men home, "they had now turned an interesting sideshow into the main event. The press, which had been only mildly interested to this point, was now fully involved in the drama, obliged to offer commentary and insight" (p. 178).

That commentary and insight broadly supported expulsion. Peterson (2009) notes that Brundage and the IOC drew a favorable response from prominent U.S. sports journalists for ejecting Smith and Carlos from the Olympics. One of America's most respected sports columnists proclaimed Smith and Carlos "stood on the podium with heads bowed in defiant refusal to look at the American flag while it was being raised" (as quoted in Hoffer, 2009, p. 161). Once they returned to the U.S., neither Smith nor Carlos enjoyed widespread support. Carlos (2011) stated that "once you got even five minutes from our neighborhood" in San Jose, it was clear hatred was everywhere (p. 132). "We were un-American," Carlos concluded (2011, p. 132). And given no media or other major platform, including social media, to express in their own words why he and Smith protested as they had, their side of the story, in effect, was not allowed to be told.

The cold shoulder also came from Blacks, with Smith (2007) noting that "I found out there were more blacks than whites who didn't want anything to do with me" (p. 180). He added, "The people that I had turned to for support left me with nothing" (p. 183). Smith eventually went "underground" (p. 201) for six years, taking a coaching job at Ohio's Oberlin College. He eventually was denied tenure because "my teaching and coaching were below departmental standards," an assertion he mocks in his autobiography (p. 204). He later took a similar position at Santa Monica College in southern California, where he coached for more than 25 years in part because "opportunities were never available to me at the bigger schools" (p. 236). Carlos (2011) also felt the lack of financial security, noting that dinner at times was "oatmeal and cream of wheat. The lack of money translated into unbearable tension in our family" (p. 149).

Peterson (2009) examined newspaper coverage of Smith and Carlos' actions in 1968, concluding that "sportswriters, in general, objected to Smith and Carlos's demonstration and failed to contextualize the political statement behind their act . . . sportswriters viewed the protest as a damning blow to the Olympic spirit" (p. 115–116). Journalists from across the U.S. expressed anger at the track stars. One Associated Press reporter stated that Smith and Carlos's raised fists were "Nazi-like" (Peterson, 2009, p. 107). One *Los Angeles Times* reporter noted he was "sick of apologizing for the state of blacks in the United States" (Peterson, 2009, p. 110). The *Chicago Tribune* suggested Smith and Carlos were "renegades" who would be considered "heroes by fellow extremists" (Peterson, 2009, p. 111).

According to Hoffer (2009), one *New York Times* columnist saw it differently: Robert Lipsyte suggested what Smith and Carlos had done was "the mildest, most civil demonstration of the year" (p. 175). Lipsyte was among the few in the sports journalism profession who asserted Smith and Carlos— especially during the tumultuous year 1968 was in America—were men who ought to be looked at favorably.

The media in 2016 were more supportive of Kaepernick than their colleagues had been in 1968 to Smith and Carlos. A systematic content analysis of media coverage of Kaepernick was not conducted for this chapter; however, a constructed week sample that considered stories written by journalists (letters to the editor, for example, were not reviewed) was created. The author used the ProQuest Newsstand database to generate the stories using "Kaepernick" as the search term. The results indicate firm approval of Kaepernick using his public status to protest what was happening to many African Americans across the country.

One report stated that Kaepernick was doing what other recent and current black athletes were not: publicly taking a stand on controversial racial issues (Perez, 2016). One columnist in Wisconsin, Kaepernick's birth state, wrote, "Sitting during the national anthem isn't giving a middle finger to every current and former service member who sacrificed his or her life to protect our freedoms" (Dombeck, 2016, para. 17). Another columnist mocked East Carolina University officials for not supporting 19 members of the school's band who had copied Kaepernick and had taken a knee during the national anthem. The columnist noted that the First Amendment was alive and well with the only negative voices "on social media and radio talk shows" (Brennan, 2016, para. 3). A third columnist refuted arguments that Kaepernick's protest was turning fans away from the game; the journalist suggested the overall poor quality of games was, in fact, the cause (Collins, 2016). One of the few stories critical of Kaepernick identified during the constructed week appeared in the *Washington Examiner*, a conservative news website and magazine. In the story, multiple Pittsburgh-area residents question whether any protest involving the national anthem is appropriate (Zito, 2016).

In short, the principal theme to sports media coverage in 2016 indicated Kaepernick's peaceful and legal actions deserved broad support, and Kaepernick should be considered a role model for using his fame and his money to call attention to the ill-treatment too many African Americans had received. No such positive sentiment was offered to Smith and Carlos in 1968; the hostile media reaction they received when compared to the favorable reaction Kaepernick received offers yet another reason that the narrative equating the three men is unwise.

CONCLUSION

More than 50 years have passed since Tommie Smith and John Carlos did what Olympic officials at that time demanded never be done—using sport to advance a political agenda. Described by the Associated Press in 1968 as leveling "a bitter racial blast at the white structure" (Grimsley, 2018, para. 7), Smith and Carlos stood silently, each with a fist covered in a black glove raised high in the air, to call attention to the plight of human rights miseries in the United States and around the world. As Smith stood, he feared he'd soon be felled by a bullet (Smith, 2007, p. 1). Neither man knew wealth as a child: Smith was a "sharecropper's son" and Carlos grew up "on the tough streets of Harlem" (Almond, 2018, para. 1). Deemed by Olympic officials and prominent American sportswriters as unworthy of being called an Olympian, each suffered personal and professional setbacks in the years following their protest. It took decades, but "their legacies have been restored" (Almond, 2018, para. 13), most symbolically with a 22-foot sculpture of them displayed at San Jose State University, where both were students in 1968.

Jackson (2018) has succinctly stated:

> OPHR's actions before the Games offer today's athletes a playbook for collective action. And unlike the amateur athletes competing in the Olympics in the 1960s, professional athletes today have the economic and cultural capital to achieve even broader advancements. Unlike OPHR, they won't run out of resources, even if actions spark a fierce backlash like the podium protests did. (para. 9)

This statement crystallizes why assertions that Colin Kaepernick is the heir to the protest legacy created by Tommie Smith and John Carlos come up short.

Smith and Carlos suffered for their actions in ways Kaepernick never will. That statement does not mean they were more honorable, noble or sincere than Kaepernick in what they sought to accomplish; rather, it acknowledges that in 1968 two amateur athletes, who were born poor and marginalized, were denied any social, political or economic benefits that might derive from their athletic accomplishments. In effect, they had committed a sin worthy of expulsion from the flock. A man with $39 million in his bank account already had the social, political, and economic benefits when he, in effect, also was expelled from the National Football League.

Christopher Petrella is a professor at American University. He has worked with Kaepernick in creating a "Know Your Rights" camp, which educates young African Americans on how to "properly interact with law enforcement in various scenarios" (KnowYourRightsCamp.com). He understands why Kaepernick is linked with athletes who have publicly protested but disagrees with such an association. He thinks Kaepernick's name ought to be alongside Ella Baker's (Branch, 2017). Baker worked with multiple civil rights groups in the 1960s; *TIME* identified her as "the mother of the civil rights movement" (Scelfo, 2017). Petrella told the *New York Times:*

> Just as Colin tends to eschew the spotlight, Baker operated under the principle that "Strong people don't need strong leaders," Petrella wrote. Baker once said that "People must fight for their own freedom and not rely on leaders to do it for them." This approach seems consistent with Colin's principle of believing in the capacity of ordinary people to grow into leaders, to self-advocate and to lift as we climb. (Branch, 2017, para. 98)

Significant parts of America refused to accept that idea in 1968 and again in 2016. For these Americans, the principles outlined in the First Amendment were forgotten as rage and hate spewed forth against three men who believed the country and the world could do better in its treatment of the marginalized and the less fortunate. Smith, Carlos and Kaepernick demanded that justice triumph over inequality. In this effort, what each man did was linked. Nevertheless, powerful factors undermine any attempt to further associate Smith and Carlos and 1968 with Kaepernick and 2016.

REFERENCES

49ers.com (2017, March 3). Colin Kaepernick opts out of contract, becomes a free agent. 49ers.com. Retrieved from https://www.49ers.com/news/colin-kaepernick -opts-out-of-contract-becomes-a-free-agent-18611631

Almond, E. (2018, October 17). Fifty years later, Tommie Smith and John Carlos relive the protest. *San Jose Mercury News*. Retrieved from https://www

.mercurynews.com/2018/10/17/fifty-years-later-tommie-smith-and-john-carlos
-relive-the-protest/

Al Jazeera (2016, September 22). US: Colin Kaepernick says he has received death
threats. AlJazeera.com. Retrieved from https://www.aljazeera.com/news/2016/09/
nfl-kaepernick-received-death-threats-160921152934415.html

Amdur, N. (2011, October 11). Olympic protester retains passion. *New York Times*.

Barca, J. (2018, February 1). Colin Kaepernick not stopping, donations roll past $1
million. *Forbes*. Retrieved from https://www.forbes.com/sites/jerrybarca/2018/02
/01/colin-kaepernick-not-stopping-donations-roll-past-1-million/#4a94544b1668

Barra, A. (2008, August 23). Fists raised, but not in anger. *New York Times*.

Belson, K. (2016, September 15). N.F.L. fines two Broncos for head hits to Panthers'
Cam Newton. *New York Times*. Retrieved from https://www.nytimes.com/2016/09
/16/sports/football/nfl-fines-two-broncos-for-head-hits-to-panthers-cam-newton
.html

Bien, L. (2013, February 4). Super Bowl XLVII: Colin Kaepernick shines in losing
effort. SBNation.com. Retrieved from https://www.sbnation.com/nfl/2013/2/4
/3949488/super-bowl-2013-colin-kaepernick-49ers

Blackistone, K. (2016, September 4). Colin Kaepernick challenges sport's nationalism, and our notion of it as safe space. *Washington Post*. Retrieved from https://
www.washingtonpost.com/sports/colin-kaepernick-challenges-sports-nationalism
-and-our-notion-of-it-as-safe-space/2016/09/04/7a312dac-71fd-11e6-be4f
-3f42e5a49e_story.html?utm_term=.43fd0cc981f8

Bloom, J. and Willard, M.N. (eds.). (2002). *Sports matters: Race, recreation and
culture*. New York: New York University Press.

Branch, J. (2017, September 7). The awakening of Colin Kaepernick. *The New
York Times*. Retrieved from https://www.nytimes.com/2017/09/07/sports/colin
-kaepernick-nfl-protests.html

Brennan, C. (2016, October 5). East Carolina officials miss point on national anthem
protest. *USA Today*. Retrieved from https://search.proquest.com/usnews/docview
/1826352535/D2C169AB090F40C8PQ/13?accountid=28365

Carlos, J. (2011). *The John Carlos story: The sports moment that changed the world*.
Chicago: Haymarket Books.

Collins, D. (2016, November 36). Collins: Debunking the week's biggest sports
myths. *Times-Tribune*. Retrieved from https://search.proquest.com/usnews/
docview/1835762051/2F3659B895094E59PQ/4?accountid=28365

Corsello, A. (n.d.). Mr. Colin Kaepernick. Mr.Porter.com. Retrieved from https://www
.mrporter.com/journal/the-look/mr-colin-kaepernick/535?cm_mmc=PartnerizeAM
-_-skimlinks_phg-_-True+Content-_-305950&setupsession=false

Dombeck, T. (2016, September 5). Colin Kaepernick a patriot for taking a seat.
Herald Times Reporter. Retrieved from https://search.proquest.com/usnews/
docview/1816645445/90F178D1777A412DPQ/23?accountid=28365

Draper, K. & Belson, K. (2019, February 15019). Colin Kaepernick and the N.F.L.
settle collusion case. *New York Times*. Retrieved from https://www.nytimes.com
/2019/02/15/sports/nfl-colin-kaepernick.html

Fucillo, D. (2016, August 27). NFL issues statement on Colin Kaepernick not standing during the National Anthem. NinersNation.com. Retrieved from https://www.ninersnation.com/2016/8/27/12672566/nfl-statement-colin-kaepernick-national-anthem

Gaines, (2017, September 10). Colin Kaepernick received less than one-third of his "record" $126 million contract. Business Insider. Retrieved from https://www.businessinsider.com/colin-kaepernick-record-49ers-contract-2017-8

Gregory, S. (2017, December 18). Colin Kaepernick: The quarterback who upended the NFL without taking a snap. *TIME, 190,* 100–103.

Grimsley, W. (2018, October 16). 50 years ago today: Tommie Smith and John Carlos protested with raised fists at the 1968 Olympics. *Chicago Tribune.* Retrieved from https://www.chicagotribune.com/sports/breaking/ct-spt-tommie-smith-john-carlos-olympics-protest-20181016-story.html

Henderson, S. (2010). "Nasty demonstrations by negroes": The place of the Smith-Carlos podium salute in the civil rights movement. *Bulletin of Latin American Research, 29,* 78–92.

Hoffer, R. (2009). *Something in the air: American passion and defiance in the 1968 Mexico City Olympics.* New York: Free Press.

Jackson, V. (2018, October 3). The forgotten organization behind one of the most iconic moments in sports history. *Washington Post.* Retrieved from https://www.washingtonpost.com/outlook/2018/10/03/forgotten-organization-behind-one-most-iconic-moments-sports-history/?utm_term=.66bcbaa17690

Johnson, M. (2016, December 10). Colin Kaepernick's parents break silence: "We absolutely do support him." ESPN.com. Retrieved from http://www.espn.com/nfl/story/_/id/18247113/colin-kaepernick-parents-break-silence-speak-support-criticized-quarterback

Kaepernick, C. (2016a). Instagram post. https://www.instagram.com/p/BHhetl8g_EE/

Kaepernick, C. (2016b). Instagram post. https://www.instagram.com/p/BHkQULXAvZu/

Klemko, R. (2012, November 30) Colin Kapernick's parents upset at criticisms of son's tattoos. *USA Today.* Retrieved from https://www.usatoday.com/story/sports/nfl/2012/11/29/49ers-colin-kaepernick-tattoo-criticism-sporting-news/1736671/

Know Your Rights (n.d.) Retrieved from https://knowyourrightscamp.com/about/

Lee, E. (2015, October 8). Colin Kaepernick details racial struggle from his childhood. Us. Retrieved from https://www.usmagazine.com/celebrity-news/news/colin-kaepernick-details-childhood-racial-struggle-2015810/

Longman, J. (2018, September 6). Kaepernick's knee and Olympic fists are linked by history. *New York Times* (online). Retrieved from https://www.nytimes.com/2018/09/06/sports/kaepernick-nike-kneeling.html

Martin, S. and McHendry, Jr., G. (2016). Kaepernick's stand: Patriotism, protest, and professional sports. *Journal of Contemporary Rhetoric, 6,* 88–98.

Newkirk II, V.R. (2017, August 11). No country for Colin Kaepernick. *The Atlantic.* Retrieved from https://www.theatlantic.com/entertainment/archive/2017/08/no-country-for-colin-kaepernick/536340/

Perez, A. (2016, September 5). Why Colin Kaepernick and other athletes are more likely to address social issues. *USA Today*. Retrieved from https://search.proquest.com/usnews/docview/1816740769/90F178D1777A412DPQ/3?accountid=28365

Peterson, J. (2009). A "race" for equality: Print media coverage of the 1968 Olympic Protest by Tommie Smith and John Carlos. *American Journalism, 26*, 99–121.

Quick, S. (1990). "Black knight check white king": The conflict between Avery Brundage and the African nations over South African membership in the IOC. *Canadian Journal of History of Sport, 21*, 20–32.

Rosenberg, M. (2017, December 11). Truthteller. *Sports Illustrated, 127,* 60–62.

Scelfo, J. (2017, January 16). On MLK Day, honor the mother of the civil rights movement, too. *TIME*. Retrieved from http://time.com/4633460/mlk-day-ella-baker/

Sheehan, J. (1968, October 18). 2 Black power advocates ousted from Olympics. *New York Times*. Pg. 1.

Smith, T. (2007). *Silent Gesture*. Philadelphia, PA: Temple University Press.

Wagoner, N. (2016, August 27). Hard to see how Colin Kaepernick can overtake Blaine Gabbert now. ESPN.com. Retrieved from http://www.espn.com/blog/san-francisco-49ers/post/_/id/18885/hard-to-see-how-colin-kaepernick-can-overtake-blaine-gabbert-now

Wyche, S. (2016, August 27). Colin Kaepernick explains why he sat during the national anthem. NFL.com Retrieved from http://www.nfl.com/news/story/0ap3000000691077/article/colin-kaepernick-explains-protest-of-national-anthem

Zirin, D. (n.d.) Fists of freedom: An Olympic story not taught in school. PBS. Org. Retrieved from https://www.pbs.org/newshour/extra/app/uploads/2014/02/All-docs-for-Human-Rights-lesson-2.pdf

Zito, S. (2016, November 3). Mel Gibson movie "Hacksaw Ridge" promotes patriotism and respect for military. *Washington Times*. Retrieved from https://www.washingtonexaminer.com/mel-gibson-movie-hacksaw-ridge-promotes-patriotism-and-respect-for-military

Zukas, D. (1992). The International Olympic Committee: Tragedy, farce, and hypocrisy. *Sociology of Sport Journal, 9*, 340–353.

PART II

Refusing to "Stick to Sports"

Chapter 3

Place and Protest in the NBA's Pandemic Bubble

Anthony C. Cavaiani and Stephen P. Andon

The events of 2020 present a novel window into the study of protest and athlete activism. Given the onset of the global coronavirus pandemic, which triggered lockdowns and presented the greatest public health challenge of the last century, it is not surprising that the Carnegie Endowment for International Peace labeled 2020 as an "extraordinary year . . . [that] highlighted the resilience of protests around the globe" (Press & Carothers, 2020, para. 1). In the United States, the first five months of the year were marked by the emergence of Black Lives Matter (BLM) protests connected with the deaths of Ahmaud Arbery, Breonna Taylor, and George Floyd, among others. By June 2020, *The New York Times* estimated that between "15 million and 26 million people in the United States [had] participated in demonstrations over the death of George Floyd and others in recent weeks" (Buchanan et al., 2020, para. 2). The year operated as a significant turning point in athlete activism, 6 years after LeBron James and other NBA players wore "I Can't Breathe" t-shirts following the death of Eric Garner and four years after WNBA players began wearing Black Lives Matter warm-up shirts and NFL quarterback Colin Kaepernick launched his protest against police brutality.

With professional sports on hiatus and athletes across the sporting world locked down in their homes, there was a unique opportunity to engage in BLM protests. This activism was particularly central to professional basketball players, considering the cultural influence of the NBA and WNBA and the racial makeup of both leagues (74% of players in the NBA and 69% of players in the WNBA identify as Black or African American; Lapchick, 2020). Without the routine of team responsibilities like regular practices, games, and media availability, these players could operate with full agency to participate in protests in locations of their choosing. For example, California natives Russell Westbrook (Houston) and DeMar DeRozan (San Antonio) spoke at a rally in Compton, and Jaylen Brown (Boston) and Malcolm Brogdon (Indiana) demonstrated together among throngs of protestors in Atlanta. Brogdon addressed the crowd in Atlanta, his hometown, by invoking a particular focus on place, "We built this city. This is the most proudly black city in the world. Let's take some pride in that . . . I have a grandfather who marched next to Dr. King in the '60s. He would be proud to see us all here" (Golliver, 2020, para. 10).

Once the NBA season resumed later that summer in tightly-controlled, bubble-like conditions at Disney World, that player agency became curtailed. Despite the opportunity to wear BLM messaging on their jerseys and the NBA's efforts to put BLM markings around the arena and on television, players were much more constrained by the bubble. Given the importance of "place" in protest movements, as asserted by Endres and Senda-Cook (2011), the stifling nature of the bubble led George Hill (Oklahoma City) to say, in the wake of the Jacob Blake shooting in Wisconsin on August 23, "We shouldn't even have came to this damn place, to be honest" (Zillgitt, 2020). Three days later, the Milwaukee Bucks boycotted their game against the Orlando Magic, leading to a league-wide shutdown of the playoffs.

This chapter investigates this tension between agency and constraint that NBA players faced in the bubble through the theoretical frame of place and protest rhetoric. We first argue that activism and league-approved social justice messaging was enabled through the classical rhetorical notion of kairos. Second, we consider the implications of this rhetoric of space/place with respect to the constraints the bubble created that limited the agency of NBA players. Finally, we discuss how athlete activism in the bubble, and its corporate influence, will impact the legitimacy and effect of athlete activism moving forward.

KAIROS AND THE BUBBLE

Sport has been hailed as the common identifier for decades. Especially during crises, many people believe sport can bring people together. Brown (2004) describes how sport helps to heal group wounds to connect people, stating "Hardly offering an escape from tragedy, sport often directly addressed the nation's pain, inviting spectators to deal with their feelings from a number of perspectives" (p. 41). The NBA's restart during summer 2020, amid the global pandemic and social unrest in America, was designed, or invented, in part to help people cope with deep social isolation and to provide people with some semblance of live sports.

The classical rhetoric notion of kairos is premised on the idea of urgency and timeliness. A speaker urgently responds to a message that requires immediate attention. Miller (2002) explains how kairos is related to propriety or decorum and "becomes a principle of adaptation and accommodation to convention, expectation, predictability" (p. xi). Understanding kairos means to comprehend and acknowledge an order that is stated or given; and to violate that order results in some form of rhetorical failure (Miller, 2002, p. xi–xii). Conversely, Miller explains another competing view about kairos is its association to the unexpected and spontaneous, and that

> kairos encourages us to be creative in responding to the unforeseen, to the lack of order in human life. The challenge is to invent, within a set of unfolding and unprecedented circumstances, an action (rhetorical or otherwise) that will be understood as uniquely meaningful within those circumstances. (p. xiii)

Miller (2002) says this action cannot be understood within the context of previous actions because the action is adaptive and rhetoric becomes escapable as a result. The NBA's kairotic response to the pandemic was achieved through propriety and decorum, as the league adapted stringent health protocols required for everyone to effectively resume and sustain the restarted season in Orlando. Furthermore, the league's collaborative effort with the National Basketball Players Association (NBPA) was both adaptive in accounting for the intense racial tensions within the U.S. and creative in its response to those unforeseen circumstances resulting from the pandemic and ongoing social unrest. The league was well-aware that both situations were extremely fluid and likely to change throughout the duration of the restart. Read together, the NBA's kairotic response to the pandemic and BLM protests were adapted through particular notions of decorum—daily testing for everyone and physical distancing to name a few, and an acknowledgment about the role athlete activism would need to have in the bubble—both of which were unexpected months prior but were now required to fulfill rhetorical action and were unable to be understood through previous contexts because of the uniqueness of the moment in which the league found itself.

A statement released by the NBA detailed the reason for restarting its season in Orlando as one premised on a shared effort between the league and the players association to allow for an environment in which conversations between players and the league would be encouraged while addressing issues of racial inequalities. Commissioner Silver was quoted as saying:

> The league and the players are uniquely positioned to have a direct impact on combating systemic racism in our country, and we are committed to collective action to build a more equal and just society. A shared goal of our season restart

will be to use our platform in Orlando to bring attention to these important issues of social injustice. (NBA & NBPA, 2020, para. 5)

Names of notable players such as Chris Paul, Trae Young, and Donovan Mitchell, in addition to NBPA Chief Executive Director Michele Roberts and Diversity and Inclusion Officer Oris Stuart, appeared in the letter. This strengthened the ethos of the league by demonstrating whose input was sought when designing the bubble. The NBPA and the league also agreed to allow players to wear a social justice message on the back of their jersey where their last name would traditionally appear. The list was agreed to by both parties and included phrases such as "I Can't Breathe, Say Her Name, Breonna Taylor, Equality, Group Economics, and Black Lives Matter" (Spears, 2020). Furthermore, the release also made an explicit appeal to the unique platform the league and players have in combating systemic racism and the role the restart would play in solving that inequality.

However, the NBA's previous handling of athlete activism ran counter to its current embracing of social justice. The league suspended Mahmoud Abdul-Rauf for his silent protest of the national anthem during the 1995–1996 season, and the backlash forced him out of the league by 2001 (Spears, 2017). Craig Hodges from the famous early-1990 Chicago Bulls teams was also silenced for his freedom fighter advocacy (Tinsely, 2020). The NBA is also well-known for its failure to foster inclusivity and address racism during the Donald Sterling case, the former Los Angeles Clippers owner who made racist remarks regarding Black players. Additionally, another constraint impacting activist rhetoric in the bubble were the roles of Silver and Roberts. Since taking over as commissioner in 2014, Silver has embraced a socially-conscious players mantra. Silver expressed his support for both NBA and WNBA players' boycott in the wake of the killing of Jacob Blake in Wisconsin, saying, "While I don't walk in the same shoes as Black men and women, I can see the trauma and fear that racialized violence causes and how it continues the painful legacy of racial inequality that persists in our country" (Al-Khateeb, 2020, para. 3). Silver's ability to sympathize and identify with players regarding social justice is well-chronicled. As sports commentator Dave Zirin noted regarding the difference between the NBA and NFL, "Adam Silver has worked closely with the head of the NBA Players Association Michele Roberts to make sure that players know they are supported if they want to make statements" (Angell, 2020, para. 2). Roberts was instrumental in helping secure player voice and expression within the bubble, and her collegial and warm relationship with Silver is well-publicized (Amick, 2020). She was very visible within the bubble and is also the first woman to lead a professional sports union in the U.S., and her role in informing players about the implications of their actions in the wake of the Blake incident was invaluable in how the players responded.

In addition to the social unrest of 2020, the league also took great lengths to create a safe, healthy, and COVID-free environment for anyone who entered the bubble. Players were not mandated to enter the bubble, which began on July 7, 2020. There was, however, a financial penalty for opting out—a surrender of salary for each game missed, up to a maximum of 14 games. According to CNBC, a player who opted out from a team that played 14 or more games in the bubble would see a 15.1% salary reduction (Elkins, 2020). Thus, only a small number of players decided against joining the bubble.

Beyond financial implications, many of the guidelines presented to the NBA players by the league stipulated strict conditions for surveillance and movement. Players and personnel were required to quarantine before traveling to Orlando and, once they arrived, they had to "quarantine until they test[ed] negative for the coronavirus twice, at least 24 hours apart" (Deb & Cacciola, 2020, para. 6). Any person inside the bubble was tested daily and was required to wear a mask when not eating or playing basketball. Players were given wearable RFID bracelets that Disneyworld has standardized for use as hotel room keys, touchless purchases, and tracking visitor movements through its properties. Additionally, players were given the option to wear two different motion and health tracking smart devices: a "proximity alarm that would notify the player if he spends more than five seconds within six feet of another person wearing the alarm . . . and an Oura smart ring that tracks temperature . . . heart rate, and other health measures" (Stein, 2020, para. 11). Adding to these measures of surveillance, the NBA informed players they would use video monitoring technology for contract tracing purposes and established an anonymous hotline for anyone in the bubble to report any observed violations (Bontemps, 2020). While players were not forbidden from leaving campus, the NBA handbook stated that players should only leave under "extenuating circumstances." If a player decided to leave the bubble, for any reason, they were subject to a 10-day quarantine in which they were subject to financial punishment.

Players were not allowed to spend time with each other in hotel rooms, nor were they allowed to socialize with players from teams staying in the other hotels. They were allowed to socialize with other teams inside their hotel, as long as they maintained social distances of at least six feet. Recreation guidelines included prohibition of wearing video game headsets, playing doubles ping pong, and sharing golf equipment. Furthermore, no family members or "nonfamily members with long-standing relationships" were allowed into the bubble until the start of the second round of the NBA playoffs, which began on August 30, 2020—a period of over 50 days. Despite this, some players decided not to bring anyone into the bubble, extending their isolation, as

Goran Dragic of the Miami Heat told *The Ringer*, "I've got two young kids, I don't know what they would do here. You don't have a lot of things to do" (Uggetti, 2020, para. 2).

The amplification of the player-driven and league-sanctioned activist rhetoric in the bubble was meaningful because of its kairotic appeal, but also its deployment of space and place. This allowed the force of the activist messaging to be loud, visible, and direct. Next, we read the bubble through a close analysis of space/place scholarship.

SPACE/PLACE IN THE BUBBLE

The theoretical domain of space and place has been studied primarily by cultural geographers, who offer varying degrees of nuances in their approach to the concepts. Beginning with Yi-Fu Tuan, place is understood via a sense of attachment, akin to what one may feel for their home. This meaning, or sense of attachment, is driven primarily by "experience," (Tuan, 1975, p. 152) but that "experience takes time . . . to know a place well requires long residence and deep involvement" (p. 164). Over time individuals can cultivate an attachment or love of place, what Tuan termed "topophilia." In contrast, space for Tuan represents the freedom of wide-open expanses and to get out into the world. Cresswell (2004) summarizes this distinction succinctly, "when humans invest meaning in a portion of space and then become attached to it in some way it becomes a place" (p. 10). DeCerteau (1984) opts to focus on mobility instead of attachment, by offering a definition of place as a static, locked, stable location that is planned, while space reflects the movement one chooses to take through places. Consequently, space delivers an agency for individuals, whether to escape their confines or challenge the status quo. Building on those concepts, Marc Augé (1992) uses the examples of hotel rooms, highways, and airports as "non-places," or avenues of movement where our experience is transactional and temporary. These locales, "are spaces where people coexist or cohabit without living together" (Augé, 1999, p. 110). Notably, he asserts, your stay in a non-place like a hotel is wiped away, as if you were never there. Harvey (1996) focuses further on the idea of mobility by identifying a "tension between place-bound fixity and spatial mobility of capital" (p. 296). In so doing, he stresses that places are constantly subject to flow of capital, because old or existing places are under consistent threat of being repurposed to extract as much financial value as possible.

Addressing space and place within sport is relevant because stadiums can become like home—for many. Fans see stadiums like Madison Square Garden or Wrigley Field as sacred places, linking to Tuan's concept of topophilia. In the modern age, the replacement of older stadiums with "mallparks" and arenas provides consumer opportunities year-round while wiping away the memories of older facilities. These new places are often embedded with expansive marketing and nostalgic branding, in an attempt to imbue a feeling of experience (Andon, 2013). Reflecting on DeCerteau's understanding of place, stadiums are not built for the freedom of movement and, consequently, many sports sociologists have outlined how stadiums are highly-restrictive and controlling environments. If sport originated as play in free and open spaces without boundary, then painting lines, separating spectators from the field of play, and limiting access to stadiums in the form of tickets, club levels and luxury suites, is inherently restrictive. This control in the stadium aligns with sports geographer John Bale's (1993) understanding of stadiums as places where a dominant group attempts to wield power over people. In so doing, he analogizes the modern stadium with Foucault's prison, where stadiums are places of "containment and surveillance" (Bale, 1993, p. 122). This sterilization of the stadium, where conditions are made to perfectly replicate each other—in an effort to make stadiums uniform—is what Bale (1996) ultimately describes as placelessness. Crucially, that definition of the sterilized, repetitive stadium also applies to "a place like Disney World [that] represents the epitome of placelessness constructed, as it is, purely for outsiders and reproduced across the globe" (Cresswell, 2004, p. 45).

For NBA players, the conditions in the bubble took the sterilization and restriction of movement to a heightened level. Though they may have been accustomed to the grind of road trip travel through Auge's non-places, the regulations for entering and living in the bubble aligned more with Bale's prison analogy. While restrictions are a common feature of place, as Cresswell (2004) notes, "laws and rules pervade place" (p. 35), the NBA's approach was extensive. Inviting 22 teams to complete the 2019–2020 season in the bubble, the NBA provided a 113-page handbook of health and safety protocols that detailed everything from testing procedures, to rules for disinfecting basketballs, and recreation restrictions for players staying in the three Disney World Resort hotels (Deb & Cacciola, 2020, para. 2). While the handbook focused on the caution that was needed to resume the season amid a spike in coronavirus cases in Florida, the unprecedented approach to caution created a set of carceral conditions via a punitive approach to income, restriction and surveillance of movement, and limited social interaction.

As a result of these policies of financial punishment, surveillance, and isolation, it is difficult to see the NBA bubble as any kind of topophilic place. Despite the attempts of some NBA teams to try and make the bubble more welcoming, players did not have an opportunity to develop an attachment to the facilities of Disney World, itself a paragon of placelessness. Signaling the inability to feel an attachment to anything in the bubble, Houston Rockets forward P. J. Tucker relied on bringing an 85-inch TV for some semblance of normalcy: "I have to make it as much as home as I could" (Zillgitt, 2020, para. 11). With restrictions and punishments for movement outside of the bubble, NBA players were not granted the agency or freedom of movement needed for de Certeau's concept of space. Richaun Holmes, a center on the Sacramento Kings, discovered this restriction the hard way when he was sent into a 10-day quarantine after leaving the hotel boundary to meet a Postmates food delivery person. Holmes told the press after his quarantine, "I really wasn't too aware of the borders . . . they had to enforce the rules and I completely understand that" (Anderson, 2020, para. 4). It may be simplest to label the bubble a non-place, given its temporality and absence of human interaction, but the duration of time spent in the bubble and considerations of mobility problematize that simplification. Turning to Harvey (1996) and questions of mobility, it becomes clear that players were asked to remain fixed in place in the bubble so that the NBA, owners, and commercial partners could preserve the fluidity of capital. Faced with a loss of over $800 million in ticket sales due to the pandemic postponement of the season, *ESPN* reported that without a restart to the season, the NBA would have lost an additional $1.5 billion in revenue (Wojnarowski & Lowe, 2020). The bubble can then be understood as a salvage effort that kickstarted the flow of capital across several fronts—for the League, its teams, and its commercial partners, as well as for TV broadcasters and, finally, Disney World. The resort was reportedly paid $150 million by the NBA to use the properties for the bubble (Windhorst, 2020). The resumption of the season to prime the financial pumps around the league calls into question Massey's (2008) argument about the power dynamics at play, with the large levers of capitalism controlling the decisions to resume the season in Orlando. Quite literally, as Massey (2008) notes, some movement is privileged—capital, in this case—creating conditions of "imprisonment" for other groups.

Under the guise of safety, no matter how relevant to conducting an NBA season under extraordinary circumstances, the conditions recalled Foucault's (1979) notion of discipline through panoptic surveillance. Aware of these restrictions before entering the bubble, a handful of NBA players confirmed the analogy on various social media posts. LeBron James posted on Twitter, "Just left the crib to head to the bubble . . . felt like I'm headed to do a bid man," while Portland Trailblazers guard Damian Lillard echoed those sentiments on Instagram on the same day, "Feel like I'm going to do a bid . . . headed to the bubble" (James, 2020; Lillard, 2020).

Consequently, the players in the bubble were fixed, but not in place. Because they were largely restricted from movement and interaction, neither were they afforded the freedom of space. They faced the dehumanizing characteristics of a non-place, but not the temporality of one. Stuck in Disney

World, players were moved into the bubble to suit the will of billion-dollar corporations and a media, which demanded a paragon of discipline. This greatly impacted the players' agency, generally, in terms of their sense of empowerment, as well as their ability to voice and act in protest during the summer of 2020. As Jeremy Zimmer, the head of United Talent Agency stated, "Underneath player empowerment is . . . a real connectivity to what's happening in our country and how we're dealing with the injustice that lives underneath" (Chotiner, 2021, para. 10).

But the bubble was neither the place nor the time for NBA players to express that empowerment. This fact is perhaps best summed by New Orleans Pelicans guard Jrue Holiday, who told the *New York Times* in May of 2021, "I'm not going to lie, I didn't really want to go to the bubble. It didn't' feel like it was the time for basketball" (Stein, 2020, para. 16). The dilemma between timing, place, and player empowerment in the bubble was brought into sharp focus in the aftermath of the police shooting of Jacob Blake in Kenosha, Wisconsin on August 23. Reached for comment to ask what NBA players could do in response, Bucks guard George Hill said, "We can't do anything. We shouldn't even have came to this damn place, to be honest" (Zillgitt, 2020). Hill recognized the limitations of player agency and protest in the bubble and his mention of place underscores the powerlessness of the bubble, rendering it placeless.

The impact of this placelessness on activism and protest cannot be under-stated, especially given what Endres and Senda-Cook (2011) established, "Place is a performer along with activists in making and unmaking the pos-sibilities of protest" (p. 258). But unlike how the Castro in San Francisco became the epicenter for gay rights or how the Lincoln Memorial is forever linked with the civil rights movement, the bubble's lack of place and carceral quality denied the NBA players the agency to implement place tactically. As Endres and Senda-Cook (2011) note, place is deployed by social movements in three crucial ways: to build on the pre-existing meaning of a place, to tem-porarily reconstruct the meaning of place, and to repeat reconstructions that result in new meanings (p. 266).

None of these tactical offerings were available for NBA players. To begin, the NBA Disney World bubble is not a place of pre existing meaning; it is widely understood as perfecting meaninglessness. When speaking of the California-based Disneyland, Baudrillard (1994) decries the resorts as an "imaginary world" designed for children and "adults who go there to act the child" (p. 13), while Tuan (1998) also notes the theme park's "erasure of the present," as a means of escapism (p. 27). The players had no meaning to attach to the bubble in which they were trapped, no meaning to draw upon in a vacation destination designed to erase, ignore, and gloss over America's fraught and disturbing racial past. The restrictions on mobility denied players the opportunity to recreate meaning inside the bubble. As previously noted, going into the bubble was not a free choice for most players, faced with financial penalties, and players identified—correctly—the bubble as a prison. While Endres and Senda-Cook (2011) highlight the potential of reconstructed meaning with the examples of the American Indian Movement's takeover of Alcatraz Island and bicycle riders controlling city streets during Critical Mass, those individuals not only possessed the agency for movement but the freedom to gather. As Cavaiani (2020) notes, "when people gather in a place to protest, meaning occurs," (p. 478) but, in the case of the bubble, the players were specifically prohibited from interacting and gathering in any meaningful way outside of competitive games. Without this ability to gather, the players were robbed of their means to amplify their message.

Implications of Branding Activism

The bubble's deployment of space/place and its kairotic response to the pandemic and social unrest amplified athlete activism that occurred in Orlando. McCall (2021) argues that the NBA's embracing of social justice messaging in the bubble was more akin to a commercialized free speech campaign by stating "if the NBA wants to just run a basketball league, that is fine. But if it wants to run a free expression operation for its players and executives, it can't be picking and choosing based on which posture looks financially feasible at the moment. Free speech is a fundamental principle that remains fundamental regardless of making money or the topic of any moment" (para. 12).

The relationship between commercialization, sport, and social causes has been occurring for years. For some, it is why they enjoy attending live games or consuming sport. Media representations of sport, and causes such as breast cancer, can guide audiences' attitudes and perceptions about the role of sport in society. Rugg (2020) details the NFL's "Crucial Catch" campaign, its annual October breast cancer awareness campaign in which players would wear pink shoes and other gear, asserting how the NFL has strategically "utilized these campaigns to shape representations of the players, the league, and the sport in ways that best address the threats to the league" (Rugg, 2020, p. 614). The NFL's sports media interests are complex and their effects are significant. Additionally, Major League Soccer (MLS) attempted to curtail political signage at their games when the Portland Timbers Army displayed images of the Iron Front, a Nazi-inspired symbol with three arrows pointing down and to the left. MLS banned the display on the grounds that it violated the league's fan code of conduct on political displays, only to later pivot on the issue amidst fan backlash and allow it at games, permitting it isn't displayed throughout the broader stadium (Murray, 2019).

The NFL and MLB have both utilized overt military performances to provide the public with a covert sanctioning of war. Butterworth (2014) has documented how the MLB and NFL have helped to legitimize and sanction war in the minds of the public while constructing memories of national identity that are playful and consumable. Butterworth (2009) also analyzed how MLB and minor league baseball teams have held Christian "Faith Nights" as a strategic way to increase attendance while publicly endorsing a particular religion. The bubble was different in how it employed space/place to spur on activism—its placelessness prohibited any noticeable backlash while allowing for multiple gestures and symbols of athlete activism.

The corporation plays a pivotal role in branding an athlete-activist message. As Hayhurst and Szto (2016) contend, corporatization works within the confines of dominant political and economic ideologies without attempting to dismantle the inequalities that pervade them. The NBA's social justice-focused bubble restart operated according to a similar logic—it promoted a particular brand of athlete activism through a frame of unity while earning social capital in the minds of some audiences and simultaneously alienating others. Kimble (2020) labeled the bubble as an attempt by the league to brand itself as the unifying change agent, not the players. The bubble, he says, demonstrates the "problem with 'unity' and the limits of corporate activism" and only reinforced the perception that words like "change" and "social justice" have now become buzzwords that are worthy of marketing (Kimble, 2020, para. 4). The bubble's ability to freeze, or pause, activism and package it into a mediated display of professional sports during a pandemic summer amidst national and global lockdowns, allowed the NBA to require players to adhere to strict health testing while publicly showcasing their activism to promote their image as a socially-conscious league. The NBA upheld Hayhurst and Szto's (2016) definition of corporate responsibility as "a commitment to behave ethically and harm no one . . . it [also] means that corporations will act in accordance with approved labor codes and environmental policies and become advocates for human rights" (p. 526). The NBA accomplished this goal while assuming the position of a professional-sports-league-as-social-change-agent and fulfilling its corporate interests to offset financial loss from the cancellation of over 200 regular season games as a result of the pandemic.

While agency and choice were not the mantra of the bubble, it advocated for change through as forceful of an apparatus that it was seeking to dismantle. Butterworth (2020) asserts that anthem protests are more indicative about how sport is used to communicate a logic of consensus to advance a shared sense of unity and to consider how the quest of unity can enable sameness and a lack of acknowledgement about differences. For instance, Meyers Leonard of the Miami Heat stood during Game 1 of the 2020 bubble Finals with his hand over his heart while wearing a Black Lives Matter shirt and stood alongside his kneeling teammates, engaging in what Kurtz (2021) would call tinted dissent. The implication space/place has on athlete activism follows from Endres and Senda-Cook's (2011) notion about the ephemerality of places. What occurred in the bubble teaches us that activism in the stadium will continue to place demands on athletes, influence the speech allowed to be uttered, and have pervasive effects on our attitudes and values.

CONCLUSION

What lies ahead for sports leagues in an era now endorsing widespread acceptance—or perhaps a demand for—player activism is unclear. The NBA and the players utilized the bubble for a timely and satisfactory rhetorical response, yet despite the exigence of the pandemic and the summer of protests, player agency was stifled by the lack of the mobility afforded through the placelessness of the Disney bubble and the League's financial obligations. As the NBA returns to pre-pandemic norms, it remains to be seen how much time and space players will have to express their activism and how much the League will embrace, reject, or co-opt that activism. Indeed, the history of rhetoric is replete with examples of rhetoric flourishing as a result of democratic discourse being achieved and realized; but when attitudes—and space—are constrained and society places restrictions on discourse, rhetoric invariably wilts. The empowerment of athletes to use their platforms is a challenge to the ways in which previous athletes like Muhammad Ali, Abdul-Rauf, and Kaepernick have been outcast. But how can that empowerment and agency flourish beyond the bubble, and will teams and leagues actively respond to issues in ways that are not purely influenced from their corporate interests in athlete activism? As Adam Silver said at the start of the 2020–2021 season, "My sense is there will be somewhat of a return to normalcy, that those messages will largely be left to be delivered off the floor" (Hughes, 2020, para. 3). For many players, the dichotomy of on/off the floor does not exist, yet leagues seem poised to ensure that it does.

REFERENCES

Al-Khateeb, Z. (2020, August 8). Adam Silver responds to player boycott: "I wholeheartedly support NBA and WNBA players." *The Sporting News.* https://www.sportingnews.com/us/nba/news/adam-silver-player-boycott-support-nba-wnba-players/sxiys8l6p9ms11diomjjvupfg

Anderson, J. (2020, July 22). Kings' Richaun Holmes left NBA bubble for chicken wings; Kelly Oubre Jr. not to blame. *The Sacramento Bee.* https://www.sacbee.com/sports/article/244407577.html

Andrews, M. (2020, June 24). Dealing with racial matters will be shared goal of NBA, NBPA when season resumes. *ESPN.* https://www.espn.com/nba/story/_/id/29359197/dealing-racial-matters-shared-goal-nba-nbpa-season-resumes

Andrews, M., & Wojnarowski, A. (2020, June 16). Avery Bradley: Coalition wants NBA's plan for Black causes before restart. *ESPN.* https://www.espn.com/nba/story/_/id/29319677/avery-bradley-says-nba-players-coalition-wants-league-plan-black-causes-restart

Andon, S. P. (2013). From a secret seraglio to an open Target: A private collector's transcendent integration into a commodified baseball stadium. In K. Moist & D. Banash (eds.), *Collecting and collections: Objects, practices, and the fate of things* (pp. 133–150). New York: Scarecrow Publishing.

Angell, I. (2018, April 10). Why athlete activism looks different in the NBA. *WNYC.* https://www.wnycstudios.org/podcasts/takeaway/segments/why-athlete-activism-looks-different-nba

Augé, M. (1992). *Non-places: Introduction to an anthropology of supermodernity.* Verso.

Bale, J. (1993). The spatial development of the modern stadium. *International Review for the Sociology of Sport, 28*(2/3), 121–134.

Bale, J. (1996). Space, place and body culture: Yi-Fu Tuan and a geography of sport. *Human Geography, 78*(3), 163–171.

Baudrillard, J. (1994). *Simulacra and simulation* (S.F. Glaser, Trans.). Ann Arbor: University of Michigan Press.

Beer, T. (2020, October 15). NBA ratings drop not due to blowback over players activism, poll suggest. *Forbes.* https://www.forbes.com/sites/tommybeer/2020/10/15/nbas-ratings-drop-not-due-to-blowback-over-players-activism-poll-suggests/?sh=6ee5cd436b31

Bontemps, T. (2020, June 16). In documents, NBA details coronavirus protocls, including 2-week testing period for positive tests. *ESPN.* https://www.espn.com/nba/story/_/id/29321006/in-documents-nba-details/coronavirus-testing-process-orlando-campus-life

Brown, R. S. (2004, November). Sport and healing America. *Society, 42*(1), 37–41. DOI:10.1007/BF02687298

Buchanan, L. Bui, Q, & Patel, J. K. (2020, July 3). Black Lives Matter may be the largest movement in U.S. history. *New York Times.* https://www.nytimes.com/interactive/2020/07/03/us/george-floyd-protests-crowd-size.html

Butterworth, M. L. (2020). Sport and the quest for unity: How the logic of consensus undermines democratic culture. *Communication & Sport, 8*(4–5), 452–472. https://doi.org/10.1177/2167479519900160

Butterworth, M. (2014). Public memorializing in the stadium: Mediated sport, the 10th anniversary of 9/11, and the illusion of democracy. *Communication & Sport, 2*(3), 203–224. https://doi.org/10.1177/2167479513485735

Butterworth, M. (2009). Saved at home: Christian branding and faith nights in the "church of baseball." *Quarterly Journal of Speech, 97*(3), 309–333. https://doi.org/10.1080/00335630.2011.585170

Cancian, D. (2020, October 13). Did NBA finals rating crash nearly 70%, as Donald Trump claims? *Newsweek.* https://www.newsweek.com/fact-check-donald-trump-nba-finals-ratings-drop-1538584

Cavaiani, A. C. (2020). Rhetoric, materiality, and the disruption of meaning: The stadium as a place of protest. *Communication & Sport, 8*(4–5), 473–488. https://doi.org/10.1177/2167479519900161

Chotiner, I. (2020, May 31,). LeBron James's agent is transforming the business of basketball. *The New Yorker.* https://www.newyorker.com/magazine/2021/06/07/lebron-james-agent-is-transforming-the-business-of-basketball

Cresswell, T. (2004). *Place: A short introduction.* Malden, MA: John Wiley & Sons Ltd.

Deb, S. and Cacciola, S. (2020, June 17). The NBA is coming back. There are 113 pages of new rules. *New York Times.* https://www.nytimes.com/article/nba-return-health-rules.html

de Certeau, M. (1984). *The practice of everyday life.* University of California Press.

Endres, D., & Senda Cook, S. (2011). Location matters: The rhetoric of place in protest. *Quarterly Journal of Speech, 97,* 257–282. doi.org/10.1080/00335630.2011.585167

Golliver, B. (2020, May 31). NBA players past and present show up and out to protest George Floyd's death. *Washington Post.* https://www.washingtonpost.com/sports/2020/05/31/nba-players-protest-george-floyd-death/

Harvey, D. (1996). *Justice, nature and the geography of difference.* Blackwell Publishers.

Hayhurst, L. M. C. & Szto, C. (2016). Corporatizing activism through sport-focused social justice? Investigating Nike's corporate responsibility initiatives in sport for development and peace. *Journal of Sport & Social Issues, 40,6. 522*–544.

Hughes, C. (2020, October 8). Silver: NBA to scale back social justice messaging next year. *NBC Sports.* https://www.nbcsports.com/washington/wizards/adam-silver-nba-scale-back-social-justice-messaging-next-season

James, L. [@KingJames]. (2020, July 9). *Just left the crib to head to the bubble. Shit felt like I'm headed to do a bid man! Fr.* [Tweet]. https://twitter.com/KingJames/status/12813270493 83112705

Kelsey, E. (2014, December 13). Why the NBA is okay with I can't breathe protests by players. *The Christian Science Monitor.* https://www.csmonitor.com/USA/Latest-News-Wires/2014/1213/Why-NBA-is-OK-with-I-Can-t-Breathe-protests-by-players

Kimble, J. (2020, September 3). The NBA bubble was never the players platform to fight systemic racism. *Medium.* https://level.medium.com/the-nba-bubble-was-never-the-players-platform-to-fight-systemic-racism-5c6796952922

Kurtz, J. B. (2021). Sport, social justice, and the limits of dissent after George Floyd: A reply to Butterworth. *Communication & Sport, 9*(2), 171–187. https://doi.org/10.1177/2167479520976359

Lapchick, R.E. (2020). The 2020 racial and gender report card: National Basketball Association. *The Institute for Diversity & Ethics in Sport.* https://www.tidesport .org/nba

Lillard, D. [@damianlillard]. (2020, July 9). *Feel like I'm going to do a bid.. headed to the bubble* [Photograph]. Instagram. https://www.instagram.com/p/ CCbi4qTAeFS/?hl=en

Massey, D. (2008). A global sense of place. In T. S. Oakes and P. L. Price (eds.), *The cultural geographer reader* (pp. 257–263). Routledge.

McCall, J. M. (2021). NBA's commitment to free speech activism ends when bottom line suffers. *The Hill.* https://thehill.com/opinion/civil-rights/532307-nbas -commitment-to-free-speech-activism-ends-when-bottom-line-suffers

Miller, C. (2002). Foreword. In P. Sipiora & J. S. Baumlin (eds.), *Rhetoric & kairos: Essays in history, theory, & praxis.* State University of New York Press.

Murray, C. (2019, August 239). MLS political signage ban escalates as fans protest during Timbers-Sounders rivalry game. *Orlando Sentinel. https://www .orlandosentinel.com/sports/soccer/mls/os-sp-mls-political-signage-20200528 -hj75767nwfdqlgj6lju6d5hmjm-story.html*

NBA & NBPA advance talks on social justice. (2020, June 24). *NBA Communications.* https://pr.nba.com/nba-and-nbpa-advance-talks-on-social-justice-efforts/

Press, B. & Carothers, T. (2020). Worldwide protests in 2020: A year in review. Carnegie Endowment for International Peace. https://carnegieendowment.org/2020 /12/21/worldwide-protests-in-2020-year-in-review-pub-83445

Rugg, A. (2020). Incorporating the protests: The NFL, social justice, and the constrained activism of the "Inspire Change" campaign. *Communication & Sport, 8*(4–5), 611–628. https://doi.org/10.1177/2167479519896325

Spears, M. J. (2017, October 17). Abdul-Rauf: "It's an indication not much has changed." *The Undefeated.* https://theundefeated.com/features/abdul-rauf-protests -indication-not-much-has-changed/

Spears, M. J. (2020, October 12). "Black Lives Matter, people": How the NBA's social justice efforts dominated the season. *The Undefeated.* https://theundefeated .com/features/how-the-nba-social-justice-efforts-dominated-the-season/

Stein, M. (2020, June 16). Swabs and sensors: Memos offer details of life in NBA "bubble." *New York Times.* https://www.nytimes.com/2020/06/16/sports/basketball /nba-bubble-coronavirus-disney-world-html

Tinsley, J. (2020, June 17). Craig Hodges is still shooting his shot. *The Undefeated.* https://theundefeated.com/features/craig-hodges-is-still-shooting-his-shot/

Tuan, Y. F. (1975). Place: An experiential perspective. *Geographical Review, 65*(2), 151–165.

Tuan, Y. F. (1988). *Escapism.* Baltimore, MD: The Johns Hopkins University Press.

Uggetti, P. (2020, September 10). Families and friends have entered the bubble. *The Ringer.* https://www.theringer.com/nba/2020/9/10/21429764/nba-bubble-family -and-friends-fred-vanvleet

Washington, J. (2016, September 1). Still no anthem, still no regrets for Mahmoud Abdul-Rauf. *The Undefeated. https://theundefeated.com/features/abdul-rauf -doesnt-regret-sitting-out-national-anthem/*

Windhorst, B. (2020, July 1). Sources: Orlando bubble to cost NBA more than $150 million. *ESPN.* https://www.espn.com/nba/story/_/id/29394052/orlando-bubble-cost-nba-more-150-million

Zillgitt, J. [@JeffZillgitt]. (2020a, August 24). *Talking about what the police shooting in Kenosha, Wisconsin and what players can do, Bucks guard George Hill said, "We"* [Tweet]. Twitter. https://www.twitter.com/JeffZillgitt/status/1297997726240710657

Zillgitt, J. (2020b, July 12). Life inside the bubble with NBA players: Gold, fishing and shotgunning beers. *USA Today.* https://www.usatoday.com/story/sports/nba/2020/07/12/nba-players-life-inside-bubble-golf-fishing-shutgunning-beers/5425058002

Chapter 4

Answering the Call

Maya Moore, Religion, and the Framing of Athlete Activism

Vincent Peña

The last decade has seen a resurgence of activism in sports, especially athlete activism around issues of social injustice, police brutality, criminal justice reform, and gender inequality. Perhaps the most prominent and well-documented example of this activism was Colin Kaepernick's protest against social injustice and police brutality during the national anthem before National Football League (NFL) games in 2016. Kaepernick's protest was one of the biggest storylines of the NFL season, and his actions sparked widespread praise as well as condemnation, and ignited a national movement across the country (Hoffman & Minsberg, 2018). However, Kaepernick was not the first, nor the last, athlete to use his platform to shed a light on social issues and advocate for a solution to societal ills. But his protest and the ensuing movement have dominated discourse about athlete activists and the role of athletes as engaged members of society. The re-emergence of athlete activism, at a level not seen for decades, has been called by some a "renaissance of the activist athlete" (Khan, 2020, p. 3). Kaepernick and other athletes aside, this decade has been dominated by large social movements in the U.S. and beyond. Occupy Wall Street, the Arab Spring, the Black Lives Matter movement, the Women's March, #RedforEd, the Hong Kong Protests—all of these are examples of mass social movements brought on by social, economic, political, and cultural injustice and inequality. In the sporting realm, most of the activism has been centered around the same issues that sparked the Black Lives Matter movement, namely, police brutality. The killings of black people by police officers, often captured on video, has led to protests by countless athletes across all sports. The summer of 2020 saw a resurgence in athlete activism that surpassed all the efforts in previous years, as an international Black Lives Matter movement took center stage following the police killings of George Floyd and Breonna Taylor. But before the summer of 2020, before virtually every athlete in every major sport was throwing their support behind a movement that many were silent about just a couple years earlier, Maya Moore quietly stepped away from the sport she loved in order to fight for social and racial justice.

Moore is a living basketball legend, a star who has dominated every level of competition—from high school to the pros—and is in the prime of her career. She plays in the Women's National Basketball Association (WNBA) for the Minnesota Lynx, where she has won numerous awards, league titles and other accolades. In college at the University of Connecticut, she led the Huskies to two national titles while being honored as the women's national basketball player of the year multiple times. She has also represented the United States at the Olympics, helping lead the women's team to two gold medals. However, Moore has skipped out on the last three seasons of the WNBA to pursue much different goals than those that can be achieved on the basketball court. In 2019, Moore announced she would sit out the season to advocate for the innocence of a man she believes was wrongly convicted as a teenager, tried as an adult, and sentenced to prison for 50 years. Jonathan Irons was accused of committing an armed robbery outside of St. Louis, Missouri, during which a man was shot twice in his home in the attempted burglary. Irons was convicted despite any physical evidence (including fingerprints, footprints, DNA, or a weapon), no eyewitness testimony, or the inability to testify himself. He was found guilty by an all-white jury and spent most of his life behind bars for a crime he did not commit. Moore met Irons through her family's church ministry program and was inspired to help, which for her meant devoting her time and money to Irons' cause, as well as putting her career on hiatus (Streeter, 2019). A Missouri judge overturned Iron's conviction in March 2020, and he was released in June of the same year (Streeter, 2020).

I use Moore's activism to examine the media discourse about athlete activism when it is not necessarily an offshoot of a larger social movement. Moore's activism in this instance is an individual effort and not necessarily part of a larger movement like the one Kaepernick kickstarted or the recent Black Lives Matter movement in 2020. Her activism is a solitary activism. Therefore, understanding the media's treatment of Moore's activism, especially in comparison to examples of collective athlete activism, is vital to this chapter. Of particular interest in this essay is the discourse used to describe Moore's activism, how her actions are compared to other athlete activists, and the relative dearth of coverage from mainstream news and sports media, especially in relation to coverage of prominent male athlete activists, both currently and historically. Utilizing a theoretical framework of framing as a way to analyze a wide range of news and sports media sources, this chapter will situate Moore's activism within a broader trend of athlete activism and focus on what role her identity as a black, Christian woman plays in media discourse.

THEORETICAL FRAMEWORK

This chapter relies theoretically on the concept of framing. Reese (2001) defined news frames as "organizing principles that are socially shared and persistent over time, that work symbolically to meaningfully structure the social world" (p. 11). Generally speaking, framing simply refers to the way news media portray, discuss or describe a topic or issue, as well as what they include or exclude in their coverage. How an issue is framed implies what is deemed important or salient, and therefore can shape the way it is perceived. The framing of Moore's actions is important, as there are implications for framing her criminal justice reform efforts as activism, advocacy, fight for social justice, faith-based calling, and so on. Chief among them is that the reluctance to call what she does "activism" discursively positions it as something different from what other athlete activists do, and in doing so creates a hierarchy of activism that privileges certain forms over others (Kilgo & Harlow, 2019).

A number of scholars have examined athlete activism from an array of perspectives. Journalism scholars have looked at the way protests are covered by news media, applying a well-known framework called the protest paradigm (Coombs, Lambert, Cassilo & Humphries, 2019; McLeod & Detenber, 1999). Others have looked at the history of athlete activism (Agyemang, 2012), consequences of protesting as an athlete (Kaufman, 2008), the framing in social media contexts (Schmidt, Frederick, Pegoraro, & Spencer, 2018), as well as the ability for sports to be a venue for social change (Kaufman & Wolff, 2010).

Coombs and Cassilo (2017) analyze the media coverage of LeBron James' activism in response to police shootings of unarmed black men. They look at the 15 most-visited sports websites and outline four prominent frames that emerged from their analysis, which were: Brand LeBron; Established Voice, Higher Expectations; Attention, Not Aggression; and Community Versus Protest (Coombs & Cassilo, 2017). These frames, respectively, refer to the way activism has become part of James' brand as a global sports superstar, how his history of speaking out meant that more was expected of him as time passed, how his activism focuses on bringing attention to issues rather than being an active participant in changing them, and lastly how James prioritizes community over protest, and how that tension is articulated in other sports coverage at the expense of communities affected most by racial injustice (Coombs & Cassilo, 2017).

Centering the Activism of Women Athletes

There is no shortage of literature that focuses on male athlete activists, but far less attention is paid to female athlete activists—a trend that isn't all that surprising given the lack of attention paid to women's sports in general (Cooky et al., 2015). Much of the aforementioned research focuses heavily on examples of male athlete activism. Examples of women's activism in the realm of sports are often overlooked by the media in favor of male athlete activism. Cooky and Antunovic (2020) wrote about the exclusion of women athlete activists, especially women of color, to the benefit of men. But considering that women have often been at the center of these instances of activism in recent years, whether in the WNBA or the United States Women's National Team (USWNT), it is necessary to explore these examples as well. Ignoring female athlete activism furthers the symbolic annihilation of women that happens in many other spaces, especially in the media (Tuchman, 1981). Coombs and Cassilo (2017), in their article devoted entirely to the activism of LeBron James, note in their limitations section that not enough attention has been paid to women's activism. They state, "The athletes playing in the Women's National Basketball Association (WNBA) have been at the forefront of the Black Lives Matter movement, yet their voices have not received the same level of media attention as those of their male counterparts" (p. 440).

Although Kaepernick's protests in 2016 have come to represent a decade or so of athlete activism, it's certainly worth noting that it did not start with him. In fact, just a few months before Kaepernick, four players for the Minnesota Lynx in the WNBA—including Moore, Lindsey Whalen, Rebekkah Brunson, and Seimone Augustus—spoke at a news conference before a regular season game to bring attention to the recent spate of shootings. In the summer of 2016, two black men, Philando Castille and Alton Sterling, were killed by police officers within a week; both were caught on camera. The entire Lynx team wore black T-shirts that read "Change starts with us. Justice & Accountability" on the front, and "Black Lives Matter" on the back. The names of Castille and Sterling, as well as the Dallas police shield (representing five Dallas police officers who were killed by a sniper at a protest) were also on the back of the shirt (Ziller & Prada, 2017).

That protests in the WNBA preceded Kaepernick was not lost on some. Writing for *Glamour*, Celeste Katz (2018) noted, "Ask someone about activism in pro sports, and it's a fair bet they'll highlight someone like the NFL's

Colin Kaepernick, whose 'take a knee' protests captured the attention of the country (and the personal condemnation of President Donald Trump). But WNBA players were actually ahead of Kaepernick in using their platform to make their views known" (para. 5). Kaepernick's protest obviously became more notable, partly because of the exposure granted a league like the NFL, not to mention the prominence football holds in American culture—but probably also because he is a man. That the NFL is an exponentially more popular league than the WNBA is no surprise to anyone, nor is it shocking that Kaepernick was a more well-known athlete than many of the women who participate in the WNBA. I would be remiss, however, to ignore the fact that both of those are because of a culture and a society that privileges men over women, and certainly men's sports over women's sports (Cooky et al., 2015). The hegemony of men's sports in American sporting culture extends beyond the playing field and the paychecks, and includes the attention paid to athletes when they speak up for social change.

In addition to the Lynx, the New York Liberty sported warm-up shirts bearing the words #BlackLivesMatter and #DallasFive. Following them, several more teams, including the Indiana Fever, Phoenix Mercury, Washington Mystics, and Seattle Storm, all wore Black Lives Matter shirts in solidarity. The Lynx had prompted a wave of activism that also included teams holding media blackouts, kneeling during the national anthem, and taking a stand against racism (Gibbs, 2017). The WNBA in 2018 started a campaign called "Take a Seat, Take a Stand," which directs money from ticket sales to help form partnerships with organizations and non-profits for the purpose of advocating for issues such as sexual assault prevention and women's health (Katz, 2018). Other WNBA players, such as Breanna Stewart, have also been dubbed activists. Stewart has protested Donald Trump's Muslim ban, advocated for sexual abuse victims, and worked with an organization dedicated to ending violence against women (Hill, 2018). Interestingly, one journalist described how Stewart's whiteness makes her activism more effective. "It makes a big difference when the best player in the game is also among the most outspoken. And keeping it all the way real, it makes an even broader impact if that player is white" (Hill, 2018, para. 23).

An important task when examining how the media describe and frame athlete activism, and activism more broadly, is to define exactly what is meant by activism. The notion of activism isn't always explicitly defined, and can include protesting, speaking out publicly, volunteering for an organization, or raising awareness. The dictionary definition of activism likewise varies depending on the dictionary. It can be defined as: "a doctrine or practice that emphasizes direct vigorous action especially in support of or opposition to one side of a controversial issue" (Merriam-Webster); or "the process of campaigning in public or working for an organization in order to bring about political or social change" (Oxford English Dictionaries); or "the doctrine or practice of vigorous action or involvement as a means of achieving political or other goals, sometimes by demonstrations, protests, etc." (Dictionary. com). The key phrase in two of these definitions is "vigorous action," which would apply to traditional notions of what activism looks like (i.e., protesting, marching). As we can see, activism can take many forms, and instances of activism aren't always labeled as such. There is also a difference between activism and advocacy. Advocacy is "the act or process of supporting a cause or proposal" (Merriam-Webster). However, sometimes activism and advocacy take on similar forms.

This all raises the question of whether certain examples of athlete activism are labeled appropriately, and if that even matters. Of particular significance to this chapter is the lack of media sources labeling Moore's efforts in criminal justice reform as "activism." Some writers label it as activism, but there are few examples. This has the effect of viewing activism in strict, narrow terms, and therefore would apply only to instances such as Kaepernick, Tommie Smith and John Carlos, or Muhammad Ali. Consequently, it can lead to perpetuating the notion that male athlete activism is more important and relevant, especially in cases when women's activism pertains to issues that aren't prioritized by men (i.e., reproductive rights, sexual abuse, violence against women, gender pay inequality).

Maya Moore, Faith, and Social Justice

Maya Moore has an extensive record of standing up and speaking out for social change. Beginning with the protest with her Lynx teammates in 2016, Moore has devoted a significant amount of time on and off the court to advocate for change. Most notably, she has focused much of her attention on criminal justice reform. Although much of the public didn't learn about Moore's interest in Irons's case until she announced her hiatus from the league, she was concerned with the injustice against him for years. Moore is an evangelical Christian, and her faith is what motivates her, as evidenced by the number of articles referencing her religious beliefs and the explicit quotes in which she talks about it. "'We are to be Christ's hands and feet,'" she says. 'We're called to be loving neighbors. It might not be as popular, but we have to give a voice to the voiceless'" (Cooley, 2017, para. 31).

Moore's activism hasn't been limited to her protests with her WNBA teammates. She has spoken publicly about criminal justice reform, been featured in media panels, and has even started an organization, Win with Justice, focused solely on criminal justice reform, particularly prosecutorial reform. In 2017, Moore, along with Mark Dupree Sr. and Miriam Krinsky, penned an op-ed in *USA Today* advocating for a change in how prosecutors approach the criminal justice system. Dupree is the district attorney for Wyandotte County, Kansas, and Krinsky is the executive director of Los Angeles County's Citizens' Jail Commission on Jail Violence. They argue for a move away from a perspective that prioritizes wins and losses and toward a system that prioritizes "fairness, equity, and sensible approaches to justice system engagement" (Moore et al., 2017, para. 9). The three work together for Win with Justice, although Moore is the face of the organization. The organization's website states:

> As a professional athlete, an elected prosecutor, and a justice system leader, we work in the public eye and are privileged that our communities have bestowed tremendous trust in the work we seek to carry out. To live up to that trust, both on and off our respective "courts," we believe that we need to bring a new vision to our justice system that moves beyond simply a result-driven finish line and instead brings a broader lens to promoting safe and healthy communities. ("About," n.d.)

A notable aspect of Moore's activism before and during her hiatus from the league is the way she was often described as an activist before her departure and almost never described that way following her departure, partly due to the emphasis on her religious motivations. Given the relative lack of academic research on women athlete activists, this chapter is guided by the following research question: How is Maya Moore's activism framed in sports and news media discourse?

METHODOLOGY

To examine the media coverage of Moore, I conducted a qualitative discourse analysis, focusing on the media framing of Moore's work involving social justice and the way journalists, writers, and columnists discuss Moore in the context of other athlete activists. Qualitative textual analysis is concerned with how the practices and performances of communication are articulated and embedded within text to examine underlying assumptions, ideologies, biases, and manifestations of power. In the case of Moore, this includes assumptions and ideologies of race, gender, and religion, especially as they relate to activism. The corpus (n=50) is comprised of several media outlets, including both legacy news media and newer, digital-first media. In following Cooky and Antunovich (2020), who argue for expanding the scope of what constitutes as sports media in academic research, the corpus includes not just sports sources like ESPN or *Sports Illustrated*, but other sources and websites that covered this story, such as The Root, BET, or *Bitch Magazine*. I gathered these articles through keyword searches on databases like Factiva,

LexisNexis as well as through simple internet searches on Google, using the search terms "Maya Moore" or "Maya Moore activism." When I found a piece published within a particular outlet, I also utilized these search terms using the respective site's search function. I examined both news articles as well as opinion/commentary pieces but excluded anything that wasn't at least 300 words. I also excluded any articles that were focused on the impact of her hiatus on basketball, such as articles that focused on how her absence would impact her team. As with any discourse analysis, the goal here is to examine the overall coverage of Moore's activism and the ways that discourse creates meaning, perpetuates hegemony, and establishes difference.

Though widening the scope of what is considered sports media is important and at times necessary, it is also important to avoid excluding certain mainstream publications because the prominence of these outlets means their content is often seen by more people, and therefore have a greater likelihood of influencing discourse. It is also good, for sake of comparison, to see what they include and exclude in their coverage, and how more niche sources make up for those gaps. Cooky and Antunovich (2020) advocate for "telling stories differently," which means upending the dominant narrative usually told by sportswriters, one that privileges the experience of men and perpetuates the hegemonic masculinity inherent in sports. Similarly, McClearen (2021) argues that marginalized groups may be left out of mainstream media coverage, but that doesn't mean they aren't covered by niche outlets. She contends that it is useful to view the representation of marginalized groups (women, LGBT, people of color, etc.) as a "hierarchy of visibility" wherein certain groups receive more attention in certain media spaces than others.

ANALYSIS

There are several themes in the discourse surrounding Maya Moore, which I developed after several close readings of the articles in the corpus. She is usually framed in a way that (1) emphasizes her Christianity by describing her activism as a calling or giving a voice to the voiceless; (2) extols her efforts as exceptional due to the circumstances, including leaving her sport at the height of her career; and (3) compares her to male athlete activists.

CHRISTIANITY AS MOTIVATION FOR ACTIVISM

A notable aspect of the discourse about Moore is the seeming reluctance to label what she does as activism. It can be seen in examples across the sample of media stories about her activism. In the articles I examined as well as other media appearances, Moore herself does not usually label herself an activist, nor does she generally call what she does activism. Moore, as well as many writers, refer to her actions as "ministry" or a "calling." Another way it's often described is giving a "voice to the voiceless" (Hector, 2019). In several interviews, Moore describes her decision in this same way. In one instance, she stated, "There was a lot of attention around police shootings and officers being shot. My [Lynx] teammates and I wanted to use our voices to help those who didn't feel like they had a voice. We all need to be better but we also need accountability and we need to acknowledge what is happening to one group of people in particular" (Granderson, 2020, para. 9). That same article also quotes her as saying "I decided that it was time for me to use my voice and the resources that I had to publicly help Jonathan's cause and draw attention to criminal justice reform" (Granderson, 2020, para. 14). The writer, L. Z. Granderson of the *Los Angeles Times,* explicitly refers to her faith by saying, "she didn't walk away from a successful basketball career solely to address criminal justice reform. She left to get closer to God" (para. 20).

Other examples of this focus on faith and giving a voice to the voiceless include an article from BET, which states, "But she is strong in her faith and believes she will be called to whatever is next. In the meantime, giving a voice to the voiceless is what she is meant to do" (Hector, 2019, para. 11). Writing in the *New York Times*, Kurt Streeter (2019) notes, "She is answering what she says is a call from God. For most of her life, others have defined her: 'the Invincible Queen' and 'the Perfect Superstar.' Now she believes that God wants her to step away from the fray and consider what is truly important" (para. 8). Implicitly, the inclusion of her religious faith adds significance and value to her activism in a way that doesn't happen with athletes who aren't as forthright about their religious beliefs. Her faith seemingly makes her activism more important.

There has been little to no criticism of Moore's activism, albeit a lot of the coverage is devoted to questioning if and when she'll return to playing. But the lack of criticism is in stark contrast to the treatment of the likes of Kaepernick or soccer star Megan Rapinoe, whose activism wasn't guided by their faith, but is focused on the very same issues Moore has dedicated herself to. Granted, Kaepernick and Rapinoe's actions were different in form and substance, taking place at or before sporting events, but little, if any, of the coverage focused on their faith. They were viewed as distractions because, as the arguments went, sports aren't the place for protesting. Because Moore is an activist away from the court, at least at this point, her work becomes acceptable.

Additionally, sports media framed Moore's religious motivations in a way that implies religion is a more justifiable reason for activism than politics or social justice. Writers perhaps are reluctant to challenge someone's faith, but more readily able to contest one's political perspectives. Her activism is not necessarily "religious" activism, but the focus on her religious beliefs and her faith has the effect of obscuring the inherently political implications of her efforts, which are aligned with the goals of other athlete activists who have been politically active. This echoes previous research on the impact of religious beliefs on activism in communities of color, especially Latino and Black communities. While Moore is motivated by her faith to engage in social justice activism—and celebrated for it in media coverage—religion is not always a driving factor in activism and can in fact lead some to avoid engaging in such efforts (Harris, 1994; Beyerlein, Sikkink, & Hernandez, 2016).

Exceptionality of Moore's Activism

Another theme of the coverage of Moore's efforts to exonerate Irons is the framing of her activism as exceptional, unique and "without comparison." *Washington Post* columnist Kevin Blackistone described her activism as exceptional, in that she doesn't just talk about it, but acts on it. Whether intentional or not, it has the effect of situating Moore's activism in relation to other instances of athlete activism in a way that rhetorically gives it more importance. He wrote,

"Moore didn't stop at demonstrating before a game. She didn't start and end her protest with the donning of a T-shirt emblazoned with a slogan. She didn't just use a few minutes of time onstage at the ESPYs to demand change. No, she quit her sport, then devoted her money and all of her newfound time to the cause of criminal justice reform for cases involving black men" (Blackistone, 2020, para. 7).

While Moore herself has done all those things, Blackistone is emphasizing that speaking up about an issue or raising awareness is not as important or valuable as actively participating in work that aims to directly enact social change. Sydney Umeri (2020), writing for SB Nation, touches on a similar theme: "Moore had done so much more than just talk about the issues. She is an advocate in the truest sense of the word" (para. 12).

This discourse of exceptionality also manifests itself in relation to Moore's position among the basketball elite, and the sacrifice she made to step away from her basketball career. As many have noted, Moore was in the prime of her career, coming off a stretch of team and individual success that is largely unmatched in men's or women's team sports. Herring and Paine (2020) outlined just how rare it is for a player of Moore's caliber to step away from her sport. They note that other prominent athletes, such as Muhammad Ali, Curt Flood, Tommie Smith, John Carlos, or Kaepernick have sacrificed their careers for a larger purpose, but that Moore's decision is even more noteworthy because of her status as a women's professional basketball player. They further state, "Beyond that she plays a pro sport that pays far less than others—one in which the salaries have been so low on a relative scale that many players go overseas during the offseason to play, even though that increases their injury risk. Moore walked away from the game despite having less of a chance than her male counterparts to build up financial security" (Herring & Paine, 2020, para. 12).

Moore's hiatus from basketball for social justice reform isn't just seen as exceptional because so few athletes have gone that far, but also because unlike men's basketball players who make vastly more money, she doesn't have that luxury. Her age at the time of her hiatus, 29, also lends to her "exceptionality" because she didn't have to step away yet. As Herring and Paine (2020) note, "Moore is special because she could have gone about her business as one of the best players in WNBA history, but instead she chose to lend her voice and platform to victims of injustice" (para. 18).

Dave Zirin, a prominent sportswriter, writes about Moore's "struggle for social justice" and notes how she has become an "activist for transforming our cruel system of criminal justice" (2020, para. 8). Zirin also describes Moore's activism as exceptional, claiming there are no comparisons to what she is doing. "This is a story for the ages. There is no comparison for an all-time athlete taking this kind of extraordinary step away from their craft to pursue social justice. It makes Maya Moore a legend, on and off the court" (Zirin, 2020, para. 10). Some of these articulations of exceptionality also included the impact of Moore's activism, not just on society but on others as well. In an editorial for the *Minneapolis Star Tribune*, the editorial board (2020) wrote:

> Athletes finding their voice is a welcome development for society, and sport, and it shatters the stereotype of self-absorbed stars in the pro and college ranks. Sure, just like any cohort, there are problematic individuals, especially since so many are thrust into the spotlight at such a young age. But many more are what society urges them to be: role models. And in the process of finding their voices, these athletes can inspire teammates, as well as others in society, to find theirs. (para. 10–11)

Comparisons to Male Activists

Cooky and Antunovich (2020) write how women's activism is often situated against examples of male athlete activism. They state, "Sportswomen's social activism is understood within the context of sportsmen's social activism. Moreover, although the WNBA protests occur on the heels of the NFL season wherein Colin Kaepernick began protesting during the national anthem, sport media narratives would contextualize WNBA's actions relative to Kaepernick's" (2020, p. 10). Not surprisingly, Moore's activism is often discussed in a similar fashion. In some sense, constant comparisons to Kaepernick aren't all that surprising, especially as he has become the de facto face of this "renaissance of the athlete activism."

Media coverage of this, especially from non-traditional, non-sports outlets, has underscored the invisibility of activism by women in sports. Britni de la Cretaz of Bitch Media wrote, "Yet women athletes are also at the forefront of political activism, which goes largely overlooked as the media focus falls on male athletes such as Colin Kaepernick, Michael Bennett, and LeBron James" (2017). Of interest in Moore's case is also her allusion to Kaepernick as being an influence for her activism, despite having protested before him in 2016 with her Lynx teammates. In Granderson's piece for the *Los Angeles Times*, Moore is quoted as saying, "there's no question that Colin [Kaepernick] is a part of sparking a new wave of athletes using our voice and I definitely got courage from him. When he said 'Change starts with us,' it gave me courage to raise my voice" (2019, para. 9–10).

As noted in the section on the discourse of exceptionality, Moore's activism was described as such largely because of the comparison to other male athletes who have taken similar actions. And in a culture and society that values the actions of men over those of women, instances like Moore's activism are only validated when put in context with historical examples of male activists. As Herring and Paine (2020) wrote in the *New York Times*, "history should remember her in the same conversation as Ali and Kaepernick—a conversation that has only grown in importance over the past few weeks" (para. 18–19).

Some authors noted the harm in the viewing of women's activism only as an extension of larger efforts started by men. As one journalist wrote:

> History reflects a narrative that has underrecognized the contribution of female athletes and their activism. While many remember the pregame actions taken by the St. Louis Rams to show solidarity with protesters in Ferguson, Missouri, fewer know of the actions of Knox College women's basketball's Ariyana Smith, who was the first athlete to demonstrate during the Black Lives Matter movement. While many remember the demonstrations of NFL teams kneeling during the anthem in 2017, fewer will recall the first time an entire team knelt for the anthem: the Indiana Fever in 2016. (Hurd, 2020, para. 29)

Though Moore might reference other athlete activists at times, it's notable that mainstream sports outlets such as ESPN or *Sports Illustrated* avoided calling Moore an activist or situating her within a broader trend of athlete activism. In ESPN's case, it's not all that surprising that its coverage avoided allusions to Kaepernick and other activists, especially with its cozy relationship with sports leagues like the NFL that were adamantly opposed to athlete activism, and even more opposed to Kaepernick, as evidenced by the league's alleged collusion against him. In other words, the tendency of sports outlets and other media organizations to avoid framing Moore's actions as activism reflects broader inequities in sports media and society, both of which value the political and civic contributions of men, often at the expense of women doing the same.

DISCUSSION AND CONCLUSION

This chapter highlighted the ways Moore's actions are framed by both sports and non-sports media alike as being exceptional compared to other forms of activism, as being a product of her religious beliefs and Christianity, and as existing only in comparison with other, mostly male activist athletes. While these are the major themes throughout the media coverage, I make particular note in this chapter of what is labeled as activism and what isn't. Of interest in Moore's case is the lack of media sources labeling it as "activism" despite the fact that advocating on behalf of a wrongly convicted man can be seen a textbook example of activism. However, because Moore's actions take place away from the sporting arena, and therefore aren't viewed as a distraction— something in the way of the entertainment and escapist nature of sports—her activism is deemed acceptable, valid, and not done in a way that "disrespects" national and cultural institutions like the military, the flag, or the police. Yet, advocating for criminal justice reform, even on a granular, individual level, is inherently a critique of the system that allows for those types of injustice to happen in the first place.

Moore's activism, when it is called that, is framed in context of her religious beliefs, which both lends credibility to her actions as well as trivializes them because of their religiosity. Sports media research on women's activism has shown that while there are some positive trends in the media coverage of Moore in particular, that coverage pales in comparison to examples of male athlete activism. Even when that person is one of the most prominent athletes in sports, regardless of gender, there is still scant coverage. In following Cooky and Antunovich's (2020) call to include more sources in what is considered sports media, this chapter was able to include a variety of sources that might cover the activism of female athletes. However, it also showed the dearth of coverage from mainstream sports outlets that presumably would have devoted weeks of coverage if that athlete was a man. Overall, this paper shows how a discourse of exceptionality, especially one couched in gender and religion, reflects the broader power structures in sports media. Moore's activism is framed in such a way as to highlight the uniqueness of her activism and emphasize her religious motivations, while also downplaying it by constantly comparing it to other (male) athletes.

To be clear, Moore's activism *is* exceptional. The goal of this chapter is not to argue that it is not, but rather to examine the power of sports media to define what activism is deemed exceptional, acceptable, tolerable, or forbidden. The coverage of her activism largely focuses on her religious motivations, a discursive tactic that ascribes her efforts more significance while also delegitimizing them. Additionally, the reluctance to call what she has done activism works to distinguish her from other athlete activists and situate her activism as more worthwhile. Moore provides an example of advocacy in action that stands in stark contrast to the more disruptive and attention-grabbing forms of activism, such as protests, marches, or symbolic gestures like kneeling or raising a fist. Implicit in this distinction is that her activism is more meaningful, and therefore more acceptable, even though she is concerned with many of the same issues as other prominent athlete activists.

REFERENCES

Agyemang, K. (2012). Black male athlete activism and the link to Michael Jordan: A transformational leadership and social cognitive theory analysis. *International Review for the Sociology of Sport*, *47*(4), 433–445. https://doi.org/10.1177/1012690211399509

Beyerlein, K., Sikkink, D., & Hernandez, E. (2016). Citizenship, religion, and protest: Explaining Latinos' participation in the 2006 immigrant rights marches. *Social Problems*, *66*(2), 1–31. https://doi.org/10.1093/socpro/spx047

Blackistone, K. (2020, March 18). Maya Moore left the basketball court for criminal justice reform. She is seeing the results. *Washington Post*. Retrieved from https://www.washingtonpost.com/sports/2020/03/18/maya-moore-left-basketball-court-criminal-justice-reform-she-is-seeing-results/

Cooky, C., & Antunovic, D. (2020). "This isn't just about us": Articulations of feminism in media narratives of athlete activism. *Communication and Sport*, *8*(4–5), 1–20. https://doi.org/10.1177/2167479519896360

Cooky, C., Messner, M. A., & Musto, M. (2015). "It's dude time!" *Communication & Sport*, *3*(3), 261–287. https://doi.org/10.1177/2167479515588761

Cooley, J. (2017, April 13). Champion for change. Fellowship for Christian Athletes. Retrieved from https://www.fca.org/magazine-story/2017/04/13/champion-for-change

Coombs, D., & Cassilo, D. (2017). Athletes and/or activists: LeBron James and Black Lives Matter. *Journal of Sport and Social Issues*, *41*(5), 425–444.

Coombs, D. S., Lambert, C. A., Cassilo, D., & Humphries, Z. (2019). Flag on the play: Colin Kaepernick and the protest paradigm. *Howard Journal of Communications*, *31*(4), 317–336. https://doi.org/10.1080/10646175.2019.1567408

De la Cretaz, B. (2017, September 25). All of the work, none of the credit: Don't drop the ball on the WNBA's activism. Bitch Media. Retrieved from https://www .bitchmedia.org/article/wnba-players-on-the-frontlines

Editorial Board. (2020, July 10). Maya Moore is a hero on—and off—the court. *The Minneapolis Star-Tribune.* Retrieved from https://www.startribune.com/maya -moore-is-a-hero-on-and-in-the-court/571712072/

Gibbs, L. (2017, July 25). The WNBA has found its voice. Think Progress. Retrieved from https://archive.thinkprogress.org/wnba-activism-past-present -future-2ffed59163aa/

Granderson, L. (2020, March 14). Maya Moore left the WNBA to help free a man from prison. She might've saved his life. *Los Angeles Times.* Retrieved from https: //www.latimes.com/sports/story/2020-03-14/wnba-maya-moore-criminal-justice -reform-jonathan-irons

Harris, F. C. (1994). Something within: Religion as a mobilizer of African-American political sctivism. *The Journal of Politics, 56*(1), 42–68.

Hector, J. (2019, October 3). WNBA superstar Maya Moore put legendary career on hold to fight prisoner's conviction. BET. Retrieved from https://www.bet.com /news/sports/2019/10/03/wnba-superstar-maya-moore-put-legendary-career-on -hold-to-fight-.html

Herring, C., & Paine, N. (2020, June 11). Maya Moore gave up more to fight for social justice than almost any athlete. Fivethirtyeight.com. Retrieved from https:// fivethirtyeight.com/features/maya-moore-gave-up-more-to-fight-for-social-justice -than-almost-any-athlete/

Hill, J. (2018, August 29). Breanna Stewart, MVP and athlete activist. The Undefeated. Retrieved from https://theundefeated.com/features/breanna-stewart -2018-wnba-mvp-and-athlete-activist/

Hoffman, B., & Minsberg, T. (2018, September 4). The deafening silence of Colin Kaepernick. *New York Times.* Retrieved from https://www.nytimes.com/2018/09 /04/sports/colin-kaepernick-nfl-anthem-kneeling.html

Hurd, S. (2020, July 2). Maya Moore, the game-changer: "This is the epitome of using your platform." The Undefeated. Retrieved from https://theundefeated .com/features/maya-moore-game-changer-jonathan-irons-epitome-of-using-your -platform/

Katz, C. (2018, May 17). The WNBA is starting a new season—of activism—by asking fans to take a stand. *Glamour.* Retrieved from https://www.glamour.com/story /wnba-take-a-seat-take-a-stand

Kaufman, P. (2008). Boos, bans and other backlash: The consequences of being an activist athlete. *Humanity and Society, 32*, 215–237.

Kaufman, P., & Wolff, E. (2010). Playing and protesting: Sport as a vehicle for social change. *Journal of Sport and Social Issues, 34*(2), 154–175. https://doi.org/10.1177 /0193723509360218

Khan, A. (2020). *The renaissance of the activist athlete* [Unpublished manuscript]. Department of African American Studies, Pennsylvania State University.

Kilgo, D. K., & Harlow, S. (2019). Protests, media coverage, and a hierarchy of social struggle. *The International Journal of Press/Politics, 24*(4): 508–530.

McLeod, D., & Detenber, B. (1999). Framing effects of television news coverage of social protest. *Journal of Communication, 49*(3), 3–23. https://doi.org/10.1111/j .1460-2466.1999.tb02802.x

Moore, M., Dupree, M., & Krinsky, M. (2017, November 22). Op-Ed: WNBA star Maya Moore pushing for change to criminal justice system. *USA Today*. Retrieved from https://www.usatoday.com/story/sports/2017/11/22/op-ed-wnba-star-maya -moore-pushing-change-criminal-justice-system/887868001/

Reese, S. (2001). Framing public life: A bridging model for media research. In S. Reese, O. Gandy, & A. Grant (eds.), *Framing public life* (pp. 7–31). Mahwah, NJ: Erlbaum.

Schmidt, S., Frederick, E., Pegoraro, A., & Spencer, T. (2018). An analysis of Colin Kaepernick, Megan Rapinoe, and the national anthem protests. *Communication & Sport, 7*(5), 653–677. https://doi.org/10.1177/2167479518793625

Streeter, K. (2019, June 30). Maya Moore left basketball. A prisoner needed her help. *New York Times*. Retrieved from https://www.nytimes.com/2019/06/30/sports/ maya-moore-wnba-quit.html

Streeter, K. (2020, July 1). Jonathan Irons, helped by W.N.B.A. star Maya Moore, freed from prison. *New York Times*. Retrieved from https://www.nytimes.com /2020/07/01/sports/basketball/maya-moore-jonathan-irons-freed.html?campaign _id=9&emc=edit_nn_20200702&instance_id=19941&nl=the-morning&regi_id =68069793&segment_id=32426&te=1&user_id=7b80e6a1f9ca694733805833bf4 568fc

Tuchman, G. (1981). The symbolic annihilation of women by the mass media. In S. Cohen & J. Young (eds.), *The manufacture of news: Deviance, social problems and the mass media* (pp. 169–185). Beverly Hills, CA: Sage.

Umeri, S. (2020, December 28). Maya Moore's actions off the court made her our 2020 Athlete of the Year. SB Nation. Retrieved from https://www.sbnation.com /wnba/2020/12/28/22167945/maya-moore-jonathan-irons-activism-athlete-of-the -year-2020-wnba

Ziller, T., & Prada, M. (2017, September 14). The WNBA has been at the forefront of protesting racial injustice. SB Nation. Retrieved from https://www.sbnation.com /2017/9/24/16357206/national-anthem-protest-wnba-history-donald-trump

Zirin, D. (2020, March 11). Maya Moore saves a life. *The Nation*. Retrieved from https://www.thenation.com/article/society/maya-moore-jonathan-irons/

Chapter 5

Advantage Authenticity

Naomi Osaka's Activism for Social Justice and Mental Health

Ann E. Burnette and Anthony V. LaStrape

Naomi Osaka put the tennis world on notice with her 2018 straight-set victory in the women's final of the U.S. Open. Osaka, 20 years old and seeded 20th, beat 36-year-old Serena Williams, who was seeking her seventh U.S. Open title and 24th major title. The final of the U.S. Open was notable not only for Osaka's first major championship, but for the controversy that erupted during the match and spilled over into the trophy presentation. During the second set, chair umpire Carlos Ramos issued a warning to Williams for receiving coaching from her coach Patrick Mouratoglou, who was seated in the players' box. Williams objected and argued with the umpire before resuming the match. Two games later, Williams smashed her racquet on the court in frustration during a changeover and Ramos penalized her one point for a second code violation. Williams again objected and vented her anger at Ramos. Ramos penalized Williams one game for verbal abuse. Osaka maintained her composure to clinch the victory and become the first Japanese tennis player to win a Grand Slam tournament. However, the fans in attendance had become riled during the interactions between Williams and Ramos and continued to boo loudly during the remainder of the match and the trophy ceremony. As the trophies were presented, Osaka cried and Williams put her arm around Osaka while imploring the crowd, "Let's make this the best moment we can" (as cited in Roenigk, 2018). With this match, and the controversy surrounding it, Osaka became a global public figure.

The characteristics Osaka displayed that night—her grit and vulnerability—have continued to be dominant parts of her image as she has won more major titles, become an international influencer, and used her celebrity to advocate for social change. This chapter analyzes how Osaka, on her Twitter feed and in her public statements, constructs an ethos of authenticity by communicating intimacy, ordinariness, and immediacy to her followers. We examine how Osaka uses her ethos of authenticity to advocate for racial justice and mental health awareness. We argue that, in her advocacy, Osaka displays embodied authenticity as well as commodified authenticity. The texts we analyze are Osaka's tweets and posted statements on her official Twitter feed from January 2020 until December 2021, as well as an essay Osaka wrote and published in *Esquire* in 2020, and one she wrote and published in *TIME* in 2021.

NAOMI OSAKA

Naomi Osaka was born on October 16, 1997, in Osaka, Japan. Her mother, Tamaki Osaka, is Japanese, and her father, Leonard Maxime François, is Haitian. The couple had two daughters; Naomi is 18 months younger than her sister Mari Osaka. Osaka's parents used the name "Osaka" for both of their children to make life for them easier in Japan. The family moved to Long Island, New York, when Naomi was 3 years old. Both girls started playing tennis and the family moved to Florida in 2006 to give them more opportunities to train. Like Serena Williams, one of Naomi Osaka's idols, Naomi did not come up through the junior circuit but instead debuted on the International Tennis Foundation (ITF) Women's Circuit in October 2011. She went pro in September 2013, shortly before her 16th birthday. In 2016, the Women's Tennis Association (WTA) named her the Newcomer of the Year, and she entered the WTA's top 50 in rankings. After her breakthrough win in the 2018 U.S. Open, Osaka won the 2019 Australian Open and became the first Asian tennis player to be ranked No. 1 in the world. She has since won the U.S. Open again in 2020 and the Australian Open in 2021, bringing her total of Grand Slam titles to four thus far in her career. As of May 2020, Osaka became the highest paid female athlete ever and was the 29th highest paid athlete in the world (Bridges, 2021).

Growing up, Osaka held both U.S. and Japanese citizenship. When Osaka demonstrated potential as a successful tennis player, her father urged her to represent Japan because it would afford her more possibilities (Sarkar, 2016). When Osaka turned 22, she was required by Japan's Nationality Act to renounce her American citizenship if she wanted to retain her Japanese citizenship, so she did. Osaka frequently reflects on the complexities of her experience as a biracial and multinational person. In one interview she observed, "When I go to Japan people are confused. From my name, they don't expect to see a black girl" (as cited in McCarvel, 2016, para. 4). Her intersectionality, according to her agent Daniel Balog, "makes her very marketable on several different levels" (as cited in McCarvel, 2016, para. 19).

Osaka's Ethos as an Influencer

As a social media personality on Twitter, Naomi Osaka comes across as a young woman who shares many of the same interests and concerns as fans her age. Osaka's voice is at once ingenuous and polished. In her tweets she expresses her love of fashion, music, animé, and sports. She shares selfies and TikToks of herself, her family, and her friends. In contrast to these similarities, Osaka's Twitter feed also highlights the differences between Osaka and her fans. She tweets about her cover photos, interviews and photo layouts in *Vogue*, *GQ*, and the *WSJ Magazine* Women's Fashion Issue. She also describes her participation in Fashion Week, a Netflix documentary about her, her encounters with celebrities such as Jay-Z, and her friendship with Kobe Bryant as well as her grief at his death. She is a brand ambassador for international companies including Nike, Yonex, Citizen, Nissan, Mastercard, ADEAM, BODYARMOR Sports Drink, TAG Heuer, Workday, Louis Vuitton, Frankies Bikinis, sweetgreen, Hyperice, Mattel, Panasonic, and Levi's.

Naomi Osaka has become a public figure whose statements and actions are parsed by fans and critics around the world. As an athlete, she has significant rhetorical influence on debates of the day. Grano and Butterworth (2019) have noted that sport is "a rhetorical site that is constitutive of political culture" (p. 5). Osaka has chosen to use her platform to advocate for racial justice and mental health awareness. The very fact that she has chosen to speak on these issues frames them as important. Moreover, she is able to advance her advocacy of these issues through her ethos of authenticity.

Authenticity is a powerful dimension of the ethos of public rhetors. Scholars of political communication argue that authenticity is a label that Americans use to evaluate political rhetors. Luebke (2021) provides a useful discussion of the rhetorical qualities that connote political authenticity. These qualities can also convey authenticity for other public rhetors. Osaka demonstrates many of these characteristics, which enhances her persuasive ethos. Luebke (2021) argues that consistency, intimacy, ordinariness, and immediacy are the dimensions of authenticity; the characteristics of intimacy, ordinariness, and immediacy are strong themes in Osaka's rhetoric. Intimacy is the perception that a public figure has invited their audience to see the figure in the private sphere. This fosters a feeling of authenticity because "one is less subject to public expectations in private settings, making it more likely that people show their real and authentic self" (Luebke, 2021, p. 643). Public figures who share personal details about their lives communicate this sense of intimacy (Luebke, 2021). The quality of intimacy accords with what scholars of social media identify as the "visibility mandate"—the expectation that a social media influencer must "put oneself out there" (Duffy & Hund, 2019, p. 4984). The second aspect of authenticity that Luebke describes is ordinariness. A public figure can convey ordinariness by communicating their imperfections, their down-to-earth qualities, and their amateurism (Luebke, 2021). Finally, Luebke (2021) defines immediacy as "the construction of authenticity as a direct translation of the inner self to other" (p. 645). Public rhetors can accomplish this through real-time responses to events and by using social media platforms that enable rhetors to communicate without being edited or filtered (Luebke, 2021).

In her tweets and in her essays, Osaka employs strategies of intimacy by sharing behind-the-scenes moments with her followers. She posts frequent selfies and shares TikToks of herself with her mother, her sister Mari, and her boyfriend, the American rapper Cordae. Osaka also provides commentary on her private behavior which creates the impression that she is sharing insight into her private moments and motivations. For instance, she reported via Twitter, "I hate watching tennis when I'm rooting for someone. Why are my muscles tensing up like I'm about to hit the ball?" (Osaka, October 10, 2020). Her willingness to be visible in these contexts reinforces her authenticity because she is showing herself as unguarded.

Osaka also shares her vulnerabilities with her audience, which signals that she is ordinary. She has discussed her struggle with shyness, tweeting, "Using self-deprecation as humor could potentially make you insecure and anxious in social situations. Thanks for coming to my TED talk" (Osaka, February 15, 2020). She also tweeted, "I lowkey want to start playing mixed doubles but I'm so bad at doubles I would just . . . embarrass myself the entire time" (Osaka, August 11, 2020) and "I fell on my ahaha twice today" (Osaka, May 25, 2021).

These expressions show Osaka as spontaneous and artless; they also complement Osaka's more corporate voice. Duffy and Hund (2019) note that influencers' use of social media has an "entrepreneurial" (p. 4985) aspect. In some cases, Osaka's tweets promoting products reflect her ordinary and authentic voice. She tweeted a photo of herself in front of a Nike store with an advertising image of herself in the store window with the comment, "INSANEEEEEEE" (Osaka, August 8, 2020). To announce a launch of her Nike products, she tweeted, "Im [sic] freaking out a lil [sic] bit but it's out now" (Osaka, November 16, 2020). She also advised her followers about sweetgreen, "Btw do yourself a favor and try the harvest bowl it'll change your life" (Osaka, May 6, 2021). At other times, despite appearing on her personal Twitter feed, her endorsements have the ring of corporate advertising copy. She tweeted, "@MarcusCooks taught me how to cook a recipe inspired by both of our cultures. You can watch the full video at priceless.com" (Osaka, August 6, 2020). On behalf of Nissan, Osaka tweeted, "Bold and quiet. Powerful and calm. The new @Nissan Ariya" (Osaka, April 9, 2021). Because her ordinary, authentic voice is highly marketable, it helps smooth the awkwardness of the more commercial statements.

Osaka also addresses her Twitter followers directly and casually, such as when she tweeted, "You know what I wanna say thank you guys and hope you're having a good day" (Osaka, February 22, 2020). She prefaced her announcement she would not play the 2020 French Open because of an injury by crediting her fans, posting on Twitter, "Hey guys, first and foremost thank you so much for all the support over the last 3 weeks. I couldn't have done it without you!" (Osaka, September 17, 2020). She also seeks input from her followers, tweeting, "Reply to this tweet with your most awkward encounter ever" (Osaka, May 18, 2020), and, "If I were to IG interview tennis players who would you guys want to see lol" (Osaka, May 19, 2020). This immediacy, according to Osaka, extends to her relationship with the press. She framed her media strategy in a *TIME* editorial by explaining, "I always try to answer genuinely and from the heart. I've never been media trained, so what you see is what you get" (Osaka, July 8, 2021). Her expressions of appreciation and responsiveness suggest immediacy and a desire to have an authentic connection with her audience.

Osaka's visible persona is consistent with the rise of micro-celebrities. These are people who have become famous due to their ubiquitous online presence (Nouri, 2018). Kutthakaphan and Chokesamritpol (2013) argue that public identification for micro-celebrities rests on three elements: admiration, association, and aspiration. This homespun celebrity gives rise to adaptation from traditional celebrities as the public no longer is comfortable with the distance one enjoys by being rich and famous. An athlete like Naomi Osaka exists in an advertising space where anything is possible. She is young, athletically gifted, multi-racial, and most important, candidly open with her audience.

The authenticity Osaka projects in her public persona takes two forms that we identify. Osaka enacts embodied authenticity through her presence and the use of her person to communicate her support for social justice causes. Because of her intimacy, ordinariness, and vulnerability, she is an appealing public figure with whom fans can identify. Her authenticity becomes commodified authenticity when her corporate partners utilize this persona to promote their products, services, and images.

Osaka on Racial Justice

Naomi Osaka took on the issue of racial justice at various points in 2020. On May 26, the day after the murder of George Floyd, she retweeted a video of it originally posted by StanceGrounded (Osaka, May 26, 2020). Osaka continued to tweet her commentary on reactions to Floyd's murder. Three days after Floyd's death, she tweeted, "Just because it isn't happening to you doesn't mean it isn't happening" (Osaka, May 29, 2020). On June 1, she tweeted, "I see people been ghost on twitter for a week when the events first started unfolding, but as soon as the looting started they sure are quick to give us hourly updates on how they're feeling once again" (Osaka, June 1, 2020). When activists declared Tuesday, June 2, 2020, "Black Out Tuesday" and encouraged social media users to post black squares as their profile pictures, Osaka tweeted her ambivalence about the gesture. "I'm torn between roasting people for only posting the black square this entire week," she tweeted, "Or, accepting that they could've posted nothing at all so I should deal with this bare minimum bread crumb they have given" (Osaka, June 2, 2020). In a June 4 tweet, Osaka expressed her frustration with the criticism of athletes who engage in social activism. "I hate it when random people say athletes shouldn't get involved with politics and just entertain," she declared, arguing, "Firstly, this is a human rights issue. Secondly, what gives you more right to speak than me? By that logic if you work at IKEA, you are only allowed to talk about the 'GRÖNLID'?" (Osaka, June 4, 2020).

Osaka took her social activism to other channels as well. On July 1, 2020, she published an essay in *GQ* titled, "I Never Would've Imagined Writing This Two Years Ago." She began the piece by reflecting on her identity and people's attempts to categorize her: "As long as I can remember, people have struggled to define me. I've never really fit into one description" (Osaka, July 1, 2020). She wrote that when she saw the "horrific video of George Floyd murder and torture," she "felt a call to action" (Osaka, July 1, 2020). She recounted her actions in honor of Floyd, including flying to Minneapolis to visit the George Floyd Memorial and join protesters there, as well as signing petitions, participating in protests, and donating money to the cause once she returned to Los Angeles. She then decided "it was time to speak up about systemic racism and police brutality" (Osaka, July 1, 2020). When Osaka (July 1, 2020) observed "tackling racism has been challenging for me. I have received racist comments online and even on TV," she framed her fight against racism as being personal, taking place in private and public spaces, and posing challenges that she doesn't always feel she overcomes. She emphasizes intimacy and ordinariness in this argument and thus seeks identification with her audience.

In addition to using media channels to broadcast her message, Osaka also used her appearances in—or absence from—tournaments to convey her stance. The 2020 professional tennis season, like other sport schedules, was radically affected by the Covid pandemic. Three of the four Grand Slam events were upended in different ways. The Australian Open was held during its traditional slot in late January/early February. Osaka, who had won the tournament in 2019, lost in the third round to American teenager Coco Gauff. In March, the organizers of the French Open, which traditionally begins on the fourth Sunday of May, announced that the tournament would be post-poned until September. In April, the All England Lawn Tennis Association cancelled the 2020 Championship at Wimbledon; it was the first time the tournament had not been held since World War II. There was debate and uncertainty about whether the U.S. Open would go forward (Clarey, 2020). In the end, the United States Tennis Association (USTA) chose to conduct the tournament at the usual facility, the USTA Billie Jean King Tennis Center in New York, from August 30 to September 13. In response to the pandemic, however, players would be required to limit the number of people among their support staff and no spectators were allowed in the facility. All person-nel and tennis players were required to wear masks except athletes when they were playing. The masks would serve as a vibrant medium for Osaka to make political statements.

On August 23, 2020, Jacob Blake, a 29-year-old Black man, was seriously injured in a police shooting in Kenosha, Wisconsin. As protests mounted, Osaka was playing in the Western & Southern Open, a warm-up tournament for the U.S. Open. That tournament is usually played in Cincinnati; in 2020, the tournament was held at the USTA Billie Jean King Center to provide an opportunity for players and organizers to put into practice the Covid mitiga-tion protocols for the U.S. Open. Osaka had reached the semi-finals of the Western & Southern Open when she announced that she would withdraw from the tournament in solidarity with the NBA protest against Blake's shoot-ing. Tournament organizers ultimately decided to suspend the tournament for a day to honor the protests, and Osaka won her semifinal match before with-drawing from the final because of injury (Gay, 2020). In this episode, Osaka demonstrated her willingness to sacrifice her visibility as well as her potential earnings. She embodied her protest in a literal sense: she made her argument through her physical presence or absence.

When she arrived to play at the 2020 U.S. Open, Osaka made the decision to wear her politics on her mask. Each time she arrived to play a match and departed after the match, she wore a black face mask inscribed with the name of a Black person who had been killed. Over the seven matches she played from the first round to the final, she wore the names of Ahmaud Arbery, Philando Castile, George Floyd, Trayvon Martin, Elijah McClain, Tamir

Rice, and Breonna Taylor. Here Osaka again embodied her support of her social activism by expressing her politics on her person. This embodiment relies on an enthymematic understanding of what the names represent. While Osaka's social media visibility is different from that of her fans, using masks as a form of protest is a type of activism widely available to any of her fans and thus reinforces Osaka's ordinariness.

Osaka on Mental Health

After back-to-back hard court titles at the U.S. and Australian Opens, Osaka lost on clay in the Madrid Open in early May of 2021 to a player well below her stature (Chowdhury, 2021). This upset, leading into a Grand Slam tournament on clay, brought fervent questioning from the media. In order to limit her exposure to negative questioning about her prowess on clay courts (Futterman, 2021), Osaka (May 26, 2021) informed French Open tournament officials that she would not be participating in media sessions at the French Open by releasing a statement via Twitter:

Hey everyone—

Hope you're all doing well, I'm writing this to say I'm not going to do any press during Roland Garros. I've often felt that people have no regard for athletes mental health and this rings very true whenever I see a press conference or partake in one. We're often sat there and asked questions that we've been asked multiple times before or asked questions that bring doubt into our minds and I'm just not going to subject myself to people that doubt me. . . . However, if the organizations think that they can just keep saying, "do press or you're gonna be fined," and continue to ignore the mental health of the athletes that are the centerpiece of their cooperation then I just gotta laugh.

Osaka was intimate with her audience here. She took them to the inner workings of a tournament and spoke to the climate of the press conference in a way that people outside of the sport might not be familiar with. Osaka has knowledge of what happens to athletes once press conferences end and spoke to how a kernel of doubt in the press room can manifest on the court.

Osaka also centered the athlete within the corporation of tennis. Osaka alluded to struggling with her own mental health as a result of press conferences but was not explicit in this statement. Instead, she made the argument that an athlete's well-being is the most important aspect of sport and must be protected at the highest levels. Those outside the world of professional tennis are not privy to the long workouts and recovery sessions, trainers, and dietary restrictions, and do not know what it takes to become a professional athlete or to perform on a professional stage. For those individuals who follow Naomi

Osaka's Twitter feed for recommendations on smoothies, fashion, and travel, the revelation that a multi-millionaire struggles with the constraints of her job is something unique to this generation of athlete. A statement like this one exudes authenticity because it is so vulnerable. This titan of the sport, who has been hitting tennis balls since she could pick up a racket, can be laid low by the doubt that comes from questions about her performance.

Tournament officials at the French Open responded to Osaka by quickly fining her $15,000 with the heads of all the other Grand Slam tournaments threatening expulsion from the French Open and harsher monetary penalties at tournaments moving forward (Futterman, 2021). Officials reasoned that Osaka would have an unfair advantage if allowed to skip media obligations her competitors were not allowed to avoid. Osaka (May 31, 2021) again took to Twitter stating:

Hey everyone, this isn't a situation I ever imagined or intended when I posted a few days ago. I think now the best thing for the tournament, the other players, and my wellbeing is that I withdraw so that everyone can get back to focusing on the tennis going on in Paris. I never wanted to be a distraction and I accept that my timing was not ideal and my message could have been clearer. More importantly I would never trivialize mental health or use the term lightly. The truth is that I have suffered long bouts of depression since the US Open in 2018 and I have had a really hard time coping with that. . . . So here in Paris I was already feeling vulnerable and anxious so I thought it was better to exercise self-care and skip the press conferences. I announced it preemptively because I feel like the rules are quite outdated in parts and I wanted to highlight that.

And with that, she was gone. Osaka again embodied her activist argument, in this case for mental health advocacy, by refusing to be present at press conferences. Here she explicitly told the world that she has had long bouts of depression and that her depression is directly related to tennis, specifically, her turbulent defeat of Serena Williams to win the 2018 U.S. Open. Osaka was both immediate and intimate with her audience. She was at the tournament, living with her decisions and the backlash, and she told her audience via Twitter her response to the crisis (withdrawal from the tournament) before tournament officials could release a statement at the organizational level. For Osaka's audience this behavior connotes a reverence for her Twitter followers who are in the know at the same time as her organizational bosses.

Osaka's words give voice to her innermost feelings about her place in the world as an athlete and a human. There are many things that go into being a professional tennis player that have nothing to do with actual tennis. While Osaka is having a professional dispute with her workplace, something most employees can attest to, it is rare for a medical diagnosis to be shared publicly. The intimacy displayed here reinforces Osaka's genuineness because even the most cynical observer would acknowledge that making this up to avoid a tennis tournament is unlikely. As the realization of Osaka's absence from the French Open set in, the public's attention turned to perhaps the most prestigious tennis tournament, Wimbledon, which began in less than a month. Osaka's agent revealed that Osaka would not play in Wimbledon, citing her desire to take personal time with family and friends and plan for the Olympic Games which would be played in Osaka's home country of Japan (Clarey & Rothenberg, 2021). This decision reflected Osaka's resolve regarding her mental health and the embodied authenticity she brought to the issue. Sports careers are finite and tennis careers can evaporate quickly. To withdraw from two Grand Slam events while being considered one of the favorites to win is something the public is not used to seeing, which makes Osaka's decisions all the more thought provoking.

Osaka's advocacy on this topic contributed to the larger conversation about athletes and mental health that was taking place and that American gymnast Simone Biles would further ignite at the Tokyo Olympics. Prior to the Olympics, Osaka wrote in *TIME* that "Michael Phelps told me that by speaking up I may have saved a life" (Osaka, July 8, 2021). She reiterated the intimacy, ordinariness, and immediacy of her concerns, noting, "It has become apparent to me that literally everyone either suffers from issues related to their mental health or knows someone who does" (Osaka, July 8, 2021). Osaka was the athlete selected to light the Olympic cauldron in Tokyo; she then lost in straight sets in the third round of the Olympic women's tennis singles competition. In August, Osaka entered the 2021 U.S. Open as the third seed. Osaka lost in the third round to the eventual finalist, unseeded Layla Fernandez, who turned 19 years old three days after her win over Osaka. By October 2021, Osaka's world ranking fell outside the top ten for the first time since 2018 (Agence France-Presse, 2021). Osaka's embodied authenticity was on display as she struggled to recapture the athletic success of her earlier days on the tour. She also highlighted the nature and significance of her commodified authenticity when she thanked her corporate partners and observed that she was not surprised by their support because she "purposefully chose brand partners that are liberal, empathetic and progressive" (Osaka, July 8, 2021).

CONCLUSION

Osaka uses various persuasive strategies to advance her social activism. These include messages in social media such as Twitter and mass media such as magazines. They also include embodied arguments such as her refusals to appear at tournaments and press conferences and wearing enthymematic messages on her face masks. These verbal and embodied messages are perceived as authentic because of her performance of intimacy, ordinariness, and imme- diacy. This embodied authenticity gives Osaka a unique voice on the issues of racial justice and mental health awareness; her expertise is not theoretical but lived. Osaka's authenticity also makes her more appealing as a corporate brand ambassador. The advertising messages that are true to her authentic voice help eliminate barriers between her followers and the corporations that want them as customers. In this way she is a powerful example of commodi- fied authenticity.

Professional institutions provide the benefit of both heft and scale. As institutions grow in size, the individual loses more influence. Human resource departments, while named with the individual in mind, are often put in place to uphold the prized status of the institution. When the individual and their needs supersede the needs of the institution, the individual is the one who will be forced to make concessions. Naomi Osaka is a gifted athlete, but she is also one piece of a much larger whole. While the talent on the court is what is sold to the public, the institution encompasses aspects beyond the actual proceedings on the court. Osaka's actions influence other players, venues, administrators, support staff, trainers, managers, food service, merchandisers, talent bookers, and the media.

The question then becomes, how does a cog in the machine question the machine? Osaka is an important and well-paid cog, but a cog in the overall tennis conglomerate nonetheless. A charitable reading of Osaka's requests promotes the creation of a different, more athlete-centered machine. A more critical reading is for the destruction of the machine altogether. When a dis- ruptor critiques hegemonic practices, that person's credibility comes under scrutiny. Osaka comes under scrutiny every time a tennis legend questions her commitment to the furtherance of the sport. Osaka comes under scrutiny when media members set up straw person arguments about Osaka avoiding press during a tournament but courting the press by appearing on magazine covers. Osaka comes under scrutiny by advertising her compensation and then demanding that she be grateful for the opportunity to live the life the institution has made possible for her.

Despite her appeal and power as an authentic voice, Osaka still faces the constraints of an athlete, particularly an athlete who is a woman of color. Naomi Osaka is not allowed to have views about the structure of a tourna- ment, how diverse brand partnerships are, police brutality, mental health, or reckoning with pervasive racial inequality. Osaka, as prized minority, must uphold the structure that allows for her power and status. She must show some form of athletic gratitude or be branded as selfish in more conventional circles. What makes Osaka special is that she is rejecting these conventions in an eloquent and most public way. Osaka, like many people of her generation, is challenging what it means to work in America and is willing to put her authenticity on the line in that effort.

REFERENCES

Agence France-Presse. (2021, October 4). WTA rankings: Naomi Osaka falls out of top-10 for first time since 2018. *Firstpost.* Retrieved from https://www.firstpost .com/sports/wta-rankings-naomi-osaka-falls-out-of-top-10-for-first-time-since -2018-10024151.html

Bridges, C. A. (2021, June 6). 10 things to know about tennis superstar and former Boca Raton resident Naomi Osaka. *The Palm Beach Post.* Retrieved from https:// palmbeachpost.com

Chowdhury, P. (2021, May 5). "I'm not a professional clay court player": Naomi Osaka opens up on her discomfort on clay. *Essentially Sports.* Retrieved from https: //essentiallysports.com

Clarey, C. (2020, June 15). U.S.T.A. plans to move forward with U.S. Open amid pandemic. *New York Times.* Retrieved from https://nytimes.com

Clarey, C., & Rothenberg, B. (2021, June 17). Naomi Osaka withdraws from Wimbledon but will play in Tokyo Olympics. *New York Times.* Retrieved from https://nytimes.com

Duffy, B. E. & Hund, E. (2019). Gendered visibility on social media: Navigating Instagram's authenticity bind. *International Journal of Communication, 13,* 4983– 5002. Retrieved from https://ijoc.org/

Futterman, M. (2021, May 31). Naomi Osaka quits the French Open after news conference dispute. *New York Times.* Retrieved from https://nytimes.com

Gay, J. (2020, August 31). No Rafa, no Roger, no towel service, no problem: How the 2020 U.S. Open will be different. *Wall Street Journal.* Retrieved from https:// wsj.com.

Grano, D. A., & Butterworth, M. L. (2019). Rhetoric, sport, and the political: An introduction. In D. A. Grano & M. L. Butterworth (eds.), *Sport, rhetoric, and political struggle* (pp. 1–22). New York: Peter Lang.

Kutthakaphan, R., & Chokesamritpol, W. (2013). *The use of celebrity endorsement with the help of electronic communication channel (Instagram) [Master's thesis, Malardalen University School of Business, Society and Engineering]. http://www. diva-portal.org/smash/get/diva2:626251/FULLTEXT01.pdf*

Luebke, S. M. (2021). Political authenticity: Conceptualization of a popular term. *The International Journal of Press/Politics, 26*(3), 635–653. doi: 10.1177/194016220948013

McCarvel, N. (2016, January 19). Serena Williams: Rising Japanese star tennis Naomi Osaka is "very dangerous." *USA Today.* Retrived from https://usatoday.com

Nouri, M. (2018). The power of influence: Traditional celebrity vs social media influencer. *Advanced Writing: Pop Culture Intersections, 32,* 1–20.

Osaka, N. [@naomiosaka]. (2020, February 15). *Using self deprecation as humor could potentially make you insecure and anxious in social situations. Thanks for coming to my* [Tweet]. Twitter. https://twitter.com/naomiosaka/status /1228698347059302400

Osaka, N. [@naomiosaka]. (2020, February 22). *You know what I wanna say thank you guys and hope you're having a good day today. I've been focusing* [Tweet]. Twitter. https://twitter.com/naomiosaka/status/1231319093224988672

Osaka, N. [@naomiosaka]. (2020, May 18). *Reply to this tweet with your most awkward encounter ever* [Tweet]. Twitter. https://twitter.com/naomiosaka/status /1262477434710089729

Osaka, N. [@naomiosaka]. (2020, May 19). *If I were to IG interview tennis players who would you guys want to see lol* [Tweet]. Twitter. https://twitter.com/ naomiosaka/status/1262742326700457988

Osaka, N. [@naomiosaka]. (2020, May 26). *StanceGrounded @-SJPeace- May 26, 2020 "Please, please! I can't breathe . . . My stomach hurts, my neck hurts, everything hurts"those were his last words* [Tweet]. Twitter. https://twitter.com /_SJPeace_/status/1265404784410066944

Osaka, N. [@naomiosaka]. (2020, May 29). *Just because it isn't happening to you doesn't mean it isn't happening at all.* [Tweet]. Twitter. https://twitter.com/ naomiosaka/status/1266514627934015489

Osaka, N. [@naomioska]. (2020, June 1). *I see people been ghost on twitter for a week when the events first started unfolding, but as soon as* [Tweet]. Twitter. https: //twitter.com/naomiosaka/status/1267557751187632128

Osaka, N. [@naomiosaka]. (2020, June 2). *I'm torn between roasting people for only posting the black square this entire week . . . Or accepting that they could've posted* [Tweet]. Twitter. https://twitter.com/naomiosaka/status/1267971365115592704

Osaka, N. [@naomiosaka]. (2020, June 4). *I hate when random people say athletes shouldn't get involved with politics and just entertain. Firstly, this is a human* [Tweet]. Twitter. https://twitter.com/naomiosaka/status/1268590075786326017

Osaka, N. (2020, July 1). I never would've imagined writing this two years ago. *GQ.* https://www.esquire.com/sports/a33022329/naomi-osaka-op-ed-george-floyd -protests/

Osaka, N. [@naomiosaka]. (2020, August 6). *Had a great time in @Mastercard's latest #Priceless Experience at Home! @MarcusCooks taught me how to cook a recipe inspired* [Tweet]. Twitter. https://twitter.com/naomiosaka/status /1291389606886137856

Osaka, N. [@naomiosaka]. (2020, August 8). *INSANEEEEEEE* [Tweet]. Twitter. https://twitter.com/naomiosaka/status/1292236317900734464

Osaka, N. [@naomiosaka]. (2020, August 11). *I lowkey want to start playing mixed doubles but I'm so bad at doubles I would just say, "sorry" and* [Tweet]. Twitter. https://twitter.com/naomiosaka/status/1293258639143104512

Osaka, N. [@naomiosaka]. (2020, September 17). *Hey guys, first and foremost thank [sic] so much for all the support over the last 3 weeks. I couldn't have* [Tweet]. Twitter. https://twitter.com/naomiosaka/status/1306748744604422145

Osaka, N. [@naomiosaka]. (2020, October 10). *I hate watching tennis when I'm rooting for someone. Why are my muscles tensing up like I'm about to hit* [Tweet]. Twitter. https://twitter.com/naomiosaka/status/1314929643019857926

Osaka, N. [@naomiosaka]. (2020, November 16). *Im freaking out a lil bit but it's out now* [Tweet]. Twitter. https://twitter.com/naomiosaka/status/1328385987773231104

Osaka, N. [@naomiosaka]. (2021, April 9). *Bold and quiet. Powerful and calm. The new @Nissan Ariya. #NissanAriya* [Tweet]. Twitter. https://twitter.com/naomiosaka/status/1380546501970067458

Osaka, N. [@naomiosaka]. (2021, May 6). *Btw do yourself a favor and try the harvest bowl it'll change your life* [Tweet]. Twitter. https://twitter.com/naomiosaka/status/1390269723410063361

Osaka, N. [@naomiosaka]. (2021, May 25). *I fell on my ahaha twice today* [Tweet]. Twitter. https://twitter.com/naomiosaka/status/1397154893161451520

Osaka, N. [@naomiosaka]. (2021, May 26). *Hey everyone-Hope you're doing well, I'm writing this to say I'm not going to do any press during Roland* [Tweet]. Twitter. https://twitter.com/naomiosaka/status/1397665030015959040

Osaka, N. (2021, July 8). It's O.K. not to be O.K. *TIME*. Retrieved from https://time.com/6077128/naomi-osaka-essay-tokyo-olympics/

Roenigk, A. (2018, September 1). This point wasn't up for debate: Naomi Osaka was denied her magic moment. *ESPN*. Retrieved from https://www.espn.com/tennis/story/_/id/24619049/us-open-2018-naomi-osaka-was-denied-magic-moment

Sarkar, P. (2016, May 27). Tennis—Osaka falls short of acing Japanese test. *Reuters*. Retrieved from https://reuters.com

PART III

Student Athletes Leading the Charge

Chapter 6

A Tempered Approach to Student-athlete Activism

Konadu Y. Gyamfi

INTRODUCTION

Student-athletes have come to know about the murders by law enforcement of Black people such as Eric Garner, Mike Brown, Trayvon Martin, and more and how the Black Lives Matter (BLM) movement was manifested from these cases (Reese, 2017). The emergence of BLM has been followed with a resurgence of Black athlete activism at all competition levels (Edwards, 2016). Notably, in 2015, the University of Missouri's football team demonstrated the power of the collective Black student-athlete voice by joining a protest against discriminatory practices at the university which led to the resignation of the university president and chancellor.

Although student-athletes have been known to catalyze change as in the aforementioned incidents with the University of Missouri football team, their outspokenness has been suppressed (Reese, 2017). Division I student-athletes do not believe they have enough ability to speak out on issues as the platforms that currently exist for them only question their athletic activity or incidents on campus (Arnett, 2015). They also feel restricted in their social activism because policies created and enforced by university athletic departments put them at risk of losing athletic financial aid, limited team activity, or expulsion from the team (Lomonte, 2014). Despite this, however, studies show having support from faculty and staff helps students persist as activists. As Gibson and Williams (2020) note when discussing student activism at an HBCU, "a key element in the success of this activism effort was the facilitation by faculty and staff, as students seemed to need the support of their administration to assist them in the realization of their intentions" (p. 275). Using tempered radicalism as the framework, this chapter examines how athletic department staff use strategic methods as staff members to support student-athlete activism.

THEORETICAL FRAMEWORK

Tempered radical theory (Meyerson & Scully, 1995) is a branch of grassroots leadership theory found in social movement literature in which social change is stimulated by those within an organization that lack formal authority (Kezar et al., 2011). The role of higher education staff (or administrators) fits the definition of tempered radicals and those lacking formal authority in that within the context in the United States, "staff have non-instructional responsibilities . . . and administrators have formal positions where they are delegated authority from the board of trustees and work more directly with the president and top-level leadership" (Kezar, 2011, p. 130). Staff engage in changes largely unsupported by their organizations, but when tempered, this work could lead to shifts in the values and direction of the campus (Meyerson, 2003).

Tempered radicals tend to work by staying within the organization and tempering their strategies from the bottom up (Meyerson & Scully, 1995). It shows a different approach to radical activism than the grandiose performance (Maxey, 1999). There are multiple ways one can act as a tempered radical such as quietly resisting to pursue personal congruence, using personal threats as a means to confront discriminatory practices within an organization, negotiating to find solutions to conflicts, leveraging small victories to achieve larger organizational results, and organizing actions toward a critical issue or controversy (Meyerson, 2003; Kezar, 2010). The acts of quiet resistance and using personal threats may be more ambiguous than the other tempered radical strategies; therefore, I will offer further explanation for those methods.

Wetherell (2020) explains quietly resisting for personal congruence as using small subtle strategies to resist hegemonic systems for one's personal peace. This can look like the expression of affect or emotion during a disapproving event or ceremony (Wetherell et al., 2020), decorating a space to show support for a social issue (Kezar et al., 2011), or bending but not fully succumbing to rules set within an institution by those with formal authority (Ngunjiri et al., 2012). For tempered radicals, to quietly resist is to act in discrete ways that express "personal values, subtly calling into question taken-for-granted beliefs and work practices" (Meyerson, 2004, p. 16).

The use of personal threats to confront discriminatory practices is a strategy that takes the form of using personal threats as opportunities. Ngunjiri et al. (2012) illustrate an example of this in their article about Black women church leaders as tempered radicals. Because their institution, the church, would not allow Black women to serve as preachers or mount the pulpit to preach (allowing them to only preach from the floor), Black women preachers used this personal threat to pursue opportunities by leaving and going to another church so that they can preach without restriction. Other tempered strategies they have used were speaking at camp meetings or their homes, and declining invitations to preach at churches that would not let women preach from the pulpit.

This chapter extends the use of tempered radicalism by applying it to sport, particularly collegiate sport and student-athlete activism. There are few examples of this theory's use in sport research, with one being the use of tempered radicalism to describe athlete activists such as former Major League Baseball (MLB) player Jim Bouton. Bouton was described as a social activist, bringing to light corruption that was happening in the MLB in the 1970s in his book, Ball Four. Bouton was also known for joining other sports figures as they protested against apartheid in South Africa at the 1968 Mexico City Olympics (Reed, 2019). He was tempered in the sense that he had a passionate rage, which for tempered radicals, allows them to be "angered by the incongruities between their own values and beliefs about social justice and the values and beliefs they see enacted in their organizations" (Meyerson and Scully, 1995, p. 585).

METHODOLOGY

The participants in this chapter were all given pseudonyms to keep their identities private. Each identified as athletic department staff of varying ranks, institution types, and division playing level. Journal entries were collected from each participant, asking them to focus on a specific experience they had with supporting student-athlete activism, their institution's response, if any, to their support, and their reaction to the university's response. Next, one semi-structured interview with each of the participants was conducted over Zoom. These interviews focused on institutional policies around student-athlete activism, institutional and community responses to participant support of activism, and reflections on how they have changed as a result of their actions and the events happening in society. The overall focus of both these modes of data collection was to observe how the participants may have moved in a spirit of tempered radicalism as they worked to support student-athlete activism at their institutions.

Narrative inquiry was used to analyze data in this chapter as a way of "understanding one's own or the actions of others and as connecting and seeing the consequences of actions and events over time" (Chase, 2011, p. 421). Narrative inquiry explores social, cultural, and institutional stories within one's lived experience (Jones et al., 2014) and that makes it fit for this research. It considers the stories of student-athlete activism, social injustice, current events, and institutional challenges as it considers staff experience within it.

Asking the participants to talk about how they perceive the significance of student-athlete activism, their experience with how COVID-19 and anti-Black racism impacted their support of activism and their institution's response associated with it, required the participants to narrate their motivations for engaging in this type of work. It allowed them to pay attention to temporality, sociality, and place—defining features of narrative inquiry (Jones et al., 2014).

FINDINGS

The most common method of tempered radicalism which helped shape sport staff as tempered radicals was quiet resistance. Tempered radicalism includes several other strategies, including quietly resisting to pursue personal congruence, using personal threats as a means to confront discriminatory practices within an organization, negotiating to find solutions to conflicts, leveraging small victories to achieve larger organizational results, and organizing actions toward a critical issue or controversy (Meyerson, 2003; Kezar, 2010). However, such strategies were not seen as strongly among research participants as quiet resistance. For tempered radicals, quiet resistance is to act in discrete ways that express "personal values, subtly calling into question taken-for-granted beliefs and work practices" (Meyerson, 2004, p. 18). Each participant tempered their strategies to support their student-athlete activists by reacting in small unnoticeable ways as not to bring attention or cause disruption to their work in the institution (Meyerson, 2004).

Quiet Resistance as Preferred Tempered Radicalism

Tamar

Tamar is a Director of Athlete Academic Support. Aside from signage in her office that supported different social causes, Tamar used quiet resistance as a tempered strategy while working from home due to the COVID-19 shutdown in spring 2020. The mandatory work from home order forced Tamar to become more confident in advocating for herself and thus her student-athletes because it forced her to realize the unbounded demands placed on her by her job. Tamar found that she was constantly making herself available for work, even outside of her scheduled hours. She answered the phone for colleagues whenever they called and engaged in work tasks well beyond the forty hours per week she would be paid for. Realizing this during the construct of the COVID-19 pandemic revealed to Tamar ways that she needed to advocate for herself through her work-life balance which inadvertently showed her how she could also advocate for her student-athletes with the social injustice events happening at the same time as the COVID-19 work from home order.

By personally refusing to work beyond the daily and weekly requirements in her schedule, Tamar quietly resisted the perceived demands of her work which gave her the confidence to support student-athlete activism as it began to resurge in the spring and summer semesters of 2020. She became more comfortable advocating for her student-athletes by rescheduling study hall and speaking to professors about absences due to student-athletes organizing and attending social justice marches. Tamar also became more comfortable addressing a perceived issue of racism that one of her athletes was facing in class. In an interview, Tamar said:

> I have kind of reevaluated and where forty is the limit that I'm paid for, I will either intentionally do more than the 40 hours or not. I will make a conscious decision about whether or not to respond to a coach at 10:00 PM. But that ability to kind of see where I don't stick up for myself, coinciding with this resurgence of this movement . . . It was like kind of great timing because I will say something. So, I would've been uncomfortable a year ago with the student who came up to me about his teacher. And I would have been uncomfortable asking him if he thought it was because of his race. That just feels funny. But it's a question and it's a fair question. And I hope that it's a question that helps him see like, I'm not downplaying this for you. If you think this is because of your race, then we will deal with it.

Tamar's use of quiet resistance to pursue personal congruence is seen here as she resisted the need to work more hours or beyond the hours that she was assigned. This new comfort in advocating for her personal congruence then inspired her to advocate for her student-athletes in other subtle ways. Meyerson (2004) speaks of this quiet resistance as an act of self-expression (similar to dress, language, or leadership style) which can influence others to pursue similar subtle acts. In this case, Tamar's act of resisting additional work influenced her and how she supported her student-athletes in activism.

Gabby

Quiet resistance also helped sport management professor/student-athlete tutor Gabby become comfortable in her role as a tempered radical. As a tutor, Gabby kept the news channel MSNBC on the screen and used it in conversation with the student-athletes she tutored. In her journal Gabby wrote, "in the offices when we met in-person, the television channel would be tuned to MSNBC. This allowed for conversations to evolve regarding politics, civil unrest, and racial injustice." She followed up in her interview by expressing "the cool thing was it made a very comfortable environment to talk about that stuff." Quietly resisting to pursue personal congruence is revealed here as the comfort being created in the office between the student-athletes and staff around watching and discussing issues of social injustice.

Meyerson (2004) explains that for quiet resistance, small actions by dominant cultures can be disrupted by "creating ripples that lead to significant change" (p. 17). Gabby's small action of keeping the news on created a comfortable environment and thus created ripples of change among her student-athletes. It also showed the ways in which staff "work through and with students to quietly resist the status quo" (Kezar et al., 2011, p. 148). In her interview, Gabby shares "I mean, before any of this was really brought to the forefront. These student-athletes did not care about anything. He suggested that the team get together and watch a documentary on Netflix. But it was really neat to see him like approach the coaches and say, hey, how about we do this today instead of a practice."

The news channel in the office allowed Gabby's student-athletes to be comfortable in expressing their apathy and hopelessness for the issues. However, it also allowed them to be comfortable to come back to her when a combination of events transformed the student-athletes' minds about these same issues. Gabby was able to witness, because of her small act of quiet resistance, that her student-athletes went from not caring about the issues, to becoming more concerned and taking actionable steps to create change and resist the status quo within their team.

Amma

Amma, a track and cross-country coach at an HBCU, revealed her quiet resistance in two ways: she held programming and supported activism programs created by her student-athletes. After hearing about an upcoming white supremacist rally happening near campus, Amma's student-athletes wanted to attend a counterprotest happening at the rally. Although Amma understood the importance and significance of her all-Black team attending this counter protest, Amma also felt that it could potentially become dangerous and decided to hold track practice during that time. "Once we heard got word of that [the rally] we were like, ok we definitely need to have this Saturday practice and then just let them [the student-athletes] know like, hey look, we understand, we get it. But it's just not . . . it's not going to be [safe]." Instead, Amma had conversations with the team about other ways they could be activists.

Amma supported the team with planning their own rally on campus in counterprotest to the white supremacist group's rally. She also recognized that the rally would not be impactful if it conflicted with pre-scheduled events on campus. She detailed how as a coach, she navigated her campus partnerships and learned how to help her student-athletes effectively schedule events on campus so that "student-athlete protests would not conflict with other events happening on campus/help them get the largest crowd possible."

Holding practice was Amma's form of quiet resistance and method of protecting her student-athletes from potential harm, but her personal congruence came when Amma decided to attend the rally herself. "I went. I didn't want them to go . . . what if something happens to [them]?" This act resembles the Kezar et al. (2011) example of "taking time off from work to observe important religious holidays not officially recognized by the organization" (134) as quietly resisting to pursue personal congruence. Although not exactly the same, the sentiment is similar because Amma took time to observe something that was important to her and her student-athletes. Holding practice and encouraging another form of activism to her student-athletes was Amma's act of quiet resistance and her personal congruence came from attending the rally she protected her team from attending.

Wynter

Wynter's form of quiet resistance took shape when she played a part in revising the Twitter statements of her student-athletes. After the murder of George Floyd, the women's basketball team at Wynter's university crafted a statement to post on their team's Twitter account. Wynter explained that she encouraged the team to post the message on their official account so that they could have the largest audience possible:

> We wanted to have a centralized platform for them to air their . . . what they wanted out there. We wanted to give them basically a platform where it had a lot of followers, you know? Where a lot of eyes are going to be able to see this, where people in the community obviously are the ones who will follow that account the most and a lot of alumni. So, we wanted to give them the biggest platform that they can have.

Wynter also shared how posting to the official team account and editing the student-athletes' message were intentional acts. For Wynter and her colleagues, posting on the team's official Twitter account would help shelter the student-athletes from harsh comments regarding the content of the post. Editing the tweet ensured that the content and value of the student-athletes' message was clearly stated. Wynter emphasized, "we didn't want their message to be lost in their emotion." These actions can be viewed as Wynter's pursuit of personal congruence as she intentionally wanted to keep harmful messages away from her student-athletes and ensure that their statements were being received clearly.

CLEARER VISION IN 2020: COVID-19
AND ANTI-BLACK RACISM

I acknowledge that COVID-19 and anti-Black racism are separate tragedies and have created hardships and disparities for communities and as they ran parallel to each other, they intersected many times in 2020. As the participants shared their experiences, there were moments when one pandemic stood alone and other moments when each fused into parts of the other. Whichever way people experienced the two issues, one thing in common indicated by participant Wynter was that 2020 gave many people clearer vision.

The murder of George Floyd strongly impacted the way Wynter, Amma, and their student-athletes saw anti-Blackness and racism in society. It appeared that the juxtaposition of Colin Kaepernick taking a knee with the knee on the neck of George Floyd ignited an urgency within the participants and their student-athletes to see and act on anti-Blackness differently. This new vision can be likened to quiet change tactics like psychological resistance that Lowery (2020) explains as tempered radical methods. It is here that tempered radicals experience their radicalism internally, in the form of their "thoughts or resistance to stereotypes" (Lowery, 2020, p. 362). Seeing the massive support for Floyd in the peak of Covid-19 made Amma more zealous about supporting issues in the Black community. She questioned why others were not taking action: "why aren't you marching, why aren't you voting . . . why aren't you on this side?" Witnessing people march during a pandemic is where Amma saw the need for action more clearly.

The COVID-19 pandemic gave Gabby and her student-athletes the time to pause and observe what was happening in society. Having tournaments cancelled and being sent home, away from campus and athletic activity, gave student-athletes the time to absorb information pertaining to the Black Lives Matter movement and even participate in demonstrations. Gabby spoke about how the impacts of COVID-19 and anti-Blackness made her student-athletes more concerned about social injustice. It reinforced the prior conversations she had with them in the office with MSNBC on the television.

As her student-athletes watched their professional counterparts in the NBA play in the "NBA Covid Bubble," Gabby explained how seeing images of professional athletes protesting with jersey slogans and making [social justice related] statements during press conferences instantly inspired her student-athletes. Gabby explains, "I had witnessed the shift from literally no interest to passionate [about social injustice] . . . I noticed that they began to realize how real these issues were and how easily they could be affected, due to the color of their skin."

Wynter's path to clearer vision came through witnessing student-athletes transform around issues of racial injustice. Before the murder of George Floyd, Wynter noted that her team was not very passionate about activism. "The only time social issues ever came up was when George Floyd passed; at least for our team." Afterward, Wynter saw not just her team, but student-athletes at other institutions view Floyd's murder as the pinnacle for racial justice and the time to take a stance. Wynter described the stance as, "either be with us, or you're against us . . . players were not afraid to transfer. Players were not afraid to go to the draft. Players were not afraid to opt out and say, 'hey it's because of Covid' because the NCAA gave most sports a blanket waiver and they could come back for another year."

Gabby and Tamar saw things more clearly when their tempered strategies did not feel like enough. As tempered radicals, they each participated in small wins or small experiments that promoted hope and increased progress towards change (Meyerson, 2004). Acts such as helping a team register to vote, facilitating social justice awareness in place of practice, and attending protests were seen as "nothing monumental" to Gabby. Wynter discussed that growing up, she was taught that as a Black person, she was to keep her head down and not make others uncomfortable. But with the current social climate, she feels that now is the time where she can and must do more; that it is no longer enough just to keep your head down. Wynter stated, "I think I can definitely do more . . . It's time to do something different and do something better." Even while in quarantine at home with symptoms of the COVID-19 virus, Tamar felt that she "kept it minimal" by rescheduling study hall and communicating with faculty about why certain student-athletes would be absent from class. Despite being sick, Tamar still felt that she could have done more to show her support for student-athlete activism: "I could have shared it on social media, making my support obvious . . . [It] may not have brought people from (redacted) to (redacted) for a march, but it might have spread the word about the work our students are doing to make our world better, that ignorance and hate would not be tolerated, and how much I support them."

As Meyerson (2004) describes, "even when the changes are minor- remain minor- small wins are qualitative, if not quantitative, demonstrations that things can be different" (p. 18). Although Gabby, Wynter, and Tamar saw their acts as not enough, it was enough for tempered radicals because it kept their work sustainable and led to "heightened ambition and effort to do more" (Meyerson, 2004, p. 18). These examples speak to what enough action may look like and allude to the idea that small wins could influence others to engage in continued efforts as tempered radicals for student-athlete activism. It also alludes to the idea that there is never "enough" action, and the work of social change is never complete.

IMPLICATIONS

Practical implications for sport staff as tempered radicals include methods that would help them feel more confident in their strategies that support and positively cultivate the activism of their student-athletes. Suggestions for practice include sport staff assessing activism among their student-athletes, athletic departments expressing and encouraging actions around social justice, and creating policies that clearly state the department's stance on activism.

ASSESSING ACTIVISM

Sport practitioners and athletic departments should consider assessing student-athlete activism because their student-athletes are engaged in it. Activism has been part of college campuses from as early as 1507 and students are continuing to engage as activists to confront oppression and push societal and institutional change (Carlton, 2020). As activism seems to not fade away, assessing it can give athletic departments the opportunity to work intentionally with student-athlete activists and not against them. It can provide staff with the knowledge of their student-athletes' concerns and what they need to be successful within their activist identity.

Suggestions for assessments can include a participant assessment, attitudinal assessment, or a need assessment. Assessing individual behaviors through a participant assessment can give sport practitioners an idea of the likelihood of student-athletes to engage in different activist activities. An attitudinal or climate survey can help sport staff focus on specific issues or causes their student-athletes are passionate about. Having this information can help develop programming or other supportive measures that address their interests more directly. Lastly, a needs assessment can provide more tailored information about what student-athlete activists may need to be successful. This could be an assessment soliciting the methods student-athletes use to be activists (e.g., protests, social media, marches). Some of my participants found themselves reacting to the needs of their student-athlete activists by rescheduling study hall or holding practice when they could be proactive by having systems in place that support activism.

Support for Non-Student Activism

Athletic departments and even universities should consider more expressive support for their staff that may engage in activism. Participants in this study engaged as tempered radicals in support of student-athlete activism which in itself is its own form of activism. Based on the findings, I perceive that sport staff are afraid of voicing their opinions on social issues that oppose or challenge their leadership, department, or institution because they do not want to make others uncomfortable, create a problem, or lose their job or status at their job. Their shift to being "more comfortable saying something" after the resurgence of the Black Live Matter movement reflects this assertion. Their fear resembles how student-athletes were afraid to lose athletic aid, playing time, or suffer some other repercussions for engaging in activism (Lomonte, 2014). The difference now is that athletes have been willing to put that on the line and their staff are quietly behind them. Should staff feel the liberty to stand next to or in front of the student-athlete on these issues, I imagine what the weight of their resistance would look like and if they could be free to be radical without temperament.

Practical ways that universities and athletic departments can express their support of their staff is to send out messaging that encourages their community, faculty, staff, and students to engage in social justice work. Emails from the athletic director or university president that inspire staff to converse on topics of social injustice with students can be enough for staff to feel safe enough to be tempered radicals. Other suggestions could include facilitating discussions during meetings, posting signs that support social causes in the office, providing access to view documentaries on related topics, or funding professional development in the form of conferences, trainings, or workshops on relevant topics.

Take a Stance with Policy

Athletic departments should consider creating policies that clearly state their stance on activism for both their students and their employees. This policy should not be left to individual coaches to decide for their teams. As a department and in collaboration with the university, clear messaging should permeate across the department culture so that when unfortunate issues occur on campus or in the greater community, there will be no confusion about how the department will respond because they have one unified document to refer to.

Within this policy should be specific language about the types of activism that are supported by the department while recognizing individual rights to free speech granted by the federal government and constitution. For example, activism in the policy does not need to name specific movements like Black Lives Matter, but it should clearly state support for causes that condemn the violence and oppression of marginalized groups. Athletic departments should consider creating a task force that monitors events in the media that may incite activism among students and staff and that may warrant members of the department to revisit the policy.

Lastly, this policy should include the department's staff and how they choose to engage in activism as it relates to supporting their student-athletes. It should protect staff that choose to engage in activist activities with student-athletes and protect those who may choose not to engage. The policy should allow staff to feel free to operate reasonably within their role and institution while engaging in causes that are meaningful to their beliefs and identities.

CONCLUSION

Student-athlete activism has been documented from as early as the 1960s. Without this documented history, Black athletes would be unaware of the power they have to use their sport platform for social change (Cooper et al., 2019). Staff have played a role in social movements through their involvement as tempered radicals, taking strategic steps from within the organization to influence change. This chapter explored the ways in which these tempered radicals work in support of student-athlete activism and uncovered unique perspectives of how sport staff performed such roles in the midst of a global pandemic and civil unrest. As social justice issues continue to arise and student-athletes continue to use their platform to address these issues, the work of the tempered radical for student-athlete activism will also continue.

REFERENCES

Arnett, A. (2015). Athletes and activism. *Diverse: Issues in Higher Education, 31*(25), 18–19.

Blinder, A., & Witz, B. (2020). College athletes, phones in hand, force shift in protest movement. *New York Times.* https://www.nytimes.com/2020/06/12/sports/ncaafootball/george-floyd-protests-college-sports.html?auth=login-google

Carlton, G. (2020). Student activism in college: History of campus protests. *Best Colleges.* https://www.bestcolleges.com/blog/history-student-activism-in-college/

Chase, S. E. (2011). Narrative inquiry: Still a field in the making. In N. K. Denzin & Y. S. Lincoln (eds.), *The Sage handbook of qualitative research* (4th ed.; pp. 421–434). Los Angeles, CA: Sage.

Cooper, J. N., Macaulay, C., & Rodriguez, S. H. (2019). Race and resistance: A typology of African American sport activism. *International Review for the Sociology of Sport, 54*(2), 151–181.

Edwards, H. (2016). The promise and limits of leveraging Black athlete power potential to compel campus change. *Journal of Higher Education Athletics & Innovation, 1*(1), 4–13.

Gibson, C., & Williams, F. (2020). Understanding the impetus for modern student activism for justice at an HBCU: A look at personal motivations. *Urban Review, 52*(2), 263–276.

Jones, S., Torres, V., Arminio, J. (2014). *Negotiating the complexities of qualitative research in higher education.* New York: Routledge.

Kezar, A. (2010). Faculty and staff partnering with student activists: Unexplored terrains of interaction and development. *Journal of College Student Development, 51*(5), 451–480.

Kezar, A., Gallant, T., Lester, J. (2011). Everyday people making a difference on college campuses: The tempered grassroots leadership tactics of faculty and staff. *Studies in Higher Education, 36*(2), 129–151.

Lomonte, F. (2014). Fouling the first amendment: Why colleges can't, and shouldn't, control student-athletes' speech on social media. *Journal of Business & Technology Law, 9*(1), 1–50.

Lowery, K. (2020). Critical development of courage within social justice school leaders: Silence, tempered radicals, and revolutionaries. *Handbook on promoting social justice in education*, 355–373.

Maxey, I. (1999), Beyond boundaries? Activism, academia, reflexivity and research. *Area, 31(*3), 199–208.

Meyerson, D., and M. Scully. (1995). Tempered radicalism and the politics of ambivalence and change. *Organization Science* (6), 585–600.

Meyerson, D. E. (2003). *Tempered radicals: How everyday leaders inspire change at work.* Boston, MA: Harvard Business School Press.

Meyerson, D. E. (2004). The Tempered Radicals: How employees push their companies—little by little—to be more socially responsible. *Stanford Social Innovation Review, 2*(2), 14–23.

Ngunjiri, F. W., Gramby-Sobukwe, S., & Williams-Gegner, K. (2012). Tempered radicals: Black women's leadership in the church and community. *The Journal of Pan African Studies, 5*(2), 84–109.

Reed, K. (2019). Jim Bouton's impact reached far beyond the baseball diamond. Troy Media. https://troymedia.com/viewpoint/jim-bouton-impact-beyond-baseball/#.YenLLi2cZQI

Reese, R. (2017). The lack of political activism among today's Black student-athlete. *Journal of Higher Education Athletics & Innovation, 1*(2), 123–131.

Wetherell, M., McConville, A., & McCreanor, T. (2020). Defrosting the freezer and other acts of quiet resistance: Affective practice theory, everyday activism, and affective dilemmas. *Qualitative Research in Psychology, 17*(1), 13–35.

Chapter 7

The Flag versus Football

How Mississippi State Running Back Kylin Hill Used 98 Characters to Compel the State of Mississippi to Change Its Flag

Megan R. Hill

On June 22, 2020, Kylin Hill, star-running back for Mississippi State University, replied to a tweet from Mississippi Governor Tate Reeves (R) with 98-characters of his own. They read: "Either change the flag or I won't be representing this State anymore [Hundred Points Symbol] & I meant that . . . I'm tired." After posting the tweet, Hill reportedly rolled over and took a nap, unaware of the role his message would play in finally bringing an end to the 126-year history of the Confederate battle emblem in the Mississippi state flag (Dellenger, 2020; Lee, 2021).

Within an hour, Hill was awoken to the reality of the situation, his phone's nonstop alerts indicating his tweet was going viral (Lee, 2021). If the number of retweets and likes he was receiving weren't clear enough indications of the powerful way his words were reverberating across and beyond the Internet, Hill's teammates', mother's, and athletic director's immediate reactions and concerns certainly were (Dellenger, 2020; Lee, 2021). Although their concerns were warranted,[1] Hill's tweet didn't appear in a vacuum. Rather, it appeared four days after the Southeastern Conference (SEC) and National Collegiate Athletic Association (NCAA) each announced they would reconsider hosting any championship events in the state unless the flag changed (Lee, 2021). Nevertheless, it was Hill's tweet that garnered the most attention, underscoring the growing influence collegiate athletes have to raise awareness and ultimately influence social justice issues (Kluch, 2020).

This chapter thus situates Kylin Hill's act within extant typologies of social justice activism; principally, Edwards (2016) conceptualization of the four waves of Black athlete activism in the United States (U.S.), Cooper et al.'s (2019) typology of African-American sport activism and Kluch's (2020) five different conceptualizations of social justice activism among collegiate athlete activists. In doing so, this chapter heeds Cooper et al.'s (2019) call for further exploration of activists and activism by illustrating the ways in which Hill's tweet, posted as part of his everyday use of social media, both exemplifies and extends existing conceptualizations of (collegiate) athlete activism. As someone who "wasn't looking to be an activist" (Lee, 2021, para. 21) but rather, "was venting" (Lee, 2021, para. 21), Hill's tweet and its subsequent impact illustrate the ways in which collegiate athletes, including those who do not self-identify as activists, are capable of leveraging their power and influence, through social media, to affect social change.

AFRICAN-AMERICAN SPORT ACTIVISM

Any analysis of activism in sport, in any era, would be incomplete without discussing the contributions made by renowned sport sociologist Dr. Harry Edwards. Founder of the Olympic Project for Human Rights (OPHR) (1967), Edwards positioned the Black athlete at the center of activist movements, a decision that has repeatedly withstood examination (e.g., Agyemang, et al., 2010; Moore, 2017). In 2016, Edwards gave the opening keynote address at the annual meeting of the North American Society for the Sociology of Sport (NASSS), outlining four waves of Black athlete activism in the U.S.: activists in the first wave (1900–1945) focused their efforts on *gaining legitimacy* (e.g., Jack Johnson, Fritz Pollard, and Paul Robeson) while activists in the second wave (1946-early 1960s) aimed to acquire and increase their *political visibility* (e.g., Jackie Robinson and Althea Gibson) and their counterparts in the third wave (mid-1960s–1970s) fought for *dignity and respect* (e.g., Muhammad Ali, Tommie Smith and John Carlos). The third wave was followed (1980s–early 2000s) by a significant decline in African-American sport activism, epitomized by Michael Jordan's infamous quote in 1990 when questioned about his decision not to endorse Harvey Gantt (D–North Carolina), a Black Senate candidate, in his race against Jesse Helms (R–North Carolina), a known racist: "Republicans buy shoes, too" (Lutz, 2020). Current African-American sport activists (e.g., Colin Kaepernick, Venus Williams, LeBron James) are part of the fourth wave (2005–present) and are focused on "securing and transferring power via *economic and technological capital*" (Cooper et al., 2019, p. 161). In short, Black athletes in this fourth wave are leveraging their financial power, including their own monetary assets, in combination with the strategic use of (social) media "to raise awareness of, challenge, and change oppressive structures in society" (Cooper et al., 2019, p. 163).

Building on Edwards's (2016) assessment of the four waves of Black athlete activism, Cooper et al. (2019) developed a typology of African-American sport activism centered around race and racism to connect the diverse array of actors, actions, and outcomes connected to sport activism within their appropriate socio-historical, socio-political, and socio-cultural contexts. The typology identified five types of activism: symbolic, scholarly, grassroots, sport-based, and economic. Of particular importance here, *symbolic activism* was defined as specific, public actions (e.g., protests) taken by athletes to increase awareness of social justice issues and promote substantive change while *sport-based activism* was described as "specific actions taken *by* athletes to alter and mitigate the hegemonic nature of structural arrangements, rules/policies/bylaws, and practices *through* sport organizations that serve to reinforce subordination, marginalization, and exploitation of certain groups" (Cooper et al., 2019, p. 172, emphasis in original). Prototypical examples of each type of activism include Tommie Smith and John Carlos's symbolic actions[2] while standing on the medal podium during the 1968 Mexico City Olympics (Edwards, 1980) and Curt Flood's opposition to Major League Baseball's reserve clause in 1969 (Early, 2011), respectively.

Edwards's (2016) and Cooper et al.'s (2019) work thus provides a clear foundation for understanding modern athlete activism; however, both models remain largely silent about the role and impact collegiate athletes, in particular, are playing in today's social justice movement. Cooper et al. (2019) acknowledge such limitations by positioning their typology as a building block rather than a complete framework and by pointing to areas in need of further examination (e.g., time-based activism, engagement-based activism, context-based activism). As this chapter argues, one such area is collegiate athlete activism.

COLLEGIATE ATHLETES AND SOCIAL JUSTICE ACTIVISM

Despite the multi-billion dollar revenues generated by college sports programs (Blinder, 2019; Huddleston, 2020) and the nearly half a million athletes that participate each year (NCAA, 2021), collegiate athlete activism has only recently become a focus of attention among scholars, with MacIntosh et al. (2020) arguing student-athletes should be studied as a unique group due to their visibility on and off-campus. As public facing representatives of the university at a wide range of events, student-athletes, in comparison to the non-athlete student population, are not only more likely to create social change (Kluch, 2020) but to encounter situations involving conflict, particularly when their goals and roles as university representatives and individual citizens diverge. Such situations further exacerbate the isolation student-athletes already feel from their campus communities (Bowen & Levin, 2003), accentuating the potentially devastating consequences they may face for speaking out on social justice (Kaufman, 2008). Given the potentially fraught roles student-athletes thus embody, it is critically important to understand how, why, when, and whether or not collegiate athletes engage in acts of social justice activism (MacIntosh et al., 2020).

To begin to unpack those questions, MacIntosh et al. (2020) conducted a secondary analysis of survey data collected by RISE.[3] Their analysis indicated that the 2,092 collegiate student-athletes who participated in the survey held considerably positive views of engaging in activism. There were, however, differences in the student-athletes' perceptions of social justice depending on their race and gender, with athletes of color and female student-athletes holding stronger positive attitudes toward and intentions to engage in activism in comparison to White athletes and male athletes, respectively. MacIntosh et al.'s (2020) analysis thus provided broad insight into the perspectives of student-athletes regarding activism while also highlighting the need for more in-depth examinations of student-athletes' perceptions of specific types of activism, as well as barriers to engaging in activism.

Kluch's (2020) analysis of interview data collected from 31 NCAA Division I collegiate athlete activists sought to provide such detail, with the study's athletes defining activism in multiple, intersecting ways. More specifically, the athletes' definitions fell into five overarching themes: social justice action, mentorship, authenticity, intervention, and public expressions of resistance. The first theme to emerge, *social justice action*, was consistent with extant research on activism in sport (Cooper et al., 2019; Lee & Cunningham, 2019). However, the three subthemes that emerged as part of this overarching theme further signified collegiate athlete activists' desire to *actively pursue social justice* on and off campus, to engage in *cause-specific actions* (e.g., advance the rights of oppressed, marginalized groups), and to be *trailblazers*, either on their team or in society at large. The second theme, *mentorship*, was also consistent with previous research (Cooper et al., 2019) but was further defined as taking place via two subthemes: *effort-based* mentorship and *identity-based* mentorship. Student-athlete activists identified *effort-based* mentorship as serving in a mentorship role for others passionate about similar causes while *identity-based* mentorship was defined as "serving as a mentor for individuals who shared similar identities" (Kluch, 2020, p. 578). *Authenticity* emerged as the third theme, with the student-athletes articulating their activism as a form of openly expressing their true selves. The two primary subthemes identified here were *visibility as minoritized group* and *being true to oneself.* The fourth theme, *intervention,* included the subthemes *power of one's voice* and *media as a tool of intervention.* Intervention was thus described by student-athlete activists as using their platforms, particularly their social media following, to speak up for those who cannot speak for themselves. The final theme, *public expressions of resistance*, was defined by participants as "publicly staged strikes, protests, or riots" (Kluch, 2020, p. 582) and emerged either out of *participants' own experiences* engaging in public protest or their exposure to *mediated examples of public resistance.*

Kluch's (2020) typology, like Cooper et al.'s (2019), serves as an important building block for our understanding of collegiate athlete activism. In particular, the perspectives of the 31 NCAA collegiate athlete activists Kluch interviewed illustrate the ways in which today's collegiate athletes view activism as part and parcel of their everyday lives, cultivated and strengthened by their public roles as athletes and enriched by the reach of their social media platforms. One key limitation of Kluch's (2020) typology, however, is that it relies solely on collegiate athletes who self-identify as activists. What happens when a collegiate athlete who doesn't self-identify as an activist engages in activist behavior?

KYLIN HILL TWEETS

Kylin Hill was born in Sandfield, Mississippi, a poor, historically black neighborhood just 25 miles west of Mississippi State University (Dellenger, 2020). He has the words Sandfield Baby tattooed on the inside of his right biceps (Dellenger, 2020). Rather than interesting, yet unimportant artifacts of Hill's life, these details are integral to understanding how he became involved with the Mississippi state flag. Hill himself signaled their importance when he added a second, often overlooked tweet to his first on June 22, 2020, writing, "Unlike [the] rest I was born in this state [Hundred Points Symbol] and [I] know what the flag mean" (Lee, 2021, para. 33).

It is this, Hill's second tweet, that provides the necessary context for understanding the last two words of his first, "I'm tired," by alluding to his experience growing up and living as a Black man in Mississippi, where Hill has been called the n-word (Dellenger, 2020; Lee, 2021), where "Since 2000, there have been at least eight suspected lynchings of Black men and teenagers . . . " (Brown, 2021, para. 1), and where the state flag, since 1894, had intentionally contained the Confederate battle emblem as a form of direct, symbolic defiance of the power and progress Black people gained during Reconstruction (Dellenger, 2020; Lee, 2021) despite being the state with the largest proportion of Black residents (at 39%; United States Census Bureau, 2019).

In the wake of the Black Lives Matter movement (BLM), the protests surrounding George Floyd's murder, and in light of his own experiences in Mississippi, Hill had finally had enough that Monday afternoon, firing off an authentic, almost reflexive response via his preferred medium of communication, Twitter (Lee, 2021), writing "Either change the flag or I won't be representing this State anymore [Hundred Points Symbol] & I meant that . . . I'm tired."

In doing so, Hill took aim at not only the flag, but at something even more potent in the state of Mississippi, sports; principally, college football. As Cleveland (2020) asserts, "Sports have never been only a game in Mississippi. No, sports are woven deeply into our cultural fabric, a major part of who we are and what we are about. Always have been." (para. 1). In only 98 characters, Hill had agreed, tying his athletic performance and that of the team he represented directly to Mississippi's cultural fabric, as represented by its state flag. Exploiting the power of social media to vent a personal, yet collective anger and frustration (Wahl-Jorgensen, 2019), Hill raised the stakes and pressure on Mississippi lawmakers to choose which part of their cultural fabric was more important: football or the flag?

Within a week of Hill's tweet, their decision was clear. Lieutenant Governor Delbert Hosemann (R) publicly announced his support for changing the flag while the state legislature passed House Bill 1796, officially removing the state flag from all public buildings and establishing a commission to design a new flag to be voted on in November 2020 (Lee, 2021). Only eight days after Hill's tweet, Governor Tate Reeves (R) signed the bill into law (Lee, 2021).

To be clear, Hill's tweet wasn't *the* reason the Mississippi state flag, the last state flag in the U.S. to symbolically pay tribute to slavery, to the Confederacy, to White supremacy (Dreher, 2015), was removed and a new flag adopted by Mississippi voters on November 30, 2020 (Lee, 2021). But, it was the shot in the arm the movement needed to keep the issue on the front burner (Dellenger, 2020), particularly as opposition to the change grew. Such opposition had succeeded in thwarting past attempts to change the flag, including a statewide ballot measure in 2001 that failed by a nearly 2-to-1 margin (Dellenger, 2020; Lee, 2021) and was, again, slowing momentum for change this time around, as indicated by Governor Reeves's tweet on June 22, 2020, stating, "Over the weekend there has been a proposal floating amongst some in the legislature to create a second Mississippi flag. Let's call it the

'Separate but Equal' flag option. While well-intentioned I'm sure, it does not meet the threshold."

Against this backdrop of repeated failure and waning momentum, Hill's direct reply to Reeves's tweet struck the right cord, reigniting the debate and drawing even more scrutiny from the state's high-profile athletic leaders, including Mississippi State's Athletic Director John Cohen, their head football coach Mike Leach, and the University of Mississippi's head football coach Lane Kiffin, all of whom descended on the Mississippi capital demanding the flag change (Dellenger, 2020; Lee, 2021). With the pressure mounting, with more and more businesses and organizations joining the call to change the flag, it became clear that Hill's tweet was the straw that broke the camel's back, compelling lawmakers to finally change the flag.

In short, in the span of twelve days in June of 2020, all efforts to change the Mississippi state flag seesawed from failure to victory. A movement that appeared dead in the water was first revived by SEC Commissioner Greg Sankey's announcement that the league would ban championship events in Mississippi until the state changed its flag (Cleveland, 2020). The NCAA quickly followed suit, banning all regional baseball and basketball championships from the state (Cleveland, 2020). Unfortunately, the inevitable economic fallout stemming from these decisions did little to move the legislative needle, leading many to believe the movement was, yet again, in peril. And then, a shy, yet determined young man, whose Twitter bio was simply the letters BLM with a raised fist emoji, entered the fray, venting his frustrations over 98 characters to his more than 28,000 followers (Lee, 2020), an act that turned the tide toward victory and changed the course of Mississippi history.

Contextualizing Hill's Actions

The impact of Kylin Hill's tweet will be forever immortalized in the newly-adopted Mississippi state flag, but to truly understand how and why his tweet was able to accomplish such a feat, we need to contextualize his actions within the history of African-American sports activism in the U.S.

Clearly, Hill's use of Twitter to convey his message speaks directly to Edwards's (2016) conceptualization of the fourth wave of Black athlete activism. Hill's tweets not only raised awareness of the issue, but in claiming he would no longer play football for Mississippi State University unless the stage flag changed, he used his social media platform as a tool for disruption, putting Mississippians' passion for college football in direct competition with their attitudes toward the state's flag.

Hill's ability to engage directly with his followers and by virtue of going viral, with the public at large (Poell & van Dijck, 2015), also brought the movement to the playing field, with his threat to no longer play football for Mississippi State University functioning as both a cause-specific social justice action (Kluch, 2020) and a form of symbolic activism (Cooper et al., 2019). The fact that Hill chose to extemporaneously convey his ultimatum via social media also demonstrates the authenticity of his intervention (Kluch, 2020), and by leveraging his capacity as the star running back for Mississippi State, Hill directly challenged the structures that sustained the flag's use (sport-based activism), as well as those that discourage student-athletes from developing a civic consciousness (Staurowsky, 2014).

Where Hill's actions depart from current typologies of (collegiate) athlete activism is in their relative spontaneity and intent. As Hill has made clear in multiple interviews, he did not see himself as nor was he "looking to be an activist" (Lee, 2020, para. 21). Rather, he was simply using the everyday communicative tools at his disposal (i.e., Twitter) to vent long-standing frustrations to the world. Not only did Hill not think the flag was going to change, but he has subsequently acknowledged that he likely would have played even if it hadn't (Dellenger, 2020; Lee, 2021). In other words, Hill is an unlikely activist; his actions singular in time, context, and impact. As a Mississippi native and star-athlete, Hill conveyed his message at exactly the right time (i.e., in the wake of George Floyd's murder, on the heels of the SEC and NCAA's decisions, and during a global pandemic), using exactly the right channel (i.e., Twitter), to threaten an institution (i.e., college football) that mattered even more to Mississippians than the state flag.

Hill's case thus illustrates how the modern collegiate athlete, by simply being true to themselves (authenticity) through their use of social media (media as a tool of intervention), can leverage their roles as high profile, public personalities to draw attention to, challenge, and ultimately change social justice issues in society, even if they don't consider themselves activists.

CONCLUSION

An increase in activist actions taken by professional and intercollegiate athletes the past few years has reignited the seemingly time immemorial question of whether or not sports are an appropriate site for political protest. The question and supposed debate it engenders belies reality. Sport and politics are not mutually exclusive, as extensive scholarship has documented (e.g., Allison, 1986, 1993, 2004; Coakley, 2015; Edwards, 1969; Grix, 2015; Miller & Wiggins, 2004). Rather, as Kaufman and Wolf (2010) have demonstrated, there are characteristics inherent to sport that align directly with activism, including social consciousness, meritocracy, responsible citizenship, and interdependence. These characteristics, combined with the focus of modern social justice movements (e.g., BLM) and the power of social media, have accelerated the number and array of activist actions taken by athletes at all levels of competition during this fourth wave of Black athlete activism (Edwards, 2016).

As this chapter argues, the activist actions taken by collegiate athletes, specifically, are ripe for analysis. Although collegiate athletes have always played a unique role on and off campus, their visibility and financial power are set to grow exponentially as they literally cash in on endorsement deals for their names, images and likenesses (NIL; Murphy, 2021). Such deals will inherently upend the traditional power dynamics between collegiate athletes and institutions of higher education, with potentially significant impacts on how, why, when, and whether or not collegiate athletes engage in acts of social justice activism.

This new power dynamic will take shape alongside an ever-shifting social media landscape that has already shown itself capable of serving as a form of "connective action" (Bennett & Segerberg, 2013) that requires as much effort to broadcast social and personal injustices (Henderson, 2013) as it does to organize protest actions (Yan et al., 2018). As Kylin Hill's tweets illustrate, the dynamism of social media can turn what begins as a personal vent session into a message that galvanizes an entire movement.

In fact, it is examples like Hill's, where an unlikely activist is thrust into the spotlight, that perhaps best reflect the experience of the modern (collegiate) athlete as someone who, at any time, in any place, may engage in an unplanned, yet not entirely spontaneous expression of individual identity via social media and, in doing so, tap into a collective frustration capable of building momentum toward concrete action. For Kylin Hill, tapping out 98 characters before rolling over and taking a nap in June 2020 resulted in historic change in Mississippi, and even though changing "The flag won't end racism off the bat . . . it's a start, you know?" (Kylin Hill as cited in Lee, 2020, para. 9).

NOTES

1. Offensive reactions to Hill's tweet not only appeared on Twitter, but he and his family were subject to additional acts of overt racism (Lee, 2021).

2. Tommie Smith and John Carlos each raised a fist adorned with a black glove to represent African-American strength and unity and wore black socks without shoes to represent African-American poverty. Smith also wore a black scarf while Carlos wore black beads to represent lynching victims (Davis, 2008).

3. RISE is a "national non-profit that educates and empowers the sports community to eliminate racial discrimination, champion social justice and improve race relations" (RISE).

REFERENCES

Agyemang, K., Singer, J. N., & DeLorme, J. (2010). An exploratory study of Black male college athletes' perceptions of race and athlete activism. *International Review for the Sociology of Sport, 45*, 419–435.

Allison, L. (Ed.) (1986). *The politics of sport.* Manchester: Manchester University Press.

Allison, L. (Ed.) (1993). *The changing politics of sport.* Manchester: Manchester University Press.

Allison, L. (2004). *The global politics of sport: The role of global institutions of sport.* New York: Routledge.

Bennett, W. L., & Segerberg, A. (2013). *The logic of connective action: Digital media and the personalization of contentious politics.* New York: Cambridge University Press.

Blinder, A. (2019, September 30). N.C.A.A. athletes could be paid under new California law. *New York Times.* https://www.nytimes.com/2019/09/30/sports/college-athletes-paid-california.html

Bowen, W. G., & Levin, S. A. (2003). *Reclaiming the game: College sports educational values.* Princeton, NJ: Princeton University Press.

Brown, D. L. (2021, August 8). Lynchings in Mississippi never stopped. *Washington Post.* https://www.washingtonpost.com/nation/2021/08/08/modern-day-mississippi-lynchings/

Cleveland, R. (2020, June 29). For not the first time, sports has helped Mississippians see their way to change. *Mississippi Today.* https://mississippitoday.org/2020/06/29/for-not-the-first-time-sports-has-helped-mississippians-see-their-way-to-change/

Coakley, J. (2015). Assessing the sociology of sport: On cultural sensibilities and the great sport myth. *International Review for the Sociology of Sport, 50*(4–5), 402–406.

Cooper, J. N., Macaulay, C., & Rodriguez, S. H. (2019). Race and resistance: A typology of African American sport activism. *International Review for the Sociology of Sport, 54*(2), 151–181.

Davis, D. (2008, August). Olympic athletes who took a stand. *Smithsonian Magazine.* https://www.smithsonianmag.com/articles/olympic-athletes-who-took-a-stand-593920/

Dellenger, R. (2020, September 23). How 18 words on Twitter helped change a flag and unlocked the power of the college athlete. *Sports Illustrated.* https://www.si.com/college/2020/09/23/kylin-hill-mississippi-state-flag-daily-cover

Dreher, A. (September 9, 2015). Mississippi flag: A symbol of hate or reconciliation? *Jackson Free Press.* https://www.jacksonfreepress.com/news/2015/sep/09/mississippi-flag-symbol-hate-or-reconciliation/

Early, G. L. (2011). *The level playing field.* Cambridge, MA: Harvard University Press.

Edwards, H. (1969). *The revolt of the Black athlete.* New York: Free Press.

Edwards, H. (1980). *The struggle that must be: An autobiography.* New York: MacMillian.

Edwards, H. (2016, November 3). The fourth wave: Black athlete protest in the second decade of the 21st century. Keynote address at annual conference of the North American society for the sociology of sport, Tampa, FL.

Grix, J. (2015). *Sport politics: An introduction.* London, UK: Macmillan International Higher Education.

Henderson, S. (2013). *Sidelined: How American sports challenged the Black freedom struggle.* Lexington, KY: The University Press of Kentucky.

Hill, Kylin [@H_Kylin]. (2020, June 22). *Either change the flag or I won't be representing this State anymore [Hundred Points Symbol] & I meant that . . . I'm tired* [Tweet]. Twitter. https://twitter.com/H_Kylin?ref_src=twsrc%5Egoogle%7Ctwcamp%5Eserp%7Ctwgr%5Eauthor

Hill, Kylin [@H_Kylin]. (2020, June 22). *Unlike [the] rest I was born in this state [Hundred Points Symbol] and [I] know what the flag mean* [Tweet]. Twitter. https://twitter.com/H_Kylin?ref_src=twsrc%5Egoogle%7Ctwcamp%5Eserp%7Ctwgr%5Eauthor

Huddleston Jr., T. (2020, September 2). College football stars could be earning as much as $2.4 million per year, based on NCAA revenues: Study. CNBC. https://www.cnbc.com/2020/09/02/how-much-college-athletes-could-be-earning-study.html

Kaufman, P. (2008). Boos, bans, and other backlash: The consequences of being an activist athlete. *Humanity & Society, 32*, 215–237.

Kaufman, P., & Wolff, E. A. (2010). Playing and protesting: Sport as a vehicle for social change. *Journal of Sport & Social Issues, 34*, 154–175.

Kluch, Y. (2020). "My story is my activism!": (Re-)Definitions of social justice activism among collegiate athlete activists. *Communication & Sport, 8*(4–5), 566–590.

Lee, M. (2021, January 30). Kylin Hill fought to change the Mississippi flag. Next up: The NFL. *Washington Post.* https://www.washingtonpost.com/sports/2021/01/30/kylin-hill-mississippi-flag-nfl/

Lee, W., & Cunningham, G. B. (2019). Moving toward understanding social justice in sport organizations: A study of engagement in social justice advocacy in sport organizations. *Journal of Sport & Social Issues, 43*, 1–19.

Lutz, T. (2020, May 4). Michael Jordan insists "Republicans buy sneakers too" quote was a joke. *The Guardian.* https://www.theguardian.com/sport/2020/may/04/michael-jordan-espn-last-dance-republicans-sneakers-quote-nba

MacIntosh, A., Martin, E. M., & Kluch, Y. (2020). To act or not to act? Student-athlete perceptions of social justice activism. *Psychology of Sport & Exercise, 51*, 1–8.

Miller, P. B., & Wiggins, D. K. (eds.). (2004). *Sport and the color line: Black athletes and race relations in twentieth-century America.* London: Psychology Press.

Moore, L. (2017). *We will win the day: The Civil Rights Movement, the Black athlete, and the quest for equality.* Praeger.

Murphy, D. (July 1, 2021). Let's make a deal: NCAA athletes cashing in on name, image and likeness. ESPN. https://www.espn.com/college-sports/story/_/id/31738893/ncaa-athletes-cashing-name-image-likeness

NCAA. (2021). Student athletes. https://www.ncaa.org/student-athletes

Poell, T., & van Dijk, J. (2015). Social media and activist communication. In C. Atton (ed.), *The Routledge companion to alternative and community media* (pp. 527–537). London, UK: Routledge.

Reeves, T. [@tatereeves]. (2020, June 22). *Over the weekend there has been a proposal floating amongst some in the legislature to create a second Mississippi flag.* [Tweet]. Twitter.https://twitter.com/tatereeves?ref_src=twsrc%5Egoogle%7Ctwcamp%5Eserp%7Ctwgr%5Eauthor

RISE. (n.d.). Who we are. Rise to win. https://risetowin.org/

Staurowsky, E. (2014). College athletes' rights in the age of the super conference: The case of the All Players United campaign. *Journal of Intercollegiate Sport, 7*, 11–34.

United States Census Bureau. (2019). *ACS demographic and housing estimates.* https://data.census.gov

Wahl-Jorgensen, K. (2019). *Emotions, media and politics.* New York: John Wiley & Sons.

Yan, G., Pegoraro, A, & Watanabe, N. M. (2018). Student-athletes' organization of activism at the University of Missouri: Resource mobilization on Twitter. *Journal of Sport Management, 32*, 24–37.

Chapter 8

Conditions of Voice

Black Student-Athlete Activism at The University of Alabama

Meredith M. Bagley

The summer of 2020 sweltered with racial justice activism, and college athletes joined the fray at unprecedented levels. Notable among them were hyper-elite football players, often Black, at "power 5" schools such as The University of Alabama. Football players in these large, highly commercialized athletic departments are tightly monitored, scheduled, and disciplined, leading to common critiques that they are disengaged from "real" issues of the day (see Woods & Harris, 2020). The summer of 2020 presented a significant challenge to this perception as elite college football players spoke on topics of racial equity, police violence, and broader social justice issues facing their everyday lives. In this chapter, I examine two major instances of athlete anti-racist activism at The University of Alabama in the summer of 2020: a June "Black Lives Matter" video the football team produced, and a collective student-athlete march in August 2020 that culminated in speeches by football players, the head football coach, and three administrators.

I have two goals in this chapter. One, to apply a robust and nuanced theoretical and critical frame to the rhetoric provided in these two activist instantiations, asking how elite Black male college student-athletes are expressing their civic, political "voice." Secondly, I place "voice" in quotes to bring attention to the ways scholars engage this concept. Following the work of critical rhetorical scholars such as Watts (2001a, 2001b, 2012), Grano (2009), and Flores (2016), I argue that the remarkable activism by Alabama football players illustrates that voice "is constitutive of shared experience," (Watts, 2001b, p. 187) rather than a simple instrument of individual agency. I extend

Grano's (2009) caution about over-valorizing "moral fantasies" about heroic athlete voice in times of political crisis, and I urge my peers in sport communication and sport media to attend to Flores's (2016) call for "racial rhetorical criticism" that "provides the maps through which racial publics encounter and contest dominant discourses" (p. 12).

RACIAL RHETORICAL CRITICISM
AND BLACK ATHLETE VOICE

In this analysis, I follow Watts' urging to approach voice as "a relational phenomenon occurring in discourse . . . not reducible to the subject's agency" (2001b, p. 180). Watts develops this argument by first reviewing the ways the white-dominated field of speech or communication studies conceptualized "voice" in its first century of existence. Even as modernist notions of stable subjects wielding discrete agency were dismantled, Watts demonstrates the paucity with which our understanding of voice operates. Culminating in a masterful treatment of Black aesthetics in the New Negro movement, Watts challenges communication scholars to recognize that "a condition for voice . . . is social. In a sense, voice 'exists' without an Other to recognize its emanation; but this conception is poverty. The richness of voice is endowed as a function of the social body" (2012, p. 16). He distinguishes speech from voice, just as we can distinguish emotion from affect, each pairing representing a surface-level manifestation of larger forces operating at the level of experience, the body, and relations of everyday life. He states, for instance, that

> The "kernel" of speech is "planted" in voice, and speech implies an addressee. Voice is uncontrollable and signals the undecidability of affect's aliveness, it also announces a *statement-in-the-making*. As we go about our busy lives, we are "called" by many voices, tempting, singing, and threatening voices. To the extent that we resonate with a form of speech, we become attuned to the emotions vibrating at its edges. (2012, pp. 16–17)

This approach to voice challenges us to engage Black athlete activism from a more robust theoretical framework, asking about the nature of our own experience as we seek understanding of theirs.

Watts (2012) is also careful, as many critical sport scholars are, to not conflate voice with progress or positive social impact. As an approach to publicity, the ways that moments of voice rely on a community recognizing the affect "vibrating at its edges" means that antisocial, violent, and regressive voices also come to pass in our social worlds. Watts warns of this by saying

"The emergence of a public is not necessarily, or even probably, innocent. US history alone tells us that lynch mobs and genocidal campaigns have spilled out from such occurrences" (2012, p. 17). This echoes Grano's caution that "voice is vital to structural moral fantasies in mediated sport culture, especially that an athlete-hero can return to intervene in a current political crisis," (2009, p. 193). Voice and affect are uncontrollable resources bubbling up from the varied experiences of those constituting a public; not a relied-upon resource for positive social change.

Athlete activism may have been at an all-time high in the summer of 2020 but this does not mean that athlete voice is unfettered. Grano (2009) examines how player voices are actually rarely heard in the larger sport media commentary industry, as well as ways that we discipline voice (mostly from athletes) through rules about taunting, demands for media appearances, and, in the years since his article's publication, direct or indirect punishment for political speech. Cooper, Macauley, and Rodriguez (2019) take up Edwards's famous "eras of activism" chronology to suggest a typology for ways that Black athletes enter the realm of political speech. They carefully distinguish between in-sport and out-of-sport activism, radical and liberal foundations, and caution in their conclusions that their chart is just the tip of the iceberg for the complex and ongoing ways athletes are testing the boundaries of voice (and thus, Watts would argue, affect) in sport. Finally, Butterworth (2020) ably argues for how citizenship is so closely aligned with "unity" and "consensus" that athlete activists dissenting to status quo situations such as police brutality are denied citizenship by hostile audiences.

Watts's work on voice has, surprisingly, not been picked up in the critical sport literature. This is surprising to me given the attention it receives within critical cultural scholarship on race, aesthetics, and culture. Flores (2016) points to Watts's body of work in her state-of-the-field essay calling for more overt "racial rhetorical criticism" that "is reflective about and engages in the persistence of racial oppression, logics, voices, and bodies" (p. 5). After crediting Ono and Sloop's work (1995) on "vernacular rhetoric" as foundational, Flores moves next to credit Watts for "retheorizing voice away from speaking or language toward . . . situated and communal [notions], in and on the body if also exceeding it" (p. 11). This essay attempts to show the value and utility of Watts's approach for scholars of sport rhetoric or communication.

CONDITIONS FOR THE SOCIAL VOICE: UA BLACK LIVES MATTER VIDEO

One month after George Floyd was killed by police, the official University of Alabama football team twitter account released a link to a video with the accompanying message of "In this moment in history, we can't be silent."[1] For two minutes, 17 players from the university's football team—and its legendary head coach—narrate a script written by standout offensive line- man Alex Leatherwood that addresses "racism . . . brutality . . . [and] a better world." Leatherwood wrote the prose as he processed his reactions to Floyd's murder, then approached the UA coaching staff to produce it as a team video. In the video, the heads and faces of each speaker are visible against a black backdrop with their names provided below their face at their first appearance. Each player speaks part of the script, ending with several voices stating and restating the final line of "All lives can't matter until Black lives matter." [2]

The video is remarkable, for the simple reason that at other key inflection points of racial violence and Civil Rights activism, the university football team (or athletics structure overall) did remain silent. We are told that now is different, that now the conditions warrant comment and expression. The video could also be read as highly strategic, getting ahead of a difficult situation or providing cover for larger entrenched issues at Alabama. However, applying the framework of racial rhetorical criticism and Watts's social conception of voice allows us to see the nuance and power of this rhetorical artifact.

The video demonstrates voice as "constitutive of ethical and emotional dimensions inherent in living in community with others" (Watts, 2001b, p. 180). Its opening lines provide a plural personal pronoun—"we"—as the voice of the video as the prose delineates the diverse racial identity of the team: "We are a team. Black, white, brown. Together we are a family. We are brothers." The somewhat prosaic nature of this opening line is deepened, however, by the embodied delivery of voice in the video: Alex Leatherwood opens the video (in his only appearance) as a large, deeply dark-skinned man, followed by the pale complexion of starting quarterback Mac Jones, then the "brown" shade of lineman Emil Ekiyor. The quick succession of these athlete bodies, combined with the prominence of their names and positions on the team, tells the audience this is a unique message and begins to perform the social, communal voice Leatherwood crafted for the statement.

As additional faces of players appear and rotate past the viewer (always one at a time), the prose demonstrates Watts's insight that "'voice' is constitutive of shared experience" (2001b, p. 187). The athletes—after the opening trio we see and hear Evan Neal, Slade Bolden, Patrick Surtain, Devonta Smith, Thomas Fletcher, Cam Latu, Major Tennison, Josh McMillon, Stephon Wynn Jr., Jaylen Waddle, Jarez Parks, DJ Dale, Ale Kaho, and Dylan Moses—first tell us about the community to which they belong: "We represent ourselves, our families and hometowns, our university and our country." They speak to the lineage of these social connections: "We stand on the shoulders of giants. Our grandparents and parents. Our ancestors, our heroes, Alabama alumni and former players who have changed the world." This introduction section closes with a nod to space and context: "Beginning on our historic campus, we speak as one. Acknowledging our history. Honoring their legacy, building a better, more just future."

This peroration moves between familiar sport phrases about representing home and school to broader and more unusual invocations of "ancestors" and "grandparents" that—depending on the student—links their voices and bodies to the disparate experiences of segregation. Are the white players invoking their ancestors who could have played football at UA in generations past? Are Black players nodding to those talented predecessors who were denied opportunity? White quarterback Mac Jones delivers the direct reference to "our historic campus," prompting the listener to recall histories of racial hierarchy but also hearing Jones acknowledge that history while offering his face and voice for an experience of commonality. Black teammate Josh McMillon emphasizes "their" in the statement about legacy and provides a strong delivery of the aspiration for a "just future."

As the narrative washes over the listener and racial exclusion references are understood, the determinedly multi-racial performance from the players shifts the video from an expression of Black oppression, or of white support, to a social, connected, ethical expression of living in community with others. During the opening lines we hear from four white players (Jones, Bolden, Fletcher, Tennison), eight Black players (Leatherwood, Ekiyor, Neal, Surtain, Smith, McMillon, Wynn, and Waddle) and one AAPI player (Latu). These are the student-athlete bodies, each racialized in their own ways, that "speak as one" about the "just future" they want to build.

The participation of (white) head football coach Nick Saban is noteworthy on its own but also allows us to see the utility of Watts's conception of voice. Like the white players that participated in the video, the powerful voice and face of Saban reinforces the message of social connection and lived experience that the Black players provide, challenging an individuated and separatist reading of Black voice as only serving Black interests.

Saban first appears at the 0:40 mark of the video with the lines "And in this moment in history, we can't be silent. We must speak up for our brothers and sisters, for our sons and daughters." Arguably the most influential person in the video, perhaps at the whole university, delivers the central argument of the video, the caption that introduced it on twitter: we can't be silent. Saban speaks in his typical voice, rate, and expression, slow enough to be heard clearly with no signs of discomfort or haste. The second line Saban provides is notable for its gender inclusion and its communal focus: he, we, all of us have brothers, sisters, sons, daughters. A viewer who was confining the video's message to elite male college athletes is challenged to hear the social, communal entailments of how race, racism, and violence impacts all of us. The inclusion of sisters and daughters also challenges the hypermasculinity of football by invoking deaths and violence to Black women in the team's call for action.

Just after Saban's appearance, the script gives its first overt link to race and racism. Prior to these lines it is strongly implied, between the timing of its release and its twitter caption, that the video is aligned with Black Lives Matter activism. However, the key expression of the video's motivating topic bears scrutiny. On one hand, star (white) quarterback Mac Jones delivers the "we stand against racism" phrase, providing a high profile white voice and face for the central crux of the message. The reference to "brutality," however, does not specify police as perpetrators, softening the message's direct focus on police forces and broadening to a more generic pattern of antagonism. Black players delivering this section of the script are superstar receiver Devonta Smith and linebacker Jarez Parks (who will speak at the August rally). These voices add resonance to the message via star status and activist commitments, but the decision to not directly name the police is notable.

As the piece continues, I'd argue that the focus remains consistent with Watts's insights on voice, especially for Black communities, in that we cannot conceive it purely as an instrumental tool but must attend to ways voice is "a relational phenomenon occurring in discourse . . . not reducible to the subject's agency nor does it reflect a limitless range of signification" (Watts, 2001b, p. 180). I do not know if Leatherwood's original script called out the police; what we know is that the version delivered collectively by the team did not, and I'm not willing to dismiss the video for that one omission. It is quite possible that Leatherwood was working within the relational aspect of voice as he crafted this, thus limiting his discursive agency but engaging the collective, multifaceted experience and viewpoint that his teammates shared to the world. Evidence for this is the lines right after racism is explicitly mentioned. The players tell us that "When we see our families, our neighbors, our classmates subjected to violence, we recognize the fear in their eyes." The focus remains relational, communal, social. The invocation of fear, from giant muscled elite athletes, is also profound: it acknowledges that racial violence, whether from institutional actors like the police or peers or local residents, can strike fear in even the largest or most protected of us. This line continues to bring the players into the impact of racial violence: AAPI athlete Ale Kaho and the extremely dark-skinned defensive captain Dylan Moses share that "And when we experience racism, it hurts." Two players of BIPOC identity, delivering the truth that Alabama football players are not immune from this treatment, and then expressing the human vulnerability of feeling pain. This type of voice is not demanding or name-calling, but it is a significant mode of public voice all the same.

If the "we experience racism" line is the emotional highpoint of the speech, it closes on a more hopeful note, but one rooted in complexity and gravitas.

Saban returns for a final appearance, speaking for the white ally role with the words "Until I listen with an open heart and mind, I can't understand his experience and his pain." In this line, we hear Saban perform compassion, reflexivity, and empathy while asking for the simple, powerful task of listening. The emotional vulnerability remains but is delivered squarely and without shrinking from it. The players take up the message to the close, telling us "We choose to listen, we choose to hear, and to understand others' perspectives." They express resolve that, "We believe the solutions to our challenges are within us." Both of these lines can slide into weaker positions that allow white-dominated public spaces, like police forces, legislatures, or Board of Trustees, to not be named as extending white-dominant policies or practices. But nuance remains in these lines and when viewed with Watts' reminders in mind, we see depth to them not recognized by quick comment board reactions; we hear that elite Black college football players see themselves as part of solutions, that we should listen to them—better, we should hear them—and that they are committed to change.

The video closes with six different players reciting the closing line, "All lives can't matter until Black Lives Matter," and the video goes dark to reveal these words in the background as soft piano music closes the entire piece. Jones remains the white voice and face in this final montage, amid BIPOC teammates Waddle, Dale, Kaho, and Smith. Adaptations of the phrase "Black Lives Matter" have been controversial as they typically express disdain for the basic premise of the movement to value and protect Black citizens (see Carney 2016, Kil 2019). The UA football video flirts with this line, but I'd argue that the use of "can't" preserves a defensible level of anti-racist activism. It is not the watered-down inclusivity of "all lives matter" and it inserts a temporality, a timeline that indeed all lives cannot matter *if we do not* protect and value a specific portion of our community.

CONDITIONS FOR PUBLIC VOICE "HAPPENING": UA ATHLETES PROTEST MARCH

On the afternoon of Monday, August 31, 2020, varsity student athletes, including coaches, trainers, and athletics staff, marched from the Mal Moore Athletic Center (home to weight training, dining facilities, coaches' offices) approximately two blocks up Bear Bryant Drive and turned into campus for another block to arrive at the historic Foster Auditorium, site of Gov. George Wallace's failed 1963 attempt to block enrollment of African American students at UA. The march was highly organized and controlled due to pandemic concerns for the athletes: all marchers wore masks, only athletics personnel were in the march, barricades kept onlookers back at the rally site, and no

significant contact was made between student- athletes and onlookers. Video
and photography records suggest that over 200 student-athletes marched,
with perhaps 50 coaches and staff. Head football coach Nick Saban walked
at the front with players who lead the effort, including star running back
Najee Harris. Men's basketball head coach Nate Oats (also white) walked,
and players from men's and women's track and field, women's soccer, men's
basketball, cheerleading, and swimming/diving can be identified based on
team attire.[3] Signs with racial justice messages, as well as t-shirt slogans and
images, underscore the event's "Black Lives Matter" focus.

At Foster Auditorium, the marchers gathered near the main doors where
a stage had been constructed with a speaker podium. Media and general
onlookers stood behind metal barricades approximately 20 to 25 yards away
from the athletes. With the delayed start of fall sports, online format of most
instruction, and reduced on-campus residence, UA campus was much quieter
on this day than a typical fall semester. Perhaps 100 additional onlookers
attended the rally, and the overall feel of the event was somber and serious.
There were no yells, no chants, no inflamed pleas for action. Eight individuals
spoke at the rally, four Black and four white. Coach Saban spoke first, followed in order by Harris; university president Dr. Stuart Bell; football player
Jarez Parks; campus police chief John Hooks; athletic director Greg Byrne;
football player Chris Owens; and vice president for diversity, equity, and
inclusion Dr. G. Christine Taylor.

A brief pause for context is warranted. Prior to the summer of 2020, athletes, including those in college, were not just speaking out on political issues
but their speech and symbolic actions were becoming coordinated, or at least
informed and influenced by other athletes in equally unprecedented ways.[4]
An undeniable context for the UA athlete protest was the August 23 shooting
of Jacob Blake in Kenosha, Wisconsin. The day following Blake's shooting,
NBA stars voted to not play their playoff game, a historic climax to an already
unprecedented summer of activism. Blake's shooting, on top of ongoing
Black Lives Matter activism on college campuses, led to rallies and marches
occurring on other college campuses, including SEC members Missouri,
Tennessee, Vanderbilt, Mississippi, Mississippi State, and Florida.[5] Indeed,
since 2017, the SEC had been commemorating the desegregation of football
teams in the league, honoring past players and coaches and creating films
and special events to reckon with the league's racial history.[6] In the summer
of 2020, the conference launched a SEC Racial Equality and Social Justice
council[7] made up of head coaches and student-athletes with a corresponding
website page tracking events and progress around racial equity topics.[8] The
difficult work of contextualization is part of the intervention I urge sport communication scholars to do: we have to challenge our own approaches when
keeping up with the powerful voice(s) and action(s) of athlete activists today.

With these contexts in mind, I assess the speeches at the August rally through Watts's lens of Black voice as a "happening" (2001b); a rhetorical moment that produces "the sound of affect" (2001b); and as an "occurrence in need of acknowledgment" (2012). As a live event and less mediated (though highly scripted), the rally is a case study in contemporary Black voice, specifically the ways young student-athletes engage affect as a way to create awareness of their social condition, their broader humanity, to demand acknowledgement (if not redress) of unjust conditions.

First, Watts asks us to approach Black voice "not [as] a unitary thing that inhabits texts or persons either singly or collectively. It is itself a happening that is invigorated by the public awareness of the ethical and emotional concerns of discourse," (2001b, p. 185). The student-athlete speakers at the rally evoked the present, the past, and their physical surroundings to require audiences to see and realize their perspectives in new ways. Najee Harris introduces himself as "a student at UA"—not an elite super star athlete—and linebacker Jarez Parks looks around the plaza while saying "I came here [to UA] just like many of you." Offensive lineman Chris Owens asked his listeners to "look around, see who's standing near you" and ask if you've done enough to make racial justice and equality a reality. While absent a laundry list of demands, the student-athlete speeches fit Watts's view of voice as "happening" by bringing affect into materiality, demanding recognition and participation from their surroundings.

Evidence of this "happening" comes from white speakers Saban and Byrne. Both men shared how much they have learned from the (Black) players. Race is evoked in these statements via the ways Saban and Byrne point to ways their whiteness limits their understanding of the world and these issues. Saban tells us "I don't get to see the world through the same lens as they do; and I respect and appreciate the lens they see the world in, the way they live the world in." Saban's use of "get" is notable here, as if he is missing out on insight and knowledge by not ever experiencing Black life. Byrne likewise speaks of learning, rooting it relationally as "talks [my wife and] I haven't had to have with our sons . . . about what to do when you're pulled over, about always keeping a receipt when you're out shopping, about being careful when you go out." Byrne refers to "the talk" that Black parents give their children, the affect of fear and constant anxiety about the specter of white violence. This is the "effect" of Black voice at the UA athlete rally: a reckoning with difference, overt effort at perspective-taking, admissions of growth.

Second, Watts calls voice "the sound of affect," stating that as "the audible projection of persons, voice announces the felt experience of one's immediate relation to and inseparability from the world and others" (2012, p. 16). The march and rally were steeped in affect, despite the carefully planned and quarantined nature of its execution. Players from many teams wore t-shirts or carried signs of racial justice, Black Lives Matters, and calls for police reform. Najee Harris spoke in a t-shirt stating "Defend Black Lives" with a raised fist image, and Jarez Parks spoke in a t-shirt stating "If only we loved Black people as much as we love Black culture." Parks's delivery was the most direct, natural, and emotional, including a moment when he paused to collect himself. He shares the ways racial terror shapes his everyday life at the very start of his comments, relating to the audience how each time he safely returns home to his apartment he thanks God. Parks describes the disconnect between promises of meritocracy and lived experience of blackness by stating "no matter how smart we are, how talented we are, my skin color can be a perception changer any minute." There is clear emotion in these words, a quality Watts suggests can be erased by overly abstract theories of voice (Watts, 2001b, p. 188). The student-athletes provide "the sound of experiential encounters in civic life" (Watts, 2001b, p. 185) as Black men—this is an affect and instantiation of voice rarely afforded them.

Finally, Parks and his teammates' urgings fit with Watts's (2001b) view of voice as an "occurrence in need of acknowledgement" (p. 192). Voice in this mode is not argument or debate; it is an embodied oral and aural insistence of one's existence. Flores (2016) highlights this aspect of Watts' work, the ways voice is rendered "answerable" (p. 11) rather than solitary or unidirectional. Black voice, Watts argues, is fundamentally rooted in the social; its affective richness demands answer. Student-athlete Chris Owens is a strong example of this aspect of voice; he speaks powerfully, with slow pacing and direct eye contact, laying out simply that "our country is not a place of equality and unity . . . [that] we are unable to achieve our goals." Owens points to "cultural norms" that Black Americans learn in order to survive, and he names "systemic inequalities" as long-term obstacles to change. Najee Harris, while speaking more from his notes and thus lacking as much affective power in his delivery, comes closest of the players in laying out demands, asking for police re-training, criminal justice reform, and community engagement. Athletic Director Byrne provides a sense of the "answer" that these moments of Black voice create: statements of being heard and believed over empty promises of change. Byrne offers a lament, of sorts, that "we love how sport brings us together . . . [but] how can we take all the support we feel on the field, the court, the pool and bring it to our daily lives?"

Watts intervenes into definitions of voice after studying the speakers of the New Negro Movement. The very term, "New Negro," he argues, was less self-chosen by leaders like DuBois than offered by White audiences who were asked—forced perhaps—to generate "new forms of perceptual care" to make sense of Black aesthetics around them (2012, p. 4). Black voice in these ways or moments is less of a clearly articulated plan for change, reform, or even revolution; it shifts the everyday terrain of recognition and identity.

It forces new categories, even if they are imperfect, for dominant classes to interpret their communities and peers. I see resemblances, especially in the words of college athletes, to this era. The players' voices operate as "a unique means for making sense of the intersection of aesthetics, rhetoric, and the lived experience" of Black Americans (Watts, 2012, p. 4). Coach Saban calls them "intelligent" and "peaceful" and "positive"—words not quickly associated with giant muscle-bound Black men in America today. Vice president for diversity Dr. G. Christine Taylor (who is Black, says they've added to her bragging rights in the SEC, that we, like they, cannot "sit on the bench" amid systemic injustice, and that "this is your time." Between the video and the march, fans and observers of Alabama football saw new sides of their star players, new skills, new emotions, new ways of being in the world. This is the power of voice, if we expand our analytical scope.

CONCLUSIONS: THE MARGIN OF ABUNDANCE & MARGINALIZATION

In this analysis, I've attempted to show that the UA athlete activism of summer 2020 was a "happening" in the sense of Watts (2001b): "not a unitary thing that inhabits texts or persons either singly or collectively. It is itself a happening that is invigorated by the public awareness of the ethical and emotional concerns of discourse" (p. 185). The accuracy of Watts's conceptualization of voice is matched only by the urgency with which we adopt his theoretical intervention. That is, as long as scholars of sport, activism, and social change insist on a concept of voice that privileges individual agency, subjectivity, or personal "style," we risk allowing dominant social conditions to persist.

Flores (2016) encourages us to think about the ways racial logics are intensely local, even as they connect to networks of national and global scale. Locality allows us to engage the complexity of voice, be it supporting or countering dominant norms, or both. As she argues, we must "see the spaces in between hegemonic and resistive, dispelling possibilities of either as pure spaces" (p. 12). SEC football players possess many privileges and uphold dominant norms in many facets of their lives. At the same time, the courage to speak publicly on these topics while in season, facing draft pressures and hostile audiences, cannot be overlooked. The sociality of these two cases is significant: the team spoke as a team and the Black players spoke up within social conditions of activism, awareness, and new commitments. The locality of speaking at Foster Auditorium adds depth and complexity to the event, as does the involvement of white UA officials and administrators. It is insufficient to dismiss this event based on the presence of those privileges, just as it is irresponsible to proclaim the march pure revolutionary politics. Racial rhetorical criticism, critical theories of voice, and analytical tools in these traditions are of paramount importance when tracing and exploring the complex layers of voice and activism happening on our campuses.

Evidence suggests that athlete activism may be here to stay. Certainly, situations of injustice, racialized or other, will not end anytime soon, but athletes are also building their identities and expectations around voice and activism. Kluch (2020) finds that college athletes are increasingly identifying themselves as activists from day one, despite any risk or stigma. Public marches and speeches are but one form of this activism, meaning our scholarly models or concepts will need to continue their own evolution as well. Kaufman and Wolff (2010), revisiting past research on the risks of activism, identify four ways in which sport is structurally oriented towards producing progressive activism (social consciousness, meritocracy, responsible citizenship, and interdependency), suggesting that sport produces (or hones) these type of actors. Butterworth (2020) argues that sport rivalry may indeed be a space in which productive, lasting "adversary" relationships are taught, rather than explosive, destructive "enemy" ones. Only time will tell where the hot summer of 2020 takes us, but scholars need to be prepared.

Race, racial justice, racialized experiences, racialized bodies—all of these ideas and realities are part and parcel of sport. As Flores (2016) and others remind us, it is not enough to "attend to" race from a standard framework such as rhetorical theory, sport communication studies, or sport media influence. This standard approach only deepens the ways Black bodies and lived experiences are too often relegated to "the spaces between, outside, and beyond the 'canon,' tokenized in readers and syllabi in that familiar pattern of one is enough" (Flores, 2016, pp. 5–6). The breadth and scope of Black Lives Matter activism in sport forces us to confront the paradox of "abundance and marginalization" that characterizes critical race scholarship: it/they are everywhere, but also not centered or made forefront. The summer of 2020 demands we do better.

NOTES

1. Video is available at https://www.youtube.com/watch?v=Pu2LOSGbNpg. Its title on youtube is "University of Alabama football team speaks out against racial inequality, injustice."

2. In its format, the video resembles a similar message produced remotely by several major NFL stars and released on twitter three weeks prior. In this video, taken primarily via smart phone cameras and edited together, major players such as New York Giants running back Saquon Barkley and Kanas City Chiefs quarterback

Patrick Mahomes not only articulate their experience as Black men in America but they directly ask NFL leaders to "listen to your players," publicly condemn racism, and stop "silencing" players from political activism. One day later NFL commissioner Roger Goodell issued his own video apologizing for the treatment of Colin Kaepernick and promising better dialogue with Black players and anti-racism actions. The NFL video is available at https://touchdownwire.usatoday.com/2020/06/04/nfl-players-create-powerful-what-if-i-was-george-floyd-video/

3. Video of the march is accessible at https://www.cbs42.com/sports/alabama/watch-live-alabama-football-team-marching-for-social-change-on-campus-this-afternoon/

4. Relevant contexts include, but may not be limited to: athlete protest to delays, cancellations, and resumption of sport activity amid the coronavirus pandemic; name-image-likeness and student athlete unionization efforts; athlete efforts in the successful campaign to change the Mississippi state flag; effects of professional sport teams being in "bubbles" that summer for competition, leading to increased and more coordinated political responses such as the NBA playoff strike the day after Jacob Blake's shooting.

5. Other campuses that saw student athlete racial justice activism included Oklahoma and Duke. See https://www.washingtonpost.com/sports/colleges/nick-saban-alabama-players-hold-protest-march-on-campus/2020/08/31/61008996-ebe2-11ea-bd08-1b10132b458f_story.html for reporting on this.

6. Alabama was due to honor John Mitchell and Wilbur Jackson, its first two African American varsity football players in 1970, in an on-field ceremony but shifted to a video tribute that debuted in Dec 2020. That video can be seen at https://www.youtube.com/watch?v=LrgyTTpzGDM.

7. See https://www.secsports.com/equality for more information.

8. See https://www.secsports.com/article/30692299/sec-pursuing-racial-social-equality-college-sports_for an account of actions taken by the SEC Racial Equality and Social Justice initiative.

REFERENCES

Butterworth, M. (2020). Sport & the quest for unity: How the logic of consensus undermines democratic culture. *Communication & Sport, 8*(4–5), 452–472.

Carney, N. (2016). All lives matter, but so does race: Black Lives Matter and the evolving role of social media. *Humanity & Society, 40*(2), 180–199.

Cooper, J. N., Macauley, C., Rodriguez, S. H. (2019). Race & resistance: A typology of African American sport activism. *International Review for the Sociology of Sport, 54*(2), 151–181.

Flores, L. A. (2016). Between abundance and marginalization: The imperative of racial rhetorical criticism. *Review of Communication, 16*(1), 4–24.

Grano, D. A. (2009). Muhammad Ali versus the "modern athlete": On voice in mediated sports culture. *Critical Studies in Media Communication, 26*(3), 191–211.

Kaufman, P. & Wolf, E. A. (2010). Playing and protesting: Sport as vehicle for social change. *Journal of Sport and Social Issues, 34*(2), 154–175.

Kil, S. H. (2019). Reporting from the whites in their eyes: How whiteness and neoliberalism promotes racism in the news coverage of "All lives matter." *Communication Theory, 30*(1), 21–40.

Kluch, Y. (2020). "My story is activism!": (Re-)Definitions of social justice activism among college athlete activists. *Communication and Sport, 8*(4–5), 566–590.

Watts. E. K. (2001a). Cultivating a Black public voice: W. E. B. DuBois and "the criteria of Negro art." *Rhetoric & Public Affairs, 4*(2), 181–201.

Watts, E. K. (2001b). "Voice" & "voicelessness" in rhetorical studies. *Quarterly Journal of Speech, 87*(2), 179–196.

Watts, E. K. (2012). *Hearing the hurt: Rhetoric, aesthetics, and politics of the New Negro Movement.* Tuscaloosa, AL: University of Alabama Press.

Woods, A. & Harris, K. (2020, December 3). Student athletes marched, but has anything really changed? *The Crimson White.* Last accessed August 14, 2021 at https://cw.ua.edu/70024/opinion/opinion-student-athletes-marched-but-has-anything-actually-changed/

Chapter 9

When the Shirt Hit the Fan

Mike Gundy and the OAN Controversy

John McGuire, Ray Murray, and
Andrew M. Abernathy

The summer of 2020 saw an awakening of political activism among athletes after the death of George Floyd. The actions of conservative news outlets that criticized resulting protests as well as the Black Lives Matter movement heightened the tensions in the country. One America News Network (OAN) was one of these networks. OAN saw itself as an alternative to an older and more successful conservative news outlet, Fox News Channel. As a result, OAN's coverage was even more critical of the protests.

During this time, Oklahoma State University (OSU) football coach Mike Gundy was seen in a photo on Twitter wearing a t-shirt with the OAN logo. Had it not been for the logo, the photo would have appeared innocent enough—taken with two other people in an outdoor setting. But those three letters were enough to trigger an online revolt from Oklahoma State football players, past and present. It became a pressing crisis for a program that had dealt with outside crises in the past, but never one that publicly pitted the head coach versus his players, as well as drawing indirect criticism from the University's President and Athletic Director on social media. The situation had potentially immense consequences for Gundy and the University. As Eitzen (2012) has noted, major college head coaches in revenue-producing sports like football are seen as part of a larger economic enterprise that places importance on winning games and generating income. The OSU football program, which generated about $37 million, or nearly 40% of the athletic department's annual revenues in 2019, was facing significant financial losses in 2020 because of the COVID-19 pandemic (Wright, 2021). Failure to deal with this crisis would possibly derail OSU's coming season (one where it expected to challenge for the Big 12 title) as well as harm recruiting. The university's leaders were also in a difficult position, for Gundy was not only the winningest coach in school history, but also popular with alumni, having been an OSU quarterback in the 1980s. Finally, Gundy had much at stake, having a contract paying more than $5 million annually.

This chapter focuses on Gundy's efforts to deal with this communication crisis, utilizing Hearit's model of apologetic ethics (1995, 2006). Hearit's approach allows the researchers not only to explore Gundy's response to the crisis, but also what Hearit describes as the ethics behind Gundy's multiple efforts at apology.

CRISIS MANAGEMENT WITHIN THE SPORTS WORLD

The management of crisis situations within all levels of sports has become a highly studied area within the sports media discipline. Such research dates to the 1990s, when Benoit and Hanzcor (1994), for example, examined Tonya Harding's *60 Minutes* interview, trying to deflect blame in the assault of rival skater Nancy Kerrigan before the 1994 Winter Olympics trials. Much of the image repair research has focused on players, including National Football League All-Pro Terrell Owens, tennis legend Serena Williams, Tour de France champion Lance Armstrong, and baseball star Mark McGwire (Benoit, 2015; Brazeal, 2008; McGuire et al., 2013). There also has been research about sports organizations engaging in image repair, such as the National Hockey League trying to restore trust with its fans after a bitter lockout of players resulted in cancellation of the 2004–2005 season or the New Orleans Saints organization when it had to explain offering players bounties for taking opposing players out of games (Benoit, 2015; DiSanza et al., 2013). It is curious individual coaches have rarely been the focus on these types of studies because of the unique role such individuals play in sports organizations, particularly in the head coach's typical role of communicating with multiple stakeholders (e.g., players, fans) more often than anyone else in the organization (Comeaux, 2015; Smith, 2009). Although Benoit (2015) discussed Saints coach Sean Payton, it was part of an overall examination of image repair of multiple individuals within the Saints organization. Armfield et al.'s (2019) examination of the New England Patriots and Deflategate looked at the image repair efforts of Coach Bill Belichick as well as quarterback Tom Brady and owner Robert Craft. Gundy's situation is unique because of the conflict with his players as well as the financial and reputational peril created for Gundy and OSU's athletic department.

Crisis Communication and Apology Ethics

There are many academic approaches to understanding and analyzing the practice of apologia in communication. For example, Benoit's (1994) theory of image repair is a prominent method for studies where individuals or corporations try to deal with negative communication situations (most of the above cases relied on Benoit's theory).

Hearit (1995; 2006) has offered another model that can be used in such situations, drilling down on the intent, execution, and quality of apologia in crisis communication, which he called apologetic ethics. Within this approach, Hearit has identified standards such communication must achieve to be seen as authentic and reach its desired goals. Hearit argued his method allowed a way to "ethically judge the apologetic decision making offered by individuals and organizations" while acknowledging there may be factors that complicate such efforts (Hearit, 2006, p. 77). The assertion that victims be considered as the top priority in such situations, as opposed to one's individual or corporate interests, is one distinction in Hearit's method (Hearit, 2006).

Hearit's apologetic approach has three distinct levels, with the first addressing the manner of the apology (2006). Although Hearit suggested no one trait enjoys supremacy over the others, such apologia has greater success when all or most of these traits are present. Truthfulness, for example, is critical as any obfuscation of the facts could damage how people view the apology. Sincerity is judged as communicating understanding about the offense committed and offering regret and a commitment to repair the damage caused. Hearit also stated such communication from the offender needed to be voluntary (not coerced) and timely (though some may see doing it too soon as paying lip service to the offense). Hearit also made note of the need for an appropriate context for the apology. Hearit described the context as a situation where the offender makes a public apology (e.g., widespread dissemination through the media) unless the number of stakeholders is limited. In such instances, the manner of apology may be private in nature.

The second level in Hearit's approach (2006) focused on the content of the apologetic communication. For example, Hearit declared the individual or corporate transgressor must be unequivocal in what is expressed (e.g., acknowledging wrongdoing and regret, fully accepting responsibility). The individual/corporation must identify action steps for resolving the behavior (e.g., offering corrective action and/or appropriate compensation; addressing expectations of stakeholders). For an individual transgressor, Hearit also suggested such communication content be empathetic (e.g., identifying with injured stakeholders) and be proactive in repairing the existing relationship (e.g., seeking reconciliation, asking for forgiveness). As noted above, the

Table 9.1. *Hearit Model of Judging Apologetic Ethics*

Considerations	Conditions
Manner of the Apology	*Truthful, Sincere, Voluntary, Timely, Addresses all Stakeholders, Performed in an Appropriate Context*
Content of the Communication	*Explicitly acknowledges wrongdoing; Fully accepts responsibility; Expresses regret; Identifies with injured stakeholders; Asks for forgiveness; Seeks reconciliation with stakeholder; Fully discloses information related to the offense; Provides explanation addressing legitimate expectations of the stakeholders; Offers to perform corrective action; Offers appropriate compensation*
Complicating Circumstances	*Catastrophic financial losses; Grave liability concerns; A moral learning curve; Problem of full disclosure; Discretion*

Sources: Frandsen and Johansen (2007); Hearit (2006)

ethical nature of the apology can be viewed more positively by achieving these traits in the communication.

The third level in Hearit's model (2006) examined what may detract from the efficacy of the other levels. Hearit identified five such circumstances, with the first two focusing on economics (i.e., catastrophic financial losses, liability concerns). Two other factors deal with what can be said (or not said) in such situations (i.e., lack of full disclosure, discretion). The other complicating factor, a moral learning curve, identified the possibility an individual or corporation does not immediately recognize or address all injured parties or relationships, and whether efforts are made to rectify such mistakes because of what has been learned from the original offense (Hearit, 2006).

Applying Hearit's Model to Sports Figures. Hearit used his model to examine circumstances surrounding Atlanta Braves pitcher John Rocker who in December 1999 was caught up in controversy after making racist comments about ethnic populations and the LGBTQ+ community in New York City (2006). Various stakeholders directly (e.g., those in the baseball industry) and indirectly (e.g., politicians such as New York Mayor Rudy Giuliani) involved expressed outrage with Rocker's comments. Rocker made an initial apology Hearit judged as failing ethically in multiple ways (e.g., manner in the way apology was made and its content, seen as being too defensive and lacking mortification). Rocker's second attempt at expressing an apology came a few weeks later during a January 2000 interview with ESPN's Peter Gammons. Rocker specifically stated he was apologizing but also sought to minimize his transgression by citing times when he felt New York fans had mistreated him. Hearit's assessment of Rocker's 2000 apology redux "although not ethically ideal, did reach standards of moral acceptability" (2006, p. 99). Rocker engaged in the act of apology on one more occasion: the first time the Braves went to New York to play the Mets in 2000. Hearit identified this strategy as successful, for there were no significant problems with the New York crowd when Rocker entered the game.

Frandsen and Johansen (2007) look at the apologetic ethics in a crisis communication situation involving a popular handball team in Denmark. Coach Anja Andersen had pulled her players off the court in the middle of a game in protest of several officiating calls. The team later returned to the court to finish the match it eventually lost. Controversy surrounded the decision and the team's chief communication person in a postgame setting, offered an explanation, saying though the decision to pull the players was unconventional, the behavior of the officials created the situation (Frandsen & Johnasen, 2007). Danish newspapers and officials for the Danish Handball Federation said Andersen's behavior was "a disgrace to the sport" (Frandsen & Johnasen, 2007, p. 98). As the initial attempt to quell the controversy had failed, Andersen, while not explaining her reasoning to pull the players out of the match for a time, took blame in a second statement: "I would like to apologize to all persons who are in need of an apology" (Frandsen & Johnasen, 2007, p. 98). The authors, using Hearit's (2006) model, suggested the coach's explanation (or lack thereof) created problems with the apologetic ethic of being truthful. The coach's apology was lacking in other ways based on Hearit's model (e.g., seeking reconciliation). As a result, the Danish coach was seen as doing more harm than good, hurting her reputation with those she offended (e.g., fans of the club and the local press).

A CHRONOLOGY OF THE GUNDY-OAN CRISIS AND RESPONSE(S)

Gundy was no stranger to controversy since his hiring as OSU football coach in 2005. In 2007, Gundy created a social media sensation with his "I'm a man, I'm 40!" rant after a game, attacking a female sports columnist's article about quarterback Bobby Reid. Gundy and the rest of the athletic department also faced scrutiny after a series of *Sports Illustrated* articles in 2013 alleging illegalities before and after Gundy's hiring. While most of the charges were unfounded, it cast the program in a negative light. But unlike these other situations, the controversy Gundy faced in summer 2020 originated within the program itself.

Day 1: The T-Shirt Hits the Fan

Gundy's t-shirt photo first appeared on Twitter on June 10, 2020. Five days later on the morning of June 15, a reporter retweeted the photo, noting Gundy was wearing an OAN t-shirt. Although not a newsworthy item unto itself,

Gundy had told reporters in April 2020 about his appreciation of OAN and the way it covered news. In that instance, he stated, "They just report the news. There's no commentary" (Unruh, 2020a, para. 20). Those comments resulted in OAN contacting Gundy and sending the t-shirt in question (Brown, 2020). That America was in the midst of a social reckoning after George Floyd's death at the time made matters worse. OAN anchors and reporters were critical of protesters affiliated with the Black Lives Matter (BLM) movement, with one OAN host referring to BLM as "a criminal organization" (Reimer, 2020, para. 15). OSU players reacted within hours to the t-shirt photo. The first, and most prominent reaction, came from junior running back Chuba Hubbard, a prospective All-American who had returned to OSU despite an opportunity to enter the 2020 National Football League (NFL) Draft. Hubbard tweeted, "I will not stand for this. This is completely insensitive to everything going on [in] society and it's unacceptable. I will not be doing anything with Oklahoma State until things CHANGE" (Hubbard, 2020). A wave of supporting tweets from Black and White Cowboy players expressed support of Hubbard's stance. One of the team's defensive leaders, Amen Obongamega, retweeted Hubbard's tweet and stated, "I stand with him!" and star wide receiver Tylan Wallace proclaimed, "It's About Way More Than Football!!!" (Obongamega, 2020; Wallace, 2020). Former Oklahoma State running back Justice Hill supported his former teammate in his tweet, hinting the program had other issues beyond Gundy's choice of T-shirt: "OSU Athletics and University need major change. 100% support brotha" (Hill, 2020). Another former player who had recently left the program for the pros stated, "Can't stay silent Anymore! Call a Spade a Spade!!" (Green, 2020). As the number of tweets on social media grew, the University's administration felt compelled to comment. University President Burns Hargis tweeted, "I hear and respect the concerns expressed by our Black student-athletes. This is time for unity of purpose to confront racial inequities and injustice. We will not tolerate insensitive behavior by anyone at Oklahoma State" (Hargis, 2020). OSU Athletic Director Mike Holder said in a statement "the tweets from the current and former players are of grave concern" (Unruh, 2020b, para. 11).

Athletic department officials were ramping up a crisis communication response from the time they became aware of the apparently offensive tweet. Internal emails later made public showed officials were attempting to craft a statement for the head coach to read that day. By 7:00 that evening, Gundy, along with Hubbard, engaged in his own crisis management in an amateurly shot video posted to Hubbard's Twitter account. Gundy, speaking first, focused on what he had learned about OAN from talking with Hubbard and other players but did not offer a specific apology:

In light of today's tweet with me, a t-shirt I was wearing, um, I met with some players and I realized it's a very sensitive issue with what's going on in today's society, and so we had a great meeting and made aware of some things that, uh, players feel like that can make our organization, our culture even better than it is here at Oklahoma State and I'm looking forward to making some changes, and it starts at the top with me, and we got good days ahead.

Then when Hubbard spoke, he was the one who was offering an apology—about his initial tweet: "I'll start off first saying that I went about it the wrong way by tweeting . . . I'm not someone, you know, has to tweet something that makes change, I should have went to him, as a man, and I'm more about action, so that was bad on my part . . . " (KJRH-TV, 2020).

Gundy's failure to directly express regret or to ask for forgiveness can be viewed through Hearit's (2006) model as sabotaging the video's purpose, especially in its content. In attempting to focus on team and team culture, Gundy did not directly address his transgression (e.g., wearing the OAN t-shirt) against the primary stakeholders (his team) and instead sought to emphasize the positive (that "he had a great meeting" with the players and "we got good days ahead"). Gundy's first statement failed to fully accept responsibility or even address the wrongdoing that had occurred or that he even fully accepted responsibility. The manner of the apology was also problematic, as the content of the first video and its rushed nature (recorded a few hours after Hubbard's initial tweet) called its sincerity into question, which in turn weakened the authenticity of Gundy's statement.

Day 2: An Actual Apology

In the age of 24-hour sports talk on radio and television, Gundy's t-shirt and his June 15 video became topic du jour. As Hearit (2006) noted, the media will often act as a "third party," joining stakeholders and taking offense (p. 84). Television programs like *First Take* on ESPN and *Undisputed* on FS1 spent extended time on the topic, especially because there was little else to discuss in sports because of the pandemic. Co-host Max Kellerman went off on Gundy on the *First Take* program: "There was only one person basically apologizing. Not the coach who owes an apology, but the player who did not!" (ESPN, 2020). On *Undisputed*, co-host Skip Bayless also criticized Gundy's lack of remorse in the June 15 video while suggesting the coach was potentially facing dismissal (*Undisputed*, 2020). Sports talk radio programs around Oklahoma spent multiple hours rehashing the tweets and previous day's video. *The Oklahoman* sports columnist Berry Trammel wrote Gundy was putting the University and its athletic department in a bad situation, and not for the first time (Trammel, 2020).

It was obvious Gundy would need to say more, and in a far different format, and one athletic department employee suggested better production values were needed (Brown, 2020). Thus, Gundy went into the athletic department's video studios and did a short video the next day (June 16). Gundy spoke into the camera and no one else appeared. An OSU logo appeared at the end of the video, signifying the official nature of the statement. What Gundy read sounded similar to rough drafts floating around the day before:

> I had a great meeting with our team today. Our players expressed their feelings as individuals and as team members. They helped me see through their eyes how the T-shirt affected their hearts. Once I learned how that network felt about Black Lives Matter, I was disgusted and knew it was completely unacceptable to me. I want to apologize to all members of our team, former players and their families for the pain and discomfort that has been caused over the last two days. Black lives matter to me, our players matter to me. These meetings with our team have been eye-opening and will result in positive changes for Oklahoma State football. I sincerely hope the Oklahoma State family will accept my humble apology as we move forward (Gundy, 2020)

Gundy's second public statement regarding the controversy can be seen as being far more effective through Hearit's (2006) apologetic model, particularly in its content. A primary requisite in Hearit's model is that victims are the primary focus of such apologies. Current Cowboy players were singled out as well as players' families and former players. The content of Gundy's second statement presented an apology, acknowledging his wrongdoing (wearing an OAN T-shirt without knowing the network's editorial views), expressing regret for it, and accepting responsibility for the offensive event. Gundy's new statement discussed reconciliation with his players and addressing their expectations (meeting with players, listening to their feelings about race relations in the country). Gundy's second statement specifically stated the phrase "Black lives matter to me" to address the expectations of behavioral change on the part of players while repeating his previous pledge of "positive changes for Oklahoma State football."

Gundy's second statement is also more effective in the manner it was presented compared with the first statement. Gundy's university-produced video, where he is speaking into the camera, allowed this effort to come across to the intended audience as more truthful and sincere. Gundy's solo appearance on camera also suggested he was trying to place responsibility on himself for his action; as a result, the production values suggested the apology was presented in an appropriate context. Another of Hearit's (2006) steps is also met. As noted above, Gundy addressed multiple stakeholders, including the parents of players. Had Gundy given this sort of statement first, one could have also argued it was timely.

Regarding complicating circumstances, the problem of full disclosure is the only applicable factor in Hearit's (2006) model that could be applied here. Gundy's second statement goes only as far as saying there would be "positive changes," but without specifics.

Gundy's Consequences

The t-shirt controversy triggered an internal athletic department review by Oklahoma State's Athletic Director's office. Although there was no finding of problems related to race within the football program, players offered criticism of Gundy's aloof nature and lack of communication (Unruh, 2020c). The conclusion of the investigation allowed the University to circle the wagons around its coach, with a supportive statement from University President Hargis. And though never directly connected to the controversy or subsequent review, Gundy proposed and accepted a $1 million reduction in his yearly salary as well as reducing the length of his rollover contract from five to four years and reducing the buyout amount in the event the university sought to terminate him without cause (Unruh, 2020c). The researchers suggest at least two of these actions (e.g., reducing the length of contract and buyout amount) could be seen as performing corrective action and offering appropriate compensation. Although the salary reduction was done at a time of fiscal difficulties for OSU and all athletic programs, the other actions dealt directly with Gundy's employment status and did not impact the immediate financial state of university athletics.

DISCUSSION

Hearit's (2006) apologetic ethics model allows researchers to drill down on the use of apologies in managing crises, whether at the individual or corporate level. In Mike Gundy's case, the researchers see similarities with other examples presented above regarding the cases of Atlanta Braves pitcher John Rocker and Danish handball coach Anja Andersen. Just as Rocker and Andersen, Gundy needed not one, but two tries at trying to make an apology. A failure to go far enough in identifying, admitting to, and promising or engaging in corrective action spoiled the first effort at apology from all three of these figures. Thus, one of the findings that can be drawn from these cases is that the idea of a timely apology should be secondary to one that gets the content of the apology correct—thereby enhancing the chances of an immediate and positive outcome. In Gundy's case, the researchers regard his second communication (and later action related to his contract) as generally effective, meeting many of the conditions of Hearit's model. The involvement of outside parties in working with improving the manner and content of Gundy's apology was a significant difference in these statements. Where Gundy's first video statement failed to put the offended stakeholders front and center in both content and the manner it was presented, the second statement addressed the players and other parties and more importantly, got Gundy to admit to his wrongdoing and acceptance of responsibility, which is key in Hearit's model.

While judging Gundy's second effort at apology as more effective, the judgment carries with it one caveat—lack of full disclosure as to corrective actions. This caveat suggests there are barriers for researchers to effectively gauge the effectiveness of apologia strategies or outcomes within the sports team setting, regardless of the theory being applied. While Gundy stated that certain efforts "will result in positive changes for Oklahoma State football," these changes were never publicly shared. The internalization of such actions does not allow for a fully accurate analysis of the apologetic ethics in these situations, as opposed to a corporation or government agency that may be subject to greater scrutiny (as discussed below). It could be suggested that Gundy's ability to hold his team together after the flare-up over his OAN T-shirt is evidence that whatever actions were undertaken were successful.

One other conclusion from this research is that Gundy's behavior should be considered within an athletic team structure. One can suggest Gundy, the son of a football coach, a high school and college football star, and a lifelong career as an assistant or head coach, is likely a strong advocate for what DeSensi (2014) called the "sport ethos" (p. 58). This ethos can be described as a structure offered through sport, particularly the teaching and learning of team play and the discipline to follow rules restricting behaviors. In sports, locker rooms are often viewed as sanctuaries, where signs on the wall implore players that "what you see here, what you hear here, stays here." While the phrase is associated with support groups, the phrase also reflects the sports ethos where the idea of team is first and foremost. In both of Gundy's public statements, he fell back on descriptions of "our organization" and "our culture." For Gundy, he likely saw this crisis through a "team" perspective, where the issue could be resolved internally through the team structure. This perhaps explains why Gundy thought the initial video shot June 15 discussing these ideas might offer an adequate response. The fact there were more stakeholders to be addressed and the realization that the manner and content of that first communication was lacking resulted in a more formal and highly crafted second statement.

The 2020 season ended up a mixed bag for Oklahoma State in college football's most bizarre season. Gundy guided OSU to another winning season and it won its bowl game against Miami (FL) but fell short of the preseason goal of winning a Big 12 championship. Chuba Hubbard struggled through injuries, announcing before the season ended he was leaving the team to get healthy and prepare for the 2021 NFL Draft. The OSU football program retained the large majority of players despite the t-shirt controversy and pandemic and had a successful recruiting effort in the fall of 2020, landing a top-40 class (Nagel, 2020). The 2021 season was even better, with Gundy's team, loaded with veteran players, winning 10 games, finishing runner-up in the Big 12 Conference and winning the Fiesta Bowl.

Ultimately, the OAN t-shirt controversy at Oklahoma State raised awareness about media coverage of those protesting George Floyd's murder. In addition, OSU players' threat to boycott participation with the team demonstrated the potential power that athletes at all levels of sports possess.

REFERENCES

Benoit, W. L. (2015). *Accounts, excuses, and apologies: Image repair theory and research* (2nd ed.). SUNY Press.

Benoit, W. L., & Hanzcor, R. (1994). The Tonya Harding controversy: An analysis of image repair strategies. *Communication Quarterly, 42*, 416–433. https://doi.org/10.1080/01463379409369947

Brazeal, L. (2008). The image repair strategies of Terrell Owens. *Public Relations Review, 34*(2), 145–150. DOI: https://doi.org/10/1016/j.pubrev.200.03.021

Comeaux, E. (2015). Practitioner views of college head coaches: A stakeholder management perspective. *Journal for the Study of Sports and Athletes in Education, 9*(2), 102–116. DOI: 10/1179/1935739715Z.00000000038

DiSanza, J. R., Legge, N. J., Allen, H. R. and Wilde, J. T. (2013). The puck stops here: The NHL's image repair strategies during the 2004–2005 lockout. In J. Blaney, L. R. Lippert, & J. S. Smith (eds.), *Repairing the athlete's image: Studies in sports image restoration* (pp. 319–358). Lanham, MD: Lexington Books.

Eitzen, D. S. (2012). *Fair and foul: Beyond the myths and paradoxes of sport.* Lanham, MD: Rowman & Littlefield.

ESPN. (2020, June 16). *First Take reacts to Chuba Hubbard's calling out Mike Gundy about wearing an OAN shirt.* [Video]. YouTube. https://youtube.com/watch?v=t41y59oFNho

Frandsen, F., & Johansen, J. (2007). The apology of a sports icon: Crisis communication and apologetic ethics. *Hermes-Journal of Language and Communication in Business, 20*(38), 85-104. https://doi.org/10.7146/hjlcb.v20i38.25906

Gundy, M. [@CoachGundy]. (2020, June 16). [Video Attached] [Tweet]. Twitter. https://twitter.com/CoachGundy/status/1273002885283020809

Hargis, B. [@burnshargis]. (2020, June 15). *I hear and respect the concerns expressed by our Black student-athletes. This is a time for unity of purpose* [Tweet]. Twitter. https://twitter.com/burnshargis/status/1272646557930831878

Hearit, K. M. (1995). "Mistakes were made": Organizations, apologia, and crises of social legitimacy. *Communication Studies, 46*(1–2), 1–17. https://doi.org/10/1080/10510979509368435

Hearit, K. M. (2006). *Crisis management by apology: Corporate response to allegations of wrongdoing.* Lawrence Erlbaum Associates.

Hill, J. [@jhill21_]. (2020, June 15). *OSU Athletics and University need major change. 100% support brotha.* @Hubbard_RMN [Image attached]. [Tweet]. https://twitter.com/jhill21_/status/1272606883027746817

Hubbard, C. [@Hubbard_RMN]. (2020, June 15). *I will not stand for this..This is completely insensitive to everything going on society and it's unacceptable.* @Kyle_Boone [Image attached] [Tweet]. Twitter. https://twitter.com/Hubbard_RMN/status/ 1272601786449264642

KRJH-TV (2020, June 15). *Chuba Hubbard, Mike Gundy meet, post video promising change* [Video]. YouTube. https://www.youtube.com/watch?v=gO6d-8g2Zuk

McGuire, J., McKinnon, L., & Wanta, W. (2013). "Big Mac" with a side of steroids: The image repair strategies of Mark McGwire. In J. Blaney, L. R. Lippert, & J. S. Smith (eds.), *Repairing the athlete's image: Studies in sports image restoration* (pp. 27–40). Lexington Books.

Nagel, C. (2020, December 16). Where does Oklahoma State's 2021 recruiting class rank? *Pokesreport.com.* https://247sports.com/college/oklahoma-state/Article/Oklahoma-State-football-recruiting-class-rankings-National-Signing-Day-2021-156926557/

Ogbongbemiga, A. [@closedprayer]. (2020, June 15). *I stand with him!* @Hubbard_RMN [Tweet]. Twitter. https://twitter.com/closedprayer/status/1272601961725034496

Reimer, A. (2020, June 16). If Mike Gundy loves OAN, then Chuba Hubbard is right to think about boycotting Oklahoma State. *Forbes.com.* https://www.forbes.com/sites/alexreimer/2020/06/16/if-mike-gundy-loves-oan-then-chuba-hubbard-is-right-to-think-about-boycotting-oklahoma-state/?sh=a6096cc601f1

Skip and Shannon. (2020, June 16). *Undisputed-Skip & Shannon talking Mike Gundy's latest debacle: The t-shirt isn't only issue.* [Video]. YouTube. https://youtube.com/watch?v=YyhCCfhh_J4

Smith, J. G. (2009). NFL head coaches as sensegiving change agents. *Team Performance Management, 15*(3–4), 202–214. https: doi. org/10.1108/13527590910964964

Trammel, B. (2020, June 16). OSU football coach Mike Gundy needs to give his school some relief. *The Oklahoman.* https://oklahoman.com/article/5664777/osu-personnel-don't-need -gundy-problems-during-a-pandemic

Unruh, J. (2020a, April 8). OSU coach Mike Gundy's full opening statement on coronavirus and football. *The Oklahoman.* https://www.oklahoman.com/article/5659723/osu-football-read-the-entirety-of-mike-gundys-viral-opening-statement-on-coronavirus-and-football

Unruh, J. (2020b, June 15). OSU football: Mike Gundy says Cowboys have "good days ahead" after talk with Chuba Hubbard. *The Oklahoman.* https://www

.oklahoman.com/article/5664666/osu-football-chuba-hubbard-says-he-wont-par-ticipate-in-activities-due-to-mike-gundys-oan-shirt.

Unruh, J. (2020c, July 3). OSU football: Mike Gundy's contract reduced by $1M and one year following internal investigation. *The Oklahoman.* https://www.oklahoman.com/article/5665986/osu-football-mike-gundys-contract-adjusted-following-internal-investigation

Wallace, T. [@OfficialTylan2] (2020, June 15). *It's About Way More Than Football!!! @Hubbard_RMN* [Tweet]. Twitter. https://twitter.com/OfficialTylan2/status1272642783203950595

Wright, S. (2021, February 4). Despite Oklahoma State athletics turning a profit for 2020, Mike Holder is bracing for shortfall this fiscal year. *The Oklahoman.* https://www.oklahoman.com/story/sports/college/cowboys/2021/02/05/despite-oklahoma-state-athletics-turning-profit-2020-mike-holder-bracing-shortfall-this-fiscal-year/325848007/

PART IV

Gender Equity Issues

Chapter 10

The Motherhood Punishment

How Alysia Montaño & Allyson Felix Compelled Nike to Provide Maternity Protections in Female Athlete Sponsorship

Andrea Fallon-Korb

By 2017, Allyson Felix was one of Nike's most marketed athletes with good reason—at that time, she was the most decorated female track-and-field athlete in Olympic history with six gold medals and an 11-time World Champion. When Felix revealed her pregnancy to Nike during sponsorship contract negotiations in 2018, she asked Nike to guarantee she would not be punished for lower levels of performance in the months following childbirth, but talks stalled (Felix, 2019). This was not the first time Nike enforced penalties on pregnant athletes. They informed Alysia Montaño, a Nike-sponsored track athlete, in 2013 that if she were to get pregnant, Nike would pause her sponsorship contract and stop payment because she would not be competing or meet the predetermined performance threshold for support (Montaño, 2019). This "motherhood punishment" was potentially career-ending, not because of the physical repercussions of pregnancy and the difficulty to return to elite form, but because professional athletes of Felix and Montaño'scaliber rely on sponsorships to pay for coaching and training as well as basic living expenses.

Being an elite athlete comes at a high cost, and most elite athletes struggle financially. In a recent survey, 58% of Olympians state they are not financially stable and over half do not believe they receive enough compensation from the International Olympic Committee or national federations (Pells,

2020). Despite stipend programs to help cover training and medical expenses (see USATF, 2021), 60% of U.S. Olympians make less than $25,000 per year, which is not enough to pay for training, travel, and basic living necessities (Burton, 2021), forcing some Olympians to apply for food stamps (Whiteside, 2013). For example, in the 2016 Rio Olympics, over 100 U.S. athletes created GoFundMe campaigns to try and make ends meet (Itkowitz, 2016). As a result, many elite athletes rely on sponsorships to survive (West, 2019). Sponsored athletes are not employees of a business, but rather operate as independent contractors. As a result, if sponsored athletes become pregnant, they will not qualify for federal programs like paid family leave (West, 2019). Consequently, if a pregnant or new mother is not able to compete or reach a specific performance threshold set by a sponsor, they will lose both their contract and financial support. This system is inherently inequitable for pregnant and postpartum mothers, and it is imperative that athletes are protected from this motherhood bias.

This chapter will apply the Theory of Planned Behavior (TPB) to Nike's sponsorship of athlete-mothers. It will describe (1) how workplace norms and attitudes helped to maintain Nike's discriminatory practices toward pregnant elite athletes; (2) how perceived control, attitudes, and norms maintain a harmful status quo for elite pregnant and postpartum mothers; and (3) how Montaño and Felix created public pressure to shift public norms and attitudes, forcing Nike to create more inclusive practices in women's sponsorship contracts.

THEORY OF PLANNED BEHAVIOR

Ajzen's (1991) TPB explains that intentions, and the subsequent motivation and effort that derive from intentions, drive behavior. Intention is determined by three factors: subjective norms for the behavior, attitude toward the behavior, and perceived behavioral control over the behavior. Subjective norm describes the perceived social pressure to perform a behavior and is influenced by the perceptions of what others think, motivation to comply with others' expectations, and the observable behavior of others. Attitude is a positive or negative evaluation of a behavior and is determined through expected outcomes and emotional responses. More specifically, expected outcomes are what is anticipated to be gained or lost from a behavior while affective responses are the expected emotional responses to a behavior. The importance or weight these are given influences how an activity is evaluated. Lastly, perceived behavioral control represents how much control an individual believes they have. For all factors, the more strongly that attitude, subjective norm, and perceived behavioral control exists, the more likely the intention will be acted upon.

TPB in the Workplace

To establish the subjective norms within Nike, it is important to investigate common practice towards pregnant and working mothers. Bias is pervasive in the workplace, as mothers are frequently undervalued and discriminated against. Felix and Montaño, elite athletes of color, are at a greater disadvantage, as the intersectionality of race and motherhood act against them, an issue White athletes do not encounter. As a result, corporations like Nike did not experience any social pressure to change common practice for pregnant and postpartum mothers.

Due to frequent unjust practices in the workplace, the Pregnancy Discrimination Act (1978) was passed to prohibit discrimination based on pregnancy or childbirth in any aspect of employment. Despite this law, pregnancy discrimination has regularly increased and is pervasive, averaging more than 6,000 claims each year (National Partnership for Women and Families, 2016), which is close to an all-time high (Kitroeff & Silver-Greenberg, 2019). African American women are disproportionally affected, making up 28% of claims filed while only representing 14% of the female workforce (National Partnership for Women and Families, 2016). After childbirth, women in the workforce are financially penalized for having children. A "motherhood penalty" exists that contributes to unequal pay structures. For example, in 2019, women, regardless of parenthood status, made only 82 cents for every dollar men made. Looking specifically at working parents, mothers were paid 75 cents for every dollar fathers received, resulting in a yearly disparity of $15,300 (Ewing-Nelson, 2021). This trend has been labeled the "mommy penalty" and, on average, working mothers earn three percent less than non-mothers (Joint Economic Committee Democratic Staff, 2016). An important juxtaposition of the "mommy penalty" is that fathers earn a "daddy bonus" and receive on average 15% more than non-fathers (Joint Economic Committee Democratic Staff, 2016). This results in a sharp contrast in earnings both between working mothers and non-mothers as well as mothers and fathers. This pay disparity dramatically increases when looking at racial inequities with Black mothers being paid only 52 cents for every White father's dollar (Ewing-Nelson, 2021).

Not only is there a substantial pay gap, but there is also a disparity in career advancement opportunities. Nearly three quarters of parents believe that women are penalized in the workplace for starting families (Bright Horizons, 2019). Six in 10 workers in the U.S. have witnessed opportunities given to less-qualified employees rather than being given to mothers (Bright Horizons,

2019). Most working mothers believe that being a parent has made it harder for career advancement (Parker, 2015). Pregnant and working mothers experience discrimination, a reduction in pay, and limited career advancement opportunities in a wide array of careers, including those who are elite athletes. Moreover, it has been shown that discrimination is higher in male-dominated industries (McCann & Tomaskovic-Devey, 2021), like sports. As a result of these practices, corporations like Nike, until recently, have not experienced any social pressure to change their discriminatory, common practice.

In addition to standard industry inequities, working mothers also battle against negative attitudes and perceptions. The "maternal wall bias" is an assumed belief that mothers are less competent and less committed to their work (Williams, 2004). Many employers expect working mothers will have lower levels of commitment and competence than non-mothers (Ali, 2016; Budig, 2014) and may even pause their career to care for children (Budig, 2014). This is demonstrated with 41% of workers believing that working mothers are less devoted to their work (Bright Horizons, 2019). Part of this stems from a second assumption that mothers will be constantly distracted by their children and will not be productive in the workplace (Ali, 2016). The belief that working mothers are less competent, less committed, and more distracted creates negative outcomes for working mothers. Put a different way, businesses feel that working mothers will hurt productivity, which will in turn impact the bottom line of the business.

The ramifications of these negative attitudes serve to further perpetuate and exacerbate subjective norms (see above) and can have far reaching negative consequences for working mothers. Correll et al. (2007) conducted a study in which participants viewed two similar resumes, the only difference being that one cover letter indicated the potential female employee was a parent. The working mother application was 79% less likely to be hired, half as likely to be promoted into a higher position, and offered $11,000 less salary than a woman who did not have children with similar credentials. In other words, working mothers are less likely to be hired and promoted, and have a lower recommended salary than other female employees. An interesting contrast in attitudes towards working parents is the comparison of the negative maternal wall bias with the positive expected outcomes for working fathers. The same bias does not exist for working fathers. In fact, fatherhood is typically valued by employers, as it is perceived to signify work commitment, stability, and deservingness (Budig, 2014).

When examining current subjective norms and attitudes toward pregnant and working mothers in the workplace, it is evident that there are no incentives to change current practices. There is no pressure to modify policies, and there is an overwhelmingly negative evaluation of expectant and working mothers.

TPB for Elite Athlete-mothers

Elite athlete-mothers, like Felix and Montaño, are defined in research literature as athletes who competed at the professional or Olympic level pre- and post-pregnancy. Before children, being an athlete is often the central identity by which elite female athletes define themselves (Appleby & Fisher, 2009). Becoming a mother usually causes a dramatic shift in perspective not only in the creation of a new identity as a mother, but simultaneously maintaining multiple identities of mother and athlete (Appleby & Fisher, 2009; Palmer & Leberman, 2009). These identities of athlete and mother are often found to be at odds with one another and incompatible (Appleby & Fisher, 2009). As a result, many athlete-mothers perceive they cannot be both and are forced to choose between the two identities (Darroch & Hillsburg, 2017; McGannon et al., 2012; McGannon et al., 2019), perpetuating the belief that women's true calling is motherhood, which is more important and more meaningful than sport (Appleby & Fisher, 2009; McGannon et al., 2012; McGannon et al., 2018).

The intention to maintain a sole identity or, alternatively, hold two identities can be explained through perceived behavioral control. If an athlete perceives the identities of mother and athlete as incompatible, then they are likely to feel little control over either identity and feel compelled to pick only one, typically choosing motherhood over sport due to societal pressure. However, if the athlete chooses to see herself as multidimensional or reframe the situation to see the positives of being an elite athlete-mother, then she is more likely to engage in both motherhood and athletic activities.

There are wide ranging social and cultural beliefs associated with motherhood and preferred behaviors. Because these are culturally bound, there is substantial social pressure to perform "good" mother behaviors. One of these cultural beliefs is the traditional view that fathers are the providers for their families, while mothers are the primary caregivers (Dixon & Wetherell, 2004). There is an assumption that "good" mothers should place the needs of their family ahead of their own, an expectation to sacrifice their own needs for the good of the family (Choi et al., 2005), and are to be constantly present in their children's lives (Appleby & Fisher, 2009). As a result, women, regardless of competitive level, have traditionally felt they do not have a right to or time for exercise (Miller & Brown, 2005; McGannon & Schinke, 2013). This belief centers motherhood as a primary identity and severs the athlete identity.

Because elite athlete-mothers must manage the competing expectations of being a "good" mother while also achieving competitive success, they anticipate and experience many negative affective responses. They describe this tension of clashing pressures with words like compromise, juggle, balance

(Palmer & Leberman, 2009), and personal sacrifice (Appleby & Fisher, 2009; Darroch & Hillsburg, 2017; Palmer & Leberman, 2009). Feelings of guilt arise when athlete-mothers are not present as children achieve developmental milestones, must rely on others for childcare, or must spend time away from their child for training (Darroch & Hillsburg, 2017; Palmer & Leberman, 2009). Guilt often increases when others help because athlete-mothers are not able to "do it all" and feel selfish that they are not being a "good" mother by putting the child and family's needs first (Darroch & Hillsburg, 2017). This likely will harm athletic performance as guilt is connected to increased psychological distress and negatively associated with psychological well-being in sport contexts (Rice et al., 2021). Additionally, working mothers "doing it all" is a myth that will be discussed in detail later.

This dichotomy creates a unique catch-22 for elite athlete-mothers. Athlete-mothers could choose to put more emphasis on being a "good" mother and their caregiving responsibilities at the expense of their own training. This would alleviate the expected emotional responses of feeling guilty and selfish, but would jeopardize future competitive success, sponsorship, and financial stability. In contrast, athlete-mothers could continue to complete the necessary training required at the elite level but be ostracized for putting too much time and energy into their sport to the detriment of the child. They would be labeled a "bad" mother, leading to negative feelings like guilt and selfishness (Darroch & Hillsburg, 2017). In this situation, the athlete-mother is expected to spend the necessary time away from her child for training and competition but pay a price for it.

The "good" and "bad" mother label, or positive and negative evaluation, that athlete-mothers experience is reinforced and perpetuated through media portrayals, further increasing the social pressures athlete-mothers feel to perform the desired "good" mother behaviors. There have been limited depictions of elite athlete-mothers and when the media does cover them, the narratives are limited to three primary storylines: (1) motherhood as transformative experience, (2) motherhood and sports being dichotomous, and (3) supermoms.

A common storyline for athlete-mothers is that of a transformative journey (McGannon et al., 2015). In this context, athletes underwent a life-changing physical and mental experience during pregnancy and after becoming mothers. As a result of this dramatic shift, if the athlete-mother does return to competition, it is framed as a "come back" (McGannon et al., 2015; McGannon et al., 2017). Implied in this storyline is the belief that there are physical and mental challenges due to female fragility that must be overcome with special precautionary medical care to attempt to reach past performance standards (McGannon et al., 2015).

A second narrative is that motherhood and athletic competition are incompatible. An overt example is when an athlete is portrayed as a "bad" mother when she competed, but became a "good" mother once she retired and put the needs of her children ahead of her own athletic aspirations (Cosh & Crabb, 2012). These storylines highlight the clashing demands of sport and motherhood, downplay athletic goals and ambitions, and compel women to choose between career and motherhood (McGannon et al., 2015). A focus is often on the guilt experienced by the athlete-mother when she is away from her children to train or compete, but it is noted that this distress can be reduced or even disappear after children's needs are placed first (McGannon et al., 2015). Again, this reinforces the idea that mothers need to be self-sacrificing and the importance of adhering to the "good" mother ideals.

The final theme is athlete-mothers being supermoms when they excel in both athletic and motherhood realms (McGannon et al., 2015; McGannon et al., 2017). In this narrative, athlete-mothers are portrayed as being highly successful in the athletic domain while simultaneously also achieving the "good" mother standards (McGannon et al., 2017). As this is such a rare and exceptional feat, a female athlete can only achieve this if she has superpowers. This is often associated with the idea that women can "have it all"—thriving in all of life's domains, which is often equated with female life fulfillment (McGannon et al., 2012; McGannon et al., 2015; McGannon et al., 2017). These superhuman standards are an illusion and unattainable as it is impossible to do everything perfectly (McGannon et al., 2015) and are typically only applied to women, as men are not expected to "do it all." They present significant harm, potentially causing additional distress for those trying to emulate such a balance (McGannon et al., 2012; McGannon et al., 2015; McGannon et al., 2017).

In becoming mothers, elite athletes undergo a shift to hold multiple identities. Remaining an elite athlete while also being a mother is not easy when there is substantial cultural pressure to adhere to "good" mother norms. Negative affect may occur if athlete-mothers prioritize their athletic career, and are in a catch-22 dilemma with competing priorities and outcomes.

PRESSURE FOR NIKE TO CHANGE

Alysia Montaño

The momentum pregnant and mother athletes began building in 2013, when Montaño informed Nike that she wanted to start a family. Nike indicated they would suspend her contract during pregnancy and would resume payment when she returned to competition (Jackson, 2019). Essentially, Nike declared they would not pay athletes unless they met a predetermined performance threshold and would not financially support athletes during pregnancy or maternity. Montaño left Nike and signed with Asics as they appeared more accommodating, telling Montaño "not to worry about [her] contract" after she disclosed her pregnancy (Collie, 2019, para. 12). To ensure compensation for basic living and medical insurance, Montaño continued to run and train under medical supervision, gaining widespread attention when she ran the 800m at the U.S. Track and Field Championships in 2014 while eight months pregnant (Phillip, 2014), thus deemed "the pregnant runner" (West, 2019). Montaño was largely hailed for her efforts and received a standing ovation, even as she was the last runner to finish the race (Associated Press, 2014). Months after the birth of her daughter, Asics informed Montaño they would reduce payment based on her 2014 performance as she failed to reach the performance goals outlined in the contract, citing a race Montaño ran hours before going into labor (Collie, 2019). Due to financial strain, Montaño returned to competition as soon as possible, taping her abdominal muscles together as she was recovering from diastasis recti, a separation of the abdominal wall muscles resulting from her pregnancy (Moore, 2019). Ten months postpartum, Montaño won the 800m U.S. national title and a month later competed in the IAAF World Championships in Beijing, pumping breast milk to ship home to her daughter (Moore, 2019).

Montaño did not share her experience at the time due to a nondisclosure agreement with Nike and Asics but decided to break this silence by publishing a *New York Times* article on Mother's Day 2019 (Felix, 2019). In the article, Montaño (2019) claimed that athletic sponsors are duplicitous. Companies presented themselves as being supportive, praised women and mothers in public, even featuring them in ads. However, they did not guarantee salary protections for these same individuals during pregnancy and postpartum. Athletes were not given exceptions for pregnancy or maternity, as they are only paid if they compete and reach predetermined performance thresholds. As a result, athlete-mothers were forced to choose to be with their newborn children or resume training shortly after giving birth to receive sponsorship money, financially support their family, and continue their career. Montaño cited Olympian Kara Goucher's experience of feeling compelled to leave her ailing newborn in the hospital so she could return to training.

Recently, Montaño described Nike and Asics's practices of withdrawing or denying sponsorships as motherhood discrimination. She stated that athlete-mothers' contracts are not renewed because they are not perceived to be "dedicated" to their sport and do not "have as much value" (Sheinin et al., 2021, para. 7). Not only do they lose sponsorship contract, but the financial ramifications are that they "get kicked out of the sport" (Sheinin et al., 2021, para. 7). Montaño is not alone in this belief. Phoebe Wright, a national champion in the 800m, stated that, "Getting pregnant is the kiss of death for a female athlete. There's no way I'd tell Nike if I were pregnant" (Montaño, 2019, para. 8).

Allyson Felix

Felix went to great lengths to keep her pregnancy a secret in 2018 and continued to compete in meets. She went out of her way to conceal her pregnancy by training in the early morning so nobody would see her, wearing baggy clothing, and limiting those who knew. She even went so far as to not allow guests to bring phones to her baby shower (Gregory, 2021).

Felix credits her advocacy for maternal education and protections to her first-hand experience of racial disparities during pregnancy and delivery. After being severely preeclamptic, causing her daughter's heart rate to slow, Felix required a life-saving emergency C-section (Campoamor, 2020). Despite being an elite athlete in great physical shape and having consistent high-quality medical care, she was surprised, as her "eyes were completely opened . . . no one is immune from this reality and that Black women face significantly higher risks—ones I wasn't really aware of and looking for" (Campoamor, 2020, para. 7). Felix discovered that Black women are three times more likely to die from pregnancy-related complications than White women (Centers for Disease Control and Prevention, 2017), 60% more likely to experience preeclampsia than White women (Fingar et al., 2017), and are 27% more likely to develop preeclampsia than Black women who immigrate to the U.S. (American Heart Association, 2020). After her experience, Felix stated that it "really ignited the fire . . . to share my experience and to be an advocate for mothers everywhere" (Campoamor, 2020, para. 10).

Felix's first act of advocacy was testifying at the House Ways and Means Committee hearing on racial disparities in maternal health. She shared her personal experience and her lack of awareness of the racial differences in maternal health and mortality (O'Neal, 2019). A week later, Felix published her *New York Times* article. In the article, Felix (2019) described that her Nike contract expired in December 2017 and during contract renegotiations in 2018, she felt pressure to return as quickly as possible after delivery since she was not receiving sponsorship income. Nike eventually offered to pay Felix 70% of her previous contract before pregnancy but talks stalled when Felix asked for maternity protection—that Nike guarantee she would not be punished for lower levels of performance in the months following childbirth. Felix was surprised to be viewed as expendable by Nike despite her past athletic success. She stated, "If I, one of Nike's most widely marketed athletes, couldn't secure these protections, who could?" (Felix, 2019, para. 9).

NIKE'S SEX DISCRIMINATION

Nike has a history of supporting female empowerment publicly through ad campaigns, but behind closed doors their actions do not match their image. This duplicity is one of Montaño's (2019) primary assertions in her *New York Times* article and supported by Felix's direct experience. During Felix's tense renegotiations with Nike declining to provide maternity protections, Nike asked her to be spotlighted in female-empowerment ads that supported female athletes at all stages of life overcoming sex discrimination (McLaughlin & Cash, 2021).

This likely continued a trend of sexism and misogyny at Nike not only with female athletes, but also with female employees. In 2018, female employees at Nike covertly surveyed colleagues, with results showing extensive experiences of sexual harassment and gender discrimination (Creswell et al., 2018). Female employees had lower salaries, fewer opportunities for promotion, and experienced overt sexual harassment and bullying by their male colleagues (Creswell et al., 2018). As a result of the survey, six senior-level male employees resigned, and an apology was issued for not taking harassment complaints seriously and fostering a culture of exclusion (Creswell et al., 2018). Nike then announced pay increases for 7,000 employees, 10% of which was designed to ensure equal compensation for the same job (Thomas & Lucas, 2018). A systematic gender discrimination class action lawsuit was also filed (Meyersohn, 2018) and is still open.

An important juxtaposition is Nike's ongoing financial support of Colin Kaepernick. Nike kept Kaepernick as a sponsored athlete when he was not playing in the NFL and thus not able to reach any performance thresholds. Yet, he was featured in a commercial that subsequently won an Emmy (O'Kane, 2019), and Nike released a limited-edition Kaepernick jersey (Dodson, 2019). This occurred a few months before Montaño and Felix's *New York Times* articles were published. If the same pay-for-performance contract clause used to discriminate against pregnant athletes was applied to Kaepernick, he would have been dropped as a Nike sponsored athlete in 2016, nearly two years prior to both releases. In drastic contrast to Kaepernick, it took significant public pressure for Nike to give support to female athletes who are mothers.

SHIFT IN INTENTION: NIKE PROVIDES
MATERNITY PROTECTIONS

Within days of Montaño's article, there was significant public support of athlete-mothers. Athletic brands Nuun (Rutherford, 2019), Burton (Burton, 2019), Altra (Altra Running, 2019) and Brooks (Brooks Running, 2019) announced guaranteed financial security for their sponsored athlete-mothers and revisions to sponsorship policies for all female athletes. Some companies went so far as to state they would assure that pregnancy and postpartum recovery would not impact any current or future contracts and no financial penalties if an athlete was unable to reach certain performance thresholds due to pregnancy or postpartum recovery. Co-chairs of the Congressional Caucus on Maternity Care sent a letter of inquiry to Nike regarding "pay fairness policies and company contracts with female athletes who are pregnant, breastfeeding, or in the postpartum period," asking CEO Parker to respond to multiple questions and pointing out Nike's misrepresentation of female empowerment in ads compared to their treatment of female athletes (Herrera Beutler & Roybal-Allard, 2019, para. 1). This public pressure forced Nike to consider revising their policy and stance on sponsorship of athlete-mothers. Despite this mounting pressure and public outcry, it took Felix publishing her article a week later before Nike released a public statement.

Ironically, due to increased media exposure through Nike's ad campaigns featuring Felix, her recognizability in the published *New York Times* article increased both exposure and backlash of Nike's exclusive practices (Chavez, 2019). Many consumers expressed negative perceptions of the brand and negative attitudes toward Nike. This negative evaluation would likely result in a change in intention for consumers to stop or limit purchases of Nike products. The fear of decreased brand favorability, negative press, and public pressure drove Nike to break their silence in order to improve public perception.

Two days after Felix's article was published, Nike's pregnancy protections were finalized (Draper, 2019). This was communicated through an internal Nike memo addressing Montaño's and Felix's critiques. The memo, which was picked up by the press, stated that Nike had started to change its pay-for-performance policy in 2018 after realizing it harmed pregnant athletes, although this was never communicated to sponsored athletes (Draper, 2019). In the maternity protection policy, Nike stated it would waive the performance requirement for 12 months (Draper 2019). Almost two months later, Nike released specific contract language and extended protections for performance deductions to 18 months, broken down to eight months of pregnancy and ten months postpartum (Chavez, 2019).

WATERSHED MOMENT

Montaño's and Felix's advocacy created a watershed moment to help pave the way for other elite athlete-mothers. As a result of their candid articles and public support, there has been increased exposure and advocacy for many athlete-mothers. In the lead-up to the 2020 Tokyo Olympics, a COVID-19 policy was created to restrict spectators, but it also prevented nursing athlete-mothers from bringing their babies with them (Associated Press, 2021). This forced several athlete-mothers to choose between continuing to breastfeed their child by remaining at home or attending the Olympics as an athlete (Associated Press, 2021). U.S. marathoner Aliphine Tuliamuk was one of several athletes who advocated to change the Olympic policy. She credits Felix and Montaño, stating, "Thankfully Allyson Felix . . . and Alysia Montaño talked about their stories because it changed the conversation and made things possible for me" (Sheinin et al., 2021, para. 16). Quanera Hayes, U.S. 400m Olympian, thanked Felix for a visual representation showing that being an elite athlete-mother is possible (Sheinin et al., 2021). Also, British sprinter Bianca Williams says of Felix, "Without her, I wouldn't be where I am now. I'm so grateful for her for speaking up, because she has changed a lot of women's lives" (Gregory, 2021, para.9).

The impact and the shift in discourse has been far reaching. Since 2019, two professional women's leagues created landmark maternity protections for athletes. The precedent-setting WNBA Collective Bargaining Agreement includes fully paid maternity leave, standard accommodations for athlete-mothers who are nursing and pumping, an annual childcare stipend, as well as housing assistance (Cash, 2020). Athletes Unlimited, an organization that runs professional women's sports leagues of softball, volleyball, and lacrosse created an all-encompassing pregnancy and maternity leave policy where athletes can receive unlimited paid parental leave during the season and accommodations for breastfeeding and childcare (Cash, 2021). Additionally, elite athlete-mothers are increasingly being portrayed in traditional media and social media in tennis (Serena Williams), WNBA (Dewanna Bonner, Skylar Diggins-Smith, Derica Hamby, Candace Parker, Diana Taurasi), and the NWSL (Ashlyn Harris, Ali Krieger, Sidney Laroux, Alex Morgan). All of these athletes are regularly seen with their children before and after competitions, during training, and in everyday life.

Despite substantial cultural, workplace, and media discrimination, Montaño and Felix were able to overcome negative working mother and athlete-mother subjective norms, attitudes, and perceived behavioral control. Through vulnerability and openly sharing their personal stories, Montaño and Felix's advocacy triggered a turning point in sport sponsorship that already has, and will continue to, influence future generations of athlete-mothers.

WHERE ARE THEY NOW?

In the months following the *New York Times* articles, Montaño found financial stability by signing a new deal with Cadenshae (Chochreck, 2019). Felix inked a new sponsorship deal with Athleta, the first athlete to ever sign with the brand (Chavez, 2019), opening the door for Simone Biles to also leave Nike sign with Athleta, citing a desire to be aligned with a sponsor focusing on women (Draper, 2021). In the run up to the 2020 Tokyo Olympics Felix expanded her brand by launching Saysh, her own signature shoe (Gregory, 2021). Additionally, in 2021, Felix partnered with Athleta and the Women's Sports Foundation to launch the Power of She Fund, a first of its kind grant to support elite athlete-mothers pay for childcare expenses, committing $200,000 to the endeavor (Women's Sports Foundation, 2021). During the 2020 Tokyo Olympics, Felix became the most decorated woman in track and field history and the most decorated U.S. track athlete of all time, earning her eleventh Olympic medal.

REFERENCES

Ajzen, I. (1991). The theory of planned behavior. *Organizational Behavior and Human Decision Processes, 50,* 179–211.

Altra Running [@AltraRunning]. (2019, May 17). We support all female athletes before, during and after pregnancy and maternity [Tweet]. Twitter. https://twitter .com/AltraRunning/status/1129535651517304832

American Heart Association. (2020, November 9). U.S.-born Black women at higher risk of preeclampsia than Black immigrants. *American Heart Association.* https: //newsroom.heart.org/news/u-s-born-black-women-at-higher-risk-of-preeclampsia -than-black-immigrants

Appleby, K. M., & Fisher, L. A. (2009). "Running in and out of motherhood": Elite distance runners' experiences of returning to competition after pregnancy. *Women in Sport & Physical Activity Journal, 18*(1).

Associated Press. (2014, June 27). Thirty-four weeks pregnant Alysia Montaño runs 800m at US race. *The Guardian.* https://www.theguardian.com/sport/2014/jun/27/ thirty-four-week-pregnant-montana-800m-us-race

Associated Press. (2021, June 24). Canadian basketball player being forced to choose between "being a breastfeeding mom or an Olympic athlete." *USA Today.* https://www.usatoday.com/story/sports/olympics/2021/06/24/olympics-2021-need -breastfeed-may-block-canadians-path-tokyo/5339417001/

Bright Horizons (2019). Modern Family Index 2018. *Bright Horizons*. https://www
.brighthorizons.com/-/media/BH-New/Newsroom/Media-Kit/MFI_2018_Report
_FINAL.ashx

Brooks Running [@brooksrunning]. (2019, May 17). *At Brooks, we support our athletes and their dreams, including starting a family* [Tweet]. Twitter. https://twitter
.com/brooksrunning/status/1129451368840925189

Budig, M. J. (2014, September 2). The fatherhood bonus and the motherhood penalty:
Parenthood and the gender gap in pay. *Third Way*. https://www.thirdway.org/report
/the-fatherhood-bonus-and-the-motherhood-penalty-parenthood-and-the-gender
-gap-in-pay

Burton. (2019, May 16). How we're supporting women and families on the Burton
team. *The Burton Blog*. https://www.burton.com/blogs/the-burton-blog/how-were
-supporting-women-and-families-burton-team/

Cash, M. (2020, January 14). The WNBA has a new CBA that increases player salaries, ensures maternity leave, and improves marketing and travel for the league.
Business Insider. https://www.businessinsider.com/new-wnba-cba-improves
-salaries-maternity-leave-marketing-travel-2020-1

Cash, M. (2021, May 9). Athletes Unlimited is enabling professional athletes to
become mothers without compromising their sports careers. *Business Insider*.
https://www.insider.com/athletes-unlimited-pregnancy-policy-enables-pro-athlete
-mothers-2021-5

Campoamor, D. (2020, August 4). Olympic star Allyson Felix speaks out about her
traumatic birth experience. *Today.com*. https://www.today.com/parents/allyson
-felix-olympic-star-traumatic-birth-experience-t188436

Centers for Disease Control and Prevention. (2017, November 14). Meeting the
challenges of measuring and preventing maternal mortality in the United States.
Centers for Disease Control and Prevention. https://www.cdc.gov/grand-rounds/
pp/2017/20171114-presentation-maternal-mortality-H.pdf

Chavez, C. (2019, August 16). Nike removes contract reductions for pregnant athletes
after backlash. *Sports Illustrated*. https://www.si.com/olympics/2019/08/16/nike
-contract-reduction-pregnancy-protection-athlete-maternity-leave

Chockrek, E. (2019, September 25). Track star who criticized Nike pregnancy policy
inks new athletic deal. *Footwear News*. https://footwearnews.com/2019/business/
power-players/alysia-montano-nike-pregnant-athlete-cadenshae-1202845509/

Choi, P., Henshaw, C., Baker, S., & Tree, J. (2005). Supermum, superwife, super-
everything: Performing femininity in the transition to motherhood. *Journal of
Reproductive and Infant Psychology, 23*, 167–180.

Collie, M. (2019, May 31). Olympian Alysia Montaño claims Nike, Asics paid her
less because she was pregnant. *Global News*. https://globalnews.ca/news/5338038
/runner-alysia-montano-pregnant-asics/

Correll, S. J., Benard, S., & Paik, I. (2007). Getting a job: Is there a motherhood
penalty? *American Journal of Sociology, 112*(5), 1297–1338.

Cosh, S., & Crabb, S. (2012). Motherhood within elite sport discourse: The case of
Keli Lane. *Psychology of Women Section Review, 14*(2), 41–49.

Creswell, J., Draper, K., & Abrams, R. (2018, April 28). At Nike, revolt led by women leads to exodus of male exeutives. *New York Times.* https://www.nytimes.com/2018 /04/28/business/nike-women.html

Darroch, F., & Hillsburg, H. (2017). Keeping pace: Mother versus athlete identity among elite long distance runners. *Women's Studies International Forum, 62,* 61–68.

Dixon, K., & Wetherell, M. (2004). On discourse and dirty nappies: Gender, the division of household labour and the social psychology of distributive justice. *Theory and Psychology, 14,* 167–189.

Dodson, A. (2019, February 20). Nike drops limited-edition Colin Kaepernick "icon" jersey. *The Undefeated.* https://theundefeated.com/features/nike-drops-limited -edition-colin-kaepernick-icon-jersey/

Draper, K. (2019, May 24). Nike says it will end financial penalties for pregnant athletes. *New York Times.* https://www.nytimes.com/2019/05/24/sports/nike-pregnant -athletes.html

Draper, K. (2021, April 23). Simone Biles Leaves Nike for a sponsor that focuses on women. *New York Times.* https://www.nytimes.com/2021/04/23/sports/olympics/ simone-biles-athleta-nike.html

Ewing-Nelson, C. (2021, May). Even before this disastrous year for mothers, they were still only paid 75 cents for every dollar paid to fathers. *National Women's Law Center.* https://nwlc.org/wp-content/uploads/2021/04/EDPFS.pdf

Felix, A. (2019, May 22). Allyson Felix: My own Nike pregnancy story. *New York Times.* *https://www.nytimes.com/2019/05/22/opinion/allyson-felix-pregnancy-nike .html*

Fingar, K. R., Mabry-Hernandez, I., Ngo-Metzger, Q., Wolff, T., Steiner, C. A., & Elixhauser, A. (2017, April). Delivery hospitalizations involving preeclampsia and eclampsia, 2005–2014. *Healthcare Cost and Utilization Project.* https://www.hcup -us.ahrq.gov/reports/statbriefs/sb222-Preeclampsia-Eclampsia-Delivery-Trends .pdf

Gregory, S. (2021, July 8). Motherhood could have cost Olympian Allyson Felix. She wouldn't let it. *TIME.* https://time.com/6077124/allyson-felix-tokyo-olympics/

Gregory, S. (2021, June 23). Allyson Felix launches her own shoe company after breaking up with Nike. *TIME.* https://time.com/6073949/allyson-felix-launching -saysh-shoes/

Herrera Buetler, J., & Roybal-Allard (2019, May 17). *U.S. Congresswoman Jamie Herrera Buetler.* https://jhb.house.gov/uploadedfiles/05_17_19_letter_to_nike.pdf

Jackson, V. (2019, May 23). Opinion: Stop penalizing female athletes for getting pregnant. *Global Sport Matters.* https://globalsportmatters.com/opinion/2019/05 /23/opinion-stop-penalizing-female-athletes-for-getting-pregnant/

Joint Economic Committee Democratic Staff. (2016, April). Gender pay inequality: Consequences for women, families, and the economy. *Joint Economic Committee, United States Congress.* https://www.jec.senate.gov/public/_cache/files/0779dc2f -4a4e-4386-b847-9ae919735acc/gender-pay-inequality----us-congress-joint -economic-committee.pdf

Kitroeff, N., & Silver-Greenberg, J. (2019, February 8). Pregnancy discrimination is rampant inside America's biggest companies. *New York Times.* https://www.nytimes.com/interactive/2018/06/15/business/pregnancy-discrimination.html

McCann, C., & Tomaskovic-Devey, D. (2021, May 26). Pregnancy discrimination at work: An analysis of pregnancy discrimination charges filed with the U.S. Equal Employment Opportunity Commission. *Center for Employment Equity.* https://www.umass.edu/employmentequity/sites/default/files/Pregnancy%20Discrimination%20at%20Work.pdf

McGannon, K. R., Curtin, K., Schinke, R. J., & Schweinbenz, A. N. (2012). (De)Constructing Paula Radcliffe: Exploring media representations of elite athletes, pregnancy and motherhood through cultural sport psychology. *Psychology of Sport and Exercise, 13,* 820–829.

McGannon, K. R., Gonsalves, C. A., Schinke, R. J., & Busanich, R. (2015). Negotiating motherhood and athletic identity: A qualitative analysis of Olympic athlete-mother representations in media narratives. *Psychology of Sport & Exercise, 20,* 51–59.

McGannon, K. R., McMahon, J., & Gonsalves, C. A. (2018). Juggling motherhood and sport: A qualitative study of the negotiation of competitive recreational athlete-mother identities. *Psychology of Sport and Exercise, 36,* 41–49.

McGannon, K. R., McMahon, J., Schinke, R. J., & Gonsalves, C. A. (2017). Understanding athlete-mother transition in cultural contexts: A media analysis of Kim Clijsters' tennis comeback and self-identity implications. *Sport, Exercise, and Performance Psychology, 6*(1), 20–34.

McGannon, K. R., & Schinke, R. J. (2013). "My first choice is to work out at work; then I don't feel bad about my kids": A discursive psychological analysis of motherhood and physical activity participation. *Psychology of Sport and Exercise, 14*(2), 179–188.

McGannon, K. R., Tatarnic, E., & McMahon, J. (2019). The long and winding road: An autobiographic study of an elite athlete-mother's journey to winning gold. *Journal of Applied sport Psychology, 31,* 385–404.

McLaughlin, K., & Cash, M. (2021, July 8). Olympian Allyson Felix says Nike was "beyond disrespectful" when asking her to be in female empowerment ads while privately disputing maternity protections. *Business Insider.* https://www.insider.com/olympian-allyson-felix-criticizes-nike-maternity-protections-dispute-2021-7

Meyersohn, N. (2018August 108). "Women are devalued and demeaned" at Nike, two ex-employees say in lawsuit. *CNN.* https://money.cnn.com/2018/08/10/news/companies/nike-gender-discrimination-bias-lawsuit/index.html

Miller, Y. D., & Brown, W. J. (2005). Determinants of active leisure for women with young children—an "ethic of care" prevails. *Leisure Sciences, 27,* 405–420.

Montaño, A. (2019, May 12). Nike told me to dream crazy until I wanted a baby. *New York Times.* https://www.nytimes.com/2019/05/12/opinion/nike-maternity-leave.html

Moore, P. (2019, May 29). Alysia Montaño called out Nike for not supporting parents. Many Americans can relate. *Washington Post.* https://www.washingtonpost.com/

lifestyle/2019/05/29/alysia-montao-called-out-nike-not-supporting-parents-many
-americans-can-relate/

National Partnership for Women and Families. (2016). By the numbers: Women
continue to face pregnancy discrimination in the workplace. *National Partnership
for Women and Families.* https://www.nationalpartnership.org/our-work/resources
/economic-justice/pregnancy-discrimination/by-the-numbers-women-continue-to
-face-pregnancy-discrimination-in-the-workplace.pdf

O'Kane, C. (2019, September 16). Colin Kaepernick's Nike ad wins and Emmy
for outstanding commercial. *CBS News.* https://www.cbsnews.com/news/colin
-kaepernick-nike-ad-won-an-emmy-for-outstanding-commercial-creative-arts
-emmy/

O'Neal, L. (2019, May 16). Olympic champion Allyson Felix tells congress about
the black maternal health crisis. *The Undefeated.* https://theundefeated.com/whhw
/olympic-medalist-allyson-felix-tells-congress-about-the-black-maternal-health
-crisis/

Palmer, F. R., & Leberman, S. I. (2009). Elite athletes as mothers: Managing multiple
identities. *Sport Management Review, 12,* 241–254.

Parker, K. (2015, March 10). Despite progress, women still bear heavier load than
men in balancing work and family. *Pew Research Center.* https://www.pewresearch
.org/fact-tank/2015/03/10/women-still-bear-heavier-load-than-men-balancing
-work-family/

Phillip, A. (2014, June 27). Olympian Alysia Montano runs an 800-meter race while
34 weeks pregnant. *Washington Post.* https://www.washingtonpost.com/news/early
-lead/wp/2014/06/27/olympian-alysia-montano-runs-an-800-meter-race-while-34
-weeks-pregnant/

Pregnancy Discrimination Act of 1978, 42 U.S.C. § 2000e-(k) (1978).

Rice, S. M., Treeby, M. S., Olive, L. Saw, A. E., Kountouris, A., Lloyd, M., Macleod,
G., Orchard, J. W., Clarke, P., Gwyther, K., & Purcell, R. (2021). Athlete experiences of shame and guilt: Initial psychometric properties of the athletic perceptions
of performance scale within junior elite cricketers. *Frontiers in Psychology, 12.*

Rutherford, K. (2019, May 15). #WeStandByHer. *Nuunlife.com.* https://nuunlife.com
/blogs/news/westandbyher

Sheinin, D., Berkowitz, B., & Maese, R. (2021, July 20). They are Olympians. They are
mothers. And they no longer have to choose. *Washington Post.* https://www
.washingtonpost.com/sports/olympics/interactive/2021/olympics-mothers/

Thomas, L. & Lucas, A. (2018, July 23). Nike is about to give 7,000 employees
raises. *CNBC.* https://www.cnbc.com/2018/07/23/nike-to-adjust-salaries-bonuses
-for-employees-to-address-pay-equity.html

Thomas, L. (2019, July 31). Ga's Athleta brand lands its first sponsored athlete:
Olympic track champion Allyson Felix. *CNBC.* https://www.cnbc.com/2019/07/30
/gaps-athleta-brand-signs-sponsorship-deal-with-olympian-allyson-felix.html

West, J. (2019, May 25019). Athletes speak out against Nike's lack of maternity leave
protection, other companies make change. *Sports Illustrated.* https://www.si.com
/olympics/2019/05/24/nike-maternity-protection-sponsorships-contract-allyson
-felix-alysia-montano

Williams, J. C. (2004). The maternal wall. *Harvard Business Review.* https://hbr.org/2004/10/the-maternal-wall

Women's Sports Foundation. (2021). The power of she fund. *Women's Sports Foundation.* https://www.womenssportsfoundation.org/wsf_program_categories/power-of-she-fund/

Chapter 11

Playing Here Doesn't Pay My Bills

An International Conversation of Pay Equity as a Discursive Practice

Katherine L. Lavelle, Korryn D. Mozisek, and Beth Fielding-Lloyd

In her justification for the 2017 Team USA hockey boycott to protest pay inequity, player Jocelyne Lamoureux-Davidson stated: "This transcends one sport. This is for women's sports" (Berkman, 2017a, para. 28). In addressing pay inequity, female athletes in the United States and United Kingdom challenge the differential treatment that sees them as less than. Despite the success of women's team sports in the United States and United Kingdom, female athletes are paid less and receive fewer benefits, support, and accommodations to help extend their careers (Culvin; 2019; Saxena, 2017).

Using cross-cutting examples from three sports, we examine women's fight for benefits and salaries commensurate with their success. WNBA (Women's National Basketball Association) players in the United States used their social media platforms to expose their pay inequities and substandard travel conditions in the summer of 2018 (Lough, 2018). The USWNT (U.S. Women's National Soccer Team), despite winning Olympic and World Cup championships with some of the most recognizable American athletes, sued their national federation in 2016 and 2019 for wage discrimination (Peterson, 2016; Kliegman, 2019). After decades of consistent success in international competitions, U.S. Women's Hockey players threatened to boycott the 2017 International Hockey Federation tournament in Michigan after fourteen months of unsuccessful negotiations to secure a living wage and financial support for girls' hockey (Berkman, 2017a). And in England, even after the Football Association (FA) launched the Women's Super League (WSL) in

2011 with a £1.5 million per year investment, inferior support for player development and continued financial instability remains (Fielding-Lloyd & Woodhouse, in press). WSL clubs and players consistently battle with the FA for material benefits, salaries, and even the ability to play during the COVID-19 pandemic, like the men's Premier League ("Women's Super League," 2020).

As scholars reflecting on the scope and significance of social justice activism in sports, we assert that these protests across different sports and nations are linked: "Women's sport does not exist in a vacuum, it informs, and is informed by, broader feminist movements of the day, and collective action has been reinvigorated as the tool of choice for catalyzing social change" (Szto et al., 2020, p. 6). The standing and perception of women on the pitch and on the court examined in sociology (Allison, 2016; 2018), communication (Lavelle, 2015), and media (Cooky & Antunovic, 2020; Cooky & Messner, 2018) research highlight shifts in acceptance and positive perceptions of female athletes over the past decades. But as Cooky and Messner (2018) observe, "just below the surface of this dramatic sea change, we can observe currents that run counter to the achievement of gender equality" (p. 10).

Examining pay equity protests in conversation helps identify the connections and divergent strategies used to advocate for better pay and working conditions. We examine these protests together because our analysis demonstrates that they share similar barriers and assumptions against the legitimacy of their claims, including pay inequity operating as material practice. As our chapter will illustrate, these instances demonstrate that female athletes are no longer willing to stay silent and are organizing for change through varying forms of activism that challenges systemic inequality.

CONSTRICTING RHETORICS SURROUNDING THE FEMALE ATHLETE

Women's team sports have become increasingly visible and successful, particularly in North America and Europe. However, there are several persistent issues that hamper their development and visibility that individual players and teams have publicly criticized and protested against. First, there is very little media coverage of women's sports. In their longitudinal study, Cooky et al. (2021) found that while U.S. media coverage increased since their 2015 study, it remains at 5.7%, despite increasing use of sport social media and increases in participation of elite female athletes. These conditions support the perception that female athletes do not deserve equitable pay and benefits because they receive less coverage than their male counterparts. Even when coverage occurs, it frequently reinforces gendered discourses perpetuating inequalities (Evans, 2017).

Second, female athletes are often expected to express gratitude for opportunities to participate in professional leagues and discouraged from advocating for appropriate compensation for their athletic abilities (Allison, 2016, 2018). For instance, pioneering WNBA players were described as "humble exceptions, socially responsible and willing role models for young girls seeking gender fairness in sport" (McDonald, 2000, p. 42). By characterizing players as role models, instead of successful and talented athletes, it obscures the work-like structures that are inherent in sports (Rigauer, 1981) and treats them as symbols instead of providing financial compensation worthy of their talents.

Third, female professional athletes (especially outside of basketball, tennis, and golf) cannot be full time athletes because their pay is so low. In their study of Canada's women's hockey players' pay equity fight, Szto et al. (2020) found that "the struggle to create sustainable and equitable women's professional hockey is one symptom of a society that continues to devalue women's experiences and contributions simply because they are women" (p. 6).

Finally, professional women's sports face significant pressure to be successful and profitable immediately, a standard not applied to men's sports (Cooky et al., 2021). For example, Major League Soccer (MLS) lost nearly $1B in 2020; instead of making budget cuts, the league used higher expansion fees to generate more money (Ruthven, 2021). This overinvestment and speculation on the future of the MLS is in contrast to the investment struggles of the National Women's Soccer League (NWSL) who, despite their well-known stars, have only recently attracted high profile investment (Marthaler, 2020). The perpetuation of differences between male and female athletes upholds economic inequalities as women's sports are expected to succeed without equivalent financial support (Evans, 2017).

Ultimately, we found our various examples were spurred on by these issues and responded in an attempt to validate female athletes' worth and pay equity claims. We examine how these three sports' efforts function by conceptualizing pay inequity as discursive and material rhetoric. Clair and Thompson (1996) characterized pay inequity as "a discursive and material practice whose ties to both patriarchy and capitalism need to be untangled" (p. 8). Pay inequity is endemic for women (Graham Davis et al., 2018), permeating a wide range of professional environments (Evans, 2017), and inherently connected to patriarchy (Graham Davis et al., 2018). Critically, "[w]omen's worth has been measured through and by their bodies" (Crowley, 1999, p. 358). Within sport, scholars have examined how pay inequity fights have occurred in hockey and soccer (Koller, 2019), professional tennis (Lavelle, 2015), and hockey (Szto et al., 2020). In engaging material rhetoric as a framework, our analysis also illustrates the ways in which pay inequity affects the material bodies of female athletes and how they become a site of protest (Crowley, 1999). As a result, this chapter evaluates the various strategies used by four women's sports teams in different contexts in their fight for pay and benefit equity, as well as how their discourse and bodily rhetoric operate as a rebuttal to the sexist assumptions about their sport.

In order to study these issues, we conducted a thematic analysis of the common and connected strategies used by Team USA hockey players during the 2017 near-boycott of the International Hockey Federation tournament, the U.S. Women's National Team's 2016 and 2019 pay discrimination filings against U.S. Soccer, WNBA players' public arguments against their salary restrictions and structural inequities in 2018, and efforts by the English Women's National Team (EWNT) to attain pay and support commensurate to their success representing a relatively new domestic league (the WSL). These four populations of athletes were selected because they share parallels in terms of conflicting demands in their positions as role models versus workers fighting to earn salaries worthy of their talent and abilities. By examining the social media posts, media coverage, and discourse of federation officials, particularly of men's leagues with supervisory power over women's sports, we can explicate how pay inequity discourse functions to impact female athletes' material lives.

CONFRONTING INEQUITY: VARYING STRATEGIES

Our collective case studies illustrate how the myth of pay equity progress becomes exposed through direct confrontation and reified when players engage in polite negotiation. As we'll discuss, pay equity is more than the numbers on a paycheck, but rather a discursive affirmation of players as valued and respected or dismissed as secondary and undeserving of respect.

Direct Confrontation and the Leveraging of Social Media

Through direct, public confrontations in the collective bargaining space, female athletes reveal systemic structures in their sports as undervaluing and dismissive of their participation. By leveraging social media pressure, boycotts, and lawsuits, female athletes highlight the ways in which their leagues or national associations view them as less than their male counterparts, thus instigating public ridicule of their organizations as well as an acknowledgment of the systemic issues women face.

In their use of social media, female athletes aimed to sway public opinion, provide a way for fans to engage in their confrontation, and to directly respond to dismissive rhetoric, thus taking on patriarchy and capitalism head on. Such direct confrontation puts the women at risk of public ridicule as well. For WNBA players, they faced significant criticism for their pay equity advocacy and were told to stay in their lane or "stay in the kitchen" (Marchant, 2019, para. 10). Such rhetoric aimed to demean players and reassert a hierarchy where female athletes are secondary, but the players challenged such efforts. A'ja Wilson, 2018 Rookie of the Year and future 2020 WNBA Most Valuable Player, called out her critics using a crying-laughing emoji and cautioning: "I pray for your future daughters wanna play basketball then maybe you'd chill on all the hate and get a better understanding" (Zucker, 2018, para. 8). Wilson's teammate, Kayla McBride, also responded to these insults, telling them to, "Stay in your lane homie because you not out there hoopin every night. Like I am" (Lough, 2018, para. 5). The players' comments challenge persistent assumptions about the inferiority of women's basketball, as compared to men's basketball at any level (Lavelle, 2012).

As noted by WNBA Player Union president Nneke Ogwumike (2018), players were not demanding "LeBron Money" (in reference to the $154M he received in his 2018 contract), but more equitable compensation for their work. In support, WNBA player Kelsey Plum tweeted: "I'm tired of people thinking that us players are asking for the same type of money as NBA players. We are asking for the same percentage of revenue shared within our CBA" (Similien, 2018). Unfortunately, WNBA players faced the misperception that they wanted the same pay as their male counterparts, thus their advocacy for equity was not supported. This allowed the WNBA to continue to "suppre[ss] the values of the league's top players" (Barnes, 2018, para. 9) and criticism of the league continued. As Ogwumike wrote in a public essay: "Everyone is going to talk about the bad things about the WNBA, maybe because it validates their belief that they don't feel the league is viable" (as cited in Weiner, 2019, para. 31).

Even worse, the criticism of the league was not only from fans, but also NBA Commissioner Adam Silver, as he made two primary public criticisms of the WNBA. First, he thought ticket sales did not generate enough revenue (Weiner, 2019) despite the significant cost differences between WNBA and NBA tickets (Berri, 2018), the shorter WNBA season, and in some cases, playing in smaller arenas ("Some WNBA teams," 2018). Second, he was concerned that the WNBA had lost money every season it had existed (Fader, 2018), even though some individual teams were profitable (Voepel, 2018). He lamented that "at the end of the day, the consumer always wins, and right now, we don't have a winning consumer proposition" (as quoted in Fader, 2018, para. 35). This reflects a common criticism facing women's leagues even though nine out of 30 NBA teams lost money during the 2016–17 season (Windhorst & Lowe, 2017). Silver's WNBA criticisms operate as "the maintenance of privileged systems of capitalism" (Clair & Thompson, 1996, p. 17). This differential treatment exemplifies how gender essentialism is a "market ideology," where the "gender-neutral market principles now argued to account for gender disparities in investment resources between elite men and women's sports" (Allison, 2018, pp. 137–38). Instead of considering structural inequities faced by women's leagues, financial losses are used as proof of their unsustainability and lack of worth.

In contrast, the U.S. women's national teams in hockey and soccer both successfully leveraged public support via social media using clear and consistent social media messages. Hockey players used the same tweet in their 2017 call to action: "Today I will do what others won't do so tomorrow, I can change what others can't. I said no to USAH (USA Hockey) and will not play in the 2017WC #BeBoldforChange" (Springer, 2017, para. 11). As explained by team captain Hilary Knight, this hashtag was utilized because after years of quietly fighting for better treatment, players needed a more effective approach (Reslen, 2017). USA Hockey had a long history of minimizing the achievements and, as will be illustrated in the next section, even the existence of the women's team.

Beginning in 2016, the women's soccer team began using the hashtag: #equalplayequalpay (Sauerbrunn, 2016). The use of the hashtag coincided with players Alex Morgan, Hope Solo, Megan Rapinoe, Carli Lloyd, and Becky Sauerbrunn filing a "charge of discrimination" with the U.S. Equal Employment Opportunity Commission (McCann, 2016, para. 2). The hashtag also coincided with the five players wearing shirts with the statement. The action followed prior American players' advocacy for equality in relation to field surfaces for the 2015 World Cup, including photos of turf burn and the gaps in turf fields (Dockterman, 2015). And, as the team explained in a *Player's Tribune* article, women playing on any surface or inferior field is expected from women but not men, despite the risks to player safety (USWNT, 2015). Importantly, the hashtag and its broader message transcended social media; it was chanted at games, a talking point around the team, and even mentioned in a major Nike ad after the 2019 Women's World Cup that referenced a glass ceiling breaking and ended with "This team wins. Everyone wins" (CNN, 2019). The hashtag continues to be used by fans in posts on Twitter about the team.

These three examples illustrate the ways that female athletes used social media to force the conversation regarding their collective bargaining agreements. In the case of women's hockey, players negotiated with USA Hockey for more than fourteen months (Reslen, 2017) and pushed for improved salary and benefits for a decade (Berkman, 2017a), which as we'll see later, matches women's soccer's efforts. The women's hockey team also received strong support from other professional sports player unions, such as the NBA, MLB, and NFL (Littlefield, 2017). In the WNBA, the most high-profile players advocating for pay equity (Liz Cambage, A'ja Wilson, and Skylar Diggins-Smith) are black women, who face intersectional racism and discrimination based on racism and sexism in the workplace outside of sports (Parker, 2013). While these approaches make players vulnerable to criticism, they also make the inequities transparent by bringing forward their dismissal through overt rhetoric they face from their organizing bodies.

Boycotts and Lawsuits as a Challenge to Ideology of Gratitude

Female athletes have also engaged in boycotts to challenge the expectation of gratitude. The ideology of gratitude promotes slow and incremental change, but in boycotting, female athletes highlight how patriarchy and capitalism undervalue their efforts. USA Hockey forced women's players to choose between their Olympic dreams and earning a living wage. With insufficient financial support, women's players could not train and play hockey full-time like their male counterparts. In justifying these low stipends, USA Hockey argued that no player received a salary; stipends only provided Olympic training support (Berkman, 2017a). In contrast, men's players can earn a living wage in their professional league as the lowest salary in the NHL is $575,00, whereas the top salary in the NWHL was $17,000 (McDermott, 2017). This inequity and lack of support inspired the women's team's boycott of an international tournament, thus exposing USA Hockey's insufficient support to grow the women's game and unwillingness to support female athletes comparably to their male counterparts. By denying players a living wage, it perpetuates the assumption that players are expected to function as exemplars for children while not properly compensated for their work as professional athletes (Allison, 2016).

The boycott also served to spotlight the slow process of negotiation between the players and federation. As observed by Jocelyne Lamoureux-Davidson, "we hope eventually they want to give us a call and give us a talk . . . we're ready to sit at a table and figure this out" (Berkman, 2017b, para. 17). Team captain Meghan Duggan urged USA Hockey to "stop treating us like an afterthought" (para. 3) because "we have represented our country with dignity and deserve to be treated with fairness and respect" (Berkman, 2017a, para. 2).

Part of Lamoureaux-Davidson and Duggan's motivation was due to the numerous resources provided to male players. For example, USA Hockey provided U.S.$3.5 million to facilitate training and support boy's hockey and another U.S.$1.4 million supporting a U20 men's hockey league (Reslen,

2017). While USA Hockey Executive Director Dave Ogrean emphasized the rise in girl's hockey in public statements during contract negotiations, this increase was not due to USA Hockey's financial support (Berkman, 2017a). As explained by U.S. Women's captain Kacey Bellamy, the threatened boycott aimed to secure more equitable resources to subsidize girls' hockey (Saxena, 2017). Instead, this lack of resources "creates a bottleneck that keeps women from pursuing the sport professionally" (Saxena, 2017, para. 6). By withholding equitable financial support, USA Hockey contends that the women's league is unimportant and promotes the "assumption that female athletes lacks value" (Allison, 2016, p. 255).

In response to the boycott, USA Hockey began reaching out to youth players, but such efforts were thwarted by national team members as younger players understood and endorsed the boycott (Berkman, 2017b; Wattles, 2017). For instance, team captain "Meghan Duggan called every single player down to the U18s to ensure the boycott succeeded," while simultaneously coaching college hockey and playing professionally (Linehan quoted in Johnson, 2018, para. 13). This parallels efforts that the U.S. women's soccer team engaged in prior to the 1996 Olympics (Wahl, 2019) and undermines the patriarchal emphasis on gratitude by ensuring a boycott's success.

Ultimately, the boycott resulted in sixteen U.S. senators indicating that USA Hockey was in violation of the Ted Stevens Olympic and Amateur Sports Act and the women's team "deserve[d] fairness and respect" (Howard, 2017, para. 31). This public pressure from players and allies resulted in a last minute agreement (McDermott, 2017), thus providing a "win" for the players over an ideology of gratitude and a response to the assumptions about the perceived lack of value of women's sports (Allison, 2016).

The USWNT has long faced the obstacle of a federation that wanted to leverage the popularity and public support of the team while dismissing calls for equity by characterizing boycotting players as choosing "not to play for their country" (Soccer America, 2000, para. 6). Such characterization aimed to deflect blame from the organization and undermine the players' boycotting position while reinforcing the ideology of gratitude. But that characterization didn't gain traction as the framing of the resulting agreement was of players ending the boycott (Longman, 2000). Both U.S. national teams' efforts illustrate how boycotts can advance female athletes' interests in equity; they both also illustrate how it has always been about more than pay and about respect for them, their efforts, and the future of their games.

After years of responding to pushes for pay equity by noting the team had the highest financial support of any women's team internationally (Soccer America, 2000), the frustration toward an expectation of gratitude and incrementalism from U.S. Soccer bubbled over in 2016 and 2019 with multiple lawsuits and more aggressive, direct confrontation in an attempt to force accountability. As Michelle Akers noted in 2016, the EEOC filing directly confronted an expectation of gratitude, "It's so frustrating, and it's surprising. Now? Still? It's been so many years and we've had so much success and there have been so many changes . . . But the stance is a constant: 'Look, you guys are lucky to play. You guys should be grateful to play'" (Peterson, 2016, para. 3). The EEOC filing was framed as the "latest salvo in what has been a long-simmering issue for the national team" (Peterson, 2016, para. 12). The women's collective frustration and anger over their dismissal and disrespect was central to both filings, illustrating how it was always about more than their individual salaries. As highly decorated player and team leader Alex Morgan offered on Facebook: "This is not only about equal pay—we get paid less than half of our male counterparts—but also equal treatment. We deserve to play in top-notch, grass-only facilities like the U.S. Men's National Team, not dangerous turf fields. We want to have decent travel accommodations" (quoted in Peterson, 2016, para. 23).

The USWNT players' 2019 lawsuit was initiated on International Women's Day, its own symbolic declaration that incrementalism hasn't led to change. What has changed over the years is "how the country sees the USWNT. . . . [T]he USWNT is more famous than ever—but that doesn't mean they're now actually getting paid anything near what they're worth" (Kliegman, 2019, para. 8). The change in the team's public perception was illustrated by chants for equal pay that followed them throughout the 2019 Women's World Cup and at their victory parade. As will be contrasted with England, this previous patient push by the U.S. team bubbled over with the lawsuit and served as a catalytic moment.

As highlighted in the recent documentary, *LFG*, the very public dispute between USWNT and U.S. Soccer served to expose the sexism at the root of U.S. Soccer (Fine & Fine, 2021). U.S. Soccer president Carlos Cordeiro was roundly booed while speaking at the victory parade while star player Megan Rapinoe remarked that she was sure that the two parties would smooth things out. But as the film illustrates, tensions escalated between the players and organization. The confrontation culminated in the team turning their warmup tops inside out at the 2020 SheBelieves Cup following a filing from U.S. Soccer that indicated women players are physically inferior to their male counterparts as justification for the inequitable pay and treatment. The players' action used their physical bodies as a site of confrontation—each providing stern looks into the camera with only the four stars and crest outline visible in pre-game photographs. This bodily performance went viral and led many sponsors to further support the players and their pay equity advocacy. In forcing a response from U.S. Soccer (and Cordeiro's subsequent resignation), the lawsuit's direct confrontation forced the federation to publicize their

perceptions, thus revealing the patriarchy women face, although with capital-
ist forces siding with the players as they are better for business.

Polite Negotiation and the Continuation of Inequity

While in the United States, basketball, hockey, and soccer players have
recently used direct confrontational strategies that are in line with the type
of sport discourse that is common, this contrasts with the polite advocacy of
the EWNT. Ultimately, such polite negotiation reinforces inequity because it
characterizes incremental changes as improvements to be grateful for rather
than spurring conversations about how dominant sport institutions repeatedly dismiss female athletes and their labor. Like we saw with USA Hockey
and U.S. Soccer, the FA advances an ideology of gratitude by emphasizing
incremental change; when taken up by the players, the focus shifts on how far
things have come rather than how far they must go.

The EWNT negotiated a £4,000 pay increase to their central contracts up
to £20,000 a year and the number of hours players could work in secondary jobs to supplement their income was raised from 18 to 24 hours a week
(Magowan, 2013). The deal was successfully negotiated by then England
player Eniola Aluko, a qualified lawyer, whose teammates unanimously
voted her as their representative for negotiations. Alongside increased pay,
gradual improvements in the EWNT's facilities and work conditions, such
as routine premium class flights to matches overseas and access to the FA's
St George's Park training, sport science and rehabilitation facility, occurred.
It must be noted, however, that such provisions are far from widespread at
the club level. For example, players at the top tier finally received mandatory medical care provisions in 2019, while players in other clubs have had
to crowdsource funding for their own medical treatment for injuries (Wrack,
2019). Further incremental progress has since occurred with the FA paying
the EWNT the same match fees and bonuses as men for international games
outside of major tournaments since January 2020, despite vast differences
remaining in major tournaments overseen by FIFA and UEFA (Taylor, 2020).

While the FA's provision of high quality facilities for the men's game is
taken as given, the introduction of such provision for the EWNT was celebrated by the FA and the football press (Black & Fielding-Lloyd, 2019).
The relatively muted celebration of steps taken towards more equitable pay
structures are emblematic of the general lack of debate about pay structures in
women's English football. After her successful negotiation of increased central contracts for the EWNT, Eni Aluko was not celebrated as an advocate or
role model for gender equality in either football popular culture or the mainstream press. There was actually much bemusement that no formal announcement occurred by the FA of their policy change to equal international match

fees in January 2020. Rather than taking the opportunity to promote and celebrate their increasingly equitable treatment of national players, the increased payments were only made public nine months later when the FA was directly asked if they intended to follow Brazil's lead in providing equal pay for international caps (Taylor, 2020). As a result, the opportunity was missed, or more likely avoided, by the FA to elevate public conversations about pay equity that may have been expected following the professionalization of women's football.

Indeed, since the launch of the WSL in 2011, the rhetoric of pay equity has been a tentative, polite and patient advocacy, which is exemplified below by former Manchester United Women's Head Coach Casey Stoney: "I think we will only get paid the same when we bring in the same sort of revenue as the men's game. We need to work on our marketing and we need to become more visible; we have to get more people into our games before we can start talking about equal pay" (Wilson, 2020, para. 4). Similarly, even Aluko, the player who negotiated the central pay increase for the EWNT in 2013, is muted in her demands for equal pay. While conceding that the women's game in England is poorly administered which limits fan attendance, she states that "we are paid less, but that's because we don't bring anywhere close to the same amount of crowds, and that's just a fact" (quoted in Ellis-Petersen, 2016, para. 24).

In minimizing opportunities to highlight conversations about pay equity, and treating it as a straightforward gender-neutral economic issue, rather than a discursive one, the root cause of inequity isn't exposed. The WSL players' and coaches' apparent acceptance of the rhetoric that pay inequity is a simple matter of market values is, as discussed above, a common trope within equity debates. However, there needs to be a critique of precisely who the "we" is in the above quotes that must "work on the marketing" or "bring in the crowds." It is difficult to see how players and coaches have the capacity to make such changes without the sustained investment that English men's elite football has enjoyed in recent decades. Unfortunately, the emblematic quotes above suggest a perception that accountability for progress in women's football rests with the women themselves rather than their governing organization.

It is ironic that Casey Stoney has since protested the substandard investment in her own team, Manchester United, which thwarted their progress. After what were described as "several polite attempts" by Stoney and the players to request improvements to their training facilities and housing, and contemplating a pre-season strike (Crafton & Whyatt, 2021), Stoney resigned as team manager and at the time of writing has accepted a position as the head coach of San Diego Wave FC in the U.S.

The acceptance of pay inequity as, for the moment, fair and something that should be accepted while being patient for incremental change, tells us much about the prevailing culture of English football and how its hierarchies are maintained despite the potential benefits that professionalization may bring to the women's game. In contrast to other examples provided in this chapter, polite advocacy silences arguments for equal pay in favor of reproducing an ideology of gratitude.

In conjunction with polite advocacy, and similarly to the popular representations of women hockey and soccer players in the United States as inspiring people (Peterson, 2016), professional women's football in England has been promoted in recent years by both the FA and the mass media as a site for the construction of "role models" for young women and girls who will inspire the next generation of women football players. Interestingly, such inspiration is not represented by stories of striving for social justice or equal access to play and resources, but about the women's game being a bastion for wholesome personal betterment and morally superior play (Black & Fielding-Lloyd, 2019). For example, on the day of the EWNT's return from a successful World Cup campaign in 2015, the FA tweeted "Our #Lionesses go back to being mothers, partners and daughters today, but they have taken on another title - heroes" ("England can go," 2015). On the same day, the FA also launched the "We Can Play" campaign that presented the players as inspirational role models:

> Before going their separate ways, head coach Mark Sampson and his squad came together for one last time to show their support for a campaign that is close to their hearts in the hope that they have inspired a new generation of women footballers to take up the beautiful game. ("Lioness return and," 2015, para. 2)

As a result, it would seem in bad taste and ungrateful of players to explicitly position themselves as workers and demand improved pay and conditions, despite their recent professionalization, in an environment where they are celebrated for their positive impact on young girls. However, as Rigauer (1981) points out, characterizing athletes as socially responsible role models obscures the work structures of sport. Thus, the EWNT are presented as symbols of incremental progress, but only in ways that support the status quo and minimize any disruption to both the organization and the prevailing gender order of the sport. The polite negotiation of pay structures in English women's football and the muted compliance with role model discourses ultimately fail to expose the current realities of inequity in the sport. Incremental improvements are successfully reified as something to be grateful for (how far things have come) rather than as instigating conversation as to how female athletes and their labor continue to be trivialized (how far there is to go).

The tensions between advancing equal treatment for themselves as workers and supporting the organization that governs their sport were laid bare in 2017 when the EWNT played Russia. At the time, Aluko had recently accused then England coach Mark Sampson of racism, harassment, and bullying. When Nikita Parris scored the EWNT's first goal, the entire team of eleven players ran to celebrate with Sampson, who was standing on the sidelines, and embraced him as a group. Parris subsequently admitted that the group gesture was intended to indicate support for Sampson (Skilbeck, 2017). While Parris herself was not a team member at the time of the alleged incidents, several other team members were.

The player's bodily and public endorsement of Sampson, and seemingly direct rebuttal of Aluko's allegations, were criticized by Aluko and Lianne Sanderson (a black teammate who supported Aluko's allegations). Aluko noted the irony of the EWNT's claims of "togetherness" when, as detailed above, it was Aluko who had negotiated the increase to their central contracts on the team's behalf ("England women's celebration," 2017). Sanderson claimed that the EWNT endorsed Sampson because they feared that they would be dropped otherwise; not an unreasonable conclusion since Aluko never played for England again after making her allegations (Skilbeck, 2017).

We would argue that the team's actions that day were a physical manifestation of the expectations that many female athletes internalize: be grateful for the, albeit inferior, support they receive for playing their sport professionally or face consequences. The team's actions also served to attack dissenters to the governing institution (the FA) and its culture. The symbolic attack on Aluko was particularly troubling given the specific nature of her allegations and the current lack of racial diversity within the EWNT (Wrack, 2021). It should be noted that Parris, who is also black, has since apologized for her actions apparently as a result of reflecting on current debates around the Black Lives Matter movement in sport culture (de Menezes, 2020). Furthermore, in their analysis of media narratives of the allegations, Velija and Silvani (2021) demonstrate how Aluko was framed as an outsider to the game through her race, the validity and seriousness of her claims were delegitimized, and that Aluko herself was presented as the problem rather than Sampson and the culture of elite women's football itself. They argue that such framings deny those who are critical of powerful sport institutions (such as the FA) a voice and, we would add, minimize the potential for critiquing the status quo.

CONCLUSION

The advocacy for pay and benefit equity in the WNBA, the U.S. and U.K.'s women's football teams, and U.S. women's hockey all demonstrate that despite differing contexts, they face similar types of discrimination and dismissal. They are discouraged from pushing too much against misogyny, racism, and for equitable pay and support by focusing less on their specific demands and instead comparing them to men's sports (without considering the differential resources devoted to them) and by treating them as symbols of equality and role models for young girls instead of as athletes. In this chapter, we explored the ways in which the ideology of gratitude is upheld in discourse and decision making in regard to pay and benefit equity in women's team sports. Small, incremental levels of support have enabled powerful institutions of sport, in these cases U.S. Soccer, WNBA, USA Hockey and the FA, to divert attention from, and their accountability for, the outstanding need for significant and fundamental change to actual support and investment in women's sports.

Cultural change in women's sports means that there needs to be "an influx of capital and an organizational commitment to invest and take risks" (Johnson, 2018, para. 26). Instead of treating women's sports and their pay inequity as a "rational market" (Clair & Thompson, 1996, p. 5), scholars must explore the systems of inequity that perpetuate pay inequity. Pay equity operates as a material rhetoric that denotes worth. Pay and benefit equity are fundamental issues for sustaining women's sports leagues as well as their impact beyond sports. If women cannot earn a living wage to be full-time athletes like their male counterparts, their progress will stall. If women's team sports in the U.S. and UK are to dismantle an ideology of gratitude to become athletes who are fairly compensated for their work, they need to have the recognition, support, and equitable pay that they deserve as professional athletes. And if women's sports are to be respected as a sphere of economic and cultural worth, the powerful institutions of sport need to not settle for gradual, incremental change but ambitiously invest with all the risk that it may entail.

REFERENCES

Allison, R. (2016). Business or cause? Gendered institutional logics in women's professional soccer. *Journal of Sport and Social Issues, 40,* 237–262. https://doi.org/10.1177/0193723515615349

Allison, R. (2018). *Kicking center: Gender and the selling of women's professional soccer.* New Brunswick, NJ: Rutgers University Press.

Barnes, K. (2018, April 20). A shift in the WNBA season? Show me the money. *ESPNW.com.* http://www.espn.com/wnba/story/_/id/26545363/mvp-stewart-ruptures-achilles-likely-19

Berkman, S. (2017a, March 15). U.S. Women's Hockey Team plans to boycott World Championship over pay dispute. *New York Times.* https://www.nytimes.com/2017/03/15/sports/hockey/team-usa-women-boycott-world-championships.html

Berkman, S. (2017b, March 16). Women's national team stands firm in face of U.S.A. Hockey's deadline. *New York Times.* https://www.nytimes.com/2017/03/16/sports/hockey/usa-hockey-women-boycott.html

Berri, D. (2018, September 4). WNBA players are simply asking for a greater share of WNBA revenues. *Forbes.com.* https://www.forbes.com/sites/davidberri/2018/09/04/what-wnba-players-want/#2c47573f33eb

Black, J. & Fielding-Lloyd, B. (2019). Re-establishing the "outsiders": English press coverage of the 2015 FIFA Women's World Cup. *International Review for the Sociology of Sport, 54,* 282–301. https://doi.org/10.1177/1012690217706192

Clair, R. P. & Thompson, K. (1996). Pay discrimination as a discursive and material practice: A case concerning extended housework. *Journal of Applied Communication, 24,* 1–20.

CNN. (2019, July 8). *Nike releases empowering ad after Team USA's win* [Video]. CNN. https://www.cnn.com/videos/business/2019/07/08/nike-ad-uswnt-womens-world-cup-team-usa-equal-pay-stewart-binks-sot-nr-vpx.cnn

Cooky, C. & Antunovic, D. (2020). "This isn't just about us": Articulations of feminism in media narratives of athlete activism. *Communication & Sport, 8,* 692–711. https://doi.org/10.1177/2167479519896360

Cooky, C., Council, L. D., Mears, M. A., & Mesnner, M. A. (2021). One and done: The long eclipse of women's televised sports, 1989–2019. *Communication & Sport, 9,* 347–371. https://doi.org/10.1177/21674795211003524

Cooky, C., & Messner, M. A. (2018). *No slam dunk: Gender, sport and the unevenness of social change.* New Brunswick, NJ: Rutgers University Press. https://doi.org/10.1177/21674795211003524

Crafton, A. & Whyatt, K. (2021, July 10). Inside the chaos at Man United women: Talk of pre-season strike, crisis talks with Ed Woodward and substandard training facilities. *The Athletic.* https://theathletic.com/2698027/2021/07/10/inside-chaos-at-manchester-united-women/?article_source=search&search_query=CASEY%20STONEY

Crowley, S. (1999). Afterword: The material of rhetoric. In J. Selzer & S. Crowley (eds.), *Rhetorical Bodies* (pp. 357–364). Madison: University of Wisconsin Press.

Culvin, A. (2019). *Football as Work: The new realities of professional women footballers in England.* [Doctoral thesis, University of Central Lancashire]. Semantic Scholar.

de Menezes, J. (2020, June 14). Eni Aluko accepts Nikita Parris's apology over Mark Sampson celebration and says "black women should always strive for unity." *The Independent.* https://www.independent.co.uk/sport/football/womens_football/eni-aluko-mark-sampson-celebration-nikita-parris-apology-twitter-a9565621.html

Dockterman, E. (2015, December 8). US Women's Soccer Team refuses to play on turf. *Time.* https://time.com/4140786/womens-soccer-team-turf/

Ellis-Petersen, H. (2016, June 11). "I won't be paid the same as Wayne Rooney, because I'm not Wayne Rooney." *The Guardian.* https://www.theguardian.com/football/2016/jun/11/eniola-aluko-i-wont-be-paid-the-same-as-wayne-rooney-because-im-not-wayne-rooney

England "can go back to being mothers, partners, and daughters" says FA tweet. (2015). *The Guardian.* https://www.theguardian.com/football/2015/jul/06/england -women-twitter-world-cup-mothers-partners-daughters

England women's celebration surprises Mark Sampson, angers Eni Aluko. (2017, September 19). *ESPN.com.* https://www.espn.com/soccer/england/story/3208535/england-womens-celebration-surprises-mark-sampson-and-angers-eni-aluko

Evans, M. (2017). *The persistence of gender inequality.* Cambridge: Polity Press.

Fader, M. (2018, October 29). Inside the WNBA's fight for higher pay. *BleacherReport.com.* https://bleacherreport.com/articles/2802759-inside-the -wnbas-fight-for-higher-pay

Fielding-Lloyd, B. & Woodhouse, D. (in press). Responsibility and progress: The English Football Association's professionalization of women's soccer. In A. Bowes & A. Culvin (eds.), *International perspectives on the professionalization of women's football.* Bingley, UK: Emerald Publishing.

Fine, A. N. & Fine, S. (Directors). (2021). *LFG* [Film]. HBO Max.

Graham Davies, S., McGregor, J., Pringle, J. & Giddings, J. (2018). Rationalizing pay inequity: Women engineers, pervasive patriarchy and the neoliberal chimera. *Journal of Gender Studies, 27,* 623–636. https://doi.org/10.1080/09589236.2017.1284048

Howard, J. (2017, March 29). With deal reached, U.S. women's national hockey team will play at world championships. *ESPN.com.* https://www.espn.com/olympics/story/_/id/19026627/usa-hockey-us-women-national-team-reach-agreement-avoid -boycott

Johnson, K. (2018, February 20). The legacy of this U.S. Women's Hockey Team is already secure. *The Ringer.* https://www.theringer.com/olympics/2018/2/20/17031044/united-states-women-hockey-winter-olympics-sport-future

Kliegman, J. (2019, June 10). Nothing and everything has changed for the USWNT. *The Ringer.* https://www.theringer.com/soccer/2019/6/10/18656696/us-womens -national-team-world-cup-lawsuit-1999-megan-rapinoe

Koller, D. (2019). The new gender equity in elite women's sports. In N. Lough & A. N. Geurin (eds.), *Routledge handbook of the business of women's sports* (pp. 217–227). London: Routledge.

Lavelle, K. L. (2012). Great Expectations: An analysis of the fan base for WNBA's Expect Great. In A. C. Earnheardt, P. M. Haridakis, & B. S. Hugenberg (eds.), *Sports Fans, Identity, and Socialization* (pp. 237–254). Lanham, MD: Lexington Books.

Lavelle, K. L. (2015). As Venus Turns: A feminist soap opera analysis of *Venus Vs. Journal of Sports Media, 10,* 1–16. https://doi.org/10.1353/jsm.2015.0010

Littlefield, B. (2017, March 29). On hockey boycott: "Sometimes athletes lead the way." *WBUR.org.* https://www.wbur.org/onlyagame/2017/03/28/women-usa -hockey-national-team

Lionesses return and back we can play campaign. (2015, July 6). *The FA.* https://www.thefa.com/news/2015/jul/06/england-women-world-cup-squad-return-and -back-we-can-play-campaign-060715

Longman, J. (2000, January 30). Women's team ends boycott, agreeing to a contract. *New York Times.* https://www.nytimes.com/2000/01/30/sports/soccer-women-s -team-ends-boycott-agreeing-to-a-contract.html

Lough, N. (2018, August 9). The case for boosting WNBA player salaries. *The Conversation.* http://theconversation.com/the-case-for-boosting-wnba-player -salaries-100805

Magowan, A. (2013, January 15). England women footballers secure central contract increase. *BBC.* https://www.bbc.co.uk/sport/football/21010984

Marchant, B. (2019, April 2). "I'll clap back": A'ja Wilson takes on "trolls" and the pay gap in return to Columbia. *The State.com.* https://www.thestate.com/news/ politics-government/article228578784.html

Marthaler, J. (2020, December 11). Investors give NWSL the financing it deserves to develop league. *The Star Tribune.* https://www.startribune.com/investors-give -nwsl-the-financing-it-deserves-to-develop-league/573376031/

McCann, M. (2016, March 31). What's next in USWNT's wage discrimination case vs. U.S. Soccer? *SI.com.* https://www.si.com/soccer/2016/03/31/uswnt-us-soccer -wage-discrimination-equal-pay-eeoc-legal-analysis

McDermott, J. (2017, March 31). Sexism plagues hockey. *The Oberlin Review.* https: //oberlinreview.org/13182/sports/sexism-plagues-hockey/

McDonald, M. G. (2000). The marketing of the Women's National Basketball Association and the making of postfeminism. *International Review for the Sociology of Sport, 35,* 35–47. https://doi.org/10.1177/101269000035001003

Ogwumike, N. (2018, November 1). Bet on women. *The Player's Tribune.* https: //www.theplayerstribune.com/en-us/articles/nneka-ogwumike-wnba-cba-bet-on -women

Parker, K. (2013, December 11). On pay gap, millennial women near parity—For now despite gains, many see roadblocks ahead. *Pew Research Center.* https://www .pewsocialtrends.org/wp-content/uploads/sites/3/2013/12/gender-and-work_final .pdf

Peterson, A. M. (2016, April 16). History repeats: US women's soccer team still in wage fight. *AP News.* https://apnews.com/article/10df9310269c4d808e65637b799 6a70e

Reslen, E. (2017, October 2). The U.S. women's hockey team has no regrets about fighting for equal treatment. *Marie Claire.* https://www.marieclaire.com/culture/ a12655144/us-womens-hockey-team-equal-treatment-team-usa-media-summit/

Rigauer, B. (1981). *Sport and Work.* New York: Columbia University Press.

Ruthven, G. (2021, April 5). Investors have paid $325m for a place in MLS. But for how much longer? *The Guardian.* https://www.theguardian.com/football/2021/apr /05/mls-cost-for-new-team-soccer-us

Saxena, J. (2017, March 16). The U.S. Women's Hockey Team's boycott is about more than money. *Elle.* https://www.elle.com/culture/career-politics/news/a43860 /us-womens-hockey-teams-boycott-about-more-than-money/

Sauerbrunn, B. (@beckysauerbrunn). (2016, March 31). *Five players signed the complaint, but the decision to file was wholeheartedly supported by the entire team*

#equalplayequalpay #thegals [Tweet]. Twitter. https://twitter.com/beckysauerbrunn
/status/715525948075089920?s=20

Similien, C. (2018, October 25). Sexism keeps its chokehold on the WNBA with
gender wage disparity. *Ebony.com.* https://www.ebony.com/entertainment/sexism
-keeps-its-chokehold-on-the-wnba-with-gender-wage-disparity/

Skilbeck, J. (2017, September 20). Eniola Aluko accuses England Women of "disrespect" after goal celebration. *Evening Standard.* https://www.standard.co.uk/sport/
football/eniola-aluko-accuses-england-women-of-disrespect-after-goal-celebration
-a3638876.html

Soccer America. (2000, January 10). *Women's boycott: Behind the pay dispute.* https:
//www.socceramerica.com/publications/article/14512/womens-boycott-behind-the
-pay-dispute.html

Some WNBA teams downsizing arenas to help bottom line. (2018, July 9).
USA Today. https://www.usatoday.com/story/sports/wnba/2018/07/09/some-wnba
-teams-downsizing-arenas-to-help-bottom-line/36737011/

Springer, S. (2017, March 31). Women's hockey: Team USA boycotts like a girl—
and wins. *WBUR.org.* https://www.wbur.org/cognoscenti/2017/03/31/us-womens
-national-hockey-team-shira-springer

Szto, C., Pegoraro, A., Morris, E., Desrochers, M., Emard, K., Galas, K., Gamble, A.,
Knox, L., & Richards, K. (2020). #ForTheGame: Social Change and the Struggle
to Professionalize Women's Ice Hockey. *Sociology of Sport Journal.* Advanced
Online Publication. https://doi.org/10.1123/ssj.2020-0085

Taylor, L. (2020, September 3020). England women's and men's teams receive same
pay, FA reveals. *The Guardian.* https://www.theguardian.com/football/2020/sep/03
/england-womens-and-mens-teams-receive-same-pay-fa-reveals

USWNT. (2015, December 7). Equal footing. *The Player's Tribune.* https://
www.theplayerstribune.com/articles/uswnt-match-canceled-field-conditions?utm
_source=theplayerstribune&utm_medium=now-trending-banner&utm_campaign
=now-trending

Velija, P. & Silvani, L. (2021). Print media narratives of bullying and harassment at
the Football Association: A case study of Eniola Aluko. *Journal of Sport and Social
Issues, 45,* 358–373. https://doi.org/10.1177/0193723520958342

Voepel, M. (2018, November 7). Adam Silver isn't "disappointed" that WNBA
players opted out of CBA. *ESPN.com.* https://www.espn.com/wnba/story/_/id
/25205141/commissioner-adam-silver-disappointed-wnba-players-opted-cba-says
-nba-support-wnba-remains-firm

Wahl, G. (Host). (2019, May 22). *Throwback* [Audio podcast]. *SI.com.* https://www
.si.com/soccer/2019/05/22/throwback-podcast-sports-history

Wattles, J. (2017, March 17). Pay fight between USA Hockey and women's players
intensifies. *CNN.* https://money.cnn.com/2017/03/18/news/usa-womens-hockey
-equal-pay/index.html

Weiner, N. (2019, May 24). The WNBA is at a turning point, and the stakes could not
be higher. *SBNation.com.* https://www.sbnation.com/2019/5/24/18637167/state-of
-the-wnba-2019

Wilson, P. (2020, September 4). Manchester United's Casey Stoney: "We have some catching up to do in WSL." *The Guardian.* https://www.theguardian.com/football/2020/sep/04/manchester-united-casey-stoney-we-have-some-catching-up-to-do-in-wsl

Windhorst, B. & Lowe, Z. (2017, September 19). A confidential report shows nearly half the NBA lost money last season. Now what? *ESPN.com.* https://www.espn.com/nba/story/_/id/20747413/a-confidential-report-shows-nearly-half-nba-lost-money-last-season-now-what

Women's Super League & Women's Championship seasons ended immediately. (2020, May 25). https://www.bbc.com/sport/football/52797022

Wrack, S. (2019, September 17). Neglect of player welfare is something women's football must address fast. *The Guardian.* https://www.theguardian.com/football/blog/2019/sep/17/player-welfare-womens-football-medical-care-insurance

Wrack, S. (2021, February 25). English women's national team predominately white . . . *The Guardian.* https://www.theguardian.com/football/2021/feb/25/england-women-all-white-xi-shines-light-on-a-deep-rooted-problem

Zucker, J. (2018, July 2). WNBA stars sound off on pay gap in wake of LeBron James deal. *High Post Hoops.* https://highposthoops.com/2018/07/02/wnba-stars-pay-gap-lebron-james-deal/

Chapter 12

Standwith Caster

Twitter, Intersectionality, and the IAAF's DSD Policy

Alison N. Novak

On an overcast day in Monaco on April 26, 2018, International Association of Athletics Federations (IAAF) leader Sebastian Coe announced new eligibility regulations for female classification in sports (Bloom, 2018). The new policy would restrict any female-identifying athlete with above average levels of androgens like testosterone from competing in IAAF running events from 400m to one mile in distance (IAAF, 2019). For many, the IAAF's announcement was clearly directed to one athlete who served as the focus of a 10-year debate on biology and gender identity in sports: Caster Semenya (Jackson, 2019). The South African middle-distance runner held records in several distances, all between 400m and the mile (BBC Sport, 2019). She also has elevated levels of testosterone, a likely result of a condition called hyperandrogenism (although she has never publicly confirmed this diagnosis; Jackson, 2019). Since 2009, her dominance in track was criticized by competitors, journalists, and members of the IAAF who argued that her elevated testosterone levels give her an unfair advantage in the sport (Palacios Ibañez, 2018). Since 2011, the IAAF supported controversial guidelines which prevented her from participating in women's track events (Dworkin, 2013). Although early restrictions were overturned through a legal appeals process, most recent rules established in 2018 (currently appealed) bar her from entry into races including Olympic trials (Mather & Longman, 2019).

Throughout this process, Semenya has been subjected to debates over identity, social categorization, and inclusivity in sports.[1] Debates on these topics occur between athletes and professional sporting organizations, journalists, and members of the public. At various points over the past decade, #CasterSemenya, #StandWithCaster and #HandsOffCaster trended on Twitter (Palacios Ibañez, 2018). Embedded in Twitter posts are messages that challenge and renegotiate the intersectional categories of identity based on perceptions of Semenya's experience. As noted by previous research, this renegotiation process is critical to understanding how discourses about Semenya materialize and reflect intersectionality in sports (Berger & Guidroz, 2009; Dworkin et al., 2013; Voelker & Harvey, 2018). Therefore, studying Twitter conversations about Semenya provides insight into how users renegotiate categories against the backdrop of evolving regulations (Ibañez, 2018; Dworkin et al., 2013).

This chapter seeks to answer the following questions: How do users invoke Semenya to challenge or renegotiate the categories of race and sex? How do users characterize their support or opposition to IAAF regulations? These questions are important as Twitter users consider ways to protest or advocate against the IAAF's rulings, which previous scholarship suggests may be the beginning stages of social movements (Dagkas, 2016). Through a critical discourse analysis adapted from Gee (2010) of #CasterSemenya tweets, this chapter provides insights into intersectionality in sports and regulations in international competition.

Caster Semenya

Semenya is a middle-distance track runner who holds the world record in the 600m and national records in the 400m, 800m, 1000m, and 1500m events. She also won Olympic gold medals in 2012 and 2016 in the 800m.

Initial scrutiny developed after her record-breaking performance in the 800m and 1500m races at the 2009 World Championship. In addition to beating her personal best by eight seconds in the 800m and 25 seconds in the 1500m (set just one month prior), news media characterized her changing appearance as more masculine with darker facial hair on her upper lip, a deeper voice, and a more severe jawline (Kessel, 2009; Fordyce, 2009). To address athletic and media concerns, the IAAF announced it would require a sex verification test to confirm her identity as a woman (IAAF, 2009). *Guardian* reporter Smith (2009) noted, "The IAAF says it was obliged to investigate after Semenya's . . . dramatic breakthroughs that usually arouse suspicion of drug use." However, others cautioned that the IAAF's investigation was motivated by racism: "many in South Africa believe it has a racial dimension" (Smith, 2009, para. 4). These critiques were propelled by the head of South African athletics, Chuene, who called the IAAF's actions racist and added, "Who are white people to question the makeup of an African girl?" (Smith, 2009, para. 12).

The sex verification test took months and required reports from a gyne-cologist, endocrinologist, psychologist, internal medicine specialist, and gender expert (Bennet, 2015). On July 6, 2010, Semenya was cleared for competing in women's athletic events, although the results of her tests were never shared due to privacy restrictions. In 2011, the IAAF established a framework for determining if female athletes with hyperandrogenism could compete in athletic events. The rule established, IAAF "shall recommend that the athlete is eligible to compete in women's competition if: (1) She has androgen levels below the normal range; or (2) She has androgen levels within the normal range but has an androgen resistance such that she derives no competitive advantage from having androgen levels in the normal male range" (Erdener, 2015).

However, in 2015, the IAAF was forced to suspend policies on hyperan-drogenism after the Court of Arbitration for Sport decided "Dutee Chand v. Athletics Federation of India (AFI) & IAAF." The court ruled Chand, a junior runner with hyperandrogenism, should be allowed to compete in women's events, despite her above-normal levels of testosterone (Hutcheon, 2015): "The court found that "the Regulations—in taking effect to bar some ath-letes from participating in any competitive athletics, whether in the male or female category, in their natural state—were 'antithetical to the fundamental principle of Olympism that *'Every individual must have the possibility of practicing sport, without discrimination of any kind,'* and imposed a 'signifi-cant detriment' on the athletes concerned" (para. 2). The court also found that the IAAF's claim, that hyperandrogenism improves athletic performance by 12%, was insufficiently supported (Hutcheon, 2015).

After winning a silver medal in 2012 in the 800m event (upgraded to gold after Russian gold medalist Savinova was banned for doping), Semenya won a gold medal in 2016 in the same event. Moments after the race, sixth-place finisher, Lynsey Sharp, gave an emotional interview reflecting, "Everyone can see it's two separate races so there's nothing I can do" (Stevens, 2016, para. 11). This was echoed by other finishers including fifth-placed Jozwik (Poland) who argued she was the first European finisher and considered herself a white silver medalist in the same event (Critchley, 2016). Karkazis (2016) reflected that the aftermath of the 800m event was one of the "most vitriolic media and social media uproars I can recall, one in which the athletes were the casualties. And . . . IAAF did nothing to quell it."

In April 2018, IAAF leader Coe announced rules focused on "differences on sex development" (DSD) which required athletes with testosterone levels of 5 nmol/L and above to take medication to reduce testosterone levels when competing in events between 400m and one mile (IAAF, 2019). The rules reflected findings from IAAF research that, "concluded that female athletes with naturally high testosterone levels in those specific disciplines benefited from an advantage over their rivals" (Bloom, 2018). Young (2018) reflected,

> But the decade-in-the-making legal standard announced today boils down to *Caster Semenya can't run because she has the characteristics of Caster Semenya*. In other words, she's too good, so she must be stopped . . . The IAAF found something about her, and arbitrarily decided that was the difference between a woman and a man. She's black and "breathtakingly butch" and from rural Africa, so instead of marketing her like Ledecky, her sport decided to spend nine years digging into her biology in an effort to find something, anything, to justify getting her off the track. None of those attempts have stuck yet, although this looks like it has the best shot. And no athlete in history has a more credible claim that the people who run her sport are simply out to get her.

Two months later, Semenya challenged the IAAF's new regulations in international court. However, on May 1, 2019, the Court for Arbitration of Sport announced it would reject her challenge, allowing the new rules to take effect in May 2019. After Semenya appealed the decision to the Federal Supreme Court of Switzerland, the court suspended the DSD rules with respect to Semenya until it issued a ruling (BBC Sport, 2019). However, on July 31, 2019, the court reversed its earlier decision, leaving Semenya ineligible for races between 400m and one mile until it concluded the case. The IAAF welcomed the court ruling and argued "there are some contexts, sport being one of them, where biology has to trump gender identity" (IAAF, 2019; Mather & Longman, 2019).[2]

Intersectionality

Gregory (2019) reflects "Her case has stirred passions around the world, as it touches on essential questions about genetics, race, gender identity and fair play. Is it even possible to classify athletes as men and women when the human body sometimes sends out more complicated signals?" As this question highlights, the nature of intersectional human identity and its role in sports triggers debate on the topic of gender and racism. Due to the contentious history of hyperandrogenism in sports, athletes, governing bodies, journalists, and members of the public are left without consensus on who should be allowed to participate in each sport and what qualifications those individuals may need.

Berger and Guidroz (2009) argue intersectional communication theory helps address the complex contemporary categories of identity within the context of a world increasingly defined by its use of digital communication technologies. These frameworks note, in part, that identity cannot be divided into separate categories, but need to be understood contextually and situationally. Novak and El-Burki (2016) argue in intersectional communication theory, an individual is not simply an answer to a set of categories, but rather a reflection of how those categories are discursively constructed, negotiated and interpreted by the individual, members of the identity groups, and non-members of the identity groups. The theory also notes that identity categories are not stagnant or permanent, but evolve over time, particularly in response to challenges of the expectations of gender, race, or class.

Dagkas (2016) argues that intersectionality in sport is a growing area of scholarly interest because professional athletes increasingly challenge traditional stereotypes of gender, race, and class. As a result, athletes and fan communities must redefine or interrogate the traditional structures of identity to understand and make-meaning of athletic performances (Abdel-Shehid & Kalman-Lamb, 2017). Blodgett et al. (2017) note that female athletes are rarely identified singularly by gender, but are also identified by their race, class, and masculine or feminine appearance.

Palacios Ibañez's (2018) dissertation on Semenya suggests that Twitter conversations about the runner reflect changing understandings and acceptance of athletes who challenge traditional gender stereotypes. Dworkin et al. (2013) argue that members of the public turned to Twitter because a lack of consensus was demonstrated by elite athletes, journalists, and sport organizers. Although Semenya was far from the first athlete to challenge gender norms, she drew international attention on Twitter because of the platform's intersectional nature and relationship to categories of race and class (Dworkin et al., 2013). Camporesi and Maugeri (2010) note that Semenya is appealing to Twitter users because of the controversial nature and variety of interpretations of each category and its place in sports. Vannini and Fornssler (2011) argue that Semenya is subject to additional public discourse and debate because of the failure of her sport to articulate consistent, clear and uncontroversial guidelines for participation. While a study of tweets from this period cannot help clarify IAAF regulations or court decisions, it can aid understanding of how the public will accept or reject upcoming rulings on the issue. It can also give insight into the contemporary treatment of gender and race in sports.

Importantly, intersectionality also reflects on the historical treatment of social identity, especially as legacies of inequality continue to permeate contemporary structures. The IAAF's rules, although largely directed toward Semenya, are far from new, especially when examining the historical treatment of African women in global competition. Karkazis and Jordan-Young (2018) reflect that historically, organizations like the IAAF have sought to bar African women from competition and "traces the inspections of women athletes to a 'familiar prurient/Enlightenment will-to-know' which . . . works in tandem with racialized ideals about women's bodies to construct women who do not fit the ideal as 'pre-modern' and 'reinforce a post-imperial sense of the 'natural' global order.'. . . . In this context 'the untamed, 'simple' African body is one that has not yet been streamlined into 'modern' norms" (para. 14). In short, the IAAF regulations reflect historical tensions between the inclusion of female African athletes in athletics. *Slate* journalist Jackson (2019) writes,

> There is a long history of questionable science—or, more accurately, scientifically unfounded ideas presented by scientists and medical doctors—used to police and "protect" female athletes. The result has been circular reinforcement: Culturally informed bad science about women creates sports policies toward women, which influence cultural ideas about women, which inform bad science . . . and so on and so forth. (para. 12)

This historical pattern of inequality and exclusion illustrates why Semenya is now at the center of debates on the role of gender and race in contemporary identity.

Twitter in Intersectionality

While more research on intersectionality and the construction of gender and race is needed in sports communication, previous research demonstrates Twitter as a platform where these constructing conversations take place. Brown et al. (2017) argue that the public turns to online social media platforms like Twitter in instances that challenge traditional gender norms or roles. In these instances, users engage in re-negotiation of categorical identifiers to reduce the dissonance between the case and the social category. Because of the global instantaneous communication potential of Twitter, these re-negotiations take place very quickly among a geographically disparate public. Although there are questions regarding if these re-negotiations manifest in changes in public acceptance or support outside of Twitter, the digital platform remains a critical space for scholars to examine how users debate challenges to traditional gender markers and identity.

Re-negotiation of categories such as gender and race take many forms on social media. Typically, a current event motivates users to first post and share their interpretation. Users then respond to each other, identifying other users interested in the topic with keywords or hashtags. These responses develop into conversations, which motivate additional postings. Rice (2013) reflects that as responses on a topic grow, more individuals are pulled into the discussion, thus broadening the scope and encouraging users to re-define, through negotiation, the categorical markers of race, gender, age, and class. In short, Twitter serves as an online platform for users to discuss athletes like Semenya and re-negotiate characteristics like race and gender. Iveson (2017) notes that although consensus is rarely reached in these re-negotiations, the process of re-negotiation is critically important because it often motivates groups of supporters (and opposition) of an individual, who can be mobilized outside of Twitter. Iveson (2017) calls for more research that examines this re-negotiation process before mobilization to better understand how individuals become the foci of the re-negotiation of social categories.

METHODOLOGICAL APPROACH

This study examines a dataset of public tweets using the #CasterSemenya, #HandsOffCaster, and #StandwithCaster hashtags to examine how users discursively constructed Semenya, the IAAF, and reflected intersectionality. Using a critical discourse analysis technique adapted from Gee (2011), this study presents a set of five discourses. Discourse analysis of Twitter hashtags provides valuable insight into re-negotiation and reflection on current events. To perform the critical discourse analysis, a team of three researchers read through all posts collected in the dataset and applied Gee's (2011) seven meaning-making tasks: significance, practices, identities, relationships, politics, connections, and sign systems/knowledge. A description and example of each task is found in Appendix A.

The dataset includes all mentions of #CasterSemenya, #StandwithCaster, and #HandsOffCaster between April 1, 2018 (the creation of the DSD policy from the IAAF) and June 21, 2019 (the ruling from the Swiss Court). While Semenya and IAAF were the foci of digital content since August of 2009, the dates reflect the most recent structural changes that directly impact Semenya's participation. Additionally, Twitter mentions of Semenya grew 1045% on the day of the 2018 IAAF rule change.

The dataset includes all 4,590 public tweets that used the three hashtags between these dates. This includes tweets from individual users, journalists, organizations, and posts from Semenya. With a goal of describing Twitter discourses about Semenya, this variety in types of users reflects the diversity of individuals and organizations who contributed to discussions on Twitter. To perform the analysis, all 4,590 tweets were collected using the twitteR package from Cran and archived as posts (complete with text, public user data, hyperlinks, and images). In addition to providing quotes for qualitative reliability, limited descriptive statistics are available through the discursive coding process and are included in the following section. A step-by-step methodological reflection is in Appendix B.

DISCOURSES

Discourse One: Information Sharing

A common form of tweet about Semenya included Tweets that linked to news articles or shared updates with followers. In most cases, users shared information about the policy, and framed it as "breaking news" to post timely and relevant information. For example, one user posted "BREAKING NEWS: A Swiss court has suspended the implementation of the IAAF's gender rules until #CasterSemenya's appeal against the rules has been finalized" on June 3, 2019, just minutes after the Swiss Court gave its ruling.

Importantly, the majority (65%) of posts that used an information sharing discourse were from official news or journalist accounts. Beyond general fans or followers of Semenya's career, these news outlets also participated in the discursive construction by invoking the "breaking news" phrase. In total, 598 (13%) tweets used the term "breaking news," making it the most common set of words included in this dataset (besides "Caster Semenya"). Posts about Semenya by news outlets serve two functions within this digital space. First, news outlets can extend the reach of Semenya's story by sharing it with followers who may not already be familiar with it. This is evidenced by the variety of news outlets that covered the story, including eNCA (a 24-hour news channel in South Africa), *Sunday Times* (a popular newspaper in South Africa), and 7Q2 (a popular radio station in South Africa). These news outlets cover stories outside of sports, thus ensuring the attention of additional followers who hold interests beyond Semenya and helping broaden the information sharing about the policy. Second, by covering Semenya and the policy, journalists legitimize the story and validate it as important news for followers to know about. The news outlets selected the story to include in their digital agendas, demonstrating its importance and prominence to readers.

Discourse Two: Supporting Semenya

For many users, Twitter was an outlet to express (often emotionally) their support for Semenya in her legal and athletic endeavors. Many users reflected on their own emotions in their support for Semenya. For example, this user posted, "When my husband and I heard the news on the radio in the car about #CasterSemenya We couldn't stop smiling. We love you @caster800m!!!!!" to describe her family's emotions after hearing the Swiss Court would allow Semenya to continue to compete. For users, Semenya's treatment was emotional, invoking their own feelings of happiness when she was victorious in court.

Support was also subtler and appeared in the specific selection of words that highlight Semenya's accomplishments and her successes. For example, "What a huge moment for #CasterSemenya and for the greater athletics community. Her ruling has successfully been appealed. She will now be allowed to compete in races ranging from 400m-1500m WITHOUT testosterone blockers." In this example, the use of "huge moment" frames the user as a supporter that reflects on the "success" of her appeal. This includes emphasizing "WITHOUT" to demonstrate frustration with earlier rulings requiring testosterone blockers. Discursively, these posts of support demonstrate the emotional labor of following Semenya's career, as well as the feelings of collective triumph when she succeeds in court and in races.

Discourse Three: Semenya's Ethnicity

While many users identified themselves from regions around the world, many tweets also reflected on Semenya's relationship to South Africa and how her experiences relate to South African culture and social politics. In these instances, users added reflections on Semenya's relationship to South African athletics and culture. For example, one user reflected on her athletic achievements and considered her a leader in sports besides track: "#CasterSemenya should Captain all the South African Squads. Soccer, Rugby and Cricket. She has the resilience." For this user, Semenya's resilience embodies the nature and ethos of South African sports, making her an ideal athlete in all fields. While statements like this are clearly hyperbolic and no one suggests she should change or add athletic events to her program, the term "resilience" appears in 409 (8.9%) posts in the database. This term is always linked to reflections of Semenya's South African heritage and desire for her to represent the country because of the strength of her character.

Beyond references to South Africa, many users also reflected on how Semenya reflects the history of oppression and challenges female, black, South African athletes have faced throughout history. In these tweets, Semenya is a new example of the historical treatment of this group: "Black woman you are a threat. If they don't vilify you and tarnish your image, they create laws to stop your greatness. What a threat you must be and how powerful you are. #CasterSemenya still you rise." In this tweet, the user reflects that women like Semenya were historically vilified, and today this vilification continues in the creation of structures that prevent athletes from entering competition.

Semenya's identity as a black woman in South Africa was also contrasted with the structures of whiteness across society. For example, "Remember, whites dont [sic] need qualifications to run institutions! Education is just for the darkies..Their superiority all over, and if they dont [sic] win, they quickly change the rules of the game, like in #CasterSemenya, and now with the @ PublicProtector, to come out superior!" In posts like these, users reflect on the structures that prevent black success in areas outside of athletics. This user reflects on their perception that white individuals are rarely asked to demonstrate their qualifications, while black individuals must routinely overcome these barriers (including the changing of rules).

While many users sought to define Semenya within historical treatment, others used this reflection to discuss her resilience and character: "She Took All the pains; She took all the Insults; She took all the Negativity; Just like dust, she Rose; Her Name Is, Caster Mokgadi Semenya. A Black South African Woman. A Queen #CasterSemenya." Like previous tweets that reflected on her resilience as a South African trait, Semenya is characterized for both her emotional strength as well as her physical abilities. Importantly, the use of "queen" appears frequently in the dataset, with 114 users referring to her as "Queen Caster" in their tweets. The use of "queen" in this dataset is interesting, considering there are only a few posts that reflect specifically on her gender or sex, despite hormones being at the heart of the IAAF's controversy. The embrace of the term "queen" reflects the public's embrace of her gendered identity and perhaps a rejection of the IAAF's controversial rulings regarding hormones and sex. In this way, although sex or gender is rarely reflected upon in the dataset, users subtly reinforce their support of her through this term. As an additional note, there are no instances of the gendered terms "king" or "prince."

Discourse Four: IAAF Criticism

First, many users criticized the motives of the IAAF in its requirement of Semenya to take testosterone blockers. For example, one user reflected, "#CasterSemenya IAAF used her as a human guinea pig and fears others are at risk." Here, the user suggests that the IAAF's motivations for the testosterone blockers may be more sinister than just suppressing Semenya's performance. The user links to an article that demonstrates the unreliability of testosterone blocking science, and how the medicines are untested in female athletes. The user implies that the IAAF may want to test this science in Semenya, thus motivating their ruling.

Other users connected the IAAF regulations to historical patterns of oppression, adding that the organization was motivated by hatred, racism, and bigotry: "What the #IAAF is doing #CasterSemenya is a human rights violation. It's similar to what countries in the West used to do to South Africans like Sarah Baartman. It's a modern kind of humiliation disguised as regulations . . . " Posts like these were common, with users reflecting that there were racist motivations for the IAAF regulations. Importantly, no user called out specific members of the IAAF when alluding to these racist practices, but instead users constructed the whole organization as racist.

This was not to say that other individuals were not called out and labeled as racists. The second form of the criticism discourse demonstrates that users criticized athletes who stood with the IAAF or supported the recent ruling against Semenya. Olympian Lynsey Sharp, who called Semenya's testosterone levels an unfair "advantage" in a 2016 interview and called Semenya "difficult to compete against" in 2019, was frequently called "racist" and a "sore loser." For example, "Lynsey Sharp defended her comments about #CasterSemenya as 'honest & diplomatic.' I think she misspelled 'ignorant' & full of crap.'" Here, users construct Sharp as an adversary to Semenya, not just because they compete against each other, but because they represent dueling ideologies of who should be allowed to participate in the sport.

Sharp is also woven into reflections on the IAAF's motivations. One user reflected a common sentiment that the IAAF was motivated to act against Semenya because of comments by athletes like Sharp: "Everytime I think about #CasterSemenya and what she went through, I can't help but wonder if Seb Coe was motivated more by Lynsey Sharp's tears than by anything else. The IAAF are going to regret this, history will judge them." Here, users argued that Sharp's tear-filled interview after the 2016 Olympics (and subsequent races) motivated the IAAF to take racist actions against Semenya.

Third, users also criticized the IAAF and supportive athletes by equivocating the discrimination facing Semenya to other athletic feats. For example, "Because Caster is stronger and faster than most female athletes, now the IAAF wants her to take medication to make her weaker. That's like telling Messi & Ronaldo to get amputated so other players can get a chance to be just as good. Fuck you all at the IAAF. #CasterSemenya." In these instances, users proposed outlandish modifications to other athletes that would hinder their performance and almost certainly increase the odds for competitors. This includes, making Usain Bolt shorter and giving Simone Biles vertigo. Other comparisons included Michael Phelps, whose body produces less lactic acid than other swimmers. Users argued that athletic organizations do not require Phelps to increase his lactic acid to even the playing field. These exaggerations serve to demonstrate user frustrations over the scrutiny of Semenya, when other athletes are praised for the bodily advantages that help them succeed.

Fourth, users also adopted humor and sarcasm to critique the IAAF and its supportive athletes. After the Swiss Court overruled the IAAF decision, many users tagged the IAAF's twitter account to share news of Semenya's victory. For example, "Has anyone checked on Sebastian Coe's pulse yet? And Lynsey Sharp?Is she still breathing? #CasterSemenya #IAAF" and "Yo @iaaforg IAAF, how are you guys doing over there? #CasterSemenya."

Antagonistic posts like these use humor to celebrate the Swiss ruling and call out the oppositional forces against Semenya.

Discourse Five: Criticism of Semenya

While most posts supported Semenya or stayed neutral in their reporting of breaking news, a small minority of posts (87 or 1.9%) criticized Semenya or her hormone levels. Unlike posts criticizing Sharp, these posts never criticized Semenya's character or even her dedication to the sport, but rather reflected on the controversy surrounding her hormone levels. For example, "#CasterSemenya Congratulations on the ruling but how can any female fairly compete with you when they know they have already lost." In these posts, the term "fair" and "advantage" appear frequently, as users grappled with any possible advantages from her hormone levels. These users equate Semenya's heightened testosterone levels as an unfair advantage against the other athletes. Implied in these references is that Semenya is an outlier to "normal" athletes. Some users even use the "normal" terminology to justify the reflection that her achievements were accomplished because of an unfair advantage: "Another unfair contest! Testosterone filled South Africa's #CasterSemenya wins again against other normal females!! #Unfair #GoldCoast2018 #CommonwealthGames." Again, these posts are uncommon, but they reflect a juxtaposition between Semenya and other athletes because of biological differences. The use of "normal" to describe her competitors implies that Semenya is not normal, and her accomplishments are unfair.

In addition, users praised the IAAC and the testosterone blockers as champions for female athletes. For example, "A win for the @iaaforg and for female athletes everywhere. #CasterSemenya will need to take testosterone blockers to compete internationally. Experts say it will make her 7 seconds slower and an also-ran. Should Semenya's past performances be allowed to stand?" Posts like this argue that the IAAC is an advocate for female athletes who aims to make play fair by addressing athletes with heightened testosterone levels. The seven-second delay statistic is referenced eight times in the dataset, although none of these posts cite a source. This post also asks followers if Semenya's past accomplishments, including her Olympic medals should be disqualified because of the IAAF's ruling, which serves to discredit her past accomplishments.

Discourse Six: Intersectionality

Finally, many of the posts wove criticism of the IAAF and athletes like Sharp into larger arguments about the contemporary and historical treatment of queer, African women in sports. As noted in earlier research about intersectionality, Twitter users approach identity as a combination of categories, rather than singular identifiers. For example, "#CasterSemenya is a cisgender black queer woman who happens to naturally produce high levels of testosterone. Biological sex is more complex than the binary, and racism, misogyny, and homophobia make a shifty brew. The #IAAF decision is targeted discrimination." Here, users approached Semenya as representative of intersectionality identity that challenges the traditional boundaries of sporting categories. As a result, the new IAAF regulations are labeled as "discriminatory" because they fail to recognize the contemporary ways that identity manifests in athletes like Semenya.

Many users noted that the new policies of the IAAF may be a reaction because leaders fail to understand or accept Semenya's identity. The IAAF's actions were discriminatory because they are rooted in larger systems of oppression faced by minorities: "there is a deep rooted system of hate that is directed towards Black + Women + Queer + Excellent + People and we are going to destroy this system of hate." The IAAF's policies were part of larger systems that struggle to understand, accept, and support athletes who do not fit traditional identity categories. Further, users argued Semenya embodies this treatment because of her status as a minority figure in multiple identity categories: "A triple minority #black #queer #woman #CasterSemenya." Her status as a black, non-feminine woman intersect and illustrate the discrimination that individuals in each category face.

For users, this was an issue beyond the boundaries of the IAAF but a reflection on larger social treatment of individuals who are part of minority groups. There were many references that this discrimination was a result of white fears of physical competition with African individuals: "Such is the modus operandi of whiteness, to protect unseasoned white women from their own mediocrity and protect them from being out-shined by a queer black woman." Semenya was the foci of these reflections on inequality even outside of sports, particularly as it fits within larger patterns of discrimination.

REFLECTION

Throughout the Twitter posts, users primarily voiced support for Semenya while criticizing the actions and motivations of the IAAF and athletes like Sharp. Importantly, most of the posts within the #CasterSemenya dataset were supportive of the athlete or critical of the IAAF or competitors. While this is certainly not a generalizable reaction amongst the public, it does demonstrate that the athlete has cultivated a community of digital supporters and fans throughout the decade. This cultivation of supporters may be important as the digital community considers actionable steps beyond Twitter. As noted by Burnap and Williams (2016), many social justice movements begin with conversations on social media platforms. There are several calls throughout the #CasterSemenya posts for actions that resonate in other spaces. For example, "Dear @AthleticsSA_, can we please stage a protest against the @ iaaforg for the unfair ruling on #CasterSemenya by not participating in an #IAAF organized event? Really, this is too much." Beyond calls for protest, other users took actions within their own personal networks: "My students & I organised a protest demonstration in solidarity with @caster800m #CasterSemenya #CasterShouldRun #SayNoToGenderTest." Although small in scope, these steps towards mobilizing the advocacy and support found on Twitter may foreshadow larger movements dedicated to Semenya, the IAAF, or gender in sports.

Finally, descriptions on Twitter seemingly reinforced that users approached Semenya using intersectional language to re-negotiate the norms and expectations of queer African women. Rather than single out a specific identity marker, users broadly included descriptions of her race, sexuality, and gender identity as a cohesive group. This is reflected in the use of "our African Queen" and language that relates Semenya to African female royalty.

For many users, the IAAF's treatment of Semenya was symbolic of the historical treatment of African women in sports. Eight users directly referenced Saartjie Baartman and generalized the fear that English or white culture felt when encountering the strength of African women. To users, Semenya's treatment was part of a long history of exclusion based on inaccurate and racist science that served to reinforce white bodies as dominant and hinder the equality and strength of African women. Importantly, users tied this treatment to other categories beyond race. For users, attributes like gender, class, and religion were also prone to forced inequality based on the policies of white society.

While Semenya continues to challenge current IAAF rulings that bar her from entry in track and field events through the legal system, digitally, fans turned to Twitter to support her and adopted intersectional language and ideology to criticize the forces restricting her. Semenya was ineligible for the 2020 (2021) South African Olympic team due to the IAAF restrictions, which rendered her ineligible to defend her world record and gold medal in the 800m. Future work should examine how discourses about Semenya evolve in her absence from arguably the most well-known sporting platform around the world. In addition, as she pursues other athletic opportunities such as football, scholarship should examine how a change in her athletic context may impact Twitter discourses. It is likely that discussions of Semenya will continue through Twitter and will help shape how future athletes are identified and supported by the public.

APPENDIX A: GEE'S (2011) DISCURSIVE CATEGORIES

Task	Description
Significance	Text reflects importance of issue, experience, or individual
Practices	Text describes the issue, experience, or topic for other users; or describes the application of a discourse to a set of actions; or engages/provides action for other users in conversation
Identities	Text uses nouns and adjectives to describe the issue, experience, or individuals
Relationships	Text connects issue, experience, or topic to other events, or foci
Politics	Text reflects on the social, historical, civic, or political nature of the issue, experience, or topic
Connections	Text discusses the relevance of the issue, experience, or topic by comparing or relating to other issues
Sign systems and knowledge	Text common language practices, jargon, or cultural knowledge within tweet

APPENDIX B: METHODOLOGY, STEP BY STEP

1. Tweets were collected from April 1, 2018, and June 21, 2019, using the Twitter package from Cran. Data includes all mentions of #CasterSemenya, #StandwithCaster, and #HandsOffCaster. Total collection is 4,590 public tweets.
2. Three researchers independently read all tweets to code for Gee's seven meaning making tasks (see appendix b for description and examples). Tweets were assigned one, two, or three tasks each.
   a. As a qualitative project, the goal is not statistical coding, but seeking out patterns of how uses invoke each task to create discourses
3. Researchers meet to review findings and identify discourses based on the patterns of use of each meaning making task.
4. Six frequent discourses were identified by researchers to identify how speakers invoked, constructed, and reflected on fitness trackers.
5. Researchers independently re-read the dataset to find examples and quotes that invoke each discourse for inclusion in the written paper.

NOTES

1. As adopted from articles by Karkazis and Jordan-Young (2018), "in writing of Semenya, we risk repeating the problems raised so eloquently by Neville Hoad and Keguro Macharia including our own 'participat[ion] in an ongoing spectacularization.'" This project acknowledges this risk and attempts to explore the topic for deeper understanding of how the "spectacularization" of an athlete who challenges traditional identity categories takes place in a digital space. Further, this article reflects that its use of "case study" and "case" throughout the project can be "a distancing, medicalizing and, ultimately, dehumanizing way to refer to her." Therefore, the project seeks to include "dominant story with counternarratives, details, and context that seek to underscore the human(s) at the core of this regulation without recapitulating harm and without erasing what is ugly and painful."

2. Since the IAAF ruling in 2018, three independent researchers have challenged the findings of the IAAF backed study on testosterone in athletic performance and called for the study's retraction from the *British Journal of Sports Medicine* (Pilke et al., 2019). Although the journal has yet to release a statement on the demands for retraction, the IAAF maintains the accuracy of the research and the corresponding regulation.

REFERENCES

Abdel-Shehid, G., & Kalman-Lamb, N. (2017). Complicating gender, sport, and social inclusion: The case for intersectionality. (Commentary)(Essay). *Social Inclusion, 5*(2), 159–162. https://doi.org/10.17645/si.v5i2.887

BBC Sport. (2019, June 4). Caster Semenya: Olympic 800m champion can compete after Swiss court ruling. *BBC Sport.* Retrieved from https://www.bbc.com/sport/athletics/48504205

Bennet, A. C. (2015). Dutee Chand v. IAAF and AFI. *Court of Arbitration for Sport.* Retrieved from https://web.archive.org/web/20170704221029/http://www.tas-cas.org/fileadmin/user_upload/award_internet.pdf

Berger, M. T., & Guidroz, K. (2009; 2010). *The intersectional approach: Transforming the academy through race, class, and gender.* Chapel Hill: University of North Carolina Press. doi:10.5149/9780807895566_berger

Blodgett, A., Ge, Y., Schinke, R., & Mcgannon, K. (2017). Intersecting identities of elite female boxers: Stories of cultural difference and marginalization in sport. *Psychology of Sport & Exercise, 32*, 83–92. https://doi.org/10.1016/j.psychsport.2017.06.006

Bloom, B. (2018, April 25). Caster Semenya to be forced to lower testosterone levels or face 800m ban. *The Telegraph.* Retrieved from https://www.telegraph.co.uk/athletics/2018/04/25/caster-semenya-forced-lower-testosterone-levels-face-800m-ban/

Brown, M., Ray, R., Summers, E., & Fraistat, N. (2017). #SayHerName: A case study of intersectional social media activism. *Ethnic and Racial Studies, 40(*11), 1831–1846. https://doi.org/10.1080/01419870.2017.1334934

Camporesi, S., & Maugeri, P. (2010). Caster Semenya: Sport, categories and the creative role of ethics. *Journal of Medical Ethics, 36*(6), 378–379. https://doi.org/10.1136/jme.2010.035634

Critchley, M. (2016, August 22). Rio 2016: Fifth-placed Joanna Jozwik "feels like silver medallist" after 800m defeat to Caster Semenya. *Independent.* Retrieved from https://www.independent.co.uk/sport/olympics/rio-2016-joanna-jozwik-caster-semenya-800m-hyperandrogenism-a7203731.html

Dagkas, S. (2016). Problematizing social justice in health pedagogy and youth sport: Intersectionality of race, ethnicity, and class. *Research Quarterly for Exercise and Sport, 87*(3), 221–229. https://doi.org/10.1080/02701367.2016.1198672

Dworkin, S., Swarr, A., Cooky, C., & Dworkin, S. (2013). (In)Justice in sport: The treatment of South African track star Caster Semenya. *Feminist Studies, 39*(1), 40–69. Retrieved from http://search.proquest.com/docview/1684423510/

Erdener, U. (2015). IOC consensus meeting on sex reassignment and hyperandrogenism. *International Olympic Committee.* Retrieved from https://stillmed.olympic.org/Documents/Commissions_PDFfiles/Medical_commission/2015-11_ioc_consensus_meeting_on_sex_reassignment_and_hyperandrogenism-en.pdf

Fordyce, T. (2009, August 19). Semenya left stranded by storm. *BBC Sport.* Retrieved from https://www.bbc.co.uk/blogs/tomfordyce/2009/08/semenya_left_stranded_by_storm.html

Gregory, S. (2019, July 18). Caster Semenya won't stop fighting for her right to run, just as she is. *TIME.* Retrieved from https://time.com/5629249/caster-semenya-interview/

Hutcheon, D. (2015, August 7). Hyperandrogenism in athletics: A review of Chand v. IAAF. *Law in Sport.* Retrieved from https://www.lawinsport.com/content/sports/item/hyperandrogenism-in-athletics-a-review-of-chand-v-iaaf

IAAF. (2009, September 11). Statement on Caster Semenya. *IAAF.* Retrieved from https://www.iaaf.org/news/news/statement-on-caster-semenya

IAAF. (2019, July 31). IAAF response to Swiss Federal Tribunal's decision. *IAAF.org.* Retrieved from https://www.iaaf.org/news/press-release/swiss-federal-tribunal-decision

Iveson, M. (2017). Gendered dimensions of Catalan nationalism and identity construction on Twitter. *Discourse & Communication, 11*(1), 51–68. https://doi.org/10.1177/1750481316683293

Jackson, V. (2019, May 1). The decadelong humiliation of Caster Semeny. *Slate.* Retrieved from https://slate.com/technology/2019/05/caster-semenya-testosterone-gender-appeal-ruling.html

Karkazis, K. (2016). The ignorance aimed at Caster Semenya flies in the face of the Olympic spirit. *The Guardian.* Retrieved from https://www.theguardian.com /commentisfree/2016/aug/23/caster-semenya-olympic-spirit-iaaf-athletes-women

Karkazis, K., & Jordan-Young, R. (2018). The powers of testosterone: Obscuring race and regional bias in the regulation of women athletes. *Feminist Formations, 30*(2), 1–39. https://doi.org/10.1353/ff.2018.0017

Kessel, A. (2009, August 19). Caster Semenya wins 800m gold but cannot escape gender controversy. *The Guardian.* Retrieved from https://www.theguardian.com /sport/2009/aug/19/caster-semenya-800m-world-athletics-championships-gender

Mather, V. & J. Longman. (2019, July 31). Ruling leaves Caster Semenya with few good options. *New York Times.* Retrieved from https://www.nytimes.com/2019/07 /31/sports/caster-semenya.html

Novak, A. & El-Burki, I. J. (2016). *Defining identity and the changing scope of culture in the digital age.* IGI Global: New York.

Palacios Ibañez, C. (2018). "I am Mokgadi Caster Semenya. I am a woman and I am fast." *Dissertation.* Retrieved from Uppsala University Library.

Rice, R. (2013). Mediated disclosure on Twitter: The roles of gender and identity in boundary impermeability, valence, disclosure, and stage. *Computers in Human Behavior, 29*(4), 1465–1474. https://doi.org/10.1016/j.chb.2013.01.033

Smith, D. (2009, August 22). Caster Semenya row: "Who are white people to question the makeup of an African girl? It is racism." *The Guardian.* Retrieved from https:// www.theguardian.com/sport/2009/aug/23/caster-semenya-athletics-gender

Stevens, S. (2016, August 21). Rio 2016: Caster Semeny victory in 800m reduces Team GB athlete Lynsey Sharp to tears. *Independent.* Retrieved from https://www .independent.co.uk/sport/olympics/rio-2016-caster-semenyas-800m-win-lynsey -sharp-tears-intersex-debate-a7202251.html

Vannini, A., & Fornssler, B. (2011). Girl, interrupted: Interpreting Semenya's body, gender verification testing, and public discourse. *Cultural Studies ↔ Critical Methodologies, 11*(3), 243–257. https://doi.org/10.1177/1532708611409536

Voelker, D., & Harvey, S. (2018). *Women in pursuit of the sports coaching profession: challenges and solutions.* London: SAGE Publications: SAGE Business Cases Originals.

Young, D. (2018, April 26). The only point of track's dumb new testosterone rules is to make it illegal to be Caster Semenya. *Deadspin.* Retrieved from https://deadspin .com/the-only-point-of-track-s-dumb-new-testosterone-rules-i-1825546141

PART V

Athlete Activism in the Online Space

Chapter 13

"If You Aren't Upset About This Problem, Then You're a Part of It"

NCAA Athlete Activism on TikTok

Shannon Scovel and Carolina Velloso

INTRODUCTION

When Oregon women's basketball player Sedona Prince posted a TikTok on March 18, 2021, highlighting the inequities between the men's and women's facilities at the National Collegiate Athletic Association (NCAA) tournament, she sparked a national conversation about equality and opportunity. Her short, selfie-style TikTok reframed the focus of the tournament away from the games and towards improving conditions and support for women's sports. Prince, however, is far from the only athlete to use this platform for social justice.

TikTok, a video-based app released by ByteDance in 2016, more closely resembles the now-defunct short-form video app Vine as opposed to other text and photo-sharing apps like Twitter, Instagram, and Facebook because of the creative focus and freedom in video creation (Anderson, 2020). TikTok is ideal for sharing entertaining posts for public engagement, and athletes, in particular, have embraced this space as a chance to continue their "role as opinion leaders alongside being amplifiers" for individual causes (Abidin, 2020, p. 84). Popular discursive, authentic videos on TikTok allow for more substantive activism by deemphasizing formal aesthetically pleasing images and instead rewarding rawness and voice from users.

TikTok is steadily becoming a favorite for athletes and celebrities, as it enables them to offer commentary in real time. Videos on TikTok are also particularly sharable, a key feature of platforms that promote virality, visibility and attention (Vázquez-Herrero, 2020; Large, 2020). The nature of the app produces "creative chaos" (Anderson, 2020, p. 10) in that users can access an endless range of video content because the algorithm governing the site is analogous to a "meme factory, compressing the world into pellets of virality and dispensing those pellets" with every scroll (Tolentino, 2019, para. 12). Through this simple interface as well as hashtags and challenges, users are drawn into the platform and encouraged to be active participants in content creation.

Previous research suggests that capturing user attention and inspiring new content creators are necessities for digital activism and advocacy movements on social media (Tufekci, 2013; Vázquez-Herrero et. al, 2020). While this statement can be applied broadly to national and international political struggles, the essence that attention and engagement are required for activism stands. Clark (2016) notes that activist posts on social media serve as "artifacts of engagement" (p. 244) that inspire others, particularly young people, to join a given cause. Thus, the ways in which college athletes—those young stars who are finding their voice on a big stage—have used popular platforms like TikTok to share political and social messages warrants study.

Scholars argue that sports stars have become more comfortable showing off their personal lives and authentic hobbies outside of the athletic arena across all social media platforms to develop a growing online relationship between athletes and fans (Pegoraro, 2010; Geurin, 2017), but little research has been done to explore the ways in which athletes are using the TikTok platform for athlete activism. Building on Bourdieu's (1986, 1993) theory of social capital and Goffman's (1959) theory of self-presentation, this chapter will take a critical perspective on social media and sport, advancing the limited existing literature on TikTok by offering new insights on the use of this social media app for social change.

THEORETICAL FRAMEWORK

Social Capital

Pierre Bourdieu (1986, 1993) developed the concept of "capital" as an explanatory framework for the relations of power between social actors. According to Bourdieu (1986), capital is the basic organizing unit of society and determines social positions within it. Capital can be symbolic, relating to the non-economic advantages that people can accumulate within a society.

Social capital—one of the three main forms of capital—is "the aggregate of the actual or potential resources which are linked to possession of a durable network of more or less institutionalized relationships of mutual acquaintance and recognition" (Bourdieu, 1986, p. 248). In other words, the network of people to whom one has access influences one's amount of social capital. In addition, different groups can have representatives who come to advocate for the group's interests and can obtain their own influence due to their position. Crucially, the forms of capital are designed to self-reproduce; that is, they are not of equal access and serve to maintain class power (Bourdieu 1986, 1993).

Previous studies have suggested that athletes can possess higher amounts of social capital than nonathletes, especially at the collegiate level (e.g. Clopton, 2012; Forbes-Mewett and Pape, 2019). Social capital is correlated to the athletes' prominence (in other words, the more famous the athlete, the higher amount of social capital), but other factors are also crucial, including sex, race, sexuality, and social status (Carter-Francique et. al., 2015). Although notions of capital are deeply rooted in hegemonic (White and male) ideologies, student-athletes who are marginalized along one or more identity axes can compensate through affiliation with a collegiate sports team (Clopton, 2011).

Representation and Identity Performance

Social capital and power can impact self-representation choices, as well as a willingness to engage in outward activism online. Goffman (1959) focused specifically on this relationship between public and private presentation, arguing that individuals engage in "an ongoing juggling of identity performance" to develop a "desirable image" for themselves and for others (Hayes Sauder & Blaszka, 2016, p. 180); he suggests that each person balances a "front stage" identity, one that is more polished and professional, with a "backstage" identity that is personal and intimate.

In a sports context, scholars have applied this concept to suggest that frontstage branding and promotion involves any content related to on-the-field performance or competition while backstage performance encompasses anything related to family life or non-athletic experiences (Goffman, 1959; Hayes Sauder & Blaszka, 2016; Lebel and Danylchuk, 2012). Though his work focuses specifically on representation and presentation in the theatre, Goffman's (1959) concepts of frontstage and backstage representation apply to athlete activism as individuals make decisions about when to use their voices and how to maximize specific social media platforms to reach a targeted audience. Athletes perform for a crowd in an arena, but activist and storytelling efforts by athletes online serve as a backstage performance brought to the forefront, one in which they can use their voice for more personal purposes on platforms like TikTok.

METHODOLOGY

Through a critical case study analysis and a close reading of sport as text for three specific instances of TikTok activism—Sedona Prince's criticism of unequal NCAA facilities, UCONN basketball's Christyn Williams's viral "Black Lives Matter" informational post, and TJ Bleichner's LGBT+ advocacy—this chapter will demonstrate the unique affordances of TikTok as a social media platform for athlete activism. Each of these case studies represented a critical moment during the 2020–2021 athletic season when NCAA student-athletes used digital media platforms, specifically TikTok, to speak up for social justice and advocate for a specific group marginalized in the existing sports landscape.

Case study research involves "intensive analyses and descriptions of a single unit or system bounded by space and time" to unpack the meaning embedded in a given incident (Algozzine et al., 2017, pp. 9–10). The three cases in this chapter each involve a single TikTok but are distinct from one another, as the first case addresses gender equality, the second centers on racial equality, and the third focuses on sexuality and inclusion. The authors recognize the importance of intersectionality (Crenshaw, 1991) across these three case studies, acknowledging the way that identity factors into athlete activism (Allen, 2021; Cooky & Antunovic, 2020). Power and privilege impact an athlete's ability to speak up and be heard, and these examples show the ability of the social media platform TikTok to amplify those previously marginalized voices and inspire meaningful change.

Each of the three cases in this study were chosen because of their reach—13,000+ views on TikTok—and because of the ways in which the athletes used TikTok's short video format to convey their message as student activists. Large (2020) argues that the potential for content to go viral on TikTok and reach a broader audience is what makes the platform particularly alluring for athletes. Virality can be defined as both a "network-enhanced word of mouth" and "a social information flow process" (Nahon et al., 2013, p. 1, 6) by which content reaches other uses; the athletes in this chapter used the viral nature of TikTok to share information related to their social justice cause with their growing audiences. (Bruns et al., 2015). The researchers also selected these particular case studies on TikTok because of the way they responded to distinct contemporary social debates.

Reading these athlete activist TikToks as text enables researchers to "[find] the cultural meanings that circulate within narratives of particular incidents" and dissect those complex, interesting and overlapping meanings contained in each text in a deeper way (Birrell et al., 2000, p. 11; Hudson, 2018). As a method, exploring sport as text helps amplify and re-center voices that may have been overshadowed by "hegemonic forces" and unpack the ways in which identities intersect in the larger historical sports media and social justice complex (Birrell et al., 2000, p. 11). The athletes in this chapter disrupted power structures with their voices and used their position to advocate for social justice and change in the NCAA and beyond.

ANALYSIS

"If You Aren't Upset About This Problem, Then You're a Part of It": Sedona Prince & Gender Equality

Sedona Prince—a forward for the Oregon women's basketball team—first made her foray onto TikTok in December 2019 when she posted a humorous dance video alongside her teammate Hillary Ellman, showing off her personality and creating light-hearted content (Prince, 2020). This simple clip brought Prince on to the app and marked the first step in her journey toward what would ultimately lead to Prince using TikTok as a platform for social justice.

Abidin (2020) notes that TikTok provides a platform for early activism from young people because of the proliferation of entertaining context mixed in with "palatable" calls to action (p. 84). Nothing about Prince's brand was aggressive; rather, she was personal, speaking directly to a group of followers and engaging in advocacy via social media. Over the course of the 2019–2020 and 2020–2021 basketball seasons, again showing herself in a full, authentic way, Prince posted more dance videos with friends and highlighted the successes that her Oregon team had throughout the season. She built a humble audience of viewers who were drawn to her content for a range of purposes, but her social capital online likely played a role in her popularity.

As a member of the nationally ranked Oregon Ducks, Prince was aspirational. Her community and associated organization held cultural power, and by representing the Ducks through her clothing and her comments across her TikTok feed, she capitalized on that power. As a woman athlete, Prince experienced less social capital than her male peers because of the gendered nature of sports and sports media (Creedon, 1994), but Prince embraced the cultural capital that she had as a successful athlete and channeled that status into her messaging. Her popularity as an athlete, activist and social media star expanded dramatically less than 18 months later, though, when Prince used her brand to not just entertain, but to inform and to advocate.

Prince's viral post, published on March 18, 2021, lasted just 38 seconds, but sent a strong message to the NCAA that the treatment of women athletes was inequitable and disgraceful. Smiling facetiously throughout the clip, Prince recorded herself as she stared into the camera on her smartphone. "I got something to show y'all," she said, panning the phone away from her face and toward the empty hotel ballroom behind her with just one small weight rack in the frame (Prince, 2021). Prince went on to explain that, as a Division I women's basketball player, the NCAA tournament was the biggest event of her season. The problem was that the NCAA provided the women athletes with far less athletic resources than the men's players, who were provided with a full weight room that included squat racks, exercise machines and a full collection of weighted plates, bars, and dumbbells. Prince had something to say about that.

"Now when pictures of our weight room got released versus the men, the NCAA came out with a statement saying that it wasn't money, it was space that was a problem. Lemme show y'all something else," she said in the post (Prince, 2021). Prince then brought the viewer along, taking them inside her emotions and thoughts. The tone and facial expressions shared in the video conveyed her feelings, as she used the video feature of TikTok to scan all of the open space in the women's practice facility, allowing the viewer to see inside the room and note the empty, available space. Su (2020) argues that humor and voice in TikTok videos "closes the distance between fans and the athlete and adds a level of authenticity" to an athlete that increases engagement with a cause, brand or organization (p. 442). Prince offered a specific, subtle activist tone by calling out the NCAA without attacking individual members: she showed the impact of NCAA policies, identified an equity problem, and left her video just open-ended enough to spur journalistic commentary and discussion (Prince, 2021).

Wang (2020) notes that the casual self-presentation and the acerbic tone of Prince's video aligns with the TikTok brand of "quirky videos, most of which were not too professionally or aesthetically produced" (p. 2). The value in TikTok lies less in the video, but more in the power of the video to connect with users on a personal level. Prince circumvented the mainstream news by using her individual platform to take a stand, but by simultaneously catching the attention of media decision-makers, Prince was able to elevate her impact. She capitalized on her complex social capital and leveraged her position and her voice for change. Because of her successful TikTok and the consistency of her brand before and after this critical incident, Prince maintained high visibility online and transformed herself into an internet celebrity (Abidin, 2020).

Antunovic and Linden (2014) thus explain that social media apps can be useful forums for demonstrating interest in, and importance of, women's sports in a media complex that frequently overlooks women. From a feminist perspective, Cooky and Antunovic (2020) argue that scholars should be cognizant of the new, emerging ways that women are sharing their stories and work to recenter media analysis on the actions and content of women, as opposed to reproduced heteronormative, patriarchal frames of analysis in which women's stories are told in relation to men. Antunovic and Linden (2014) noted that the power of digital "feminist advocacy lies in the opportunity to bring the visibility of fans and advocates of women's sports to mainstream media outlets" (p. 157), and while their work focused exclusively on one women's sports hashtag, that same conclusion about the power of visibility relates to Prince's TikTok as well. Prince utilized her status as a nationally competitive student-athlete competing in the biggest women's collegiate event in the country to raise awareness, through TikTok, of the issue of inequality for women in sports.

Following Prince's TikTok and the subsequent public outcry, the NCAA did hire a law firm to conduct an external investigation on gender inequity in college sports—the organization released a report on August 6 detailing the investigation's findings. The executive summary of the 2021 External Gender Equity Review compared Prince's TikTok to "the shot heard round the world," in that it generated national dialogue and brought to light an issue that remained pushed under the rug for far too long (Kaplan, Hecker & Fink, 2021, p. 1). Authors of the report recommended that the NCAA act to improve gender equity in revenue distribution, structural support, and championship planning across all three divisions (Kaplan et al., 2021). The NCAA was forced to respond, largely because of the impact produced by a 38-second video. Athlete activism comes in all forms, but the spreadability of media, particularly TikTok, can be a powerful force. Sedona Prince proved this.

"This House Is On Fire, and People's Lives Are at Stake": Christyn Williams & #BlackLivesMatter

On June 2, 2020, Christyn Williams, a guard on the University of Connecticut (UCONN) women's basketball team, posted her own 37-second video on TikTok explaining why the phrase "all lives matter" is an inappropriate response to "Black lives matter." She used the popular analogy of a burning house, which originated in a Kris Staub comic strip, to illustrate her point (Lopez, 2020). The analogy essentially goes: if a house is on fire, it needs to be tended to urgently. This does not mean that *only* this house matters, or that all houses don't matter. The house on fire simply needs the most immediate attention.

"We are not saying that only Black lives matter, nor are we saying that all lives don't matter. That's not what we're saying," Williams told *USA Today* in a June 8 interview (Bailey, 2020). "When people say, 'Black lives matter,' they're simply bringing attention to all of the Black lives that have either died or endured police brutality, social injustice or even the systemic racism that is in this country. So when you hear people saying, 'All lives matter,' it is repugnant and quite frankly disrespectful to the Black community" (Williams, 2020).

In her TikTok video, Williams alternates between standing in front of a digital background of a house on fire and a house not on fire. The video is cut to simulate the "two" Christyns having a conversation:

Intact-house Williams (IW): "Hey. What are you doing?" ["Listen to how dumb y'all sound" superimposed]

Burning-house Williams (BW): "Oh, this house is on fire, so we're going to go help them, we're going to go put out the fire."

IW: "Well, what about my house?"

BW: "What?"

IW: "What about my house? Doesn't it matter?"

BW: "Is . . . is your house on fire?"

IW: "No, but, like, it still matters."

BW: "Nobody said that it didn't. It's just that this house is on fire, and people's lives are at stake if we don't do something about it."

IW: "Okay, all houses matter."

BW: [Blank stare with "everytime y'all say 'all lives matter'" superimposed]

The video went viral on TikTok, amassing over 13,000 views to date. Spreading to other social media platforms like Instagram and Twitter, it gained even more attention, garnering more than half a million views on the latter.

The response to Williams's video also prompted an acknowledgement from the official Twitter account of the UCONN women's basketball team. Writing that "Christyn Williams was one of the first players to call for universities and teams to acknowledge social injustice," the Twitter thread also linked to the video with the caption "Christyn used her skills on TikTok to go viral about #BlackLivesMatter." The response from UCONN came June 19, 2020, in honor of Juneteenth, and while the team's post generated significant engagement, including 620 likes and 65 retweets, the UConn account's reposting of William's video hardly matched the impact of Williams herself.

Williams used the social capital she was conferred as a prominent member of a highly popular and successful collegiate athletic team to weigh in on a watershed moment of racial reckoning in the U.S. (Carter-Francique, 2015;

Bourdieu, 1986). Much like Prince, Williams's video showed her wearing UConn team gear, and she represented the Huskies in separate outfits as she switched between her intact-house commentary and burning house commentary. These specific clothing choices both offered a specific representation of self (Goffman, 1959)—that of a socially-conscious student-athlete—and reinforced her social capital as a Division I basketball player. Williams' performance in the video represents a gray area between Goffman's (1959) two presentation styles, frontstage and backstage, with the former focusing on scripted performance and the latter representing a more personal, unfiltered view into an individual's image. In this case, Williams is neither formal in her statements, nor is she overly personal. She is straightforward and is simply educating the audience on a platform that she built with content and capital.

Social capital involves utilizing networks and access to resources to find success in modern society, but Carter-Francique et. al (2015) argues that "community cultural wealth" is actually a more appropriate term for this process, as the later term avoids reproducing harmful power dynamics (p. 160). Community cultural wealth further serves as a holistic, complex lens through which to view an individual's ability to navigate and maximize social relations, resources, language and knowledge to create advantages. Carter-Francique et. al (2015) suggests that "the ability for Black student-athletes to access social capital through intimate networks is an essential component to the overall development of the athlete both academically and athletically" (p. 161) and this TikTok reveals that embracing these digital spaces can also lead to the development of an athlete activist. Williams leaned into her digital networks through the power of the TikTok platform and built a community of viewers and audience members who consumed her content.

Williams's post shows how TikTok is a useful platform for social justice work in that her content captures her in-the-moment and ongoing frustration with myths and misconceptions around Black Lives Matter. She uses her platform and voice on this topic to push for change. Hautea et al. (2021) notes that viewers can consider each TikTok a "dot in the mosaic of larger social patterns" that can motivate people, particularly young people to take direct material action towards change via increased activism (p. 12). TikTok provided the ideal platform through which Williams could transmit her message to a large audience of viewers. The "humorous and casual nature" of the app allowed for Williams to express her opinions on a serious and fraught subject in a creative and entertaining way (Su et al., 2020, p. 438). Williams specifically experimented with the visual effects function of TikTok by superimposing herself on a background of a house on fire throughout the video. She also used editing techniques to simulate a conversation between two characters she played herself; these specific editing skills further elevated her capital and expanded her narrative. Abidin (2020) argues that "TikTokers who display this technical expertise are often lauded and celebrated on the app," leading to a rise in celebrity status, visibility and thus increased social capital (p. 80). Williams leveraged her technical skills and her status as a Division I basketball player to gain an audience and then used the TikTok platform to present herself to a growing viewership as a relatable activist, capturing national attention for her perspective on the #BlackLivesMatter dialogue.

Clark (2016) explained that #BlackLivesMatter activism among young people online is not new, as students have been building upon the community nature of these platforms and designing their own protest movements within schools and neighborhoods. Her work looks specifically at the role that Snapchat, Facebook, and Twitter played in using "artifacts of engagement" to motivate others to take action, but Williams's post shows that TikTok is relevant in the activism conversation as well (Clark, 2016, p. 236). Williams is also older than the students evaluated in Clark's study and younger than the athletes assessed in Geurin (2017) or Pegoraro's (2010) work. Instead, she and Prince represent a new generation of collegiate athlete activists, engaging with the platforms at their disposal to not just brand themselves, but use TikTok as an important tool for athlete activism.

"Straight Girls Be Like . . . ": T. J. Bleichner & LGBT Representation

While Williams and Prince took to TikTok to raise awareness of gender and racial discrimination, T. J. Bleichner, then a track-and-field athlete at Louisiana State University, posted a TikTok on March 29, 2021, to increase holistic representation and treatment of the LGBT community. The only text in his post was a partial caption "straight girls be like . . . ," and while his activist voice was more subtle than Prince's or even Williams's, Bleichner's expressions convey his point. His video used the app's "duet" feature, in which two videos play next to each other simultaneously. The right-hand side featured a group of women in black swimwear. On the left-hand side, Bleichner walks into the frame, and the women size him up with interest. Bleichner then puts his hand up, as if to say "stop," and, after a pause, flicks his wrist downward. The women subsequently start cheering.

The purpose of the video, Bleichner explained in an interview with *USA Today*, was to highlight what he perceives as the fetishization by women of having a gay friend. Bleichner said that some people "treat their gay friends as accessories" and that the issue "isn't talked about enough" (Hall, 2021, para. 8, 11). His video garnered over 180,000 views and 42,000 likes (Hall, 2021), and through this virality, Bleichner became a powerful voice for the LGBT community. As of January 2022, the video has been viewed over 203,500 times.

Bleichner's clip was not focused on one particular moment or current event but rather he offered commentary on the everyday lived experience of gay men in America. He embraced TikTok's distinguishing features to provide "content on a . . . serious topic . . . in a humorous way" (Wang, 2020, p. 2) and aimed to correct negative behavior from fellow young people. His mission was successful, as his TikTok turned him into a micro-celebrity (Abidin, 2020; Tufekci, 2013) and raised awareness about the need for more nuanced representations of the LGBT community.

While Bleichner's moment in the spotlight was brief, Clark (2016) would argue that activists like Bleichner, whose influence spreads in a given moment of time and encourages more long-term conversations about representation and inclusion, remain important. Through this humor and culturally relevant imagery, Bleichner engaged in "peer teaching" (Abidin, 2020, p. 85) because, as those within and beyond Bleichner's social circle shared the video, the clip "[became] imbued with meanings" that may "lead to new starting points and new conclusions" (Clark, 2016, pp. 246–247) about the experiences of student-athletes who identify as a member of the LGBT community. Bleichner's posts were playful and performative, common features of popular TikTok videos (Su et. al., 2020), and his activism came from his voice and his presence on the platform.

As a collegiate runner, Bleichner's status as an athlete gave him additional standing upon which to share his message, and he, like Prince and Williams, showcased himself as an athlete activist on TikTok. He frequently presented himself wearing school colors and highlighting his experiences as a collegiate competitor, though he never mentioned running or competition in any of his posts. His TikTok had little to do with track and field, and he never commented on performance or results, making his video a prime example of athlete backstage communication (Goffman, 1959). Bleichner's use of social capital (Bourdieu, 1986) was more subtle than Prince's, as he never posted from a meet or addressed his experiences as a Division I runner directly, but he leaned into the same kind of indirect demonstration of athletic capital as Williams by making the logo of his athletic department clear in multiple videos, including his viral post.

Prior to his viral video, Bleichner had been an outspoken advocate for LGBT inclusion on his TikTok page, including the hashtags #lgbt and #gay in some variation across all but two of his TikToks before the March 29 post. He maximized the "affordances of social media to engage in presentation of his political and personal selves to garner public attention" for LGBT inclusion throughout all of his posts and utilized TikTok as an informative platform to express his views (Tufekci, 2013, p. 850). In his viral video, however, Bleichner never told the audience he was an athlete activist; the messaging and visual representations in his posts served to suggest both his political position and his athletic affiliation. Kluch (2020) argues that athletes are aware of the ways in which their social capital and status as competitors and institutional ambassadors amplifies their ability to share social justice messaging. Bleichner's TikTok post, like other activists identified by Kluch (2020), "was not so much an expression of actions taken toward social justice but more about being visible as a tool to achieve social change" (p. 20). His position as a white, gay track runner for a major Division I program gave him a position upon which to stand and connect with viewers. His social affordances as an elite athlete cannot be divorced from the nature of his viral post, and, like the other two athletes in this chapter, he leveraged that position to use his story for activism.

CONCLUSION

Virality and social impact are challenging things to accomplish in a 30-second selfie-style video, but all three of the athletes in this study—Prince, Williams, and Bleichner—achieved this goal by maximizing the unique features of TikTok as a platform for activism. Su (2020) argues that TikTok provides an ideal place for athletes to connect with fans authentically and share messages related to off-the-court topics, and these athletes demonstrate that point. Prince, Williams, and Bleichner used entertaining and theatrical, primarily backstage content, to present themselves honestly and to convey a message without being forceful (Goffman, 1959; Su et al., 2020). The use of humor, sarcasm, and transparency helped accomplish the activist goals of these athletes and promote the values of gender, sexuality and racial equality. TikTok's younger base has also been particularly useful in reaching a new generation of progressive fans.

The case studies in this chapter show how athletes have used social media, particularly TikTok, to speak up for the singular cases of gender, racial, and sexuality equality in their three posts; all of these athletes, however, were also influenced by their intersectionality identities in the creation of their content. Future research should further evaluate the way intersectionality influences social capital (Bourdieu, 1986, 1993) and community cultural wealth (Carter-Francique et al., 2015) in case studies of athlete activism in digital media. Reading sport as text enabled a critical assessment of these three cases, but Birrell (2000) urges against the assumption that all readings of the same text will align. More research should be done to add additional voices to the qualitative study of athlete self-representation, activism, and social media advocacy.

This chapter focused specifically on college athletes because of the newsworthy debates around the power of student-athlete voice, but scholars should also consider expanding the scope of research and assess how athletes at the high school and professional levels utilize TikTok as a tool for activism. The value of athlete voice is not limited by age or experience, and scholarship suggests youth activism can, in fact, be particularly impactful in pushing political and social change (Clark, 2016; Costanza-Chock et al., 2016). TikTok, and social media more generally, serves as an accessible tool with the potential to spark a conversation around human rights and activism; its potential as activist media is limitless.

REFERENCES

Abidin, C. (2020). Mapping internet celebrity on TikTok: Exploring attention economies and visibility labours. *Cultural Science Journal, 12*(1), 77–103. doi:10.5334/csci.140

Allen, S. E. (2021). Braids, beads, catsuits and tutus: Serena Williams' intersectional resistance through fashion. In R. Margrath, *Contemporary perspectives on athlete activism* (pp. 132–143). Milton Park, UK: Routledge. DOI: 10.4324/9781003140290–13

Algozzine, B., Hancock, D. R., Algozzine, R. (2016). *Doing case study research: A practical guide for beginning researchers*. United Kingdom: Teachers College Press.

Anderson, K. E. (2020). Getting acquainted with social networks and apps: It is time to talk about TikTok. *Library Hi Tech News, 37*(4), 7–12. https://doi.org/10.1108/lhtn-01-2020-0001

Bailey, A. (2020, June 8). UConn player Christyn Williams has a simple message about Black Lives Matter. It went viral on social media. *USA Today*. https://www.usatoday.com/story/sports/college/2020/06/08/uconn-basketball-player-christyn-williams-black-lives-matter-tiktok/5318984002/

Birrell, S., Trujillo, N., McDonald, M. G. (2000). *Reading sport: Critical essays on power and representation*. Lebanon: Northeastern University Press.

Bourdieu, P. (1993). *The field of cultural production*. New York: Columbia University Press.

Bourdieu, P. (1986). The forms of capital. In John G. Richardson (ed.), *Handbook of theory and research for the sociology of education* (pp. 241–258). New York: Greenwood.

Carter-Francique, A. R., Hart, A. & Cheeks, G. (2015). Examining the value of social capital and social support for Black student-athletes' academic success. *Journal of African American Studies, 19*, 157–177 https://doi.org/10.1007/s12111-015-9295-z

Clark, L. S. (2016). Participants on the margins: #BlackLivesMatter and the role that shared artifacts of engagement played among minoritized political newscomers on Snapchat, Facebook, and Twitter. *International Journal of Communication, 10*(1), 235–253.

Clopton, A. W. (2011). Using identities to explore social capital differences among white and African American student athletes. *Journal of African American Studies, 15*(1), 58–73 https://doi.org/10.1007/s12111-010-9121-6

Clopton, A. W. (2012). Social capital, gender, and the student athlete. *Group Dynamics: Theory, Research, and Practice, 16*(4), 272–288. https://doi.org/10.1037/a0028376

Costanza-Chock, S., Schweidler, C., Basilio, T., McDermott, M., Lo, P., & Ortenburger, M. (2016). Media in action: A field scan of media & youth organizing in the United States. *Journal of Digital and Media Literacy, 4*(1–2). Retrieved from http://www.jodml.org/2016/06/27/media-in-action-a-field-scan-of-media-youth-organizing-in-the-united-states/

Cooky, C., & Antunovic, D. (2020). "This isn't just about us": Articulations of feminism in media narratives of athlete activism. *Communication & Sport, 8*(4–5), 692–711.https://doi.org/10.1177/2167479519896360

Crenshaw, K. (1991). Mapping the margins: Intersectionality, identity politics, and violence against women of color. *Stanford Law Review, 43*(6), 1241–1299. doi:10.2307/1229039

Forbes-Mewett, H., & Pape, M. (2019). Social capital and the U.S. college experiences of international student-athletes and non-athletes. *Journal of International Students, 9*(3), 777–794. https://doi.org/10.32674/jis.v9i3.772

Goffman, E. (1959). The presentation of self in everyday life [monograph]. University of Edinburgh Social Science Research Centre, 2, 1–162.

Geurin, A. N. (2017). Elite female athletes' perceptions of new media use relating to their careers: A qualitative analysis. *Journal of Sport Management, 31*(4), 345–359. doi:10.1123/jsm.2016–0157

Hautea, S., Parks, P., Takahashi, B., & Zeng, J. (2021). Showing they care (OR don't): AFFECTIVE publics and ambivalent Climate activism ON TIKTOK. *Social Media + Society, 7*(2). https://doi.org/10.1177/20563051211012344

Hudson, J. (2018). *What could have been: The mediated life and afterlife of Len Bias* [Unpublished doctoral dissertation]. College Park: University of Maryland Press.

Kaplan Hecker & Fink LLP. (2021, August 2). NCAA External Gender Equity Review. New York.

Kluch, Y. (2020). "My story is my activism!": (Re-)definitions of social justice activism among collegiate athlete activists. *Communication & Sport, 8*(4–5), 566–590. https://doi.org/10.1177/2167479519897288

Large, S. (2021, April 27). *TikTok: A level playing field in sports and social media.* Opendorse. https://opendorse.com/blog/tiktok-a-level-playing-field-in-sports/

Lebel, K. (2013). *Professional athlete self-presentation on Twitter* (Paper 1303). Electronic Thesis and Dissertation Repository.

Nahon, K., & Hemsley, J. (2013) *Going viral.* Cambridge: Polity Press.

Pegoraro, A. (2010). Look who's talking—Athletes on Twitter: A case study. *International Journal of Sport Communication, 3*(4), 501–514. doi:10.1123/ijsc.3.4.501

Prince, S. [@sedonerrr]. (2020, December 11). *concussed @hillaryellman #fyp #foryou #getsilly* [Video]. TikTok. https://www.tiktok.com/@sedonerrr/video /6769057960061619461?lang=en&is_copy_url=1&is_from_webapp=v1

Prince, S. [@sedonerrr]. (2021, March 18). *it's 2021 and we are still fighting for bits and pieces of equality. #ncaa #inequality #fightforchange* [Video]. TikTok. https:// www.tiktok.com/@sedonerrr/video/6941180880127888646?lang=en&is_copy_url =1&is_from_webapp=v1

Smith, L. R., & Sanderson, J. (2015). I'm going to Instagram it! An analysis of athlete self-presentation on Instagram. *Journal of Broadcasting & Electronic Media, 59*(2), 342–358. DOI: 10.1080/08838151.2015.1029125

Su, Y., Baker, B. J., Doyle, J. P., & Yan, M. (2020). Fan engagement in 15 SECONDS: Athletes' relationship marketing during a pandemic via TikTok. *International Journal of Sport Communication, 13*(3), 436–446. doi:10.1123/ijsc.2020–0238

ThotJay. [@tjthot] (2021, March 29). *#duet with @teresa_jack straight girls be like #gay #xyzbca #lgbt #fyp #foryou* [Video]. TikTok. https://www.tiktok.com/@tjthot /video/6945089814144371973?is_copy_url=1&is_from_webapp=v1

Tolentino, J. (2019). How TikTok holds our attention. *The New Yorker.* www .newyorker.com/magazine/2019/09/30/ how-tiktok-holds-our-attention (accessed 5 January 2020).

Tufekci, Z. (2013). "Not this one": Social movements, the attention economy, and microcelebrity networked activism. *American Behavioral Scientist, 57*(7), 848–870. https://doi.org/10.1177/0002764213479369

Vázquez-Herrero, J., Negreira-Rey, M.-C., & López-García, X. (2020). Let's dance the news! How the news media are adapting to the logic of TikTok. *Journalism,* 1–19. https://doi.org/10.1177/1464884920969092

Wang, Y. (2020). Humor and camera view on mobile short-form video apps influence user experience and technology-adoption intent, an example of TikTok (DouYin). *Computers in Human Behavior, 110,* 106373. https://doi.org/10.1016/j.chb.2020 .10637

Williams, C. [@iamchristynwilliams] (2020, June 2) *Just in case anybody is STILL confused. . . . .#BlackLivesMatter #greenscreen #fyp #foryoupage* [Video]. TikTok. https://www.tiktok.com/@iamchristynwilliams/video/6833926092156390662?is _copy_url=1&is_from_webapp=v1&lang=en

Chapter 14

"The Time Is Now to Fight for Whatever You Feel Is Right"

Lewis Hamilton's Instagram Activism in 2020

Mariann Bardocz-Bencsik, Robert
Kwame, and Tamás Dóczi

Lewis Hamilton is one of the most successful motorsport athletes of all time, and one of the very few who has reached a global celebrity status. The year 2020 was a significant one for him, both on and off the racing circuit. Not only did he win his seventh Formula 1 world championship title, tying Michael Schumacher's once seemed-to-be-unrepeatable achievement, but he broke several other records, including the most Grand Prix wins in Formula 1 history. It was a memorable year for the Brit icon outside of his racing career as well, as he was heavily engaged with various societal issues. He used his most followed social media account, Instagram, to draw attention to and share his opinion about several development topics, including the fight against social injustices and climate change. His athletic and activist achievements were recognized by a number of prestigious awards. He received knighthood from Queen Elizabeth II for his contribution to motorsports,[1] he won the 2020 BBC Sports Personality of the Year Award, he was elected British GQ's Game Changer of the Year and he made the 100 Most Influential People of 2020 list by Time Magazine,[2] just to mention a few of his accolades in that year alone.

There is no doubt that Lewis Hamilton is a phenomenal motorsport athlete; his racing results speak for themselves. Nevertheless, what makes him a global celebrity is his lifestyle and activities outside of his racing life. Since

2015, he has participated in each MET Gala, one of the most exclusive social gatherings in the world, and since 2018, he collaborates with the Tommy Hilfiger clothing brand, designing his own line for the fashion house. He socializes with high-profile individuals from all walks of life, including fellow athletes such as tennis player Serena Williams and soccer player Neymar Jr., movie stars including Millie Bobby Brown and Will Smith, supermodels like Gigi Hadid and Winnie Harlow and history-making politicians such as the late Nelson Mandela. Over the years, he has earned his development celebrity status by actively working on development-related topics in various ways, including direct donations, offering his memorabilia for auctions and raising awareness through his social media accounts.

Twenty twenty was a turbulent year across the globe due to the COVID-19 pandemic and the global revival of the Black Lives Matter movement. Among its other negative effects, the health crisis limited the ways one can support developmental causes due to social distancing measures, travel restrictions and lockdowns. Celebrities' in-person participation in field trips and awareness-raising events was limited. On the other hand, the situation provided an exceptional setting for athletes to display altruism through social media (Sharpe et al., 2020). Thus, many of them, including Hamilton, focused their development work on online activism.

In this chapter, we analyze Lewis Hamilton's Instagram posts of 2020, categorizing them according to their content and further examining the ones that have a link to one or more of the Sustainable Development Goals (SDGs) of the United Nations (2015). We use Goodman and Barnes's (2011) development celebrity concept as the conceptual basis of our research, arguing that Lewis Hamilton is a development celebrity, who actively used his Instagram account to communicate about developmental challenges in 2020. With his online activities, he drew the attention of motor sports lovers around the world to some highly important global development topics.

The Concept of Development Celebrity and the SDGs

Based on Rojek's (2001) definition, celebrity is the accumulation of attention capital, and in the case of individual celebrities, three types exist. Ascribed celebrities earn their status through their bloodline, such as kings and queens. Attributed celebrities are individuals who attain fame quickly due to their presence in the media, for instance, reality tv personalities. These so-called "celetoids" can be characterized by a short-term form of attributed fame (Turner, 2006). Finally, achieved celebrities, including sports stars, are individuals whose social impact originates from their talents and accomplishments. According to to Hart and Tindall's (2009) proposition, the more merit-based the source of the celebrity's fame is, the more likely that his/her activism will be seen as powerful and successful.

Goodman and Barnes (2011) coined the term "development celebrity," referring to celebrities who work for social development causes in the "Third World." These stars spread the word about their development activities through various media channels, including their own social media accounts. Bardocz-Bencsik et al. (2019) used the "development celebrity" concept to examine elite athletes' efforts in development, expanding its scope geographically to the entire world, not solely referring to the "Third World."

When discussing and working on development topics, scholars and practitioners use the categorization of the SDGs. These are 17 global goals included in the 2030 Agenda for Sustainable Development and they represent a call for action by all countries in a global partnership. They include strategies that aim to "end poverty, build economic growth and address a range of social needs including education, health, equality and job opportunities while tackling climate change and preserve the oceans and forests" (UN, 2015). Figure 14.1 illustrates the SDGs.

#1: End poverty in all its forms everywhere
#2: End hunger, achieve food security and improved nutrition and promote sustainable agriculture
#3: Ensure healthy lives and promote well-being for all at all ages
#4: Ensure inclusive and equitable quality education and promote lifelong learning opportunities for all
#5: Achieve gender equality and empower all women and girls
#6: Ensure availability and sustainable management of water and sanitation for all
#7: Ensure access to affordable, reliable, sustainable, and modern energy for all
#8: Promote sustained, inclusive, and sustainable economic growth; full and productive employment; and decent work for all
#9: Build resilient infrastructure, promote inclusive and sustainable industrialization, and foster innovation
#10: Reduce inequality within and among countries
#11: Make cities and human settlements inclusive, safe, resilient, and sustainable
#12: Ensure sustainable consumption and production patterns
#13: Take urgent action to combat climate change and its impacts
#14: Conserve and sustainably use the oceans, seas, and marine resources for sustainable development

Figure 14.1. The Sustainable Development Goals of the United Nations. Source: United Nations. n.d. "Sustainable Development Goals. Communications materials." Accessed January 11, 2022. Credits: United Nations, 2018. The content of this publication has not been approved by the United Nations and does not reflect the views of the United Nations or its officials or Member States. https://www.un.org/sustainabledevelopment.

#15: Protect, restore and promote sustainable use of terrestrial ecosystems, sustainably manage forests, combat desertification, and halt and reverse land degradation and halt biodiversity loss

#16: Promote peaceful and inclusive societies for sustainable development, provide access to justice for all and build effective, accountable and inclusive institutions at all levels

#17: Strengthen the means of implementation and revitalize the global partnership for sustainable development (UN website, accessed on March 25, 2021).

Considering the above presented definitions and concepts, we argue that Lewis Hamilton is a development celebrity who raised awareness to a number of development topics in 2020 through his Instagram account.

A Glimpse Into Hamilton's Instagram: Huge Followerbase, Frequent Posting, Mixed Content

Lewis Hamilton's Instagram is his most popular social media account. At the time of the analysis (January 2021), his account had 21.4 million followers. For comparison, his second most followed account is on Twitter, and it had

6.1 million followers at the time. To put the number of his Instagram followers into perspective, we looked at the follower-base of the top 12 most followed F1-drivers and other motorsport athletes. It turned out that Hamilton's Instagram is by far the most popular among them. Table 14.1 lists the F1 drivers' accounts in decreasing order of popularity. It is worth noting that the account of the F1 series (@f1) had 11.7 million followers in January 2021.

Comparing Hamilton's follower-base with those of other stars of highly popular motorsports, it turns out that seven-time MotoGP champion Valentino Rossi (@valeyellow46) got the closest to him with 9.8 million followers. He is followed by 2020 MotoGP champion Marc Marquez (@marcmarquez93) who has a 5.3 million fanbase on Instagram. Looking at these numbers, it is undeniable that currently, Lewis Hamilton has the largest Instagram follower-base in motorsports.

In 2020, Hamilton posted 253 times on his main Instagram feed. Regarding the visual content of these posts, they consisted of 113 photos, 79 galleries,[3] 46 videos, and 15 so-called Instagram TVs, practically, longer videos. His posts have diverse content, from half-naked selfies to reposted video footage about cruelty in the seafood industry.[4] In the upcoming chapter, we categorize his posts based on their overall message, and then turn toward those that are about developmental topics.

Table 14.1. *Instagram Accounts of the Most Popular Formula-1 Drivers of the 2020 Season* (in decreasing order of follower-base)

Name	IG followers as of January 3, 2021	IG handle
Lewis Hamilton	21.4 m	https://www.instagram.com/lewishamilton/
Charles Leclerc	4 m	https://www.instagram.com/charles_leclerc/
Daniel Ricciardo	4 m	https://www.instagram.com/danielricciardo/
Max Verstappen	3.9 m	https://www.instagram.com/maxverstappen1/
Lando Norris	2.4 m	https://www.instagram.com/landonorris/
Kimi Raikkonen	2.1 m	https://www.instagram.com/kimimatiasraikkonen/
Carlos Sainz	2.1 m	https://www.instagram.com/carlossainz55/
Valtteri Bottas	1.9 m	https://www.instagram.com/valtteribottas/
George Russell	1.6 m	https://www.instagram.com/georgerussell63/
Pierre Gasly	1.4 m	https://www.instagram.com/pierregasly/
Romain Grosjean	1.4 m	https://www.instagram.com/grosjeanromain/
Sergio Perez	1.4 m	https://www.instagram.com/schecoperez/

Source: Own table

METHODOLOGY

As our data collection method, the first author created a database of Lewis Hamilton's Instagram posts of 2020 (n=253) in Microsoft Excel. The database contained the following information about each post: publication date, caption, type of visual content (photo, video, gallery, Instagram TV), tagged profiles, used hashtags. Captions are texts that accompany the visual content of posts. Tagging is a widely-used tool on social media to draw attention to another profile on the same platform, while hashtags give the opportunity to social media users to join a conversation about a certain topic. Our analysis is considered secondary research as it draws on existing data collected from a social media platform and later analyzed according to a research objective (Filo et al., 2015).

Based on the research objectives, qualitative thematic analysis was chosen to serve as our analytical method. Thematic analysis is a method to identify and analyze themes in qualitative data (Clarke & Braun, 2014). Clarke and Braun claim that it can be used to address various types of research questions, including those about individuals' views and opinions.

In the existing scholarship, several types of methods have been used to examine Instagram posts. A study on athletes' self-representation on Instagram analyzed the posts' imagery and their captions separately, reasoning that the two do not always correlate (Smith, 2015). Another study of fitness-related posts was primarily based on the content analysis of the photos, while captions and hashtags were used to interpret ambiguous content and motivations behind the image (Webb, 2018). Research focusing on body positivity used a three-level coding of Instagram posts. One level solely focused on imagery, while another dealt with the complete post (including imagery, captions, and hashtags) to determine the overall theme of the posts (Cohen, 2019).

In our study, adopting and adapting Webb's (2018) approach to captions and hashtags and adopting Cohen's (2019) third level of coding, the unit of analysis was a complete Instagram post. The name "Instagram" is the portmanteau of "instant camera" and "telegram," which underpins our claim that both imagery and captions are vital elements of posts. Therefore, we argue that an Instagram post's overall message can be best captured if the unit of analysis is the whole post. The focus of posts is mostly on the imagery and the caption, but the examination of tags and hashtags are helpful in clarifying ambiguous content. This is particularly useful in the case of seemingly personal, but oftentimes paid promotional posts.

We followed Clarke and Braun's (2014) six-phase process of thematic analysis in order to code and develop the themes that emerge from the posts. At the stage of data collection, the first author read and reread the captions, looked at the photos and watched the video posts multiple times. During this process, she also made initial notes. In the second phase, she started developing initial codes, which were concise phrases that reflected the overall content of the post. In phase three, potential themes were developed, and the codes were clustered into them. In the next stage, the candidate themes were reviewed against the coded data, and then, against the whole dataset. At this stage, candidate themes were revised and adapted until the themes became coherent and reflected the most important features of the data. In the fifth stage, the first author defined and named the themes. The final phase was about 'writing up,' which still involved assembling, organizing and editing the themes. At this stage, extracts from the captions were selected in order to provide evidence for the analytic claims.

From the second phase on, the third author was consulted and in case of different opinions among the researchers, the discussion went on until agreement was reached (Table 14.2). At the final stage, two social media professionals were consulted on questions that arose during the internal discussions. These consultations focused on the theme of paid posts. Posting promotional content is a continuously evolving social media practice, which has been largely unaddressed by academia. Thus, the involvement of experts was necessary to categorize some suspectedly promotional posts.

2020: A Year of Online Development Celebrity Activism

According to Goodman and Barnes (2011), development celebrities need to be credible and authentic, and need to have some expertise about their chosen development topic to be successful. They can gain their credibility and authenticity by associating themselves with credible organizations and these qualities can be further strengthened by traditional and social media communication about the celebrities' involvement in development work (p. 75). Celebrities can gain their expertise by learning from knowledgeable organizations and individual experts and also through field trips at development projects.

Due to the global health crisis, social distancing measures were in place worldwide and international travel was restricted from the third month of 2020. It naturally led to celebrities shifting their activist work to the online sphere. Our analysis revealed that 18.2% of Lewis Hamilton's Instagram posts were dedicated to messaging about development challenges. These 46 posts were grouped into the categories of the SDGs by the first and the third author separately. One post could tackle multiple SDGs. After the separate categorization, a discussion took place among the first and the third author to tackle eventual misalignments, until full agreement was reached. The final categorization of the SDG-related posts can be found in Table 14.3.

Table 14.2. Themes of Hamilton's Instagram Posts and the Number of Posts in Each Theme

Name of theme	Definition of theme	Number of posts	% of all posts	Example post
Personal	Posts about his free time activities, such as playing music and doing sports for fun; friendships; selfies with little or no caption. This category excludes posts about his family and dog(s).	63	24.9	Imagery: Gallery of two images of Hamilton on a bike trip. Caption: Haven't been on a bike in a while, had a great workout up the mountain and got to have fun coming down. Butt sore af but gains tho [flexed bicep emoji]
Formula-1	Posts about the 2020 season, including competition and test results and other major happenings.	52	20.6	Imagery: Video of Hamilton's qualifying lap that earned him pole position Caption: 97th pole [raising hands emoji] / This track is tricky! Really blown away with all the support here this weekend. So nice to see the fans back in the stands. #TeamLH
SDGs	Posts that raise awareness about one or more of the global developmental challenges, categorized into the SDGs by the authors.	46	18.2	Imagery: A photo of Hamilton wearing an "End racism" slogan T-shirt Caption: Excited to be back! Let's do this [oncoming fist emoji] #EndRacism #BlackLivesMatter
Paid advertisement	Post that either indicate promotion with the built-in "paid promotion" labelling of IG or promotion is otherwise evident from the post.	35	13.8	Imagery: Two images of him watching tv Caption: Taking the time to rest and reflect. We all need a break, this year more than ever. Personally, I love to escape by watching TV. My #LGSIGNATURE TV creates a totally immersive experience through the crystal-clear images and premium audio; it's so easy to get lost in whatever I am watching. #LGSIGNATURExLewis #LGOLED8K

Personal about his family	Posts about his family and dog(s)	34	13.4	Imagery: A selfie video of Hamilton and his mum Caption: Mums my heart [red heart emoji]
Motivational	Posts with positive messaging, formulated to inspire his fanbase to do/be better in different aspects of life.	14	5.5	Imagery: Half-naked mirror selfie in training shorts Caption: With all that is happening in the world, my only get away is to train and channel the emotions and energy into building my body stronger. This has been the best training period I've ever had, I can't stop and I won't! Staying active both mentally and physically is so important today, I want to encourage those of you out there to keep working out even if it's only for 20 minutes. Every little helps.
Other	Posts that did not fit elsewhere, including public engagements, such as participation in award shows and other events; appearance in talk shows and on magazine covers.	9	3.6	Imagery: Gallery of four photos from the photoshoot for the British GQ magazine Caption: So honoured to be called @BritishGQ Game Changer of the Year [folded hands emoji] Thank you GQ / Story and photographs: @misanharriman Stylist: @elgarjohnson Grooming: @yukomua Hair: #KerryAnnChristopher Barber: #AinsworthRamsay
Total		253	100	

Source: Own table

Table 14.3. *Lewis Hamilton's SDG-related Instagram Posts*

Date	Broad theme	SDGs tackled
January 9	Natural disaster: Australian wildfires	13, 15
February 12	Plastic pollution	12
February 16	Animal injustice	14
February 18	Animal injustice	15
March 8	Women's empowerment, climate change	5, 13
March 9	Natural disaster: Australian wildfires	13, 15
March 10	Natural disaster: Australian wildfires	13, 15
March 16	COVID-19	3
May 30	Black Lives Matter (BLM)	10, 16
June 2	BLM	10, 16
June 5	BLM	10, 16
June 8	BLM	10, 16
June 8	BLM	10, 16
June 9	BLM	10, 16
June 9	BLM	10, 16
June 9	BLM	10, 16
June 11	BLM	10, 16
June 11	BLM	10, 16
June 16	Education for all	4
June 17	BLM	10, 16
June 21	BLM	10, 16
June 28	Pride	10, 16
June 29	BLM	10, 16
July 2	BLM	10, 16
July 3	BLM	10, 16
July 5	BLM	10, 16
July 13	Women's empowerment	5, 10
July 19	BLM	10, 16
July 19	BLM	10, 16
August 3	BLM	10, 16
August 5	Man-made disaster: Beirut explosion	17
August 10	BLM	10, 16
August 16	Natural disaster: Mauritius coral reefs' damage	13, 14
August 17	BLM	10, 16
August 27	BLM	10, 16
August 30	BLM	10, 16
September 10	Plastic pollution: beach clean-up	12, 14
September 13	BLM	10, 16
September 13	BLM	10, 16
September 17	Man-made disaster: Amazon burning	13
September 23	Climate change emergency	13
October 4	Black history month	10
October 22	Protest against police brutality in Nigeria: (EndSARS)	16
October 25	Protest against police brutality in Nigeria (EndSARS)	16
November 3	BLM	10, 16
November 23	Wildlife protection	15

Source: Own table

"WE HAVE TO ACT NOW PEOPLE, LET'S MAKE CHANGES TOGETHER!"

This quote is from an Instagram post Hamilton published on February 12, 2020. It is a repost that contains video footage about plastic pollution in the oceans. It was originally published by Parley, an environmental conservation organization.[5] A similarly toned quote serves as the title of the chapter—"the time is now to fight for whatever you feel is right"—which was posted by Hamilton and accompanied a mirror selfie in a racing suit. It was published on July 19, and it encouraged the readers to fight against discrimination.[6]

These two posts, along with 44 others are all elements of Hamilton's online development celebrity work that he carried out on Instagram in 2020. In the following section, we have a look at the development topics he most frequently tackled.

Reducing Inequalities and Advocating for Strong and Just Institutions: Black Lives Matter and Other Social Justice Topics

The Black Lives Matter (BLM) movement was founded in 2013 and it focuses on protesting against white supremacy and police brutality against African-American people. Therefore, it is advocating for SDG 10 (Reducing inequalities) and SDG 16 (Peace, justice and strong institutions). The movement took momentum in late May 2020 after the killing of George Floyd, an African American U.S. citizen, by police officers. Protests against the murder and similar brutal acts were organized globally, despite the challenging circumstances due to the world health crisis. Moreover, the topic of racial injustice against African American people began trending on social media, and posts were often accompanied by the movement's official hashtag, #blacklivesmatter.

The revival of the BLM movement certainly inspired many elite athletes and teams all over the world to react and stand up for equal rights. During the decades of the Millennium, scholars observed a lack of activism by African American athletes (Agyemang, 2012); however, the year 2020 changed all of that. As Powell (2008) described it, the Black male athlete has "a comfortable standard of living, a fair degree of fame, a healthy amount of respect from the public, and because he doesn't want to jeopardize any of that, he also has a severe case of laryngitis" (p. 25). Even so, the upsurge of social media, the murders of George Floyd and Breonna Taylor,[7] and the subsequent nationwide protests demanded that celebrity athletes also take a stand. Change in the state-of-affairs is well illustrated by the fact that while

LeBron James refused to comment on the Darfur issue at the 2008 Olympics, claiming that "Sports and politics just don't match" (Agyemang, 2012, p. 442), he has been at the forefront of athlete activism in the past few years (Coombs et al., 2019).

Having first-hand experience in racial discrimination as a mixed-race athlete in a predominantly white sport (in motorsport) and society (in the United Kingdom), tackling the topic was evident for Hamilton as well. He engaged in the movement both online and in person. During the summer break of the Formula 1 season, he took part in a peaceful protest in London, which he later chronicled on Instagram.[8] Additionally, in the second half of the racing season, he led commemoration events within Formula 1 and supported the BLM movement by wearing promotional clothing[9] and with other non-verbal means.[10]

Posts about the BLM movement dominated his development-related communication on Instagram, with 25 out of his 46 development-themed posts (54.3%) drawing attention to the movement. His BLM posts also represent 9.9% of all of his posts in 2020, further showing that the topic has been of great importance to him in his overall online communication. Furthermore, #blacklivesmatter was his second most frequently used hashtag: he used it 15 times, only five times less than #TeamLH, his own hashtag as a racing driver. In addition to #blacklivesmatter, on five occasions, he used the #justiceforbreonnataylor hashtag, which is also related to the movement.

Hamilton showed all three features of successful development celebrities when he talked about the BLM movement. His expertise comes from his background as a mixed-race person, having experienced racist attitudes toward himself as a young kid. In a post on June 5, he shared footage of a short BBC documentary on him at the age of 12. In the clip, he talks about having been exposed to racist demeanor within his sport. The caption of his post presents the significant impact this experience had on him:

> I have spoken so little about my personal experiences because I was taught to keep it in, don't show weakness, kill them with love and beat them on the track. But when it was away from the track, I was bullied, beaten and the only way I could fight this was to learn to defend myself, so I went to karate. The negative psychological effects cannot be measured. (@lewishamilton, June 5, 2020)

Hamilton's authenticity and credibility are tangible in the way he engages with the topic. He published his first BLM post only five days after George Floyd's murder and continued his online activism throughout the year. Even though support for the #BlackLivesMatter movement lost momentum by autumn (Thomas & Horowitz, 2020), Hamilton kept his strong messaging about it. On November 3, over five months after George Floyd's death, he posted a photo of himself wearing a mask and a t-shirt with a BLM message. The caption of the post indicated that he is willing to continue his messaging about the topic:

> As we continue through the year I can definitely feel the slowing in momentum of BLM. I won't stop trying to push for change. Awareness is where that starts so you'll see me there each weekend representing. #BlackLivesMatter (@lewishamilton, November 3, 2020)

On December 26, he published a gallery of ten photos to sum up his year. The gallery contained three photos about antiracism and the BLM movement, including the cover picture.[11]

Over the course of the year, Hamilton was engaged in other social justice movements on Instagram as well. In October, he posted twice about EndSARS, a social movement against police brutality in Nigeria.[12] These posts can again be linked to SDG 16 (Peace, justice and strong institutions). On one occasion, he posted about the importance of adding black history into the curriculum.[13] According to his post, it could combat racial inequalities, and therefore, it is linked to SGD 10 (Reducing inequalities).

All About the Environment—Tackling Climate-related SDGs

Environmental protection, the fight against climate change and animal injustice are topics also very close to Hamilton's heart. He adopted a vegan lifestyle in 2017 and has since continued to passionately raise awareness about global warming and cruelties in the meat and seafood industry. Understanding that his credibility and authenticity can be morally questionable as he is working in an extremely polluting industry (Edgar, 2020), in a 2020 Instagram post he reported having taken steps to reduce his impact on the environment. These measures include offsetting his carbon footprint from his Formula 1 career dating back to 2007 and using electric cars when possible.[14] Throughout 2020, he continued his activism about the environment-related SDGs, namely SDG 12 (Responsible consumption and production), SDG 13 (Climate action), SDG 14 (Life below water), and SDG 15 (Life on land).

The year 2020 started with the devastating news about the Australian wildfires. Hamilton posted three times about this natural disaster and called his followers on Instagram to make changes to their lives in the fight against climate change—the cause of many natural disasters, including the wildfires. Among these three posts, two were about his visit to a rescue center that works with animals impacted by the wildfires. Such site visits give the development celebrity some sense of authenticity and a certain level of knowledge about the topic they are addressing (Goodman & Barnes, 2011).

In a video post published on March 9, Hamilton speaks in first-person singular about his experience spending a day in the rescue center, gaining first-hand knowledge about the devastation the fires caused and meeting some rescued animals. He takes a walk in the burned-down forest, feeds and plays with the animals, and learns—and makes us learn—about the local reality after the wildfires.[15] In the post's caption he emphasized how impactful this field trip was for him, and cites some facts about the damage caused by the fires. Talking about his experience, Hamilton said, "It was one of those days that really put things into perspective. Over one billion animals were impacted by the fires and it's going to take years for Australia to recover"[16] (@lewishamilton, March 9, 2020).

According to Goodman and Barnes (2011), such presentation of field trips can be an effective strategy in the making of the development celebrity. They claim that citing well-rehearsed facts and professionally documenting the trip can make the celebrity "para-experts" on the development topic, being managed by the expert organization they represent (p. 75).

Besides his posts about the wildfires, Hamilton posted about other environment-related topics as well. On five occasions, he published posts about man-made catastrophes, namely, the deforestation of the Amazon rainforest,[17] plastic pollution,[18] and the Mauritius Oil Disaster.[19] One of these posts was a self-recorded video about his spontaneous beach clean-up. In that video he showed how much waste ends up in the ocean and encouraged his followers to shop responsibly. By this clean-up activity, he illustrated what Goodman and Barnes (2011) refer to as the "extra-ordinary" development celebrity's engagement in something "ordinary." These acts can encourage us, "ordinary" people, to do something "extra-ordinary" in order to solve the problem the celebrity is talking about.

Still related to environmental topics, Hamilton posted three times about the protection of animals[20] and twice about the dangers of global warming.[21] It means that he published 12 posts about environment-related topics over the year, which is 26% of his developmental posts and 4.7% of all of his posts in 2020.

Women's Empowerment, Health Advice and More

In addition to his social justice-themed and environmental posts, Hamilton published five times about other developmental topics. He dedicated two posts to appreciate women that he looks up to professionally,[22] raising awareness about the importance of SDG 5 (Gender equality). Both posts tackled another SDG as well, which underlines the cross-sectoral nature of gender equality. At the beginning of the global health crisis caused by COVID-19, Hamilton demonstrated the proper hand-washing technique in a video post and pointed out the severity of the world situation.[23] With this post, he communicated about SDG 3 (Good Health and well-being).

In another post, he talked about his partnership with Togetherband, a campaign that promotes the SDGs through cooperation. He is the ambassador of SDG 4 (Quality education). On June 16, he shared a video post in which he candidly talks to students about his own struggles in school due to dyslexia.[24] With this confession, he highlighted his authenticity, a key characteristic of successful development celebrities.

On June 28, he posted a short message about gay pride, the promotion of equality, and visibility of LGBT individuals. With this post, he messaged about SDG 10 (Reduced inequalities) and SDG 16 (Peace, justice and strong institutions). On another occasion, he communicated about a man-made disaster—the Beirut explosion—and encouraged his followers to help those who are affected. He invited everyone to help in various ways, including financial and blood donations. With this post, he advocated for cooperation, and thus, communicated about SDG 17 (Partnerships for the Goals).

CONCLUSION

The ongoing growth and development of social media makes it easier for celebrities to speak out on their chosen development topics and get heard (Bulck, 2020). With an arsenal of social media tools, they can speak instantly and directly to their audience, without the filters of traditional media (Bennett, 2013). Celebrities' involvement in social movements have both costs and benefits, advantages and disadvantages (Meyer & Gamson, 1995). Nevertheless, according to studies, using their social platforms, celebrities can serve as standard bearers for social movements (Duvall & Heckemeyer, 2018). Lewis Hamilton did just that in 2020, when he passionately engaged in various developmental topics through his Instagram account. He has the freedom to decide what he shares with his over 21 million followers, which also means having the power to decide what developmental causes are worth dealing with. A number of scholars have noted that highly influential individuals making these decisions indicates a shift from traditional development work that is usually led by major agencies (Goodman & Barnes, 2011; Wilkins, 2012).

As our analysis shows, Hamilton's two most frequently talked-about developmental topics are reducing inequalities—mostly related to ethnicity—and environmental protection. Advocating for certain developmental topics can have controversial outcomes as well, which may have an impact on the perception of the development celebrity. As Edgar (2020) notes, when it comes to the threat of climate change, most of us are hypocrites. It naturally includes Hamilton, who is working in a highly polluting industry. Therefore, his advocacy for climate action can be the topic of a moral debate. Similar questions could be raised from one of his most well-documented commercial partnerships, the one with Tommy Hilfiger. In 2020, he published 12 posts about his collaboration with the clothing brand. Moreover, the hashtag of their collaborative clothing collection, #TommyXLewis, was the third most used hashtag on Hamilton's profile in 2020. This collaboration could be questionable based on Hamilton's passion for antiracism. The potential moral concern is based on the urban legend on the internet that Tommy Hilfiger made racist comments about who should and should not wear his clothes, which also had an impact on sales at the time (McNeil et al., 2001). Despite there being no evidence that Hilfiger made such comments and the brand handling the rumors effectively, the reputation of the fashion house was greatly damaged, especially when it comes to the topic of antiracism.

As the global health situation is slowly improving, more opportunities will emerge for Hamilton to continue his development celebrity work in person, complementing his online activism. These opportunities will include appearances at awareness-raising events and going on field trips. Whether it will impact the level of his online activism, only time will tell. This could be a topic of future studies. Another topic for further analysis of Hamilton's development work could be on his involvement as a team founder in Extreme E, an international e-car racing series that aims to raise awareness about the impact of climate change and human activity.

NOTES

1. Euronews. (2020, December 31). *Lewis Hamilton: Formula 1 driver receives a knighthood in Queen Elizabeth II's honours list.* Euronews. https://www.euronews .com/2020/12/31/lewis-hamilton-formula-1-driver-receives-a-knighthood-in-queen -elizabeth-ii-s-honours-list

2. Formula1.com. (2020, December 30). *Arise Sir Lewis! Hamilton to be awarded knighthood after historic seventh world title.* Formula1.com. https://www .formula1.com/en/latest/article.arise-sir-lewis-hamilton-to-be-awarded-knighthood -after-historic-seventh.2oKynH8fOmJytSk8mOo0o9.html

3. Seven galleries contained video content as well. Those videos are counted among the galleries and not counted among videos.

4. Reposting is a social media activity, which is sharing another account's original content on one's own account.

5. Hamilton, L. [@lewishamilton]. (2020, February 12). *We have to act now people, let's make changes together! #Repost · · · It takes: ▪20 years for a plastic bag to* [Video]. Instagram. https://www.instagram.com/p/B8do2f8FBgr/

6. Hamilton, L. [@lewishamilton]. (2020, July 19). *The time is now to fight for whatever you feel is right, change is coming! It will take us working* [Photo]. Instagram. https://www.instagram.com/p/CC0uhjes-3S/

7. Breonna Taylor was a black U.S. citizen who was killed by police officers in March 2020. The killing became the symbol of police brutality against black people in the U.S., and therefore became strongly linked to the BLM campaign.

8. Hamilton, L. [@lewishamilton]. (2020, June 21). *Went down to Hyde Park today for the peaceful protest and I was so proud to see in person so* [Photo]. Instagram. https://www.instagram.com/p/CBtUH0OBRf3/

9. Hamilton, L. [@lewishamilton]. (2020, July 2). *Still WE Rise* [Video]. Instagram. https://www.instagram.com/p/CCJu_I7hXqF/, Hamilton, L. [@lewishamilton]. (2020, July 3). *Excited to be back! Let's do this #EndRacism #BlackLivesMatter* [Photo]. Instagram. https://www.instagram.com/p/CCLH2vtsw4R/, Hamilton, L. [@lewishamilton]. (2020, July 5). *Today was an important moment for me and all the people out there who are working for and hoping for* [Photo]. Instagram. https://www.instagram.com/p/CCReSLFBu1C/

10. Hamilton, L. [@lewishamilton]. (2020, July 19). *Today I raced for everyone out there who is pushing to make positive change and fight inequality, however, sadly, as* [Photo]. Instagram.

11. Hamilton, L. [@lewishamilton]. (2020, December 26). *A look back on what has been a crazy year . . . What's been your favourite moment from 2020? Let's* [Photo]. Instagram. https://www.instagram.com/p/CJRNbmtMqy7/

12. Hamilton, L. [@lewishamilton]. (2020, October 22). *The senseless killing in Nigeria has got to stop. My heart breaks to see innocent lives taken at the hands* [Photo]. Instagram. https://www.instagram.com/p/CGpvKdQMkZD/, Hamilton, L. [@lewishamilton]. (2020, October 25). *We all have a responsibility to educate ourselves and raise awareness of the tragedies happening in the world around us* [Photo]. Instagram. https://www.instagram.com/p/CGw6GYQMFHE/

13. Hamilton, L. [@lewishamilton]. (2020, October 4). *Great to see @ mayorofldn teaming up with @theblackcurriculum to call for more diverse history to be taught in schools. Updating* [Photo]. Instagram. https://www.instagram.com/p/CF7aSEOsOLq/

14. Hamilton, L. [@lewishamilton]. (2020, September 3). *Recently I've been making many changes In my life to reduce my impact on the environment. The first step* [Photo]. Instagram. https://www.instagram.com/p/CErWff0sA_J/

15. Hamilton, L. [@lewishamilton]. (2020, March 9). *Wires Wildlife Rescue Today, I had the incredible opportunity to visit NSW, Australia to see the admirable work @WIRESWildlifeRescue is* [Video]. Instagram. https://www.instagram.com/p/B9h09YjBhGW/

16. Hamilton, L. [@lewishamilton]. (2020, March 9). *Wires Wildlife Rescue Today, I had the incredible opportunity to visit NSW, Australia to see the admirable*

work *@WIRESWildlifeRescue is* [Video]. Instagram. https://www.instagram.com/p/B9h09YjBhGW/

17. Hamilton, L. [@lewishamilton]. (2020, September 17). #ActForTheAmazon *If we lose the Amazon, we lose the fight against the climate crisis. It's that simple. And time* [Video]. Instagram. https://www.instagram.com/p/CFO94x2lL5c/

18. Hamilton, L. [@lewishamilton]. (2020, February 12). *We have to act now people, let's make changes together! #Repost · · It takes: ▪20 years for a plastic bag* [Video]. Instagram. https://www.instagram.com/p/B8do2f8FBgr/. Hamilton, L. [@lewishamilton]. (2020, September 10). *Every single piece of plastic ever made still exists today, and a heart-breaking amount end up being discarded and polluting* [Video]. Instagram. https://www.instagram.com/p/CE9qDrBlE7P/

19. Hamilton, L. [@lewishamilton]. (2020, August 16). *The state of environmental emergency declared in Mauritius is truly heartbreaking. Their beautiful coral reefs are home to thousands of* [Photo]. Instagram. https://www.instagram.com/p/CD8wfl4MrN4/

20. Hamilton, L. [@lewishamilton]. (2020, February 16). *1,400 pounds of shark fins were seized at a Miami port. This needs attention people, this is disgusting. People are* [Video]. Instagram. https://www.instagram.com/p/B8ol0StBbKm/, Hamilton, L. [@lewishamilton]. (2020, February 18). *This is the world we currently live in where humans believe that an animals life is worth less than one* [Video]. Instagram. https://www.instagram.com/p/B8uDx_PBUSf/, Hamilton, L. [@lewishamilton]. (2020, November 23). *It's so important that we fight for those that don't have a voice, animal rights and protecting our* [Photo]. Instagram. https://www.instagram.com/p/CH8OJ1gsAei/

21. Hamilton, L. [@lewishamilton]. (2020, September 23). *WE MUST ACT NOW..REPOST . . . : @washingtonpost A new digital clock unveiled in Manhattan's Union Square over the weekend promises to* [Photo]. Instagram. https://www.instagram.com/p/CFe-E24MPkR/

22. Hamilton, L. [@lewishamilton]. (2020, July 13). *I wanted to post this because it's such an important moment. This is Stephanie who is one of my* [Photo]. Instagram. https://www.instagram.com/p/CCmEaClMuda/, Hamilton, L. [@lewishamilton]. (2020, March 8). *This International Women's Day I want to celebrate the amazing women around the world who are dedicating themselves to the* [Photo]. Instagram. https://www.instagram.com/p/B9d-ViFh28n/

23. Hamilton, L. [@lewishamilton]. (2020, March 16). *I know that Coronavirus can make people nervous, but I want to reassure you all to stay calm,* not to [Video]. Instagram. https://www.instagram.com/p/B9zjmdaBJpw/

24. Hamilton, L. [@lewishamilton]. (2020, June 16). *Everyone, no matter where they're from or the colour of their skin, should have access to a quality education* [Video]. Instagram. https://www.instagram.com/p/CBf6GiMFpWn/

REFERENCES

Agyemang, K. (2012). Black male athlete activism and the link to Michael Jordan: A transformational leadership and social cognitive theory analysis. *International Review for the Sociology of Sport, 47*(4), 433–445. https://doi.org/10.1177/1012690211399509

Bardocz-Bencsik, M., Begović, M., & Dóczi, T. (2019). Star athlete ambassadors of sport for development and peace. *Celebrity Studies*, 1–16. https://doi.org/10.1080/19392397.2019.1639525

Bennett, L. (2013). "If we stick together we can do anything": Lady Gaga fandom, philanthropy and activism through social media. *Celebrity Studies, 5*(1–2), 138–152. https://doi.org/10.1080/19392397.2013.813778

Bulck, V. H. D. (2020). *Celebrity philanthropy and activism: Mediated interventions in the global public dphere* (1st ed.). London: Routledge.

Clarke, V., & Braun, V. (2014). Thematic analysis. In T. Teo (ed.), *Encyclopedia of critical psychology* (pp. 1947–1953). Springer Science+Business Media.

Cohen, R., Irwin, L., Newton-John, T., & Slater, A. (2019). #Bodypositivity: A content analysis of body positive accounts on Instagram. *Body Image, 29*, 47–57. https://doi.org/10.1016/j.bodyim.2019.02.007

Coombs, D. S., Lambert, C. A., Cassilo, D., & Humphries, Z. (2019). Flag on the play: Colin Kaepernick and the protest paradigm. *Howard Journal of Communications*, 1–20. https://doi.org/10.1080/10646175.2019.1567408

Duvall, S. S., & Heckemeyer, N. (2018). #BlackLivesMatter: Black celebrity hashtag activism and the discursive formation of a social movement. *Celebrity Studies, 9*(3), 391–408. https://doi.org/10.1080/19392397.2018.1440247

Edgar, A. (2020). Sport and climate change. *Sport, Ethics and Philosophy, 14*(1), 1–3. https://doi.org/10.1080/17511321.2020.1694601

Filo, K., Lock, D., & Karg, A. (2015). Sport and social media research: A review. *Sport Management Review, 18*(2), 166–181. https://doi.org/10.1016/j.smr.2014.11.001

Goodman, M. K., & Barnes, C. (2011). Star/poverty space: The making of the "development celebrity." *Celebrity Studies, 2*(1), 69–85. https://doi.org/10.1080/19392397.2011.544164

McNeil, K. R., Johnson, O. E., & Johnson, A. Y. (2001). "Did you hear what Tommy Hilfiger said?" Urban legend, urban fashion and African-American generation Xers. *Journal of Fashion Marketing and Management: An International Journal, 5*(3), 234–240. https://doi.org/10.1108/eum0000000007289

Meyer, D. S. (1995). The challenge of cultural elites: Celebrities and social movements. *Sociological Inquiry, 65*(2), 181–206. https://doi.org/10.1111/j.1475-682x.1995.tb00412.x

Powell, S. (2008). *Souled out?: How Blacks are winning and losing in sports.* Champaign, IL: Human Kinetics.

Rojek, C. (2001). *Celebrity*. London: Reaktion Books.

Sharpe, S., Mountifield, C., & Filo, K. (2020). The social media response from athletes and sport organizations to COVID-19: An altruistic tone. *International*

Journal of Sport Communication, 13(3), 474–483. https://doi.org/10.1123/ijsc
.2020-0220

Smith, L. R., & Sanderson, J. (2015). I'm Going to Instagram It! An Analysis of
Athlete Self-Presentation on Instagram. *Journal of Broadcasting & Electronic
Media, 59*(2), 342–358. https://doi.org/10.1080/08838151.2015.1029125

't Hart, P., & Tindall, K. (2009). Leadership by the famous: Celebrity as political capital. In J. Kane, H. Patapan, P. 't Hart (eds.), *Dispersed leadership in democracies*
(pp. 255–278). Oxford: Oxford University Press.

Thomas, D., & Horowitz, J. M. (2020, September 16). *Support for Black Lives
Matter has decreased since June but remains strong among Black Americans.*
Pew Research Center. https://www.pewresearch.org/fact-tank/2020/09/16/support
-for-black-lives-matter-has-decreased-since-june-but-remains-strong-among-black
-americans/

Turner, G. (2006). The mass production of celebrity. *International Journal of Cultural
Studies, 9*(2), 153–165. https://doi.org/10.1177/1367877906064028

Webb, J. B., Thomas, E. V., Rogers, C. B., Clark, V. N., Hartsell, E. N., & Putz, D.
Y. (2018). Fitspo at every size? A comparative content analysis of #curvyfit versus
#curvyyoga Instagram images. *Fat Studies, 8*(2), 154–172. https://doi.org/10.1080
/21604851.2019.1548860

Wilkins, K. (2012). Is the development industry taking care of business?—Why we
need accountability in communication for social justice. *Glocal Times.*

United Nations. (2015). *Transforming our world: The 2030 agenda for sustainable development.* https://sdgs.un.org/sites/default/files/publications/21252030
%20Agenda%20for%20Sustainable%20Development%20web.pdf

United Nations. n.d. 17 goals to transform our world. Accessed March 25, 2021. https:
//www.un.org/sustainabledevelopment/

Chapter 15

Mapping the Terrain of Athletes and Sports Organizations as Influential Figures in Online Conversations Around Social Justice Issues

Brandon Boatwright and Virginia S. Harrison

INTRODUCTION AND CONTEXT

Athlete activism has a long history. From Vietnam War protests and social justice commentary by Muhammed Ali to Tommie Smith and John Carlos' demonstration at the 1968 Olympics to Billie Jean King's call for gender equality, athletes have used their platforms to call attention to the political or social justice issues of their time (Billings et al., 2018; Cooper et al., 2019; Mueller, 2021). While the social justice activism we see from athletes today has roots in these examples, today's athlete activism takes a different form. With the advent of social media, athletes now have unfiltered, direct access to their fans and the general public through their platforms (Galily, 2019; Kassing & Sanderson, 2015). Athletes simply posting on social media are now newsworthy events (e.g., in 2016, ESPN wrote an article about famous athletes' best first tweets[1]). Modern social justice protests like Colin Kaepernick's kneeling for police brutality or Megan Rapinoe's call for equal pay are thus amplified by social media conversations, both by the athlete themselves and the witnessing public (Frederick et al., 2018; Johnson et al., 2020; Sanderson et al., 2016; Schmidt et al., 2019). Thus, the age of social justice activism closely relies upon the incredible access and voice athletes have to reach audiences inside and outside sport.

A clear example of the power of athlete voices on social media surrounds the death of George Floyd and the Black Lives Matter movement. George Floyd, a black man, was murdered by a white Minneapolis police officer, Derek Chauvin, on May 25, 2020, in the midst of his arrest for a forgery charge (*BBC News*, 2020). Chauvin placed a knee on Floyd's neck for nearly 10 minutes, despite Floyd's pleas that he couldn't breathe. If not for a witness filming the incident with her smartphone and posting it to social media, the truth about the death of Floyd may not have been known (Treisman, 2021). During the ensuing days, athletes took to social media to express outrage and calls for change (Lauletta, 2020). In the months that followed, athletes took to the streets to participate in Black Lives Matter marches and posted continued messages of protest on social media (Deb, 2020).

When Chauvin was convicted of second-degree murder on April 20, 2021, athletes again used their platform to react and renew calls for change (*Los Angeles Times*, 2021). The conviction of a police officer for murder is incredibly rare in the United States (Tucker et al., 2021). This chapter looks specifically at the day of Chauvin's historic conviction to analyze just how prominent athletes figured into the conversation about social and racial justice. During the year between Floyd's death and Chauvin's conviction, athletes had cemented their role in the conversation about racial justice, with players canceling NBA and WNBA games in the wake of Jacob Blake's shooting by a white police officer (Voepel, 2020); the Atlanta Dream campaigning for black Senate candidate Raphael Warnock in Georgia (Gregory, 2021); and college athletes marching on campuses across the country (Nietzel, 2020). Thus, April 20 offers a focal point in the social justice conversation which highlights the role of social media in providing a platform for athletes to take a prominent role in advocating for political and social change.

This chapter will begin with an overview of athletes as activists throughout history and the critical intersection of athlete activism and social media networks changing the way athletes and sports organizations engage with societal issues. The study detailed in this chapter will add to the conversation about athletes' networked activism around racial justice issues. While we may anecdotally believe that athletes are leading the social justice charge after the murder of George Floyd, our study will empirically investigate just how athletes are situated in this conversation on social media. Specifically, we use social network analysis of Twitter data from April 20 to see how athletes, sports organizations and media personalities are positioned in the social media conversation about Chauvin's conviction and how these messages influence the overall structure of the network.

LITERATURE REVIEW

Athletes as Activists

This chapter focuses specifically on athlete activism as defined by Cooper, Macaulay, and Rodriguez (2019): "engagement in intentional actions that disrupt oppressive hegemonic systems by challenging a clearly defined opposition while simultaneously empowering individuals and groups disadvantaged by inequitable arrangements" (pp. 154–155). Thus, when we consider the history of athlete activism in sport in this chapter, we are concerned specifically with athletes, organizations, and media personalities who speak out against the status quo and challenge power dynamics in society. Indeed, activism is different than athlete citizenship (e.g., Agyemong, 2014) or athletes acting in corporate social responsibility (e.g., Agyemong & Singer, 2011; Giannoulakis & Dryer, 2009), which are concerned with positive athlete behavior and with the community image of athletes, respectively. Additionally, this chapter focuses on activism from athletes related to racial injustice. While activism certainly includes discussions of gender issues like equal pay or hypermasculinity, equal rights for the LGBTQ+ community, or economic disparity, our examination focuses on racial injustice due to the focal point of athlete activism around the Floyd murder and Chauvin's subsequent conviction. Protests over Floyd's murder were some of the largest since the Civil Rights Era in the United States (Silverstein, 2021), and professional sport leagues in the United States like the NFL include a majority of minority athletes (Mueller, 2021). Thus, racial justice is a critical issue through which to examine athlete activism.

Scholars have indicated that athletes are entering a "fourth wave" of activism, characterized by the rise of the Black Lives Matter movement in 2013 (Cooper et al., 2019; Edwards, 2016; Mueller, 2021). The seminal moment was when members of the NFL's St. Louis Rams raised their fists during pregame ceremonies to demonstrate solidarity with protesters in Ferguson, Missouri, after the shooting death of a black teenager by white police officers (Frederick et al., 2018). Just a few years before, LeBron James and fellow NBA players posted protest images to social media after the shooting death of Trayvon Martin, a black teenager, by a white man (Galily, 2019). This fourth wave is characterized by the "economic and technological transfer of power" based on the resources afforded black athletes in the modern era, including their access to social media (Cooper et al., 2019, p. 161). Because the Black Lives Matter movement utilized social media to mobilize demonstrations, the door opened for athletes to use this tool to do likewise. Scholarship has demonstrated the power of social media in athlete activism in two ways: (1) athletes can mobilize efforts like protests and demonstrations, e.g., college athletes at the University of Missouri organizing protests against racist leadership (Frederick et al., 2018; Yan et al., 2018), and (2) athletes have a platform to speak up about issues and concerns, for example, LeBron James criticizing racist actions of President Trump (Galilly, 2019). Importantly, while narratives tend to prioritize the voices of men in activism, black women have been vocal and active advocates for racial justice and other socio-political issues like equal pay (Cooky & Antunovic, 2020). WNBA players were some of the most outspoken on Twitter in 2016, leading the conversation about Black Lives Matter in sport, although their words were often overlooked by the mainstream press.

Despite the rise of the fourth wave of athlete activism, support for athletes and their messages is not universal. Recent scholarship (e.g., Frederick et al., 2018; Galily, 2019; Mueller, 2021; Park et al., 2020; Sanderson et al., 2016; Sappington et al., 2019; Schmidt et al., 2019; Smith & Tryce, 2019) has investigated fan reaction to activism and perceptions of activist athletes. Beliefs about patriotism and racism may play a role in these reactions. Fans who did not support NFL player Colin Kaepernick's protests during the national anthem indicated stronger feelings of "uncritical patriotism" or unquestioning nationalism, while those who supported his protests tended to show more "constructive patriotism" (Smith & Tryce, 2019). Generally, fans who support athlete activism may already have stronger support for social justice issues overall (Sappington et al., 2019). Additionally, some fans still feel that protesting or activist messaging is not appropriate in sports. When analyzing fan comments on social media about athlete activists, fans criticized the players for speaking up in an athletic venue or event (Sanderson et al., 2016; Schmidt et al., 2019) or attacked the messaging and purpose of Black Lives Matter (Frederick et al., 2018). On the other hand, fan support for protests may be tied to non-issue-related reasons like social desirability bias (Mueller, 2021). Fans of color may feel compelled to support athlete activists who look like them (Mueller, 2021) or support leagues who employ these athletes (Harrison & Erlichman, in press). However, other analyses offer hope for athlete activism in the age of social media.

ONLINE OPINION LEADERSHIP AND THE NETWORKED INFLUENCE OF ATHLETES

Extant research on social media activism has shown that highly active users engage in online conversations around social and political issues by commenting, liking, and sharing indexed content (e.g., hashtags) around particular subjects (Xiong et al., 2019). By engaging in these conversations on social media platforms like Twitter, athletes, sports organizations, and media personalities become influential participants in the way issues are framed and, consequently, play a vital role in civic engagement around these issues. For example, while social media can be used to criticize and propagate racist rhetoric (Frederick et al., 2018; Kassing & Sanderson, 2015), sports superstars like LeBron James may be able to break down political silos that exist on social media by using these platforms to speak out (Galily, 2019). Their celebrity status may actually heighten awareness for the issues, like racial justice, on which they speak (Johnson et al., 2020). Under this assumption, it stands to reason that athletes, organizations, and media personalities involved in the online conversation around the Chauvin verdict leveraged their popularity to advance their own beliefs and ostensibly shape those of other users. In other words, athletes, organizations, and media outlets take on the role of *online opinion leaders*.

Advancements in digital technology and social media platforms have underscored the importance of online opinion leadership. By providing a more efficient means to connect with others and present oneself as an expert in a particular area, social media platforms have led scholars to explore the concept of *networked influenc*e (Gruzd & Wellman, 2014; Schäfer & Taddicken, 2015). In a special issue on the subject in *American Behavioral Scientist,* Gruzd and Wellman (2014) argued that social influence has given way to networked influence. They suggested that:

> Influence is no longer one person being influenced by mass communication or one person influencing another one-to-one. Rather [networked influence] shows the impact of network size, strong ties, mutual awareness . . . socially similar (homophilous) network members, clusters of ties, bridges across clusters, and how people navigate among clusters in their complex networks. (p. 1256)

Because of their immense popularity and notoriety, tweets from athletes, sports organizations, and media personalities do not exist in a vacuum. Rather, they are consumed, affirmed, challenged, distorted, and advanced as various users engage with them across digital platforms. To that end, we are interested in exploring the extent to which athletes, sports organizations, and media personalities account for the broader conversation around the Chauvin verdict and identify specific accounts that were influential in the way users made sense out of the verdict. Consequently, we advance the following research questions:

> RQ1: How prominently are athletes, sports organizations, and media personalities featured in the Twitter conversation around the Chauvin verdict?

RQ2: What are the most popular sports related accounts involved in the conversation?

METHODOLOGY

Overview of SNA

Social network analysis (SNA) builds on and uses concepts from the mathematics of graph theory to explore the structure of the relationships between social actors. In a social network, a person or entity is considered a *node* or *vertex*, and a relationship between people and/or entities is called a *link* or *edge*. SNA looks at a collection of ties among a population and creates measurements that describe the location of each person or entity within the overall network. Hansen et al. (2011) contend that the "position or location of a person or vertex in relation to all the others is a primary concern of social network analysis" (p. 32). For instance, the concept of network centrality consists of a series of metrics that characterize the degree to which a social network is centered around one or more important people. This, in turn, allows researchers to identify users who play influential roles in the spread of information (del Fresno García et al., 2016). A growing body of sports communication research has applied SNA to better understand the spread of information and resources within the sport industry (e.g., Hambrick, 2012; Wäsche et al., 2017).

Data Collection

We used a third-party social analytics software, Sprinklr, to harvest Twitter mentions and replies that contained the terms "Chauvin," "George Floyd," and/or "#GeorgeFloyd" between a six-hour span on April 20, 2021 (from 4 to 10 p.m. [EST]), reflecting the highest peak in conversation around the Chauvin verdict. In all, this scrape resulted in 60,433 tweets. In order to conduct the analytics detailed below, we chose to harvest Twitter users' interactions, specifically in the form of direct mentions and replies between users.

According to Himelboim and Golan (2019), the practice of mentioning users on Twitter using the @ symbol serves two main purposes: "First, it associated a post with another user (e.g., an individual, an organization, a brand), serving as metadata for the tweet. Second, it serves as a secondary route of content distribution. When a tweet mentions a given user, that tweet will appear on the recipient's Notifications tab and Home timeline view if the author of the tweet follows the sender" (p. 5). Conceptualizing mentions on Twitter as interactions in a social network captures the importance of users connecting with one another to spread information, ideas, and opinions. Thus, this analysis is appropriate for determining how athletes are situated in the Twitter conversation related to Chauvin's verdict on April 20. We then used an open-source data cleaning program called OpenRefine to clean the data and format it into an adjacency list suitable for social network analysis through Gephi, a social network analysis program.

Data Analysis

To address RQ1, modularity for the network was calculated to identify structurally similar groups or clusters. According to Rim, Lee, and Yoo (2020), modularity "measures how good the division is, or how separated the different vertex [i.e., node] types are from each other . . . Networks with high modularity have dense connections between the nodes within modules but sparse connections between nodes in different modules" (p. 5). Kadushin (2012) suggested that structural similarity refers to instances when "nodes with similar patterns of relationships with other nodes are grouped together" (p. 50). In SNA, these groups are commonly defined as *communities*, or "a set of nodes that have a higher likelihood of connecting to each other than to the nodes of other communities" (Perez & Germon, 2016, p. 121). Specifically, we used an open-source social network analysis program (Gephi) to perform the Louvain algorithm for fast community detection (Blondel et al., 2008).

To address RQ2, eigenvector centrality was calculated for each node in the network to identify figures in the conversation that were influential in the overall network. In essence, eigenvector centrality is considered a measure of a node's prestige or popularity within a network. According to Hansen et al. (2020), eigenvector centrality takes into consideration not only how many connections a node has, but also the centrality of the nodes that it is connected to. Prior research in sports communication has shown that athletes have the potential to occupy important positions in a social network around social issues through node-level eigenvector centrality measures (e.g., Yan et al., 2018; Yan et al., 2019).

RESULTS

RQ1 sought to explore the overall structure of the network in order to identify the composition of various community clusters embedded in the conversation around the Chauvin verdict. To do this, the modularity of each network timeframe was calculated. Modularity values range from -1 to 1, with values closer to 1 indicating strong community structure (Newman & Girvan, 2004). According to Newman (2006), any modularity value above 0.4 is generally a good indicator of community structure. Modularity for this analysis was 0.901. Nodes within each community were manually identified in order to explore the composition of the ten largest topical communities within each network.

In all, a total of 9,753 communities were identified. Table 15.1 provides a list of the top 10 communities which, altogether, accounted for roughly 25% of the overall network. The community accounting for the highest percentage of the network (modularity class 2, 6.47%) primarily revolved around reactions to Rep. Nancy Pelosi's comments that George Floyd "sacrificed himself" for justice (Slisco, 2021). The community with the second-highest percentage (modularity class 161, 3.09%) centered on comments Rep. Maxine Waters made calling for protesters to become more "confrontational" should no guilty verdict be reached in the trial (Duster, 2021). Other communities also revolved around political figures (modularity class 192, 2.74%), left-leaning media outlets and personalities (modularity class 1388, 2.72%; modularity class 1415, 1.67%), network media outlets and personalities (modularity class 415, 1.81%), right-leaning media outlets and personalities (modularity class 10, 2.11; modularity class 1402, 1.51%) and British media outlets and personalities (modularity class 166, 1.30%). Interestingly, though, athletes, sports organizations, and media personalities (modularity class 5167) accounted for 1.48% of the overall network and were the ninth-highest ranked community.

RQ2 sought to identify who the most important sports figures and organizations were in the overall network. Since modularity class 5167 was primarily comprised of such accounts, we identified the top 20 Twitter accounts associated with sports figures, organizations, and media personalities using their eigenvector centrality scores (see Table 15.2). LeBron James (@kingjames) was the most prominent figure in this community. James tweeted a simple, one-word message following the Chauvin verdict—ACCOUNTABILITY (see Fig. 15.1).

James also generated a lot of attention for a tweet he later deleted that called for accountability in the fatal shooting of a 16-year-old Ohio girl after receiving backlash for telling the police officer involved that "YOU'RE NEXT" (Polus, 2021). Memphis Grizzlies guard Ja Morant tweeted simply, "justice." ESPN reporter Adam Schefter tweeted a statement from the NFL that celebrated the guilty verdict. The Pittsburgh Penguins issued a statement from their Twitter account that read, in part: "You don't need a jury trial to watch the video and see that George Floyd was murdered . . . We hope today's verdict provides some semblance of healing for the Floyd family." Each of the accounts in this community generated conversation by virtue of their prestige and their position on the verdict. Their embedded positions within the broader network are reflective of their influence in the overall conversation.

Table 15.1. *Twitter Reaction to Chauvin Verdict Network Modularity Summary*

Rank	Modularity Class	Percent of Network	Topical Characteristics	Notable Accounts in the Community
1	2	6.47	Rep. Nancy Pelosi's comments	@speakerpelosi, @alexnbcnews, @teampelosi, @thedemocrats, @dnc
2	161	3.09	Rep. Maxine Waters' comments	@repmaxinewaters, @senschumer, @senatedems, @sensanders
3	192	2.74	President Biden and VP Harris	@potus, @vp, @joebiden, @kamalaharris, @whitehouse
4	1388	2.72	Left-leaning media outlets and personalities	@msnbc, @kylegriffin1, @joyannreid
5	10	2.11	Right-leaning media outlets and personalities	@foxnews, @candaceo, @tuckercarlson, @seanhannity @bretbair, @judgejeanine
6	415	1.81	Network news outlets and personalities	@abc, @cbsnews, @gma, @abcnewslive, @abcpolitic
7	1415	1.67	CNN and CNN personalities	@cnn, @jaketapper, @cnnbrk, @sarasidnercnn, @donlemon, @chriscuomo
8	1402	1.51	Right-leaning media outlets and personalities	@nypost, @newsmax, @breitbartnews, @jennaellisesq, @theleoterrell
9	5167	1.48	Athletes, sports organization, and media personalities	@kingjames, @adamschefter, @sportscenter, @wojespn, @espn, @nhl, @penguins, @nba
10	166	1.30	British news organizations and media personalities	@skynews, @bbcworld, @updayuk, @bbcbreaking, @bbclaurak, @bbcnews, @piersmogran

DISCUSSION

Results from this study support recent research that suggests sport functions as a powerful lens through which the public interprets social issues (e.g., Broussard, 2020; TePoel & Nauright, 2021). Few studies to date, however, have sought to examine the extent to which sports figures (athletes, organizations, and media personalities) factor into the broader conversation around social issues. These findings offer a unique understanding of the ways in which sport factors into the larger discursive landscape on social

Table 15.2. Top Sports Accounts by Eigenvector Centrality

Rank	Handle	Name	Eigenvector Centrality	Rank	Handle	Name	Eigenvector Centrality
1	@kingjames	LeBron James (NBA)	0.012259	11	@spidadmitchell	Donovan Mitchell (NBA)	0.00262
2	@adamschefter	Adam Schefter (ESPN)	0.01154	12	@damienwoody	Damien Woody (ESPN)	0.002127
3	@sportscenter	Sportscenter	0.009413	13	@jamorant	Ja Morant (NBA)	0.001833
4	@wojespn	Adrian Wojnarowski (ESPN)	0.008866	14	@carichampion	Cari Champion (Podcast)	0.00158
5	@espn	ESPN	0.008373	15	@nbapr	NBA Public Relations	0.001573
6	@nhl	National Hockey League	0.005979	16	@utahjazz	Utah Jazz (NBA)	0.001566
7	@penguins	Pittsburgh Penguins (NHL)	0.005739	17	@kendrickperkins	Kendrick Perkins (NBA)	0.001566
8	@pr_nhl	NHL Public Relations	0.004433	18	@dangerusswilson	Russell Wilson (NFL)	0.0013
9	@nba	National Basketball Association	0.003926	19	@outkick	Outkick (Website)	0.0013
10	@stephenasmith	Stephen A Smith (ESPN)	0.003646	20	@jeffpassan	Jeff Passan (ESPN)	0.001067

LeBron James ✓
@KingJames

ACCOUNTABILITY

6:06 PM · Apr 20, 2021 · Twitter for iPhone

29K Retweets   **1,298** Quote Tweets   **221.3K** Likes

♡   ⟲   ♡   ↑

Figure 15.1: A screenshot of LeBron James's tweet referencing the Chauvin verdict. Source: James, L. [@KingJames]. (2021, April 20). *ACCOUNTABILITY* **[Tweet]. Retrieved from https://twitter.com/kingjames/status/1384629525749788676**

media. While not the largest community within the network, the fact that conversations around sports figures accounted for 1.48% of the overall network structure is noteworthy considering that 98% of all other communities detected each accounted for 0.01% or less of the overall conversation. It is not especially surprising that the top communities featured conversations related to political figures and mainstream media organizations. Prior research has shown that these entities exert considerable influence to frame (Aruguete & Calvo, 2018) and set the agenda around (Feezell, 2018) topics that are widely discussed across digital media platforms. However, the fact that sports figures and organizations featured so prominently in the broader network supports the notion that sports function as a microcosm of society (Frey & Eitzen, 1991).

Social media users involved in the conversation around the Chauvin verdict turned to athletes, sports organizations, and media personalities to help make sense of the event. The networked influence of these sport-related accounts afforded Twitter users the opportunity to co-create meaning (Xiong et al., 2019) around the verdict. Tweets from notable athletes like LeBron James, Ja Morant, Kendrick Perkins, and Russell Wilson (among others) resonated with their followers and attracted both supportive commentary and criticism from other users. Similarly, sports organizations like the NHL and NBA were frequently discussed in light of public posts and comments shared by those organizations. Even notable sports media personalities like ESPN's Adam Schefter, Adrian Wojnarowski, and Stephen A. Smith played central roles in the conversation. It is important to note that not every athlete or organization included in the larger sports community cluster in the network would necessarily share the same viewpoint on the topic, however. One of the most

popular accounts in this cluster was Outkick, a sports and politics website featuring right-leaning commentators like Clay Travis. Consequently, it's worth
noting that not all users in this conversation were necessarily left-leaning or
progressive, but rather voices from sports figures and organizations carry
considerable weight regardless of political affiliation or ideological identity.
The extent to which users agree or disagree with sports figures and organizations is beyond the scope of the current study, but nevertheless serves as an
interesting outcome worthy of future consideration.

In addition to the community cluster (modularity class 5167) that primarily
revolved around athletes, sports organizations, and media personalities, there
were other, smaller clusters that also involved conversations around various
sports-related topics. For instance, another community cluster (modularity
class 2762) accounted for 1.29% of the network—the 11th largest community—and revolved around commentary about the Las Vegas Raiders account
tweeting the phrase "I can breathe" following the Chauvin verdict which generated significant backlash (Siese, 2021). Another community (modularity
class 2700) accounted for 0.35% of the overall network and included Lewis
Hamilton (Formula 1) and Bubba Wallace (NASCAR)—both prominent athletes in racing who were outspoken about the verdict.

In all, results from this study provide a helpful framework for exploring
the extent to which sports figures and organizations can influence the conversation around broader sociocultural subjects in an online environment.
Social networking sites like Twitter allow users to create public spaces where
competing ideologies and, consequently, the public's understanding of an
issue is created, debated, and spread to shape narratives around particular
social issues, especially within the context of sports (Sanderson, Frederick,
& Stocz, 2016). Prior research has revealed that social media permits athletes
and fans to engage in heated and often misinformed discussions (Kassing
& Sanderson, 2015; Schmittle & Sanderson, 2015). Nevertheless, sport is
a microcosm of society which reveals underlying values and power relations and is an arena in which issues emerge. Sports have been *shaped by*
social, economic, and political change, affected by ideologies and politics,
bureaucratization, science, technology and mass media. Results from this
analysis reveal that sports may also play a much larger role in *shaping* these
conversations.

LIMITATIONS AND FUTURE DIRECTIONS

This study is not without its limitations. By virtue of exploring one topic (the
Chauvin verdict) in a narrow time frame (a six-hour span on April 20, 2021)
on one platform (Twitter), it is heavily bound by its contextual parameters.

While the results yield valuable insight which suggests sport played a significant role in the conversation around the Chauvin verdict, they are ultimately limited to a single case. Further research is needed to evaluate the extent to which sports influence broader conversations around social and political activism. It is also worth considering that eigenvector centrality provides only one measure of influence. Because we conceptualized influence in a comparable manner to one's popularity or notoriety within a network, it does not, for example, account for the way that information is spread by "brokers" within the network (i.e., betweenness centrality). Future research should consider additional node-level centrality measures to evaluate the extent to which users are influential in a network. Finally, future research would do well to explore more predictive analytic measures to construct, test, and refine theoretical models around sport figures' participation in online activism. The current study offers a descriptive starting point highlighting the need for such research to expand.

The murder of George Floyd and subsequent conviction of Derek Chauvin resulted in a far-reaching social media conversation that was, in part, driven by athletes, sports organizations, and media personalities. Results from this analysis highlight the important role of sport in society to shape public understanding of sociocultural events and controversial issues on digital platforms. More research is needed to advance our knowledge of the role activism by sports figures and organizations plays within these social networks, but opening this line of inquiry invites further consideration of networked influence in sports and activist efforts.

NOTES

1. Walks, M. (2016, March 21). The best athlete tweets from Twitter's first decade. ESPN. https://www.espn.com/sportsnation/story/_/id/15033463/the-best-first-tweets -professional-athletes.

REFERENCES

Agyemang, K. J. (2014). Toward a framework of "athlete citizenship" in professional sport through authentic community stakeholder engagement. *Sport, Business and Management: An International Journal*, 4(1), 26–37. DOI 10.1108/ SBM-12-2011-0088

Agyemang, K. J., & Singer, J. N. (2011). Toward a framework for understanding Black male athlete social responsibility (BMASR) in big-time American sports. *International Journal of Sport Management and Marketing*, 10(1–2), 46–60.

Aruguete, N., & Calvo, E. (2018). Time to #protest: Selective exposure, cascading activation, and framing in social media. *Journal of Communication, 68*(3), 480–502.

BBC News. (2020, July 16). George Floyd: What happened in the final moments of his life. https://www.bbc.com/news/world-us-canada-52861726

Billings, A. C., Butterworth, M. L., & Turman, P. D. (2018). *Communication and sport: Surveying the field* (3rd Ed.) Thousand Oaks, CA: Sage.

Blondel, V. D., Guillaume, J. L., Lambiotte, R., & Lefebvre, E. (2008). Fast unfolding of communities in large networks. *Journal of Statistical Mechanics: Theory and Experiment, 2008*(10), P10008.

Broussard, R. (2020). "Stick to sports" is gone: A field theory analysis of sports journalists' coverage of socio-political issues. *Journalism Studies, 21*(12), 1627–1643.

Cooky, C., & Antunovic, D. (2020). "This isn't just about us": Articulations of feminism in media narratives of athlete activism. *Communication & Sport, 8*(4–5), 692–711. DOI: 10.1177/2167479519896360

Cooper, J. N., Macaulay, C., & Rodriguez, S. H. (2019). Race and resistance: A typology of African American sport activism. *International Review for the Sociology of Sport, 54*(2), 151–181.

Deb, S. (2020, June 1). As protests spur posts from athletes, N.B.A. players take to the streets. *New York Times.* https://www.nytimes.com/2020/06/01/sports/basketball/george-floyd-nba-protests.html

del Fresno Garcia, M., Daly, A. J., & Segado Sanchez-Cabezudo, S. (2016). Identifying the new Influences in the internet era: Social media and social network analysis. *Revista Española de Investigaciones Sociológicas,* (153), 23–40.

Duster, C. (2021, April 19). Waters calls for protesters to "get more confrontational" if no guilty verdict is reached in Derek Chauvin trial. CNN. https://www.cnn.com/2021/04/19/politics/maxine-waters-derek-chauvin-trial/index.html

Edwards, H. (2016). The promise and limits of leveraging Black athlete power potential to compel campus change. *Journal of Higher Education Athletics & Innovation, 1*(1), 4–13.

Feezell, J. T. (2018). Agenda setting through social media: The importance of incidental news exposure and social filtering in the digital era. *Political Research Quarterly, 71*(2), 482–494.

Frederick, E. L., Pegoraro, A., & Schmidt, S. (2020). "I'm not going to the f*** ing White House": Twitter users react to Donald Trump and Megan Rapinoe. *Communication & Sport,* 1–19. Advanced publication DOI: 10.1177/2167479520950778

Frey, J. H. & Eitzen, D. S. (1991). Sport and society. *Annual Review of Sociology, 17*(1), 503–522.

Galily, Y. (2019). "Shut up and dribble!"? Athletes activism in the age of twittersphere: The case of LeBron James. *Technology in Society, 58,* 101109. DOI: 10.1016/j.techsoc.2019.01.002

Giannoulakis, C., & Drayer, J. (2009). "Thugs" versus "good guys": The impact of NBA Cares on player image. *European Sport Management Quarterly, 9*(4), 453–468. DOI: 10.1080/16184740903331796

Gregory, S. (2021, January 7). "We did that": Inside the WNBA's strategy to support Raphael Warnock—and help Democrats win the Senate. *Time*. https://time.com/5927075/atlanta-dream-warnock-loeffler/

Gruzd, A., & Wellman, B. (2014). Networked Influence in Social Media: Introduction to the Special Issue. *American Behavioral Scientist, 58*(10), 1251–1259.

Hambrick, M. E. (2012). Six degrees of information: Using social network analysis to explore the spread of information within sport social networks. *International Journal of Sport Communication, 5*(1), 16–34.

Hansen, D. L., Shneiderman, B., & Smith, M. A. (2011). *Analyzing social media networks with NodeXL: Insights from a connected world.* Burlington, MA: Morgan Kaufmann.

Harrison, V. & Erlichman, S. (in press). NFL player protests, corporate social responsibility, and diversion in sports crisis. *Journal of Sports Media*.

Johnson, T., Reinke, L., Noble, G., & Camarillo, T. (2020). Shut up and dribble? How popularity, activism, and real-world events shape attitudes towards LeBron James and race. *The Social Science Journal*, 1–20. Advanced publication DOI: 10.1080/03623319.2020.1768484

Kadushin, C. (2012). *Understanding social networks: Theories, concepts, and findings*. New York: Oxford University Press.

Kassing, J. W., & Sanderson, J. (2015). Playing in the new media game or riding the virtual bench: Confirming and disconfirming membership in the community of sport. *Journal of Sport and Social Issues, 39*(1), 3–18. DOI: 10.1177/0193723512458931

Lauletta, T. (2020, May 28). Colin Kaepernick, LeBron James, and more athletes from across the sports world respond to the death of George Floyd. *Insider*. https://www.insider.com/lebron-james-colin-kaepernick-athletes-twitter-instagram-george-floyd-2020-5

Los Angeles Times. (2021, April 20). LeBron James, Naomi Osaka and other athletes react to Derek Chauvin guilty verdict. https://www.latimes.com/sports/story/2021-04-20/reaction-to-derek-chauvin-george-floyd-verdict-from-sports

Mueller, L. (2021). Do Americans really support black athletes who kneel during the national anthem? Estimating the true prevalence and strength of sensitive racial attitudes in the context of sport. *Communication & Sport*, 1–22. Advanced publication DOI: 10.1177/21674795211019670

Newman, M. E. (2006). Modularity and community structure in networks. *Proceedings of the National Academy of Sciences, 103*(23), 8577–8582.

Newman, M. E., & Girvan, M. (2004). Finding and evaluating community structure in networks. *Physical Review E, 69*(2), 026113.

Nietzel, M. T. (2020, June 28). Black athletes are leading the new college protest movement. *Forbes*. https://www.forbes.com/sites/michaeltnietzel/2020/06/28/black-athletes-lead-the-new-college-protest-movement/?sh=122e1ca362fa

Park, B., Park, S., & Billings, A. C. (2020). Separating perceptions of Kaepernick from perceptions of his protest: An analysis of athlete activism, endorsed brand, and media effects. *Communication & Sport, 8*(4–5), 629–650. DOI: 10.1177/2167479519894691

Perez, C., & Germon, R. (2016). Graph creation and analysis for linking actors: application to social data. In *Automating Open Source Intelligence* (pp. 103–129). Syngress.

Polus, S. (2021, April 21). LeBron deletes tweet saying Columbus police officer is "next" after Chauvin. *The Hill*. https://thehill.com/blogs/in-the-know/in-the-know/549595-lebron-deletes-tweet-saying-columbus-police-officer-is-next

Rim, H., Lee, Y., & Yoo, S. (2020). Polarized public opinion responding to corporate social advocacy: Social network analysis of boycotters and advocators. *Public Relations Review, 46*(2), 101869.

Sanderson, J., Frederick, E. & Stocz, M. (2016). When athlete activism clashes with group values: social identity threat management via social media. *Mass Communication and Society*, 19(3), 301–322, DOI: 10.1080/15205436.2015.1128549

Sappington, R., Keum, B. T., & Hoffman, M. A. (2019). "Arrogant, ungrateful, anti-American degenerates": Development and initial validation of the Attitudes Toward Athlete Activism Questionnaire (ATAAQ). *Psychology of Sport and Exercise, 45*, Advanced publication DOI: 10.1016/j.psychsport.2019.101552

Schmidt, S. H., Frederick, E. L., Pegoraro, A., & Spencer, T. C. (2019). An analysis of Colin Kaepernick, Megan Rapinoe, and the national anthem protests. *Communication & Sport, 7*(5), 653–677. DOI: 10.1177/2167479518793625

Schäfer, M. S., & Taddicken, M. (2015). Mediatized opinion leaders: New patterns of opinion leadership in new media environments. *International Journal of Communication, 9*, 960–981.

Silverstein, J. (2021, June 4). The global impact of George Floyd: How Black Lives Matter protests shaped movements around the world. CBS News. https://www.cbsnews.com/news/george-floyd-black-lives-matter-impact/

Slisco, A. (2021, April 20). Nancy Pelosi under fire for saying George Floyd "sacrificed" himself for justice. *Newsweek*. https://www.newsweek.com/nancy-pelosi-ripped-saying-george-floyd-sacrificed-himself-justice-1585213

Smith, B., & Tryce, S. A. (2019). Understanding emerging adults' national attachments and their reactions to athlete activism. *Journal of Sport and Social Issues, 43*(3), 167–194. DOI: 10.1177/0193723519836404

TePoel, D., & Nauright, J. (2021). Black Lives Matter in the sports world. *Sport in Society, 24*(5), 693–696.

Treisman, R. (2021, April 21). Darnella Frazier, teen who filmed Floyd's murder, praised for making verdict possible. *NPR*. https://www.npr.org/sections/trial-over-killing-of-george-floyd/2021/04/21/989480867/darnella-frazier-teen-who-filmed-floyds-murder-praised-for-making-verdict-possib

Tucker, E., Morales, M., & Krishnakumar, P. (April 21, 2021). Why it's rare for police officers to be convicted of murder. *CNN*. https://www.cnn.com/2021/04/20/us/police-convicted-murder-rare-chauvin/index.html

Voepel, M. (2020, April 26). All three WNBA games Wednesday postponed as part of protest of Jacob Blake shooting. ESPN. https://www.espn.com/wnba/story/_/id/29748510/all-three-wnba-games-wednesday-postponed-part-protest-jacob-blake-shootin

Wäsche, H., Dickson, G., Woll, A., & Brandes, U. (2017). Social network analysis in sport research: an emerging paradigm. *European Journal for Sport and Society*, *14*(2), 138–165.

Xiong, Y., Cho, M., & Boatwright, B. (2019). Hashtag activism and message frames among social movement organizations: Semantic network analysis and thematic analysis of Twitter during the #MeToo movement. *Public Relations Review*, *45*(1), 10–23.

Yan, G., Pegoraro, A., & Watanabe, N. M. (2018). Student-athletes' organization of activism at the University of Missouri: Resource mobilization on Twitter. *Journal of Sport Management*, *32*(1), 24–37. DOI: 10.1123/jsm.2017-0031

Yan, G., Watanabe, N. M., Shapiro, S. L., Naraine, M. L., & Hull, K. (2019). Unfolding the Twitter scene of the 2017 UEFA Champions League Final: Social media networks and power dynamics. *European Sport Management Quarterly*, *19*(4), 419–436.

Chapter 16

Athlete Activism Online

An Examination of Subsequent Fan Engagement

Lillian B. Feder and Brian G. Smith

In granting fans access to professional athletes, social media expands the capacity for a mediated connection between athletes and their supporters (Earnheardt & Haridakis, 2009). When an athlete is candid in his/her online self-presentation and posts content to social media aligning with the values held by his/her private rather than public identity, the potential for a disruption among fan-athlete relationships increases. When athletes take to social media to post politically-charged content and disclose partisanship on matters of contention, this disruption becomes almost certain. A disruption of this nature is likely to occur when the content disclosed by the athlete does not match up with fans' expectations. This may result in fans' loss of interest in the athlete, which may hold negative implications on the athlete's career trajectory. Due to the enhanced speed of escalation online, disruptions of this nature are more impactful when the offense occurs online than they would be if the disclosure had been delivered in a face-to-face interaction space and exposed through a traditional media setting, such as via televised interview (Colapinto & Benecchi, 2014). Intuitively, then, one may argue that athlete activism online yields a different set of responses from fans than do the offline activist efforts of professional athletes. For this reason, studies which serve to improve our understanding of fan response to athlete activism online are valuable.

Celebrities often find themselves under more scrutiny than the average individual (Summers & Morgan, 2008). Because celebrity careers are built in the public eye and involve the constant display of the working individual, celebrity success often depends on the established and maintained relevance of the celebrity. Resultantly, the opinions of fans are vital components impacting the longevity of celebrity careers. Professional athletes are often considered role models and serve as organizational representatives. As such, fans' social identities, which represent their senses of self in relation to others based on their group memberships (Tajfel & Turner, 1986), are tied to the length and strength of athletes' careers. The respective social identities of fans of professional athletes are in part composed of an allegiance to the athlete (Tajfel & Turner, 1986). Due to fans' lack of familiarity with athletes' personal identities, reputation is formed based on athletes' publicized social identities as a means of filling in the gaps to form and maintain a mediated connection.

Additionally, the reach of professional athletes in terms of their various followings may prove beneficial to the social movements they support. Assessing the behavioral responses of fans to politically-charged content posted online by professional athletes in direct connection to the movements addressed in athletes' posts allows for a deeper understanding of the degree to which the platform provided by social media is effective in galvanizing users to participate in social movements offline.

This chapter connects existing research broadly examining fan reactions to celebrity endorsement to studies addressing athlete activism and establishes a foundation for understanding fans' perceptions and responses to online displays of athlete activism. To conclude, the chapter highlights practical implications addressing athletes' use of social media for social movements.

LITERATURE REVIEW

Activism

Activism is characterized by conventional acts of resistance which serve to correct societal or hegemonic error (Baumgardner & Richards, 2000; Bobel, 2007). Acts of resistance are often political in nature and meant to further efforts of attaining various forms of equality (Baumgardner & Richards, 2000). Activism can take many different forms and may be demonstrated publicly in an offline setting or online through the use of the internet. Activism can be enacted in any of the following ways: communicating about an issue, "signing a petition, donating money, writing a letter, attending a meeting, being an active member of an organization, participating in a rally," or posting politically-charged content online (Savas & Stewart, 2018, p. 2; de Lemus & Stroebe, 2015).

Online displays of activism typically enlist a variety of social media. Social media are online platforms that foster social networking and provide the opportunity for users to share and generate content. These platforms stimulate social dialogues through which simultaneous feedback is provided and many individuals are able to interact with one another (Botha & Mills, 2012). Social media comprise social networking sites (SNS) through which users "debate ideas, contextualize news, and connect with like-minded individuals" (Smith & Gallicano, 2015, p. 83). The connective power of SNS is exemplified in their use to further social movements.

As such, activism is often enacted through individuals' participation in a social movement. Social movements, which are defined as "networks of informal interactions between a plurality of individuals, groups and/or organizations, engaged in political or cultural conflicts, on the basis of shared collective identities" (Diani, 1992, p. 1), can be organized online and/or offline. Social movements that are organized on SNS sometimes emerge in offline spaces through protests or demonstrations that further the movements' missions. SNS often serve as spaces through which individuals with similar beliefs come together to organize protests, which will then take place either online or onsite (Micó & Casero-Ripollés, 2013).

Of the influences on activism addressed in scholarly research to date (Bobel, 2007; Louis, Amiot, Thomas, & Blackwood, 2016; Svensson, Neumayer, Banfield-Mumb, & Schossböck, 2015; Qazi & Shah, 2018), celebrity status has been underexamined. Fan response to athlete activism has also received insufficient scholarly attention. The following section outlines existing literature on activism among celebrities and athletes.

Celebrity Activism and Fan Response

Although not a new phenomenon, celebrity activism in the form of issue politics is on the rise (Becker, 2013). The celebrity status of these individuals grants them a platform to reach the masses and garner support for the issues they value (Bourdieu, 2001; Traub, 2008). Recognizing the occupation of most celebrities as being unrelated to the political sphere, many fans regard celebrity activism as simplistic and inconsequential (Babcock & Whitehouse, 2005; Nisbett & DeWalt, 2016; Weiskel, 2005), calling the credibility of celebrity activists into question. Another area of concern for critical fans lies in the motivation of celebrities who publicly advocate for particular issues, as celebrity political involvement may serve to enhance the brand of the celebrity above all else (Brockington & Henson, 2015). Having said that, not all fans view celebrity activism through a skeptical lens.

Celebrity activism is celebrated by fans for its tendency to popularize otherwise unpopular social issues, making them more widely known and accessible to fans (Tufekci, 2013). In popularizing social issues, celebrity activists may inspire increased issue awareness and political engagement among their fans (Goodnight, 2005; Wheeler, 2012). In certain cases, celebrity activism in the form of endorsements for political candidates and social issues has been shown to impact public opinion and voting behavior (Becker, 2013; Garthwaite & Moore, 2013; Pease & Brewer, 2008).

As celebrities themselves, professional athletes who are involved in activist efforts are sure to face similar scrutiny and praise. Fan response to athlete activism has received insufficient scholarly attention. However, studies have been conducted recognizing fan reception of athlete involvement outside of the realm of athletics (Coombs & Cassilo, 2017; Haslerig, 2017; Summers & Morgan, 2008). Generally, when athletes step outside of the athletic realm to publicly comment on intellectually-charged issues, they are met with disorientation and backlash, as the "dumb jock" stereotype prevails in the subconscious of sports fans (Haslerig, 2017).

Athlete Activism

Athlete activism surged under the athletic reign of individuals advocating for civil rights in the 1960's and slowed down significantly following the 1980's (Coombs & Cassilo, 2017). Athletes like Tommie Smith, John Carlos, Bill Russell, Muhammad Ali, Jim Brown, and Arthur Ashe played a significant role in the civil rights movement by using their platform as world-class athletes to demonstrate support for racial equality (Edwards, 1969). In recent years, athletes' involvement in activism, particularly of the social justice variety, has resurged. Athletes who speak out often do so from a sense of responsibility (Agyemang, Singer, & DeLorme, 2010), using their opportunity for global reach (Rowe, 2005) to advocate for the underrepresented.

The broad reach of professional athletes uniquely positions them as effective influencers by expanding their potential to impact the attitudes and beliefs of fans and ultimately, spark social change within societies (Coombs & Cassilo, 2017; Frederick, Sanderson & Schlereth, 2017; Pelak, 2005; Melnick & Jackson, 2002; Schmittel & Sanderson, 2015). For example, Colin Kaepernick's role as a professional football player granted him a captive audience for his activist efforts. As such, Kaepernick's protests against police brutality were immediately noticed and debated. The level of access athletes have to their fans increases exponentially with the presence of social media. Athletes are no longer dependent on media sources outside of their cellphones to engage with the public. Resultantly, social media plays a large role in the current wave of athlete activism (Edwards, 2016). For example, LeBron James capitalized on Laura Ingraham's derogatory remarks by posting about them on social media. In doing so, James reclaimed the narrative of the "shut up and dribble" exchange and garnered support online, drawing from his millions of social media followers. This is the first study to examine the impact of social media—outside of its success in mobilizing large groups (Yan, Pegoraro, & Watanabe, 2018)—in its exercised use by athletes in their activist efforts.

Fan Response to Athlete Activism

Athletes who use their celebrity status to engage in activism risk rejection of their cause and degradation of their reputation. Fans sometimes have adverse reactions to athletes who publicly support social issues (Schmittel & Sanderson, 2015). These negatively charged reactions range in severity from fan disengagement to hostility. Oftentimes, athletes who openly engage in activist efforts advocating for the underrepresented come under heavy criticism and even marginalization (Frederick, Sanderson, & Schlereth, 2017; Kaufman, 2008).

Fan reactions to athlete activism efforts offline are often displayed online. In these cases, social media platforms act as interactive spaces for users to come together to manage negative reactions to athlete disclosure (Sanderson, 2013). For example, a Facebook page and Twitter hashtag denounced members of the St. Louis Rams who protested the murder of Michael Brown in 2014 (Sanderson et al., 2016). Online fan reactions to athlete activism are sometimes centered around the intent to behave in a particular way toward the athlete who has spoken out or the organization representing that athlete (Kaufman, 2008; Sanderson, 2013; Sanderson et al., 2016; Schmittel & Sanderson, 2015). Many online fan reactions disclose intent to disengage with the athlete, the organization representing the athlete, or even the sport altogether, as with fan reaction to the NFL and player engagement with the silent protests catalyzed by Kaepernick. Of course, athletes' politically-charged commentary also elicits positive fan reaction. Although Kaepernick faced mostly negative response to his initiation of protests against police brutality, his jersey sales went up during the controversy (Murphy, 2016).

Understanding Positive Fan Responses to Online Displays of Athlete Activism

Although scholarship has yet to address positive fan responses to online displays of athlete activism, prior research has addressed successful celebrity endorsement online (Chung & Cho, 2017). Successful celebrity endorsement requires positive fan reactions to endorsement-related content. As such, factors found to contribute to successful celebrity endorsement may also contribute to positive fan reaction to athlete activism online. Chung and Cho (2017) contend that celebrity-fan social media interactions, parasocial relationships, and source trustworthiness contribute to successful celebrity endorsement online. As celebrity-fan social media interactions continue to become more "intimate, open, reciprocal, and frequent," parasocial relationships between fans and celebrities are strengthened (Chung & Cho, 2017, p. 482). Source trustworthiness, which addresses the credibility of the celebrity and the inclination for fans to accept their messages as truth (Chung & Cho, 2017; Erdogan, 1999; Ohanian, 1990), is either strengthened or diminished through celebrity-fan social media interactions. Fans who maintain strong parasocial relationships with celebrities are inclined to consider their celebrity sources trustworthy (Chung & Cho, 2017).

Social media is considered "an effective tool in the fostering of parasocial relationships with celebrities" (Chung & Cho, 2017, p. 489). Social media affords celebrities the opportunity to consistently interact with their fans, disclose information about themselves to their fans, and ultimately, build or diminish their trustworthiness as sources of information for their fans. Chung and Cho (2017) also found source trustworthiness to influence fans' perceptions of brand credibility and celebrity endorsement. In addition to its application to products for common consumption, this trend may apply to social movements endorsed by professional athletes online.

Prior research has not yet addressed fan reactions to online displays of athlete activism. Due to the level of access provided by social media, which serves to expand the already abundant reach of professional athletes, and the recent resurgence of athlete activism, an examination of the response to the online activist efforts of professional athletes is warranted.

Social Media and Activism

Previous research (Chung & Cho, 2017) has demonstrated that the success of celebrity endorsement relies on celebrities' prioritization of factors such as social media interactions and parasocial relationships in their online presence. As a means of connecting celebrities with their fans, celebrity-fan social media interactions have been found to drive social media engagement among fans (Chung & Cho, 2017). Additionally, research has found that the identities of sports fans are impacted by events taking place outside of athletic competitions (Sanderson et al., 2016). Wright and Li (2011) contend that behaviors and discussions that take place offline sometimes extend to social media as well. Thus, it is plausible that fan response to athlete activism online may be influenced by social media engagement, social media parasocial relationships, and social media identity.

Social Media Engagement

Social media engagement differs from social media usage, as the former signifies a deeper level of participation by the user which sometimes occurs as a result of the latter (Paek et al., 2013; Smith & Gallicano, 2015; Smith & Taylor, 2017). Engagement can be embodied by a social media user liking, sharing, searching for, or commenting on content online (Hargittai & Hsieh, 2010; Nichols, Friedland, Rojas, Chos, & Shah, 2006; Smith & Gallicano, 2015) as well as by a social media user discussing content found online in an offline setting. Smith et al. (2015) studied engagement by associating social media activities with differing levels of engagement. A retweet with no added commentary represented the lowest level of engagement. An original tweet with a call to action represented the highest level of engagement. In this way, social media engagement can be measured by the behavioral outcomes driven by a user's response to social media consumption (Oh & Sundar, 2016; Smith & Taylor, 2017).

The study referenced later in this chapter evaluates fan response to politically-charged content posted by athletes online using engagement as a backdrop and considers the ways an athlete's social media content may elicit different levels of engagement. Evaluating online and offline responses to social media stimuli as engagement enables athletes, organizations representing athletes, and campaign strategists to effectively manage athlete disclosure online.

Social Media Parasocial Relationships

Parasocial relationships are strong one-sided connections between fans and celebrities (Horton & Wohl, 1956). These relationships "arise when individuals are repeatedly exposed to a media persona, and the individuals develop a sense of intimacy, perceived friendship, and identification with the celebrity" (Chung & Cho, 2017, p. 482). These relationships develop from spectators' attraction to and admiration for the individual in the public eye.

Fans who form parasocial relationships with professional athletes often come to regard themselves as present in the athlete's world (Earnheardt & Haridakis, 2009; Rubin, Perse, & Powell, 1985). Fans who feel deeply connected to a performer engage parasocial relationships that develop a strong level of identification as well. Further, fans' attachment to professional athletes is embodied by their identification with professional athletes. As such, identification is directly related to fandom (Earnheardt & Haridakis, 2009).

Strong levels of identification in parasocial relationships between fans and athletes have also been linked to the formation of affective bonds, which signify higher levels of engagement and attachment to the athlete on the fan's side (Pan & Zeng, 2018). Fans who identify with the athletes they admire to the degree that an affective bond is developed are likely to "desire greater similarity to athletes and take athletes' perspective" on matters of importance (Pan & Zeng, 2018, p. 196).

With parasocial relationships and affective bonds intact, fans are likely to "become involved in the narrative" delivered by an athlete—or otherwise prominent media figure—and thus become more susceptible to persuasion (Schartel Dunn, 2018). Additionally, individuals' use of the humor appeal when posting news-related content online has been found to strengthen the connection between posters and their social media followers and drive follower engagement (Highfield, 2015; Holton & Lewis, 2011). In its address of variations of politically-charged content posted online by professional athletes, the study presented later in this chapter indicates the impact of athletes' use of narrative framing and humor appeals on fan perception and response to athletes' politically-charged posts.

The strength of fans' parasocial relationships with athletes has also been positively connected to fans' likelihood to forgive athletes' ethical transgressions (Lee et al., 2018). Specifically addressing scenarios in which fans may perceive athletes' advocacy for particular social movements to characterize ethical transgressions, the study presented later in this chapter indicates how broadly applicable Lee et al.'s findings (2018) are.

Social Media Identity

According to social identity theory (Tajfel & Turner, 1986), individuals' respective identities are composed of both personal and social dimensions. A sense of personal identity comes from the "beliefs, abilities, and goals" (Barnes et al., 1988, p. 514) specific to the individual. Whereas a sense of social identity is developed through the individual's social ties, namely through their "group memberships, friends, and family" (Barnes et al., 1988, p. 514), Tajfel and Turner (1986) contend that individuals' organizational memberships and demographic classifications are strongly tied to their respective social identities. Threats to social identity comprise threats to value and distinctiveness (Branscombe, Ellemers, Spears, & Doosje, 1999). Value threats are characterized by actions or messages that diminish the value of group membership by "attacking shared group values, norms, and practices" (Sanderson et al., 2016, p. 306). Distinctiveness threats are characterized by changes in perception that diminish the uniqueness of the group (Branscombe et al., 1999).

In sports, fan identity can be impacted by events taking place both within and outside of athletic competitions (Sanderson et al., 2016). As such, the idea that fan identity may be impacted by politically-charged content from an athlete or team is plausible. Fans may react to this variety of athlete disclosure positively or negatively depending on the degree to which the content of the disclosure serves as reinforcement for or betrayal of the fan's idealization of the overall identity of the athlete in question. When the nature of the athlete's disclosure online undermines or negates the fan's idealization of the athlete, a social identity threat is posed. It is imperative to understand the reasoning behind various patterns of fan response to various forms of athlete disclosure online in order to avoid a scenario in which an athlete's fans may turn on him/her in response to a social identity threat. To preserve the empowering nature of the athlete's opportunity for online disclosure, we must recognize the simultaneous contentious nature of disclosure in general (Schmittel, & Sanderson, 2015) and understand motivating factors leading fans to react negatively to this disclosure to the degree that we may anticipate and avoid these reactions.

The remainder of this chapter focuses on establishing a foundation for understanding fans' perceptions and responses to online displays of athlete activism primarily through highlighting a study examining the fan experience of athlete activism online.

THE FAN EXPERIENCE OF ATHLETE
ACTIVISM ONLINE

This study develops an understanding of the effects of athletes' involvement in a cause via social media and stands to empower athletes, organizations, and social movement strategists to deliver effective social media communication.

The study is qualitative in nature and engages 15 semistructured in-depth interviews as its method. A structured analysis of interview transcripts and a subsequent thematic analysis of the data collected reveal four major themes regarding fan perception and response to politically-charged content posted online by professional athletes. Regarding fan perception, participants discussed their views on the responsibilities and rights of professional athletes as well as the qualities they respect and value in professional athletes and their online self-presentation. With respect to fan response, outcomes included increased interest, increased support, reinforced support, and disengagement.

The connections between the main themes found in this study and relevant theory and technique are displayed in Figure 16.1.

This study's findings generate understanding of the ways fans might interpret and respond to the online activist efforts of professional athletes, including the benefits and drawbacks of athletes' use of social media for social movements. Recognizing the inconsistency in sports fans' responses to athlete activism online, an understanding of patterns in fan perception is vital

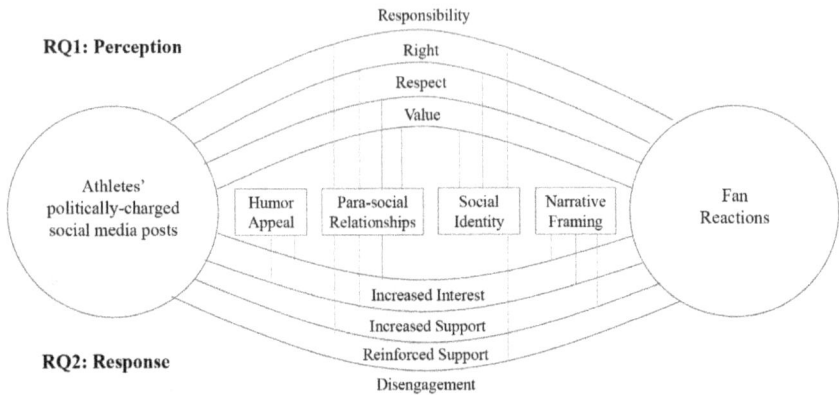

Fig. 16.1. Fan Perception and Response to Athlete Activism Online

to making sense of fan response. The findings of this study reveal that sports fans' perceptions of athlete activism online are informed by a combination of their sense of the responsibilities and rights of professional athletes and the qualities they respect and value in professional athletes and their online self-presentation.

Fans who value the maintenance of athletes' social identities tend to prefer that the content posted online by professional athletes represents athletes' single focus, or commitment to their sport above all else, while serving to maintain the escape provided to fans through their consumption of sports. These fans also tend to place a high value on modeling and consistency in the online self-presentation of professional athletes. Many of these fans choose to follow professional athletes' social media profiles to gain further access to athletes' training regimens and day-to-day sports-related practices. These fans are not interested in athletes' personal identities and believe that athletes' rights as employees of private organizations trump their rights as individual human beings. Regardless of whether teams or leagues have formally regulated athletes' online self-presentation, these fans believe athletes should avoid posting controversial content to their social media profiles. These fans typically perceive athlete activism online negatively, sometimes framing politically-charged content posted online by professional athletes as "dangerous" and "irresponsible" due to athletes' reach and lack of formal education in the political realm. Although generally opposed to the politically-charged social media posts of professional athletes, these fans are more tolerant of this content when it includes a solution to the dilemma discussed. Fans' main complaint regarding the politically-charged posts of professional athletes is that too often they are more problem than solution focused and serve to "cause a huge scene and a lot of chaos" (Participant 11).

On the other hand, fans who value gaining exposure to the personal identities of professional athletes tend to prefer that their online self-presentation
is uncensored. Many of these fans choose to follow professional athletes'
social media profiles to gain further access to athletes as whole people and are
looking to build and strengthen parasocial relationships with the athletes they
admire. In wanting to know more about athletes as whole people, these fans
value athletes' discussion of their lived experiences in the content they post
online. These fans believe that athletes' rights as individual human beings
trump their rights as employees of private organizations and view athletes as
advocates for the underrepresented. As such, these fans are supportive of athlete activism online. In circumstances in which these fans do not align themselves with the position taken by athletes in their politically-charged posts,
fans tend to remain supportive of athletes' right to post politically-charged
content. These fans typically will not perceive athlete activism online negatively unless an athlete posts offensive content revealing a racist or intoler-
ant ideology.

Four themes emerged from data analysis with respect to fan response
to athlete activism online. Three of these themes indicated positive fan
response, while the fourth theme indicated negative fan response. Positive fan
responses to athlete activism online are embodied by the increased interest of
fans, the increased support of fans, and the reinforced support of fans, all of
which can be applied to athletes as well as to social movements discussed in
athletes' politically-charged posts. Positive fan response typically comes from
fans who value gaining exposure to the personal identities of professional
athletes, as these fans perceive athlete activism online positively more consistently than fans who do not care to learn about athletes' personal identities.

Negative fan responses to athlete activism online are embodied by fans'
disengagement either with the athletes themselves, or in extreme cases, with
the sport played by the athletes altogether. Most commonly, negative fan
response comes from fans who value the maintenance of athletes' social identities. This is embodied by fans' disengagement from athletes on social media
exclusively. Scenarios in which fans disengage with athletes offline as well as
online tend to occur when athletes' self-presentation include their advocacy
for a particular cause or social movement to the degree that fans regard their
identities as no longer grounded in athletics. Scenarios in which fans disengage with the sport played by the athlete altogether occur only when multiple
athletes playing that sport participate in posting politically-charged content
online and publicly advocate for a particular cause or social movement to the
degree that fans feel the sport is becoming a platform for political discourse.

This study's results suggest a framework for understanding fan perception of athletes' politically-charged social media content. Fans who do not
take issue with athletes' inclination to post politically-charged content online

appear likely to respond positively to athletes' politically-charged posts. These fans may be likely to respond positively to posts that discuss a social movement they identify with. Fans who use sports as an escape may prefer that athletes refrain from posting politically-charged content. For fans with this opinion, social media posts may be disruptive and lead to a negative response. The framework described above is illustrated in Figure 16.2.

The eight emergent themes of this study indicate patterns in fan perception and response to athlete activism online. The study reveals that fans' sense of the responsibilities and rights of professional athletes as well as the qualities they respect and value in professional athletes and their online self-presentation shape fan perception of athletes' online activist efforts. With respect to fan response, the study has found increased interest, increased support, reinforced support, and disengagement emergent in fan behavior. These themes provide a framework from which practical implications are highlighted to inform future styles of delivery to be employed by professional athletes when posting politically-charged content online.

PRACTICAL IMPLICATIONS

Recognizing the unpredictable nature of fan response to athlete activism online, it is important to note that there is no universal norm to ensure positive fan response to politically-charged content posted online by professional athletes. Having said that, the study discussed above develops an initial understanding of how and why sports fans perceive and respond to athlete activism online in the ways they do. In evaluating fans' varying degrees of

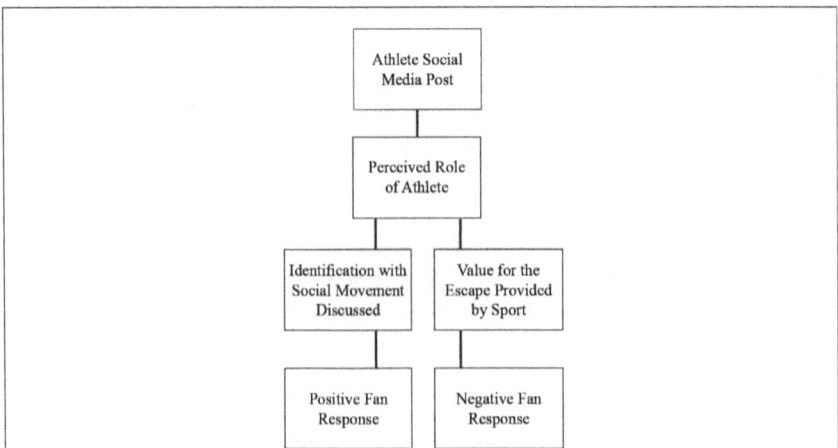

Fig. 16.2. Framework for Understanding Fan Perception of Athlete Activism Online

interest in building and maintaining parasocial relationships with the athletes they admire as a value specific to sports fans, this study provides insight with respect to the kind of athletic content sports fans would like to consume online. Further, the findings of this study disclose sports fans' varying perception and response patterns to politically-charged athlete content. The findings suggest that in order to create impact and receive positive response from sports fans, athletes who post politically-charged content online must do so with their goals and audience in mind. Knowing their goals as well as their audience grants athletes the ability to frame their content accordingly, rendering them more likely to receive positive responses to the politically-charged content they post.

Goal Orientation

The degree to which athletes are committed to the social movements they support through their politically-charged social media posts varies. Athletes thinking about posting politically-charged content online must consider the potential consequences of their actions prior to publishing their posts. Specifically, athletes should weigh the costs and benefits of publicly declaring their support and determine how committed they are to the social movement they are considering supporting online. An athlete with an unwavering commitment to the social movement, who has decided to put the movement first will have different goals with respect to the politically-charged content he/she posts online than an athlete who is only moderately committed to the movement. Due to the risk associated with an athlete's decision to post politically-charged content online, it is likely that athletes with a greater commitment to the social movement will be willing to do and say more than athletes with lesser commitments to the social movement. As such, athletes with a greater commitment to the social movement are more likely to strategically break through the echo chambers of support for the movement existing online and reach individuals who do not yet value the movement. Ideally, athletes whose goal is to garner greater levels of support for the social movement will strive to gain and maintain the attention of these individuals specifically. These athletes will walk a fine line between raising the awareness required to sway individuals to support the movement and alienating their fans.

Based on the findings of this study, athletes who are only moderately committed to the social movement they support online are least likely to elicit negative fan response, as these athletes typically post politically-charged content online infrequently. Athletes who are only moderately committed to the social movement they support online are recommended to keep public disclosure of their support primarily online and avoid disclosure within their competition space. Athletes who feel strongly about serving their communities and participating in activist efforts offline, but who are not committed to becoming outspoken activists themselves should follow suit. While successful in making a difference offline, these athletes can avoid negative fan response by limiting their public disclosure of their commitment to a particular cause. This prevents a disruption in the escapism provided to fans through their passive consumption of sports-related content.

As the commitment of the athlete to the social movement grows and the athlete's goals shift, recommendations regarding the public disclosure of the athlete's support change as well. Athletes who are committed to the social movement above all else and who strive to act as an outspoken activist are recommended to combine their approach to disclosure in both offline and online settings. The findings of this study suggest that the combination of offline and online disclosure is most effective in increasing the awareness and support of sports fans with regard to the social movements supported by professional athletes. However, combining offline and online disclosure also leaves the athlete more vulnerable to backlash, especially when their offline disclosure is delivered within the environment of their sport. Athletes can capitalize on the draw of their sport, potentially reaching individuals they may not otherwise have access to, by making politically-charged statements in press conferences as well as before and/or after competing. Additionally, the athlete's combination of offline and online disclosure speaks to the consistency of the athlete in terms of his/her commitment to the social movement, which has been found by this study to increase fans' perceptions of the athlete's credibility with respect to the movement. However, this form of public disclosure almost certainly serves as a disruption to the escapism provided to fans through their passive consumption of sports-related content and may have negative consequences on the athletic career of the athlete.

Audience Awareness

Athletes' awareness with regard to the specific audiences they are trying to reach with the politically-charged content that they post online is vital. This awareness allows athletes to frame their content to best reach the audiences whose attention they desire. The findings of this study provide insight with respect to how athletes can best reach uninterested and hostile audiences.

Many of the undergraduate students who participated in this study mentioned their inclination to tune out the politically-charged content posted online by professional athletes due to their lack of interest in politics. Fans also cited the controversial and divisive nature of politically-charged social media posts as their reasoning for scrolling past this kind of content online. However, athletes' utilization of the humor appeal got through to these fans. During their interviews, college-aged participants mentioned that a motivator in their decision to follow certain professional athletes on social media is to be kept up to date with popular culture. These fans care about being in the know and want to understand jokes that are being made by their favorite athletes. These fans mentioned enjoying sharing these jokes with their friends and disclosed an inclination to research the background of these jokes when unfamiliar with the jokes' context.

In addition to raising the awareness of otherwise uninterested fans with respect to the social movement supported by the athlete, the athlete's use of the humor appeal has been found by this study to increase fans' interest in and support for the athlete. Multiple study participants disclosed that they decided to follow Joshua Perry on Twitter after viewing a comedic, yet politically-charged tweet posted to his profile during their interviews. None of these participants knew who Joshua Perry was prior to beginning their interviews.

Participants of this study whose overall perceptions of athlete activism online were overwhelmingly negative tended to view athletes as insufficient spokespeople for social movements. These participants disclosed feeling that athletes lack credibility in the political realm and are often skeptical of the validity of the politically-charged content posted online by professional athletes. However, these fans did disclose their value for the lived experiences of professional athletes. Additionally, these fans recognize the credibility of the athlete when discussing his/her lived experience as it relates to a particular social movement.

Particularly when striving to reach a hostile audience, athletes who post politically-charged content online should frame this content as a narrative emphasizing their lived experience. In doing so, athletes overcome roadblocks, like the stereotype of the "dumb jock," which would normally prevent hostile audiences from hearing them out. In telling a story about their lived experience, athletes evade fans' inclination to question their intelligence and credibility. Engaging in storytelling also gives athletes the opportunity to employ the emotional appeal. Athletes' use of the emotional appeal has been proven by this study to be effective in reaching their fans who fall on the opposite end of the political spectrum. Sports fans with any level of respect for the athlete are often touched by this approach, which increases the likelihood that the athlete will be able to gain their support for him/herself and/or for the social movement he/she supports.

CONCLUSION

This chapter establishes a foundation for understanding fans' perceptions and responses to online displays of athlete activism. The combination of fan values and fan perception of athlete identity is found to play a large role in shaping fans' ability or aversion to digesting online displays of athlete activism. This finding emphasizes the connection between athlete activism online and research examining parasocial relationships with a focus on the link between identification and fandom. The chapter frames this understanding of patterns in sports fans' perceptions and responses to athlete activism online as influenced by the role of social identity and value threats, ultimately revealing potential benefits and drawbacks of athletes' use of social media for social movements.

The data-driven conclusions of this chapter stem from the recognition that athletes who post politically-charged content online should do so with their goals and audience in mind. Athletes who know their goals as well as their audience can frame their content intentionally, rendering themselves more likely to receive positive responses to the politically-charged content they post. The chapter establishes that athletes who frame politically-charged content as a narrative highlighting their lived experience and employing appeals to emotion and humor yield the most positive responses from otherwise uninterested or hostile fans.

The insights provided by this chapter equip public relations professionals with the knowledge necessary to represent clients who are known for athletic involvement and looking to engage in activist efforts. Public relations professionals should advise the athletes and athletic organizations they represent accordingly and strategically frame the politically-charged content included in their clients' social media content calendars.

REFERENCES

Agyemang, K., Singer, J., & DeLorme, J. (2010). An exploratory study of black male college athletes' perceptions on race and athlete activism. *International Review for the Sociology of Sport, 45*(4), 419–435. doi:10.1177/1012690210374691

Babcock, W., & Whitehouse, V. (2005). Celebrity as a postmodern phenomenon, ethical crisis for democracy and media nightmare. *Journal of Mass Media Ethics, 20,* 176–191.

Barnes, B. D., Mason, E., Leary, M. R., Laurent, J., Griebel, C., & Bergman, A. (1988). Reactions to social vs self-evaluation: Moderating effects of personal and social identity orientations. *Journal of Research in Personality, 22*(4), 513–524.

Baumgardner, J. & Richards, A. (2000). *Manifesta: Young women, feminism, and the future.* New York: Farrar, Strauss, & Giroux.

Becker, A. B. (2013). Star power? Advocacy, receptivity, and viewpoints on celebrity involvement in issue politics. *Atlantic Journal of Communication, 21*(1), 1–16.

Bobel, C. (2007). "I'm not an activist, though I've done a lot of it": Doing activism, being activist and the "perfect standard" in a contemporary movement. *Social Movement Studies, 6*(2), 147–159.

Botha, E., & Mills, A. J. (2012). Managing the new media: Tools for brand management in social media. In A. Close (ed.), *Online consumer behavior: Theory and research in social media, advertising, and E-tail* (pp. 83–100). New York: Taylor & Francis.

Bourdieu, P. (2001). The forms of capital. In R. Swedberg & M. S. Granovetter (eds.), *The sociology of economic life* (pp. 96–111). Boulder, CO: Westview.

Branscombe, N., Ellemers, N., Spears, R., & Doosje, B. (1999). The context and content of social identity threat. In N. Ellemers, R. Spears, & B. Doosje (eds.), *Social identity* (pp. 35–59). Oxford, UK: Blackwell.

Brockington, D., & Henson, S. (2015). Signifying the public: Celebrity advocacy and post-democratic politics. *International Journal of Cultural Studies, 18*, 431–448.

Chung, S., & Cho, H. (2017). Fostering parasocial relationships with celebrities on social media: Implications for celebrity endorsement. *Psychology & Marketing, 34*(4), 481–495.

Colapinto, C., & Benecchi, E. (2014). The presentation of celebrity personas in everyday twittering: Managing online reputations throughout a communication crisis. *Media, Culture, & Society, 36*(2), 219–233. doi:10.1177/0163443714526550

Coombs, D., & Cassilo, D. (2017). Athletes and/or activists: LeBron James and Black Lives Matter. *Journal of Sport and Social Issues, 41*(5), 425–444. doi:10.1177/0193723517719665

De Lemus, S., & Stroebe, K. (2015). Achieving social change: A matter of all for none? *Journal of Social Issues, 71*, 441–452.

Diani, M. (1992). The concept of social movement. *The Sociological Review 40*(1), 1–25.

Earnheardt, A. A., & Haridakis, P. M. (2009). An examination of fan-athlete interaction: Fandom, parasocial interaction, and identification. *Ohio Communication Journal, 47*, 27–53.

Edwards, H. (1969). *The revolt of the Black athlete.* New York: The Free Press.

Edwards, H. (2016). The promise and limits of leveraging Black athlete power potential to compel campus change. *Journal of Higher Education Athletics & Innovation, 1*(1), 4–13. doi:10.15763/issn.2376-5267.2016.1.1.4–13

Erdogan, B. Z. (1999). Celebrity endorsement: A literature review. *Journal of Marketing Management, 15*, 291–314.

Frederick, E., Sanderson, J., & Schlereth, N. (2017). Kick these kids off the team and take away their scholarships: Facebook and perceptions of athlete activism at the University of Missouri. *Journal of Issues in Intercollegiate Athletics, 10*, 17–34.

Garthwaite, C. & Moore, T. J. (2013). Can celebrity endorsements affect political outcomes? Evidence from the 2008 US Democratic presidential primary. *Journal of Law, Economics, & Organization, 29*, 355–384.

Goodnight, G. T. (2005). The Passion of the Christ meets Farenheit 9/11: A study in celebrity advocacy. *American Behavioral Scientist, 49*, 410–435.

Hargittai, E., & Hsieh, Y.-L. P. (2010). Predictors and consequences of differentiated practices on social network sites. *Information, Communication, & Society, 13*(4), 515–536.

Haslerig, S. J. (2017). Graduate(d) student athletes in Division I football: Redefining archetypes and disrupting stereotypes or invisible? *Sociology of Sport Journal, 34,* 329–343.

Highfield, T. (2015). Tweeted joke life spans and appropriated punch lines: Practices aroun topical humor on social media. *International Journal of Communication, 9,* 2713–2734.

Holton, A. E., & Lewis, S. C. (2011). Journalists, social media, and the use of humor on Twitter. *Electronic Journal of Communication, 21*(1–2).

Horton, D., & Wohl, R. (1956). Mass communication and parasocial interaction. *Psychiatry, 19*(3), 215–229. doi:10.1080/00332747.1956.11023049

Kaufman, P. (2008). Boos, bans, and backlash: The consequences of being an activist athlete. *Humanity & Society, 32,* 215–237.

Lee, S. H. (Mark), Simkins, T. J., Luster, S., & Chowdhury, S. A. (2018). Forgiving sports celebrities with ethical transgressions: The role of parasocial relationships, ethical intent and regulatory focus mindset. *Journal of Global Sport Management, 3*(2), 124–145.

Louis, W. R., Amiot, C. E., Thomas, E. F., & Blackwood, L. (2016). The "activist identity" and activism across domains: A multiple identities analysis. *Journal of Social Issues, 72*(2), 242–263. doi:10.1111/josi.12165

Melnick, M., & Jackson, S. (2002). Globalization American-style and reference idol selection: The importance of athlete celebrity others among New Zealand youth. *International Review for the Sociology of Sport, 37,* 429–448.

Micó, J.-L., & Casero-Ripollés, A. (2013). Political activism online: Organization and media relations in the case of 15M in Spain. *Information, Communication & Society, 17*(7), 858–871. doi:10.1080/1369118X.2013.830634

Murphy, M. (2016). Kaepernick's jersey sales soar amid anthem controversy. *New York Post.*

Nichols, S. L., Friedland, L. A., Rojas, H., Chos, J., & Shah, D. V. (2006). Examining the effects of public journalism on civil society from 1994 to 2002: Organizational factors, project features, story frames, and citizen engagement. *Journalism & Mass Communication Quarterly, 83*(1), 77–100.

Nisbett, G. S, & DeWalt, C. C. (2016). Exploring the influence of celebrities in politics: A focus group study of young voters. *Atlantic Journal of Communication, 24*(3), 144–156.

Oh, J., & Sundar, S. S. (2016). User engagement with interactive media: A communication perspective. In H. O'Brien & P. Cairns (eds.), *Why engagement matters: Cross-disciplinary perspectives of user engagement in digital media* (pp. 177–198). New York: Springer.

Ohanian, R. (1990). Construction and validation of a scale to measure celebrity endorsers' perceived expertise, trustworthiness, and attractiveness. *Journal of Advertising, 19,* 39–52.

Paek, H.-J., Hove, T., Jung, Y., & Cole, R. T. (2013). Engagement across three social media platforms: An exploratory study of a cause-related PR campaign. *Public Relations Review, 39,* 526–533.

Pan, P.-L., & Zeng, L. (2018). Parasocial interactions with basketball athletes of color in online mediated sports. *Howard Journal of Communications, 29*(2), 192–211.

Pease, A., & Brewer, P. R. (2008). The Oprah factor: The effects of a celebrity endorsement in a presidential primary campaign. *The International Journal of Press/Politics, 13,* 386–400.

Pelak, C. F. (2005). Negotiating gender/race/class constraints in the New South Africa: A case study of women's soccer. *International Review for the Sociology of Sport, 40,* 53–70.

Qazi, H., & Shah, S. (2018). Identity constructions through media discourses: Malala Yousafzai in Pakistani English newspapers. *Journalism Studies, 19*(11), 1597–1612. doi:10.1080/1461670X.2017.1284574

Rowe, D. (2005). *Sports, culture and the media* (2nd ed.). London: Open University Press.

Rubin, A., Perse, E., & Powell, R. (1985). Loneliness, parasocial interaction, and local television news viewing. *Human Communication Research, 12,* 155–180.

Sanderson, J., Frederick, E., & Stocz, M. (2016). When athlete activism clashes with group values: Social identity threat management via social media. *Mass Communication & Society, 19*(3), 301–322. doi:10.1080/15205436.2015.1128549

Savas, Ö., & Stewart, A. J. (2018). Alternative pathways to activism: Intersections of social and personal pasts in the narratives of women's rights activists. *Qualitative Psychology.*

Schartel Dunn, S. G. (2018). Parasocial interaction and narrative involvement as predictors of attitude change. *Western Journal of Communication, 82*(1), 117–133.

Schmittel, A., & Sanderson, J. (2015). Talking about Trayvon in 140 characters: Exploring NFL players' tweets about the George Zimmerman verdict. *Journal of Sport & Social Issues, 39,* 322–345. doi:10.1177/0193723514557821

Smith, B. G., & Gallicano, T. D. (2015). Terms of engagement: Analyzing public engagement with organizations through social media. *Computers in Human Behavior 53,* 82–90.

Smith, B. G., & Taylor, M. (2017). Empowering engagement: Understanding social media user sense of influence. *International Journal of Strategic Communication, 11*(2), 148–164. doi:10.1080/1553118X.2017.1284072

Smith, B. G., Men, R. L., & Al-Sinan, R. (2015). Tweeting Taksim communication power and social media advocacy in the Taksim square protests. *Computers in Human Behavior, 50,* 499–507.

Summers, J., & Morgan, M. (2008). More than just the media: Considering the role of public relations in the creation of sporting celebrity and the management of fan expectations. *Public Relations Review 34,* 176–182. doi:10.1016/j.pubrev.2008.03.014

Svensson, J., Neumayer, C., Banfield-Mumb, A., & Schossböck, J. (2015). Identity negotiation in activist participation. *Communication, Culture & Critique, 8*(1), 144–162. doi:10.1111/cccr.12073

Tajfel, H., & Turner, J. C. (1986). Social identity theory of intergroup behavior. In W. Austin & S. Worchel (eds.), *Psychology of intergroup relations* (2nd ed., pp. 33–47). Chicago, IL: Nelson-Hall.

Traub, J. (2008). The celebrity solution. *New York Times.* Retrieved from http://www .nytimes.com/2008/03/09/magazine/09CELEBRITY-t.html

Weiskel, T. C. (2005). From sidekick to sideshow: Celebrity, entertainment, and the politics of distraction. *American Behavioral Scientist, 49,* 393–409.

Wheeler, M. (2012). The democratic worth of celebrity politics in an era of late modernity. *The British Journal of Politics and International Relations, 14,* 407–422.

Wright, M. F., & Li, Y. (2011). The associations between young adults' face-to-face prosocial behaviors and their online prosocial behaviors. *Computers in Human Behavior, 27*(5), 1959–1962.

Yan, G., Pegoraro, A., & Wantanabe, N. (2018). Student-athletes' organization of activism at the university of Missouri: Resource mobilization on Twitter. *Journal of Sport Management, 32*(1), 24–37.

Index

Abdul-Rauf, Mahmoud, 44
Abidin, C., 207, 211
accountability, 246, *249*
activism: acts of resistance in, 258–59;
   assessment of, 98–99; athletic
   department's policies on, 99–100;
   by Black athletes, 104–5, 110–11;
   by Black students, 89–90; BLM in
   sport, 126, 175; branding, 50–52;
   Chauvin verdict and sport, 250–51;
   Christianity in, 64–66, 69; collegiate
   athletes, 105–7; corporate, 51;
   defining, 61–62; development
   celebrities, 225, 230–31, 234; digital,
   204; eras of, 117; fan perception
   of, *266*; Floyd murder and political,
   129; football player's racial justice,
   115–16; hierarchy of, 59; male,
   67–69; Moore using, 58–59, 66–67,
   69–70; non-student, 99; Osaka, N.,
   social strategies for, 82–83; religious,
   65–66; safe and risky, 4–5; social,
   67–69; social justice, 239–40; on
   social media, 262–65, *266*; solitary,
   58–59; sports, 104–5, 164, 250–51;
   sports with progressive, 126; of
   Stewart, B., 61; student, 206; student
   athletes attitudes toward, 12–13,
   106; symbolic, 105, 109–10; of

women athletes, 60–62. *See also*
   athlete activism
acts of resistance, 258–59
ad campaigns, 153
African Americans. *See* Black people
Ajzen, I., 144
Akers, Michelle, 170
Alabama football team, 117–18,
   120–21, 128n6
Ali, Muhammad, xi–xii; boxing
   title stripped from, 26; economic
   opportunities of, 14
Aluko, Eniola, 172, 174–75
Amma (track and cross-country
   coach), 94–96
Andersen, Anja, 133, 137
androgens, 183
anti-Black racism, 96–98
Antunovic, D., 60, 63–64, 69, 208–9
apologetic ethics: corrective actions
   in, 137–38; crisis communication
   and, 131–33; Gundy and, 135–37;
   Hearit's model of, *132*; model of,
   130; victims as focus in, 136–37
Arbery, Ahmaud, 41
Armfield, 130
artifacts of engagement, 212
athlete activism, xi; athlete engagement
   in, 16–17; of Black people, 7;

277

About the Editor and Contributors

Mia Long Anderson (PhD, University of Alabama) is an associate dean and professor in the College of Arts and Media at Sam Houston State University. Among her other duties, Dr. Anderson oversees diversity, equity, and inclusion efforts and graduate curriculum within the college. Her research interests include communication and sport, communication and race, and the intersection of communication, race, and sport. She is best known for her research on *Sepia* magazine, a Fort Worth, Texas-based, white-owned, African American targeted magazine. Dr. Anderson currently serves on the Board of Commissioners for the Commission on Sport Management Accreditation, which oversees the accreditation of sport management programs at colleges and universities. Prior to earning her doctorate at the University of Alabama, Dr. Anderson worked in sports public relations.

***

Andrew M. Abernathy is an assistant professor of professional practice at Oklahoma State University School of Media & Strategic Communications. A former magazine editor and public relations specialist, Abernathy previously taught at the University of Mississippi, where he is also a doctoral candidate in higher education policy. His research interest is focused on remediation policy in the United States and its intersection with ethics, equity, and social justice with a particular focus on its application in schools of media and mass communication.

Stephen P. Andon (PhD, Florida State University) is an associate professor at Montclair State University. Prior to his career in higher education, Dr. Andon worked in television, radio, and digital film production—with stints at WBAL-TV, WHFC-FM, and at ESPN covering the 2002 World Cup. Playing on the dynamic between popular culture and the rhetorical theories of place and memory, his research interests involve a wide array of topics dealing with sport, including the nostalgic influences of media sport, stadium narratives, sport and social media, and the development of sports fan cultures. Dr. Andon has published articles in *Communication and Sport*, the *International Journal of Sports Communication*, and *NINE: A Journal of Baseball and Culture*. His work has also appeared in a number of edited anthologies, including *Perspectives on the U.S.-Mexico Soccer Rivalry*, *American History through American Sports*, and the *Encyclopedia of Sports Management and Marketing*. As a result, his writing has been cited in outlets ranging from the *Los Angeles Times* to the *Journal of Computer-Mediated Communication* and the *Cultural Studies/Critical Methodologies* journal. His speaking engagements include over a dozen conference presentations and a guest lecture at the University of Southern California's Annenberg School of Communication.

Meredith M. Bagley (PhD, University of Texas at Austin) is an associate professor in the Department of Communication Studies at The University of Alabama. She is a critical rhetorical scholar, using critical cultural and rhetorical theory to examine artifacts and trends within sport and social change. Her current research focuses on modes of voice, both oral and embodied, within athlete activism. Her work has been featured in *Sport, Rhetoric & Political Struggle* (Grano & Butterworth Eds., Peter Lang, 2019), *Uniformly Discussed: Sportswomen's Apparel* (Fuller Ed., 2020), and, most recently *2019 Women's World Cup: Media, Fandom, and Soccer's Biggest Stage* (Yanity & Coombs Eds., Palgrave, 2021). Her teaching and activism also engage public memory on university campuses as well as LGBTQ advocacy. A lifelong athlete, Dr. Bagley most recently played and coached rugby. She lives in Birmingham, Alabama, with her wife and kids.

Mariann Bardocz-Bencsik (PhD, University of Physical Education [Hungary]) studies the role of sport in international development and high-profile athletes' involvement in development work. She holds a master's degree in international studies (2010) and a bachelor's degree in sport management (2009). Her non-academic work experience includes communication roles in various international sports organizations, including the European Non-Governmental Sports Organisation and the World Curling Federation. She is a member of the Hungarian Society of Sport Science, the International Sports Press Association and the Hungarian Sports Journalists' Association.

Brandon Boatwright (PhD, University of Tennessee, Knoxville) is an assistant professor in the Department of Communication at Clemson University. He completed his doctoral studies at the University of Tennessee, Knoxville in communication and information with an emphasis in advertising and public relations. His research focus examines the intersection of sports, social media, and opinion leadership. Dr. Boatwright also serves as the director of the Social Media Listening Center in the Department of Communication. He has published original research in *Communication & Sport*, *Public Relations Review*, *The Journal of Contingencies and Crisis Management*, *Computers in Human Behavior*, *The Journal of Public Interest Communication,* and the *Southern Communication Journal.* He is an active member of the National Communication Association and the Southern States Communication Association.

Ann E. Burnette (PhD, Northwestern University) is a Regents' Teaching Professor and Minnie Stevens Piper Professor in the Department of Communication Studies at Texas State University. She received her BA in history and MA in rhetoric and communication studies at the University of Virginia, and her PhD in communication studies from Northwestern University. Her scholarship focuses on political communication, the construction of gender in public discourse, and freedom of speech issues. Her research appears in articles in national and international journals as well as numerous book chapters.

Anthony C. Cavaiani (PhD, Wayne State University) is an assistant professor of communication at William Woods University in Fulton, MO. He teaches classes in sport communication, sports media, sports activism, communication theory, persuasive campaigns, media law and First Amendment, argumentation, and leadership communication. His research examines how sport is informed by rhetorical theories of place that foster collective identity, amplifies social justice discourse, and is used a mechanism for public deliberation about social, cultural, and political issues. His work has appeared in *Communication & Sport Journal*, edited book volumes, and he has given presentations at over 20 academic conferences. He was born and raised in metro Detroit and is an avid Detroit sports fan, in addition to rooting for Michigan State and his alma mater, Western Michigan. He lives in Fulton with his wife Megan, his son Tate, cat Thelma, and St. Pyrenees dog Lucy.

A. Michelle Clemon (JD, Columbia Law School), an experienced employment and labor law attorney and consultant with a background in Human Resources Management, received her undergraduate degree in history from Yale University and her law degree from Columbia Law School. Michelle recently earned a master's in sport management from the University of Florida, where her research interests included the intersection of elite athletes and social responsibility and the underrepresentation of minority football coaches at the intercollegiate and professional levels. Michelle is principal/

owner of The Clemon Consulting Group, a consultancy which focuses on providing HR services (including contract review, workplace investigations and workplace assessments) for companies and individuals as well as providing career planning/transition training to college and professional athletes. She is an adjunct instructor at the University of Alabama at Birmingham, where she teaches a course on the African American experience in sports. She also presents and provides legal and historical analysis around sports-related issues, including the discussion around athletes and social activism. In addition to these endeavors, Michelle is a co-host of the podcast "Black Girls Vibe," a podcast that talks sports and leisure from the perspective of black professional women.

Tamás Dóczi (PhD, University of Physical Education [Hungary)] holds an MA in sociology (2006), an MA in British studies (2005), and a PhD in sport science (2011). He currently serves as an associate professor at the University of Physical Education, Budapest, Hungary, and is a guest lecturer at the National Taiwan Sport University. His research areas include sport and globalization, the relationship of sport and national identity, the legacy of sport mega events, football fandom, and social inclusion in and through sport. In these topics he has published several journal articles and book chapters, delivered over 30 conference papers in Hungarian and English, and participated in a number of Hungarian and international R&D projects. He is also the co-author of the first Hungarian sport sociology course book, and a member of the Advisory Board of the International Sociology of Sport Association.

Andrea Fallon-Korb is a member of the Sport and Exercise Sciences Department at SUNY Oneonta, where she teaches in both the sport management and exercise science majors. Andrea has an MEd in sports psychology from the University of Minnesota, an MSW with an emphasis in clinical social work from Boston University, and a BA in psychology from Carleton College in Northfield, MN. She is currently a doctoral student at the University of Western States in sport and performance psychology, with an emphasis in positive leadership administration, and a research emphasis on equity and inclusion through the lens of sport.

Lillian B. Feder is a communication researcher with special interest in athlete activism, mindset, and performance. Her work lands at the intersection of sports communication, organizational identification, public relations, and media, and has been published in the *International Journal of Sport Communication*. Lillian is a former collegiate athlete and current athletic administrator, having held positions in collegiate athletics and the NBA. She obtained her MS from Purdue University and will return to Purdue in fall 2021 to begin her doctoral studies, continuing her inquiry into athlete identity.

Beth Fielding-Lloyd (PhD, Manchester Metropolitan University) is a principal lecturer in Sport Culture at Sheffield Hallam University. Her research has focused on gendered organizational practices in sport using methods of discourse analysis. Her current research interests are in the global development and professionalization of women's football, media representations of sport events, and social justice campaigns in sport media.

Konadu Y. Gyamfi (pronouns: she, her, hers) is an educator, social action advocate, and sport enthusiast. She has worked in both special education and higher education settings and desires for her scholarly work to be centered on examining scholar-activism and issues of social justice through sport. Her other research interests include (re)designing campus culture for students with special needs and approaches to the student affairs practice in a global context. Konadu is a Ghanaian American raised in Bronx, New York. She received her bachelor's degree in sociology from Quinnipiac University and a master's in education with a focus on sport leadership from Virginia Commonwealth University. Konadu currently attends the University of Georgia, where she is pursuing a PhD in education, specifically concentrating on college student affairs administration.

Virginia S. Harrison (PhD, Penn State University) is an assistant professor in the Department of Communication at Clemson University. She spent seven years in public relations and fundraising practice before earning her PhD at the Donald P. Bellisario College of Communications at Penn State University. Her research explores and seeks to understand the concept of stewardship in donor communications and relationship building. She also conducts research in understanding sports fan-organization relationships. Dr. Harrison's work has been published in top public relations and sports journals, such as *Public Relations Review*, *Journal of Communication Management*, and *Communication & Sport*. She has presented numerous papers at International Communication Association and Association for Education in Journalism and Mass Communication conferences, where she has won a number of awards. Dr. Harrison teaches sports and public relations courses at Clemson.

Megan R. Hill (PhD, Ohio State University) is an associate professor of communication studies at Albion College. Her research focuses on the ways in which political communication in the United States manifests across a range of areas of public life, from traditional news coverage to political entertainment programming to the type(s) of media coverage sports figures receive.

Robert Kwame (MD, Semmelweis University [Hungary]) graduated from the natural science program with English profile and mathematical section before going on to receive his doctor of medicine degree from Semmelweis University (Hungary) in 2021. His research focuses mainly on tropical diseases, in general, and malaria, in particular. Besides his medical research and practice, he is interested in the topics of social justice and anti-racism and how sport can contribute to eradicating racism-based violence. Kwame currently works as a pediatric resident in Sweden.

Anthony V. LaStrape (PhD, Tarleton State University) is an assistant professor of practice in the College of Media and Communication at Texas Tech University. He received his BA in university studies from Texas Tech University, his MA in communication studies from Texas State University, and his doctorate in educational leadership and policy studies from Tarleton State University. Dr. LaStrape has a background in rhetorical criticism, structural equation modeling, and motivational speaking. His research agenda currently includes political communication, adolescent to emerging adulthood mentoring, and the rhetoric of sport.

Katherine L. Lavelle (PhD, Wayne State University) is an associate professor of communication studies at the University of Wisconsin-La Crosse. Her previous research has explored representations of race, nationality, sex/gender in sport. She currently serves as treasurer on the Board of Directors for the International Association for Communication and Sport (IACS).

John McGuire (PhD, University of Missouri-Columbia) is a professor in the School of Media & Strategic Communications at Oklahoma State University. He has coedited two books about the impact of ESPN on the sports media business and society (*The ESPN Effect & ESPN and the Changing Sports Media Landscape*). He has also published numerous sports media research articles in academic journals, including *Newspaper Research Journal*, *Communication and Sport*, and *Journal of Radio and Audio Media*.

Anthony J. Moretti (PhD, Ohio University) is an associate professor in the Department of Communication and Organizational Leadership at Robert Morris University. He primarily teaches journalism and sport communication courses. His research interests examine the intersection of politics, sports, and media. Before entering higher education, Dr. Moretti spent more than a decade in broadcast journalism as a news and sports reporter and producer in southern California and Ohio. He earned his PhD from the E.W. Scripps School of Journalism at Ohio University.

Korryn D. Mozisek (PhD, Indiana University, Bloomington) is currently the director of integrative learning in the Office of the Vice Provost for Education and special faculty in the English Department at Carnegie Mellon University. Her research focuses on the rhetoric of sport, particularly as sport plays a role in shaping gender and sexuality norms within culture. Her dissertation titled, "Throwing Like a Girl!: Constituting Citizenship for Women and Girls Through the American Pastime," won the 2013 Cheris Kramarae Outstanding Dissertation Award from the Organization for the Study of Communication, Language, and Gender.

Ray Murray is an associate professor who teaches in the multimedia journalism and sports media sequences at Oklahoma State University's School of Media & Strategic Communications. He was a sports writer, sports editor, and copy editor while a journalist for 20 years in Montana, Florida, and Missouri. His research interests include paparazzi ethics, skills students need in an ever-evolving workplace, and newspaper readership.

Alison N. Novak (PhD, Drexel University) is an associate professor in the Edelman College of Communication and Creative Arts at Rowan University in Glassboro, NJ. She received her PhD in communication, culture, and media from Drexel University. Her work explores the intersections of digital activism, public policy, and identity. She is the author of three books, including The New Review Economy. Her work is featured in *Wired Magazine*, NBC News, and the BBC.

Vincent Peña (PhD, University of Texas at Austin) is an assistant professor in the College of Communication at DePaul University. He received his master's from the University of Nebraska-Lincoln in journalism and mass communication. His research interests lie at the intersection of sports media, culture and identity, focusing on race and gender representation as well as sports media discourse about broader social issues and athlete activism. His work has been published in journals like *The International Journal of Sport and Society*.

Shannon Scovel is a doctoral student in the College of Journalism at the University of Maryland studying the representation of women in sports and digital media. A 2017–2018 Fulbright scholar, Shannon earned her master's degree in gender studies at the University of Stirling and her undergraduate degree in journalism at American University. Her master's dissertation focused on the coverage of women during the 2008, 2012, and 2016 Olympics in The Times (UK), and her research continues to explore the relationship between gender, sport, and journalism. Shannon's interest in media studies stems from her experience as a student-athlete and college wrestling reporter for NCAA.com, and she has recently published a book chapter on women's wrestling apparel in Sportswomen's Apparel Around the World: Uniformly Discussed unpacking how gendered clothing impacts athlete identity and experience in sports.

Brian G. Smith (PhD, University of Maryland) is an associate professor of public relations in the School of Communications at Brigham Young University. Smith is an award-winning scholar and has built recognition for his research on social media engagement and activism. In 2017, he was awarded a Fulbright Fellowship to Austria to study activism and refugees in Austria. Smith's work has been published in leading public relations and communication journals, including *Journal of Public Relations Research*, *Public Relations Review*, *Computers in Human Behavior*, *International Journal of Strategic Communication*, and many others. Prior to his career in academia, Smith filled roles as an online brand marketer, marketing research manager, and managing editor.

Carolina Velloso is a doctoral student in journalism studies at the Philip Merrill College of Journalism, University of Maryland. Her research interests include representations of gender and race in the media, newsroom diversity, media history, journalism norms and processes, activist and alternative media, and sports media. Carolina has presented her research at the Association for Education in Journalism and Mass Communication (AEJMC) and the International Communication Association (ICA), among others. Her research has won several awards, including a Top Paper and a Diversity in Journalism History Research Award from AEJMC. A longtime Terp, Carolina has an MA in journalism and a BA with high honors in history from the University of Maryland.